365

DAILY DEVOTIONAL

By

Revs. Kola and Funke Ewuosho

365 Daily Devotional

www.fowm.org

ISBN: 978-0-9556597-3-7

PREFACE BY REV. KOLA EWUOSHO

To be the best or get the best out of any subject in life, we need to understand that there are usually different aspects to the subject matter. We all know we need to read our bibles and pray everyday if we want to grow to become all that God wants us to become. After getting born again through accepting Jesus Christ as our Lord and Saviour, in line with Romans chapter 10, we need to deepen our relationship with God by His Word and by His Spirit. This is one reason to read the bible and pray daily.

Devotional reading and praying should happen daily. To get a good understanding of the bible, there are various aspects to the grasping of the content of the bible. These include devotional reading, studying and the general reading of the bible; the same way prayer has different aspects like intercession, supplication as well as giving of thanks, to name a few aspects of prayer.

This book on devotional reading, helps you to draw closer to God as you internalise the principles, instructions and admonitions from God's Word. You will not only draw closer to Him but your internal conditioning will be affected too. You will learn to maintain your joy in whatever situation you face; your attitude will move from complaining to being grateful - just to mention a few benefits from cultivating a habit of devotional reading of the bible and praying. Growing up into the fullness of Christ is a lengthy process and it involves daily devotion, as we start our day with prayer and reading the scriptures and fellowship with the Lord by His Spirit who lives in us. Welcome to the process of enjoying your walk with God and growing up into Christ, enjoying the fullness of His grace and experiencing victory in many areas of your life. Enjoy God, your Heavenly Father.

Rev. Kola Ewuosho

PREFACE BY REV. FUNKE EWUOSHO

"Read your Bible, pray everyday, if you want to grow;" was the instructional song we sang regularly back in the old 'CU' (Christian Union) days. You never left your room, without having your morning devotion! However, over the years, the discipline and habit of 'morning devotion' became lost on many believers. This is attributable to a number of factors, and just to mention a few- **a**, some believers began to find it boring and irrelevant, because it became a mere religious exercise that had lost its meaning and power; **b**, life became more fast-paced and a lot of believers became caught up in the rat-race, making morning devotion of less priority. The Bible says the love of the world chokes the love of the Father in us (1 John 2:15); and **c**, Believers have become less communal and accountable in their lifestyle; and have become more independent and individualistic. For instance, back in the day; you would be asked about what you read in your morning devotion or (and) what God said to you! I remember the song, "God has something to say (to you); listen, listen, pay close attention, for God has something to say."

However, I believe it's time believers returned to the habit of having morning devotion time; for its various benefits, to mention a few: **a**, it grows you spiritually; **b**, it enhances your walk with God; **c**, it widens and deepens your knowledge of the scriptures (you would agree with me that the majority of 'modern' Christians have a very limited knowledge of the Bible!); **d**, it gives you the wisdom needed for daily living, and; **e**, it helps you develop a disciplined lifestyle.

We hope this all-year round Morning Devotional Book will encourage and aid you in achieving this goal. No one could ever and should never grow out of the simple, old, established and proven discipline of Morning Devotion.

A warm welcome to WISDOM 365!

God bless you.

Rev. Funke Ewuosho

Many thanks to the editorial team for a good job done. Special thanks to the team lead, Nicky Lawson and the FOWM - UK office team. May God reward you ALL for your good work and sacrifice of love.

Blessings!

COMMITMENT TO A DEVOTIONAL LIFE

"Now in the morning, having risen a long while before daylight,
He went out and departed to a solitary place;
and there He prayed."
Mark 1:35

We miss out a lot when we don't start the day with our priorities right — time with God. This should be our first assignment of the day. Consider the principle of sowing and reaping. "While the earth remains, Seedtime and harvest, Cold and heat, Winter and summer, And day and night Shall not cease" (Genesis 8:22 *NKJV*). We all need wisdom, guidance, counsel and direction for the things we encounter daily and it is daily that we need to sow our time, attention and affection towards God as we worship, study the Word, pray and meditate. Most of the time we encounter fleshly weakness which is the effect of a lack of waiting on the Lord. A conscious, vital and sensitive waiting on the Lord is an absolute necessity on a daily basis. The consciousness we need to develop in our minds, to replace what the world has deposited in us through the flesh, can be developed as we do the first things first. Your devotional times must become your vital link with God.

SCRIPTURE READING: Isaiah 40:28-31
PERSONAL APPLICATION: Spend time thinking about ways you can cultivate your spiritual hunger for God, then prayerfully put them into action.

HELPING THE DREAMS OF OTHERS

"So humble yourselves under the mighty power of God, and at the right time he will lift you up in honour."
1 Peter 5:6 NLT

What you make happen for others, God (through others) will make happen for you. Jesus said, "And just as you want men to do to you, you also do to them likewise" (Luke 6:31). You can't afford to be selfish. Joseph served his brothers. Joseph served faithfully as a slave in Potiphar's house and was promoted. He served faithfully in the prison and was put in charge. He served the baker and the butler by interpreting their dreams. He threw himself into service and through serving others, he broke through his own barriers. The butler remembered Joseph and Joseph was brought to interpret Pharaoh's dreams. Don't forget that Joseph helped the dreams of others even when his own dreams were yet unfulfilled! Joseph named his first son Manasseh saying that God has helped him to forget the pain of his father's house. He named his second son 'Ephraim' meaning 'fruitfulness' (Genesis 41:51-52). You can't be fruitful until you get over the pain, the hurts and the betrayals of the past! You can't help the dreams of others until you forget about your own self, your cares, your worries and your dreams. "Therefore humble yourselves under the mighty hand of God, that He may exalt you in due time; casting all your care upon Him for He cares for you" (1 Peter 5:6-7). Leave your promotion and exaltation in the hands of God. One reason why some don't serve the dreams of others is because they don't cast their own cares on the Lord. Ruth cast all her own cares on the Lord and served Naomi faithfully; even when there was nothing visible in it for her! Boaz said to Ruth, "it has been fully reported to me, all that you have done for your mother-in-law, since the death of your husband and how you left your father and mother, and have come to a people whom you did not know before. The Lord repay your work, and a full reward be given you by the Lord God of Israel, under whose wings you have come for refuge" (Ruth 2:11-12). Jesus said, "And if you have not been faithful in what is another man's, who will give you what is your own?" (Luke 16:12).

SCRIPTURE READING: Luke 6:31, Luke 16:12, 1 Peter 5:6-7
PERSONAL APPLICATION: Spend time thinking about how you can get to the place where you can sincerely help the dreams of others even when your own dreams are unfulfilled.

LIVING COURAGEOUSLY

"Have I not commanded you? Be strong and of good courage; do not be afraid, nor be dismayed, for the Lord your God is with you wherever you go."
Joshua 1:9

Courage is the ability to keep on going even when there is fear and uncertainty inside and around us. Many things in life place a demand on our courage if we are going to make much difference in our lives. It takes courage to confront yourself: your weaknesses, fears and insecurities. It takes a lot of courage to laugh at and with yourself. It takes courage to make the right decisions in life. Immediate gratification or looking for the easy way out has informed how many make decisions. The right decisions usually come with a price tag. Most of the time Satan puts pressure on us with afflictions or persecutions and his goal is primarily at our decisions. If we go the easy way out we decide for death; not life in God. Obedience to God takes a lot of courage. God told Joshua to be very strong and courageous so as to be able to carry out His assignment, that is, taking the responsibility to lead God's people after the death of Moses. There is usually an element of risk in facing the future courageously. Having courage is facing the reality that life is a risky business. At personal, corporate or family levels, risks are involved in living successfully. In fulfilling our God given assignments, we face risky situations too! So we need faith in God and His Word; we need the wisdom of God; we need to build trusted relationships around us; we need to face life fearlessly.

SCRIPTURE READING: Joshua 1:1-8
PERSONAL APPLICATION: Part of courage is having to deal with the fear or reality of failure. What if I fail? Failure is just a mere junction in the journey of life; it is not your final destination. Get up and go on!

RUNNING THROUGH A TROOP

"For by You I can run through a troop, and by my God I can leap over a wall"
Psalm 18:29

The Bible is full of people who faced barriers but, praise God, were able to break through them. God said to Jeremiah, "Do not say, 'I am a youth,' for you shall go to whom I send you and whatever I command you, you shall speak" (Jeremiah 1:7). Paul told Timothy not to allow anyone to despise his youthfulness (1 Timothy 4:12). Elizabeth, who was called barren, conceived a son in her old age (Luke 1:36-37). Sarah received strength to conceive and she bore a child "when she was past the age, because she judged Him faithful who had promised" (Hebrews 11:11). Note that Abraham was seventy five years old when he left Haran to go to Canaan. What of folks like Moses (Exodus 4:10-12), the paralytic (Mark 2:3-4), the woman with the issue of blood (Mark 5:27-34), blind Bartimaeus (Mark 10:46-52), the man at the pool of Bethesda (John 5:5-9) and a host of others, who overcame one physical disability or the other? The Bible says that when blind Bartimaeus heard that Jesus was passing by he cried out, "Jesus, Son of David, have mercy on me!" The people around him warned him to be quiet, but he cried out all the more. Then, Jesus stood still and commanded blind Bartimaeus to be called. They said to him, "Be of good cheer. Rise up, He is calling you". If you would not allow the opinion and comments of others to stop you, they will be the same ones to cheer you as you break through in life! People are fickle-minded. They change their mind so easily. Their opinion should therefore not be strong enough to stop you from going forward.

SCRIPTURE READING: Psalm 18:28-34
PERSONAL APPLICATION: Your responses are your responsibility. You may not be able to choose or determine all the events in your life, but you can choose your response to them! Ask yourself: What areas of my life have become limited because of others' opinions? What am I going to do about it?

LOOKING UNTO JESUS

"...looking unto Jesus, the author and finisher of our faith, who for the joy that was set before Him endured the cross, despising the shame, and has sat down at the right hand of the throne of God."
Hebrews 12:2

In the face of our everyday challenges, it is the easiest thing to look elsewhere. We either look to ourselves and feel sorry for ourselves, look to others and place an expectation on them that they lack the ability to bear, or look to other things. We are encouraged to look unto Jesus, the author and finisher of our faith. He, for the joy set before Him, endured the cross, despised the shame and is sat at the right hand of the Father (Hebrews 12:2). How we respond to trials, the pain of correction and pressures in general, are all determined by who or what we are looking unto. We look unto Jesus for inspiration, right motivation and choice of lifestyle. Why? He is our pattern, our model, an example of how we should live under the Father God. When we face challenges, our response depends on how matured we are. We need to rise up to do God's Word in the face of all challenges. What we behold determines what we become.

SCRIPTURE READING: 1 John 3:1-3, 2 Corinthians 3:18, Romans 8:29
PERSONAL APPLICATION: We need to identify where or on whom our focus is on. Then, make the conscious effort of shifting it onto Jesus by studying, meditating, confessing and acting on the Word.

THE WHOLE DUTY OF MAN

"I delight to do Your will, O my God,
And Your law is within my heart."
Psalm 40:8

"The conclusion of the matter is very simple; fear God and keep His commandment, for this is the whole duty of man" (Ecclesiastes 12:13). Your duty is not to impress people or to be in their good books. Your duty is not to build a big church or to have a big crowd. Your duty is not to have a lot of money. It is not to have a big household name. Your duty is not to give big testimonies in church and impress the pastor. These are the things the enemy keeps using to draw us away from the Word of God and from the straight and narrow way into the way that leads to destruction. Jesus said that many people travel on that broad way that leads to destruction. You can make a 'U' turn today. Repent. Get your priorities right. Your whole duty is to fear (love) God and keep His commandments.

SCRIPTURE READING: Matthew 7:13-27, John 14:15, Psalm 40:4-10, John 14:15
PERSONAL APPLICATION: We need to constantly examine ourselves to make sure that we always put first things first. Our relationship with God comes first—everything else is a fringe benefit. Don't mix it up.

UNDERSTANDING THE NATURE OF GOD

"For the Lord God is a sun and shield; The Lord will give grace and glory; No good thing will He withhold from those who walk uprightly."
Psalm 84:11

Many today are having problems with receiving from God. Their belief in God has been seriously affected by their experiences of prayers going unanswered. Does God still answer prayer? The answer is 'yes He does!' How can we receive from this invisible God? The first thing we need to be established in is our understanding of God's nature. He is not unwilling to give us what we need to meet our material and temporal needs. He is also interested and committed to our spiritual needs too!
God governs His Kingdom with principles. His ways can be seen in the Bible. All His operations are based on principles and we can see His patterns in the Bible.

Let us understand His nature:

1. God is unchanging in His nature (Numbers 23:19, Malachi 3:6)
2. God is benevolent (Psalm 84:11)

SCRIPTURE READING: James 1:17, Psalm 34:9-10
PERSONAL APPLICATION: For whatever you are trusting God for, find the scriptures concerning that matter and build your faith in the Word of God. If He has done it before, He can do it again!

BEYOND A SHADOW OF DOUBT

"Your eyes saw my substance, being yet unformed.
And in Your book they all were written, The days fashioned for me,
When as yet there were none of them."
Psalm 139:16

Simple as it may sound, it is very crucial that you know beyond any shadow of doubt that God has a plan for your life. You are not an accident, neither are you a mistake on earth. Even if your parents or the government didn't plan for you, God planned for you. Like He did Jeremiah, God knew you even before you were ever formed in the womb. You came out from God. The Psalmist said, "the things you planned for us, not one can recount to you" (Psalm 40:5).

Job said in his suffering, "But He knows the way I take, when He has tested me, I shall come forth as gold" (Job 23:10). He knew that God had already predetermined the way he should take. There is a way everyone should take. That's why the Bible says, "train up a child in the way he should go and when he grows up, he will not depart from it" (Proverbs 22:6).

Don't live your life aimlessly. There are some works that have been prepared for you to do even before the foundation of the earth (Ephesians 2:10). There are some things that God has in store for all those who love Him.

SCRIPTURE READING: Psalm 32:8-9, 1 Corinthians 2:1-16

PERSONAL APPLICATION: Too many people use God and don't ask God how He can use them. Changing your prayer life to ask God, "Father, what can I do for you today?", will reveal His plan for you on a daily basis.

WALKING IN FAVOUR

"For You, O Lord, will bless the righteous; With favour You will surround him as with a shield"
Psalm 5:12

When we spend time labouring for something, we can accomplish much. However, when we walk in favour, much more can be accomplished in a shorter time. Favour opens doors for you that would not usually be opened to you in normal circumstances. What God has in store for us is fully possible only with His favour upon our lives. When Esther, for example, walked in divine favour with the king, she was able to secure the release of her people, the Israelites.

SCRIPTURE READING AND PERSONAL APPLICATION: Ten benefits of walking in the favour of God:

1) Favour produces supernatural increase and promotion (Genesis 39:21).
2) Favour produces restoration of everything the enemy has stolen from you (Exodus 3:21).
3) Favour produces honour in the midst of your adversaries (Exodus 11:3).
4) Favour produces increased assets, especially in the area of real estate (Deuteronomy 33:23).
5) Favour produces great victories in the midst of great impossibilities (Joshua 11:20).
6) Favour produces recognition, even when you seem the least likely to receive it (1 Samuel 16:22).
7) Favour produces prominence and preferential treatment (Esther 2:17).
8) Favour produces petitions granted even by ungodly authorities (Esther 5:8).
9) Favour causes policies, rules, regulations and laws to be changed and reversed to your advantage (Esther 8:5).
10) Favour produces battles won which you won't even fight because God will fight them for you (Psalm 44:3). The time to favour Zion has come, yes the set time of favour is now (Psalm 102:13)

May you walk in and experience the favour of God in your life.

THE POWER OF THE TONGUE

"For he who sows to his flesh will of the flesh reap corruption, but he who sows to the Spirit will of the Spirit reap everlasting life."
Galatians 6:8

The tongue is very powerful! The Bible tells us that death and life are in the power of the tongue (Proverbs 18:21). If the Bible tells us something, we need to take it seriously! We need to watch what we say. No matter how angry you are, watch the words you say. Is it possible to be angry yet still be mindful of the words that come out of your mouth? Yes it is! The true test of maturity is in how well you can control your tongue, not in how much you know. "My dear brothers and sisters, take note of this: Everyone should be quick to listen, slow to speak and slow to become angry" (James 1:19). It is not about how fierce the storms of life are, it is about who or what has control over your tongue. Whoever or whatever has control over your tongue has control over the direction of your life. Let's submit our tongues to the Holy Spirit and receive the grace and strength that comes from Him to control and have reign over our tongues.

SCRIPTURE READING: James 3:1-12
PERSONAL APPLICATION: Pay particular attention to James 3:9-12. Ask the Holy Spirit to give you the grace and strength to watch and control the words you speak.

ACCORDING TO HIS WILL

"Therefore I say to you, whatever things you ask when you pray, believe that you receive them, and you will have them."
Mark 11:24

We need to have the basic understanding that prayer is about doing the will of God. Prayer is not just about you requesting things from God alone; it has to do with you requesting things that are in line with His will. "If you abide in Me, and My words abide in you, you will ask what you desire, and it shall be done for you" (John 15:7). There is a place where the Word of God should abide in you and when you know what God wants, you have confidence in prayer. Prayer is us participating with God for His will to be done on earth. Prayer can also be seen as the place of divine exchange. There are different kinds of prayer. There is the prayer of dedication, faith, consecration, supplication and intercession. Ephesians 6:18 tells us to pray with all manner of prayer. There is no better prayer to pray than the utterance granted to us by the Holy Ghost. He helps us to pray.

SCRIPTURE READING: Mark 11:24, John 15:7, Romans 8:26
PERSONAL APPLICATION: Have a look at Matthew 6:9-13. Who better to teach you how to pray than the Master Himself.

THE AUTHORITY OF THE WORD

"Man shall not live by bread alone, but by every word that proceeds from the mouth of God"
Matthew 4:4

It is usually very easy to think of ourselves in terms of our efforts and attempts at obedience to God. This wrongly becomes our own standard of obedience. Sometimes we compare ourselves with others and justify our efforts by theirs. Christ is the standard bearer of the Christian faith. He is the standard. His obedience is the quality expected of us by God. Christ in us is the only One who can live the Christ-life. God said, "this is my son in whom I am well pleased." The Son is still the one who pleases the Father. When we let Him live in and through us, we will be pleasing unto God as well. Jesus' obedience made a big difference in the scheme of things in God. The first Adam failed through disobedience, and Jesus, the last Adam, succeeded through obedience. Jesus did not come to die, He came to obey God and it so happened that laying down His life was part of God's plans for Jesus. How do we get into this quality of obedience? By studying how He came into this quality. Let us examine how He handled the temptation to disobey God in the wilderness of temptation (Matthew 3:13-4:11). Jesus committed to the Word of God over and above His felt needs. He shows us the way to handle such tests in our lives; to commit to every Word that comes from the mouth of God over and above our needs. It is interesting that Jesus did not mention the experience He had at the baptism of John when the scripture records that the Spirit of God came up on Him like a dove and a voice came from heaven acknowledging Him as the beloved Son. He demonstrated that His commitment was to the authority of the Word rather than to be based on the feeling He had during the experience of the dove and the spoken Word from heaven. Real as that was, He quoted the scripture that He was committed to. How committed are we to living by the standards of the Word of God? In the light of our appetites, our desires and our pride, will we give God's Word the authority in our lives? This is the way our Lord demonstrated His obedience to God and He set a pattern for us to obey likewise.

SCRIPTURE READING: Matthew 3:13-4:11
PERSONAL APPLICATION: We need to cultivate an intimacy with God that is based on His written Word and submit to the authority of God by allowing His Word to be the final authority in our lives.

THE SEED PRINCIPLE

"While the earth remains, seedtime and harvest,
Cold and heat, winter and summer,
And day and night shall not cease."
Genesis 8:22

The entire kingdom of God operates on the seed principle. Jesus made that clear in Mark 4 when He was discussing the parable of the sower. In verse 13, He asked if they understood the parable, because failure to understand it implies they may not understand the others. God Himself, in carrying out His redemption plan, planted the seed of His Son. The fundamental seed is the Word of God. He uses it for everything He does in His kingdom. If God is seed-minded, we should be too. Giving is one of the keys of the kingdom of God. The account of Matthew, showing the teachings of Christ, shows how He discusses giving, along with praying and fasting in Mark 6. He was teaching these subjects and revealing the right attitudes and heart posture we should have to do these things to get the results God wants us to get. So many realise the importance of praying and fasting, especially in dire circumstances, but fail to see the role of giving in such circumstances. In Luke 6:38, we read, "Give and it shall be given unto you, good measure pressed down and shaken together, running over shall men give to your bosom". This giving includes forgiving, not judging and not speaking evil of others. Whatever you give will be given back to you. Seedtime and harvest shall not cease says God Himself in Genesis 8:22. As I grew in my understanding of God's ways, purposes and plans, I realised that the goal of our Christian faith is not just to be blessed, important as that is, but that it also includes being conformed to the image of the Son as recorded in Romans 8:29. We please the Father when we allow His Son's image to be formed in us.

SCRIPTURE READING: Mark 4:1-33
PERSONAL APPLICATION: What does it mean to be "seed minded"? If we know that the Kingdom of God operates on the seed principle, what can we do to ensure that we sow the "right" seeds into our lives and the lives of others around us?

COME BOLDLY TO THE FATHER

"Father, I thank You that You have heard Me.
And I know that You always hear Me"
John 11:41-42

Because God is our Father, we have access to His presence. We have an open and standing invitation to come boldly, that is, fearlessly and confidently, to the throne of grace, to obtain whatever we need, whenever we need it (Hebrews 4:15-16). We've been made the righteousness of God in Christ Jesus, i.e., we have a right-standing with the Father. We are now God's children - not slaves; and we did not receive the spirit of bondage that makes us to fear, but we received the Spirit of sonship, by whom we cry out, "Abba, Father" (Romans 8:15-16). We're part of God's family. We are members of His household. How comforting and reassuring! God loves us and His love has been poured into our hearts by the Holy Spirit. The Bible says, "There is no fear in love; but perfect love casts out fear, because fear involves torment. But he who fears has not been made perfect in love" (1 John 4:18). Even when we sin and miss the mark, we can still come to God because "we do not have a High Priest who cannot sympathise with our weaknesses, but was in all points tempted as we are, yet without sin" (Hebrews 4:15).

SCRIPTURE READING: Hebrews 4:12-16, Hebrews 10:19-23
PERSONAL APPLICATION: We must not allow our sin to hinder or break our fellowship with the Father. The Bible says, "God is light and in Him is no darkness at all. If we say that we have fellowship with Him, and walk in darkness, we lie and do not practice the truth" (1 John 1:5-6). We already have an Advocate with the Father, Jesus Christ, the righteous. So all, we need to do is to humbly confess our sin to our Father and "He is faithful and just to forgive us our sins and to cleanse us from all unrighteousness" (1 John 1:9).

GUARD YOUR HEART

"Above all else, guard your heart,
for everything you do flows from it."
Proverbs 4:23 (NIV)

Whenever God wants to do a thing, He plants the seed of His Word in our hearts. The devil, on the other hand, cannot do anything unless he manipulates and influences what is in your heart. This shows that the heart is a sensitive part of our human component. In actual fact, it is the manufacturing centre for our future. You need to guard your heart by exposing your spirit to the Word of God. You must meditate in the Word constantly. The Bible says in Deuteronomy 8:3 *KJV*, "...man doth not live by bread only, but by every word that proceeds out of the mouth of the Lord doth man live." This means that our very sustenance springs from living by the Word of God. It is absolutely vital to train your spirit because that is one guarantee that you will do God's will. If you want to be a person of victory, you must feed your spirit with the Word of God. With this you enrich your inner man, thus increasing your Word level, your energy and light levels. When this increase is there, your inner man is strong and your soul is fed, thus making your mind sound. Your heart is the overlap between your spirit and soul. So, when your spirit/inner man is strong and your soul is well fed on His Word, you can be sure that your heart is well guarded. Give attention to the Word by reading, studying and meditating on it (Joshua 1:8).

SCRIPTURE READING: Proverbs 4:20-27
PERSONAL APPLICATION: Your heart is the manufacturing centre for your future. You need to give all diligence to it by guarding it. Expose it to the Word of God because that is the main source of its sustenance.

CULTIVATING INTIMACY WITH GOD

"I will instruct you and teach you in the way which you shall go; I will guide you with my eye."
Psalm 32:8

Intimacy implies familiarity, closeness, understanding, confidence and relationship. Someone called it "look into me and see". To cultivate intimacy means acceptance for, measuring worth to, and getting to recognise fine and delicate details about the one you are getting intimate with. Naturally this should happen in both parties that are coming into intimacy. This happens when the sense of worth is heightened and proper investigation is going on to know the person at a deeper level. I am sure that God's plan involves helping us cultivate this with a human being like us so we can value the quality He desires from us towards himself. The more you know, the more value you place on the intimate one. There are things about us all that are only known to the ones we are intimate with. We are moved by whatever affects our intimate partner. Intimacy is a function of quality time spent together. This requires focus and intensity. Intimacy is to be enjoyed, not endured. It can only happen when love is flowing out of a sense of deep appreciation, honour and understanding. When we direct our hearts' efforts towards God to cultivate intimacy with Him, we begin to see the deadness of religion without a personal relationship with God through the finished work of Calvary. It is not enough to have a salvation experience that is not leading us to pursue a meaningful and personal relationship with God through Christ. To have His presence, His power and see His purposes fulfilled we need to be intimate with Him. God Himself wants us to draw closer to Him and know the deep things in His heart for us, for His Kingdom and for Himself.

SCRIPTURE READING: Psalm 32:8, James 4:6-10
PERSONAL APPLICATION: How can we come to that place in our walk with God where we are so in tune with Him that we are guided by His eye? What things in our lives hinder our intimacy with God? How can we deal with them?

THE DIMENSIONS OF GOD'S MERCY

"The LORD is merciful and gracious, slow to anger and abounding in mercy."
Psalm 103:8

Recently, God began to show me that one of the ingredients that would make for victorious Christian living in these end times is His mercy; understanding and walking in it more than ever before. The Bible tells us very clearly that God is a merciful God. That is one of His many attributes and we must begin to see and know Him that way. Mercy, both in the Old and New Testaments, is defined as: compassion, pity, goodness, kindness, favour and graciousness. There are three major areas in which God shows His mercy. Firstly, in our sinfulness - even when we were sinners, before we ever believed and got saved! The Bible says that when we were still without strength, Christ died for the ungodly. "But God demonstrates His own love toward us, in that while we were still sinners, Christ died for us" (Romans 5:8). God knew that even after having been saved, we might still fall into sin, so He made a provision for that (1 John 2:1-2). Secondly, God shows us His mercy in our distresses, troubles and afflictions. "Many are the afflictions of the righteous, but the LORD delivers him out of them all" (Psalm 34:19). Thirdly, God shows us His mercy in our weaknesses. Though saved, we all have areas in which we are weak; areas where we tend to fail and to fall i.e. our faults and shortcomings (Hebrews 4:15-16). The Bible says that God is faithful. Not only will He not allow us to be tempted beyond what we are able to bear, He will also make the way of escape for us with every temptation we face (1 Corinthians 10:13). What a merciful God we serve! He is always looking out for us, not to 'get' us, but to help us out!

SCRIPTURE READING: Luke 15:11-32

PERSONAL APPLICATION: We shouldn't allow our sin or faults to drive us away from God but in spite of them, still go to Him for mercy and grace to help. The story of the prodigal son is a good example.

FREE FROM IDOLS

"At this the man's face fell, and he went away sad for he had many possessions."
Mark 10:22 NLT

Mark 10:17-30 tells us the story of the rich young ruler. Somehow this man knew that wealth had not given him eternal life. He came asking Jesus what he could do to have eternal life. Jesus told the man to keep the laws and he answered in the affirmative that he already did. Jesus told him he lacked one thing! That one thing must have been the basis for all the other things that he needed to deal with. Whenever we allow God to deal with us, He puts His loving hand on the main issues in our lives. The main issue in this man's life was his inability to give away what he had. His wealth had become his idol; it had a hold on him. To follow Jesus, he needed to be free from all the things that held him down on his inside. His obedience could not be complete while his wealth had such a hold on him. Giving away what he had was a major key to his deliverance. His obedience to Jesus to sell all he had and give to the poor meant that he would have to strip himself of the status money conferred on him. It also meant that his value system would be radically affected. A truly rich man must be rich inside his heart with a generous heart. What you are able to give, with respect to what you give, is what determines your true wealth. Jesus was giving him the missing key. Giving was the key to being set free to truly serve God. What has a hold on you can prevent you from fulfilling God's will for your life. When people have wealth without God, usually it is the wealth that has them as its slave. The only way to prevent this from happening is to be willing to give it away at any instance in obedience to God. Subject your wealth to God in obedience. Giving is a kingdom key to true abundance. Jesus was trying to teach this man how not to be enslaved by wealth by learning to give it away. When we obey and give, we give God the chance to work in us a dependence on Him, a deliverance from selfishness and to position us to let God provide for us supernaturally.

SCRIPTURE READING: Mark 10:17-30

PERSONAL APPLICATION: Allow the Holy Sprit to deal with you so that unlike the rich young ruler, you can willingly let go of anything that has a hold on you.

THE FINAL WORD

"In the beginning was the Word, and the Word was with God, and the Word was God."
John 1:1

Let the Word of God be final authority in your life. When you say Jesus is Lord of your life, understand that to mean that Jesus is the Word and the Word has final authority. That sounds very basic until you begin to consider one or two things. For example, when some people get saved, they say to themselves, "I feel saved, my feelings are changed, I experience a new birth" and people are excited. Wait until they (the same people) wake up one morning to circumstances in their lives and they don't feel saved. You then find out that their salvation was founded on their feelings; not on the Word of God. That is how simple it is. If you don't feel saved, are you saved? Make sure your foundation is not the feeling you had when you got saved. You need to labour to build that foundation on the Word. The Word says anyone who calls on the name of the Lord will be saved (Romans 10:13).

SCRIPTURE READING: John 1:1-4, Romans 10:10-13
PERSONAL APPLICATION: Think about how you can endeavour to ensure that your salvation is based on the Word of God and not merely based on your feelings or emotions. In the same way, spend time building your faith (whatever you are believing God for), on the Word of God rather than on mere feelings or experiences.

BEGIN AGAIN

"And they shall rebuild the old ruins, They shall raise up the former desolations, And they shall repair the ruined cities, The desolations of many generations."
Isaiah 61:4

Your attitude to what happens to you and your disposition to your trials will determine greatly how you come out of them. It is easier to sit around weeping than it is to rise up to begin to, "rebuild the old ruins, raise a new city out of the wreckage. They'll start over on the ruined cities, take the rubble left behind and make it new" (Isaiah 61:4 *MSG*). You don't need to run away from your problems. If you do, you will face them again. You must learn to face them! David ran towards Goliath. Someone said if the devil is after you, you are probably facing the wrong direction. Turn around and face him! The Bible says David attacked the Amalekites from twilight until the evening of the next day. "So David recovered all..." (1 Samuel 30:17-18). That is the attitude and disposition that will recover all, as opposed to the one that sits down and wonders why things are going wrong. David said, "I have pursued my enemies and overtaken them; Neither did I turn back again till they were destroyed. I have wounded them, So that they could not rise; They have fallen under my feet. For You have armed me with strength for the battle; You have subdued under me those who rose up against me" (Psalm 18:37-39). A lot of folks 'down tools' when they are going through challenges in their lives. That should not be the case if you are to see God turn your captivity around. "Those who sow in tears Shall reap in joy. He who continually goes forth weeping, Bearing seed for sowing, Shall doubtless come again with rejoicing, Bringing his sheaves with him" (Psalm 126:5-6). Even in your tears you can still sow and in your weeping you can still be bearing seed for sowing. That is the guarantee for a joyful harvest!

SCRIPTURE READING: Psalm 126
PERSONAL APPLICATION: In the midst of our trials, how can we build up and develop the right attitude and inner fortitude needed to face our Goliaths and recover all?

THE BATTLE OF THE MIND

"Casting down arguments and every high thing that exalts itself against the knowledge of God, bringing every thought into captivity to the obedience of Christ"
2 Corinthians 10:5

1 Corinthians 2:9-10 tells us that God has prepared some things for those who love Him and that He has revealed them to us through His Spirit. One of the functions of the Spirit of God is to show us the things that have been freely given to us. God has made these things available to us, but it is our responsibility to make sure we walk in the reality of these things. We need to embrace the reality of the mind of Christ because it is the mind of Christ that knows these things. Our greatest enemy is not Satan! Our greatest enemy is the man between our shoulders - our mind! If we can win that man, we have won the world. How do we change our mind? When a man first goes into the army, they subject him to things that eventually reprogramme him. It is a deception to believe that what you see or watch will not change your life. Your mind was designed to take in whatever you expose it to. To reprogramme it, we must submit to God by submitting to His Word. God has His own way of doing things. God's way with regard to finances is not the world's way. The same is true of divine protection, divine healing and so forth. We need to understand the ways of God. Often we try to force God to abide by our own programming but the truth is that God is too big to abide by our own programming. It is only when the seed of God's Word enters our hearts that our minds are forced to be reprogrammed. We will never change our mind until we change what we believe, what we say and what we do. At every given time there must be something that we are dealing with in our relationship with God and some truth that we are internalising.

SCRIPTURE READING: 2 Corinthians 5:17 *AMPC*
PERSONAL APPLICATION: How can we firstly find out and secondly walk in those things that God has made freely available to us? How do we begin the process of actively reconstructing and renewing our minds?

TAKING THE LIMITS OFF GOD

"But Jesus looked at them and said to them, 'With men this is impossible, but with God all things are possible.'"
Matthew 19:26

Today I want to share with you something I believe will set you free both spiritually and physically, to make you go for all that God wants for you. I don't want you to repeat your mistakes and failures. So, to this end I intend to share with you a principle that will enable you to take the limits off God. In Matthew 19:26, the Bible says, "with God nothing shall be impossible". For you to be able to achieve all you need to achieve in your life, you need to do things with God and be in line with His will. The Bible says in John 1:1-4 that God and His Word are one. That is to say that God is the same as His Word. Therefore to rephrase Matthew 19:26, it would read, 'WITH THE WORD nothing shall be impossible'. This should change the way you view and respect for the Word. Ask yourself, what would you attempt both for God and yourself if you had the assurance that you could never fail? What are the potentials and abilities that would be unleashed? We all know the above is true because God cannot lie. So why don't we take giant strides in God and for God? The limitations, I believe, come in through our attitude to God and His Word. Mark 4:24 *AMPC* says, "The measure [of thought and study] you give [to the truth you hear] will be the measure [of virtue and knowledge] that comes back to you—". From the above we can clearly see that it is not God that determines the measure of power, revelation and virtue that we get out of His Word, but us and our attitudes!

SCRIPTURE READING: Mark 4:24-25, John 1:1-4, Romans 10:17
PERSONAL APPLICATION: How can we actively change the way we view and value the Word of God?

NOT IN YOUR OWN STRENGTH

"So he answered and said to me: 'This is the word of the Lord to Zerubbabel: 'Not by might nor by power, but by My Spirit,' Says the Lord of hosts.'"
Zechariah 4:6

"Unless the Lord builds the house they labour in vain, who built it. Unless the Lord guards the city, the watchman stays awake in vain" (Psalm 127:1). We must start trusting God to help us raise godly children, instead of trusting in our own strength and our own know-how. "Not by might nor by power, but by My Spirit,' says the LORD of hosts" (Zechariah 4:6). God knows our children more than we do - He created them in the first place. He knows their constitution and understands their make-up. God knows what they are thinking, what they are going through and how to get across to them. If there are things you wish you could tell them or have been trying to get across to them, but haven't been able to, you can release your faith in God's Word that says, "All your children shall be taught by the Lord, and great shall be the peace of your children" (Isaiah 54:13). Ask for God's grace that brings salvation to be revealed to them, teaching them to deny ungodliness and worldly lusts and to live soberly, righteously and godly in the present age (Titus 2:11-12). Trust God to bless and prosper all your input into their lives; all the prayers, the teaching, the training, the discipline, the counselling, the love you show them, the time you spend with them, etc. Pray that they will yield the right results in their lives. Check out God's promises for your children and first of all claim them, then meditate on them, confess them over your kids and act on them. "Study this Book of Instruction continually. Meditate on it day and night so you will be sure to obey everything in it. Only then will you prosper and succeed in all you do" (Joshua 1:8 *NLT*).

SCRIPTURE READING: Isaiah 44:3, Isaiah 49:25, Joel 2:28, Psalm 112:2
PERSONAL APPLICATION: Spend time praying and entrusting the lives and futures of your children into God's hands (even if you don't yet have any of your own). Receive grace and wisdom from God to help you to raise godly children.

PUTTING FIRST THINGS FIRST

"This, then, is how you should pray:
'Our Father in heaven, hallowed be your name...'"
Matthew 6:9 NIV

"I exhort therefore, that, first of all, supplications, prayers, intercessions, and giving of thanks, be made for all men; For kings, and for all that are in authority; that we may lead a quiet and peaceable life in all godliness and honesty" (1 Timothy 2:1-2). So many times we fail to put first things first in our prayers. Prayer for those in authority is a recommended first in all our prayers. We all desire to live a quiet life in all godliness and holiness. Well, we have been told how. Pray for those in authority and for all men. That means your spouse, children and neighbours also. We need to pray in line with scripture. It is safe to say that if we pray according to His Word, we are praying according to His will. 1 John 5:14-15 says, "Now this is the confidence that we have in Him, that if we ask anything according to His will, He hears us. And if we know that He hears us, whatever we ask, we know that we have the petitions that we have asked Him."

SCRIPTURE READING AND PERSONAL APPLICATION:
Use the pattern shown in 1 Timothy 2:1-2 and spend time in earnest prayer, intercession and supplication for those in authority (governmental or otherwise) and for all men. The following scriptures are helpful in praying for family members that are about to come into the knowledge of salvation: 2 Corinthians 4:3-4, 1 Timothy 2:3-4, Acts 16:31. The following scriptures are helpful in praying for yourself and for loved ones: Ephesians 1:16-23, 3:14-19, Colossians 1:9-11. Read also Psalm 103 and Psalm 91

DEALING WITH GUILT

"There is no fear in love; but perfect love casts out fear, because fear involves torment. But he who fears has not been made perfect in love."
1 John 4:18

Guilt can produce in us a deep feeling of anger, resentment, frustration and bitterness. The deep-seated anger in many people is a product of the guilt they suffer from the unrealistic expectations and demands others have put on them at the expense of what they judged they could have done for themselves! Some people, out of guilt, spend their lives doing what they don't want to do, going where they never wanted to go, and worse still, at the expense of their own progress, they end up becoming very angry and bitter. Guilt is a wrong motivation for doing things for people. The brother of the prodigal son was very angry. He said to his father, "Lo these many years I have been serving you, I never transgressed your commandment at any time; and yet you never gave me a young goat, that I might make merry with my friends" (Luke 15:29). His father told him all he had was his! The question is, why hadn't he ever taken a young goat to make merry with his friends? So many times we place burdens or restrictions on ourselves that neither God nor anybody else has placed on us and when we find out later how much we've missed, we become angry and bitter.

SCRIPTURE READING: Luke 15:25-31
PERSONAL APPLICATION: Are there areas in your life where you are bound by guilt? As the exhortation mentions, are there burdens and restrictions that you have placed on yourself or allowed others to place on you? Spend time reading through today's scripture reading, paying particular attention to the prodigal son's brother. Then work through this question—how can I practically deal with guilt in my own life? Receive your freedom today from the bondage that guilt has placed on you (read John 8:36).

DEAD TO SIN

"Likewise you also, reckon yourselves to be dead indeed to sin, but alive to God in Christ Jesus our Lord."
Romans 6:11

The born-again man has a new and old nature living in him. He needs to know how to put one to death and how to let one come alive in him. The cross is the instrument of death for the old nature, and faith in Christ is the key to life for the new nature. Christ is to be formed in us through the process of the cross and the application of in-Christ truths in our lives. We must realise the power of the new creation and death that exists in the old creation. Sin has wrecked the old through selfishness and disobedience, and righteousness has been wrought through selflessness and the obedience of Christ. We must begin to reckon ourselves dead to sin and alive unto God. As we reckon ourselves dead, the Holy Spirit will make it a reality in our lives. We need to understand the new creation. It is by faith in Christ and it involves the suffering of the flesh, denying it and subjecting it to the reality of the Word. Whatever the old creation lost, the new regained it better than what was lost. See Romans chapters 4-6. Righteousness is more powerful than sin; faith more than fear, and love more than hate. Jesus Christ is the example of the new. He was totally subject to God, lived above sin, above Satan and above the world. He is the perfect example of the new creation. If you are born again, He is your pattern to follow.

SCRIPTURE READING: 2 Corinthians 5:16-17, Romans 4-6
PERSONAL APPLICATION: Why is it so important for us as Christians to realise the power of the new creation?

LIVING BY THE WORD OF GOD

"Man shall not live by bread alone, but by every word that proceeds from the mouth of God."
Matthew 4:4

We must live by 'every word' (not just a few agreeable words) that proceeds from God's mouth. This means, among other things, having one's life regulated, controlled and sustained by the Word of God. It means lining up your life with the Word of God. Jesus demonstrated, during the temptations, that His life was regulated and controlled by God's Word. He showed that the Word of God was the final authority in His life. He said repeatedly to the devil, "It is written" (Matthew 4:4, 7, 10). The Word of God created such a boundary around His life that Jesus wasn't going to cross even when He was hungry! The life of faith is a life of discipline. The Bible says where there is no vision or revelation, the people cast off restraint (or run wild). The life of faith is a disciplined lifestyle. Living by every Word of God is acting on it in spite of contrary evidence or what others might be saying. For example, God told Noah to build an ark when it had never rained before and he did it. Faith is having your life sustained by God's Word. Peter walked on water because Jesus asked him to come, and that word sustained Peter on the water until he began to doubt and be afraid (Matthew 14:28-31). Abraham left his country, his family and his father's house to go to an unknown land because God said so and that Word sustained him throughout! Elijah was told by God to go to the brook Cherith and then to the Widow in Zarephath and he was sustained throughout the famine period. To live by every word that proceeds out of God's mouth requires you to stay in constant fellowship with Him.

SCRIPTURE READING: Deuteronomy 8:1-3
PERSONAL APPLICATION: God has something to say to you every day about everything that concerns you, if you would listen. Confront everything in your life that hinders you from coming into alignment with the Word of God. Challenge certain mindsets you may have and/or belief systems that you have imbibed.

LIVING BY FAITH

"But solid food belongs to those who are of full age, that is, those who by reason of use have their senses exercised to discern both good and evil."
Hebrews 5:14

The Bible says, "The just shall live by faith" (Romans 1:17, Hebrews 10:38, Galatians 3:11). The Bible also says in Habakkuk 2:4, "the just shall live by his faith". This tells me first and foremost, that faith is meant to be the lifestyle of the believer, not what we do now and then or a panic button we press when we are in trouble. As a matter of fact, I suggest that if you haven't been living by faith before trouble comes, don't try to! If David had not killed the bear and the lion, it would have been presumptuous of him to try to take on Goliath. What you do at such a time is to ask around for prayers to get out of the trouble and then you can start building your faith. "He will not be afraid of evil tidings; his heart is steadfast, trusting in the LORD. His heart is established; he will not be afraid" (Psalm 112:7-8). This implies your heart must be fixed before the evil tidings come. That is the only guarantee that you won't be afraid. "In righteousness you shall be established; you shall be far from oppression, for you shall not fear; and from terror, for it shall not come near you" (Isaiah 54:14). All that stems from having been already established. I need to quickly say that one way to get your heart fixed or established is by studying and meditating in the Word of God. "But his delight is in the law of the LORD, and in His law he meditates day and night. He shall be like a tree planted by the rivers of water, that brings forth its fruit in its season, whose leaf also shall not wither; and whatever he does shall prosper" (Psalm 1:2-3).

SCRIPTURE READING: Psalm 121:1-8
PERSONAL APPLICATION: Spend time thinking about the areas of your life where you need to build your faith in God's Word.

KEEPING YOURSELF FROM IDOLS

"So the Lord alone led him,
And there was no foreign god with him."
Deuteronomy 32:12

What happens to you is not as important as what happens in you. So many times we spend time and resources on what happens to us rather than what happens in us. It is right to expect good things to happen to us but it is what happens in us that will determine what happens to us in the long run. What are your priorities? Is God your number one? What is your motivation? Is it selfish or self-centred? What is your focus? What is the fuel you are burning to do what you are doing? Is it merely emotional or spiritual? What about integrity of heart? Humility? Sincerity? Do you have the balance between principles and sensitivity to the Holy Spirit? You should have goals that will cause things to happen for you. Employ the principles but please don't forget to keep an eye on what is happening inside you. It is the lack of keeping an eye on what is happening inside us that has brought us to the place where we tolerate idols of materialism and have other gods besides Jehovah. Things become more important to us than our relationship with God. The Bible says, "little children keep yourselves from idols" (1 John 5:21). The *Amplified Bible* says, "...guard yourselves from idols—[false teachings, moral compromises and anything that would take God's place in your heart]." All the carnality that is distorting the testimony of Christians today is because these things creep up on us almost unawares. We need to keep ourselves from idols and put God first in our everyday lives.

SCRIPTURE READING: 2 Kings 5:1-27
PERSONAL APPLICATION: How can you identify and guard yourself from idols in your heart?

BECOMING FEARLESS

"The Lord is my light and my salvation; Whom shall I fear?
The Lord is the strength of my life;
Of whom shall I be afraid?"
Psalm 27:1

Fear will keep you in bondage to the devil, to people, to circumstance, to the status-quo and even to yourself! Fear will hold you back from breaking through! Fear will keep you in mediocrity. It will stop you from trying anything new, from breaking new grounds and new territories. Fear will stop you from investing in anything or anyone. Isaiah 54:2-4 says, "Enlarge the place of your tent, And let them stretch out the curtains of your dwellings; Do not spare; Lengthen your cords, And strengthen your stakes. For you shall expand to the right and to the left... Do not fear, for you will not be ashamed; Neither be disgraced, for you will not be put to shame." The question is, how much more would you be willing to do if you were sure you would not fail? Note that the children of Israel didn't enter the Promised Land because of fear! Fear is a product of unbelief and it always leads to disobedience if not overcome. To break through, you must confront and overcome your fears. Overcome the fear of people, the fear of failure, the fear of death, the fear of the future, the fear of the unknown, the fear of rejection, etc. Esther said, "if I perish, I perish" (Esther 4:16) but she never perished. The three Hebrews in Daniel 3 refused to bow to the image of gold and were thrown into the fiery furnace; but they didn't burn. If you will not bow to your fears, you will not burn! David's mighty men broke through the garrison of the Philistines to get water from the well of Bethlehem (1 Chronicles 11). Sometimes you need to break through the enemy territory to get what you need or desire! Jesus said, "Behold I give you the authority to trample on serpents and scorpions and over all the power of the enemy and nothing shall by any means hurt you" (Luke 10:19).

SCRIPTURE READING: Isaiah 54:2-4, Luke 5:1-7
PERSONAL APPLICATION: The question mentioned in this devotional is a really good one to stop and ponder on. Ask yourself sincerely, how much more would you be willing to do for God if you had the assurance that you would not fail? What are the things hindering you?

COUNT IT ALL JOY

"My brethren, count it all joy when you fall into various trials, knowing that the testing of your faith produces patience."
James 1:2-3

God's perspective on trials is, 'count it all joy'. Becoming a Christian does not automatically exclude a believer from difficulties. The proper attitude in meeting adversity is to count it all joy, which is not an emotional reaction but a deliberate intelligent appraisal of the situation from God's perspective, viewing trials as a means of moral and spiritual growth. We do not rejoice in trials themselves, but in their possible results. Testing carries the idea of proving genuineness. Trials serve as a discipline to purge faith of dross, stripping away what is false. Trials also work out endurance in us. When our Christian character goes through hardship, hope of receiving what God has promised grows stronger within us. In the trials we face, we are to ask for wisdom. Usually we do not know what to do but God does! We need to ask in faith. God wants to help us through the trials we face. Our inner attitudes of faith and endurance will help us experience the help of God. The wisdom we need here is the spiritual understanding of the purpose of trials and what to do about them. God is liberal and without reproach, that is, generous, not stingy, not condescending or begrudging. Settle it in your heart that God is not against you but for you. Don't run from Him but run to Him for all the help you need in your trials.

SCRIPTURE READING: John 15:20, 2 Timothy 3:12, 1 Peter 1:6-7, 4:12-19
PERSONAL APPLICATION: Think about ways in which, in the midst of adversity, you can give a deliberate intelligent appraisal of the situation from God's perspective rather than lending yourself to a purely emotional reaction.

UNDERSTANDING UNBELIEF

"Jesus said to him, 'If you can believe, all things are possible to him who believes.' Immediately the father of the child cried out and said with tears, 'Lord, I believe; help my unbelief!'"
Mark 9:23-24

Unbelief is a function of the thoughts we permit into our minds. These thoughts hinder our acceptance, hence believing and receiving God's truth into our hearts. This can be seen in the account of Jesus not being able to do mighty works in His hometown because of the unbelief of the people there (Mark 6:2-6). Their unbelief was a function of the kind of contrary thoughts they had permitted in their minds. What we believe and the thoughts we allow determine what is inside each and every one of us. Sometimes we do not allow beliefs that are contrary to God's Word and yet we still do not get results. This is because faith needs to have corresponding actions for the results to be seen. Many believe they do not have faith simply because they do not see results. They do not ask themselves whether they have applied themselves to corresponding actions that faith demands. So it is possible to have faith and not get results if we do not act out our faith. Faith must be based on God's Word, believed in the heart, spoken in expectation and acted upon. So we have Believing, Actions, Speaking, Expectations (BASE). Believing with the heart implies that we believe by choice and put our whole being behind it. It implies being established in the belief!

SCRIPTURE READING: Mark 6:2-6, Romans 10:9-13
PERSONAL APPLICATION: Belief and unbelief are both a function of the thoughts we think. Challenge yourself in the light of today's devotional to watch and question the thoughts you allow in your mind. Choose to think on, believe, act on, confess and expect the Word of God to come to pass in your life.

KEEPING YOUR PEACE

"Do all that you can to live in peace with everyone."
Romans 12:18 NLT

How many times have we laid awake in the night, unable to sleep, thinking about all the wrongs others have done against us? (It's even more pathetic when they don't even know they've hurt us!). And if we eventually manage to sleep off, we continue from where we stopped when we wake up! These thoughts occupy our minds and we lose our peace. Some people even find it hard to rest until they feel 'justice' has been done by them; until they've got 'an eye for an eye' and 'a tooth for a tooth.' And have you noticed the kind of bitterness that rises up in you, when you are thinking of hitting back? It's always shocking to know the evil we are capable of doing when we yield to the flesh. Getting back at someone usually robs you of your peace. How do you feel after you've just hit back at someone who wronged you; after you've just slandered them in return or shouted back at them or said an unkind word to them? Do you feel good inside? Do you feel that you've achieved something great? Are you able to have a great time of fellowship with God thereafter? It is very fleshly to retaliate and when we do that we never feel approved by God. We usually spend some time afterwards fixing a lot of damages done - done to us internally, to our relationship with God and to our relationship with others. They say, 'you might win an argument, but might have also lost a friend'; the truth is, we actually lose a lot more. It is of utmost importance for us to maintain our peace at all cost because it is one of the powerful components that make up the Kingdom of God (Romans 14:17).

SCRIPTURE READING: Matthew 5:38-42, Romans 12:18
PERSONAL APPLICATION: Romans 12:18 is a scripture not to be taken lightly for the sake of your relationship with God and with others, as well as your own peace. The key to this is learning to put the flesh under!

IDENTITY AND PURPOSE

"To Him who loved us and washed us from our sins in His own blood,
and has made us kings and priests to His God and Father,
to Him be glory and dominion forever and ever. Amen.
Revelation 1:5-6

Who are you? Who are we in Christ? Ephesians 1 has a lot to say about this. The principles of faith find their place in this stream. They are fundamental to our walk with God. We must be established in who we are in Christ. When we know who we are, we can then know what we can do. We must have the image of God in us; how God sees us in Christ. We have been made legally righteous, saved, redeemed, sanctified, blessed and empowered. We need to see these things as already settled so we can start walking in them. Know your identity in Christ. God is revealing His purpose to us in Christ. Everything God does has a purpose. The prophetic teachings coming into the Body of Christ are for a purpose. The purpose of all these teachings is Christlikeness. The changes that Moses, Joseph and others went through, before they came to the fulfilment of purpose, can be likened to the changes that produce Christlikeness in us. How do you relate with the experiences in your life? Your attitude matters a lot. How much of Christ is reflected in you? Like Esther, can you say, "if I perish, I perish"? Like Ruth, can you forsake all and follow after covenant love? We need a sense of purpose. As we act on God's Word, let us stand true to His Word and character. Read Mathew 5 and see the Beatitudes. No matter what we are going through, if we pray in the spirit, speak God's Word, keep our hearts tender before God and walk in love, God will work out His purpose in our lives.

SCRIPTURE READING: Matthew 5:1-12, Ephesians 1:1-22
PERSONAL APPLICATION: Why is it so vital for you to be established in who you are in Christ? Think about how that knowledge will transform your walk and relationship with God, and even the way you see yourself.

INTIMACY WITH GOD

"O God, You are my God; early will I seek You;
My soul thirsts for You; my flesh longs for You
In a dry and thirsty land where there is no water."
Psalm 63:1

Intimacy needs to be cultivated in any relationship we desire to have it in. Intimacy is a function of love. The scriptures say, "You shall love the Lord thy God with all your might and mind" (Matthew 22:37) and "If you love me, keep my commandments" (John 14:15). The proof of love is keeping the commandments. Our love for God will drive us to obedience. Loving God should be the basis of our obedience to Him. Real intimacy with God is guaranteed when we balance our love for God with an honour and respect for Him. This comes as a result of our fear of God. There are things that hinder intimacy. These include: not wanting to be vulnerable before another, fear of rejection, fear of being taken advantage of, suspicion and fear of ulterior motives. The love of God and the love for God are antidotes for these hindrances. When we get born again and are filled with the Spirit of God, the love of God is shed in our hearts and by revelation, the Spirit of God impresses on our hearts just how much God loves us. As we study and apply God's Word in our lives, our knowledge of Him increases and we grow in confidence towards Him. We cultivate intimacy by desiring to communicate regularly through all kinds of prayers: adoration, supplication, thanksgiving and worship. Then we ask Him questions and maintain communion with Him. Intimacy does not just happen; it takes time to build. All the factors mentioned here will lead us to intimacy and our discernment will be sharper as we grow in grace.

SCRIPTURE READING: Philippians 3:10 *AMPC*, John 14:15 *AMPC*
PERSONAL APPLICATION: How can we actively cultivate greater intimacy with God?

UNCOVERING THE TRAPS OF MONEY

"For the love of money is the root of all kinds of evil.
And some people, craving money, have wandered from the true faith
and pierced themselves with many sorrows."
1 Timothy 6:10 NLT

We need a clear understanding of God's purpose, perspective and plans for money or wealth in these last days. The love of money and the deceitfulness of riches are two traps that have the tendency to move people from one extreme to another. On one side of the extreme, some believe in being poor to be holy. The other extreme are those who think that without money nothing good can happen. So they worship money all their lives. Wherever the love of money is, greed, selfishness and covetousness are found. These all lead to being deceived by riches. You may not have anything and still be deceived. If your value system in life is governed by acquisition of wealth, external showmanship and a display of affluence, especially if your internal character (based on your relationship with God) is not the basis or foundation for your riches, you are already deceived and need a radical shake up. There are some things money can buy; others are beyond its reach. It can buy a house but not a peaceful home.

SCRIPTURE READING: Mark 10:17-30
PERSONAL APPLICATION: The main issue in the rich young ruler's life was his inability to give away what he had. His wealth had become his idol; it had a hold on him. What are the things that have a hold on your life that hinder your ability to truly follow God?

DEVELOPING A PRAYER LIFE

"Call to Me, and I will answer you, and show you great and mighty things, which you do not know."
Jeremiah 33:3

Prayer is absolutely critical for a healthy existence. It is our reality being brought into the reality of God. It is our willingness to exchange our weakness for His strength, our ignorance for His wisdom and our confusion for His clarity. How real or relevant is your prayer life? Are you really willing to learn, change or adjust as a result of your prayer? Can God show you, by His Spirit, what strongholds are operating in your life? We are the variables and God is the constant. We need the strength that comes from His dependability. We need to grow in our capacity for leadership, wisdom and understanding, and these are enhanced through an effective prayer life. Through prayer we can also extend our influence in the lives of people through praying for them. Real praying sometimes sounds like this: "Lord, why am I feeling the way I am feeling?" and answers like this can be expected: "it's your pride and selfishness that have blinded you to the contribution of others in your life. That is why you are feeling so angry, envious or offended". Now that is real praying! If you have not been hearing from God, maybe you are not really praying to Him. Jeremiah 33:3 says, "Call on Me and I will answer you and show you great and mighty things which you do not know." Luke 18:1-8 talks about praying and not giving up. God answers prayer! Pray according to His Word, aided by His Spirit, and you can expect answers from heaven.

SCRIPTURE READING: Matthew 6:5-15, Luke 18:1-8
PERSONAL APPLICATION: Prayer enhances every area of our lives. It is in that place of prayer that God can indeed show us things and deal with issues in our lives that need confronting. In the light of this devotional, challenge yourself to make your prayer life even more real and relevant to your day to day life and give God the freedom to confront every area of your life.

ENTERING INTO HIS REST

"So shall My word be that goes forth from My mouth;
It shall not return to Me void,
But it shall accomplish what I please,
And it shall prosper in the thing for which I sent it."
Isaiah 55:11

Many struggle to see God's power manifested in their lives. There is a place in God called 'entering into His rest'. After we have done our due diligence in believing, acting, speaking and expecting His Word to be fulfilled in our lives, we should labour to enter His rest. We should not allow unbelief and ignorance of His ways to derail us from experiencing His power in our lives. This is because unbelief and ignorance are two ways in which the enemy can take advantage of us. Laziness and carelessness are some other ways too. Let us not allow the enemy of our souls (Satan) to have any foothold in our lives. Satan's allies are the unrenewed mind, carnality and other fleshly tendencies not brought under the Lordship of Christ. Abraham is an example of one who entered into God's rest according to what God told him. We can learn from the father of faith. No unbelief or distrust made him waver (doubtingly question) concerning the promise of God, but he grew strong and was empowered by faith as he gave praise and glory to God. He was fully satisfied and assured that God was able and mighty to keep His Word and to do what he had promised.

SCRIPTURE READING: Hebrews 3:7-19, Hebrews 4:1-3, 10-12, Romans 4:16-21
PERSONAL APPLICATION: What does it mean to enter into the rest of God? Think about areas in your life where you need to enter into the rest of God. It could be in your finances, or your health, or regarding a certain situation... Once we have entered into His rest, we can expect His power to make the difference in our lives and situations.

THE RIGHT MOTIVE

"Talk no more so very proudly;
Let no arrogance come from your mouth,
For the Lord is the God of knowledge;
And by Him actions are weighed."
1 Samuel 2:3

Motive has to do with 'why?'. It has to do with the state of our hearts. It is the unseen force that drives what we do and say. God told Samuel not to look at Eliab's outward appearance because He looks at the heart. "Don't judge by his appearance or height, for I have rejected him" (1 Samuel 16:7 *NLT*). The LORD doesn't make decisions the way you do! People judge by outward appearance, but the LORD looks at a person's thoughts and intentions. Moses killed an Egyptian in defence of a fellow Israelite, "for he supposed that his brethren would have understood that God would deliver them by his hand, but they did not understand" (Acts 7:24-25). Though Moses had a genuine call, God still had to purify his motive. He had to flee from Egypt and for forty years he was in the wilderness before God called him to go deliver His people. Joseph interpreted the dream of the butler and said to him, "But remember me when it is well with you, and please show kindness to me; make mention of me to Pharaoh, and get me out of this house" (Genesis 40:14). Joseph spent two more years in the prison. The butler completely forgot about him until Pharaoh had a dream. I call that divine! We get disappointed because we do things out of wrong motives. God wants to purify our motives.

SCRIPTURE READING: Malachi 3:2-3, Philippians 2:1-11
PERSONAL APPLICATION: Just because we do or say the 'right' thing, does not automatically mean our motive for saying or doing that thing is correct. Think about how we can accurately identify what our true motives are for our words and actions. Ask God to purify those motives.

THE REMEDY TO SIN

"For by one offering He has perfected forever those who were being sanctified."
Hebrews 10:14

One day I had an intense insight about the plight of the human race. Sin is the root of our problem and it is one thing we don't seem to know what to do in order to stop it and its effects in our lives. Sin destroys the sinner! No matter one's race or culture, one thing all humans have in common is the sin nature. Sin is what Satan took advantage of to bring separation from God in the life of human beings. Sin gives Satan a foothold in our lives to steal, kill and destroy. No matter how good we are in other endeavors, sin will end up destroying everything good in its path. The only remedy to sin is the cross of Christ. At the cross, justice and mercy met together. The 'weakness' and 'foolishness' of God have proved to be more powerful and wiser than the wisdom of men. The cross represents God's 'weakness': the death of His Son. It also represents His 'foolishness': His death on the cross is the basis for the reconciliation of the human race and the defeat of Satan. Jesus was priest and the offering was His body and blood. Once and for all His sacrifice was made and all the provisions are eternally available to whosoever believes.

SCRIPTURE READING: Hebrews 10:5-18
PERSONAL APPLICATION: Remember that the cross of Jesus is the answer to sin. Apply the cross and everything that Jesus Christ has made available to us in your life today.

SAVED BY GRACE

"For by grace you have been saved through faith, and that not of yourselves; it is the gift of God."
Ephesians 2:8

"God saved you by His special favour when you believed. And you can't take credit for this; it is a gift from God. Salvation is not a reward for the good things we have done, so none of us can boast about it" (Ephesians 2:8-9 *NLT*). Salvation doesn't stop at the new birth; that is only the beginning. Salvation is an all-encompassing word and an on-going experience. It also includes deliverance, healing, well-being, prosperity, safety, etc. The same way we were not saved from eternal doom by our own works, we won't be saved from sicknesses, diseases, oppression, poverty and so forth by our own works! This truth set me free years ago; I stopped trying to get healed by my good works. I started to see healing also as a gift from God, through the finished work of Calvary. That to me, answered the question, "what of so and so who served God so faithfully and yet didn't get healed?" God showed me that healing is not a reward for the good things we have done; no, it is by grace! If God showed us so much mercy when we were sinners and enemies of God, how much more will He show us great mercy now that we are His children?

SCRIPTURE READING: Romans 5:9-10, Isaiah 49:14-16
PERSONAL APPLICATION: Spend time meditating on this profound statement: why would God show us so much love as sinners and then have nothing reserved for us now that He has wooed us to Himself?

HONOURED OF GOD

"Nevertheless do not rejoice in this, that the spirits are subject to you, but rather rejoice because your names are written in heaven."
Luke 10:20

The meditations of my heart on this subject started rather unexpectedly. I was thinking on the verse in Luke 10, where Jesus said the disciples should rejoice that their names were written in the book of life. It was the thought of having my name in heaven that began to fill me with honour. I am honoured to have my name written in heaven. I thought through on the basis for my name or anyone else's to be on the list in heaven. The first is salvation. When we get saved our names will be noted in heaven. Those who love God get recognized in heaven. When we get sold out on God in consecration heaven recognises us. The service we render to God with all our hearts gets us on the roll call. Heaven protects, provides, guides and reveals things to all whose names are written. Can you consider how many ways we have been honoured as believers? We are saved by the blood and kept by the power of God. Consider the love of God and all his provisions in the new covenant and imagine how honoured we are to belong to such a great God as we have. It is in the light of being honoured that I perceived the Lord saying, "how much have you honoured Me?" Do we really honour the Lord?

SCRIPTURE READING: Luke 10:19-20, Revelation 3:4-5, 20:12, 21:27
PERSONAL APPLICATION: In the light of today's devotional, sincerely ask yourself if indeed you have really honoured the Lord; not just in a select few areas of your life, but in the entirety of your life. Make a fresh commitment to God today to love, honour and to give Him precedence in your whole life.

BECOMING YOUR BEST

"For if you remain completely silent at this time, relief and deliverance will arise for the Jews from another place, but you and your father's house will perish. Yet who knows whether you have come to the kingdom for such a time as this?"
Esther 4:14

It is natural for us after a while to settle down and become very comfortable where we are. We need not only the environment of love and acceptance but also of challenge and loving confrontation. Our fears, complacency, laziness, etc., need to be confronted and our potential must be challenged. Esther had settled down to the comfort of the palace. She was too scared to do something about the plight of the Jews, but Mordecai challenged her to do something and not be silent. Esther took the challenge and her potential to save a whole race was released. You need people who will not agree with you when you say you can't, but who will look you straight in the eye and say you can! Sometimes we don't know how much potential lies within us until we find ourselves in the right environment. This is why people attend seminars, training, conferences and read books; so their potential can be challenged. Interact with people that will sharpen your potential. Rub minds with people that will always give you something to think about. Don't just stay around people who are like you or make you feel you have arrived, but around people who will stretch you and challenge you to reach out for more. It is good encouragement to know that you are not where you used to be, but you must also know you haven't yet arrived! So, keep your eye on the goal.

SCRIPTURE READING: Esther 4:1-17, Proverbs 13:20, 27:17, Philippians 3:13
PERSONAL APPLICATION: It's not easy to have people around us that confront and challenge us even though it is for our best. Learn to recognise and place a value on such relationships even when what they might tell us is not particularly palatable.

EMBRACING PROCESS

"Jesus said to him, 'I am the way, the truth, and the life.
No one comes to the Father except through Me.'"
John 14:6

Process - this is what we go through to maximize the potential that lies within us. It is the moving from phase to phase in the stages of development to fulfil purpose. We are seeing that process is the unspoken part of many statements in the Bible. It takes reading with insight to see the hidden dimension called process. Jesus says, "I am the Way, the Truth and the Life" (John 14:6). On the surface it sounds like once you come to the way you immediately know the truth and have the life. Experience has shown this not to be quite so. Moving in Christ from the stage of the way to the truth then the life is like moving from the outer court to the Holy Place to the Holiest of all. It is like having knowledge, understanding and wisdom. This is so since the Bible says God "desires all men to be saved and to come to the knowledge of the truth" (1 Timothy 2:4). Being saved and coming into the knowledge of the truth are different aspects of God's program. Many are saved, come to the way, have knowledge (without spiritual insight called understanding) and are staying in the outer court rejoicing at their salvation experience. Staying here is what constitutes the problem. We are meant to go on into the Truth and walk in the Life. Jesus says He came that we may have Life more abundantly. As we walk in the truth of who we are, who God is, who Satan is and how things are meant to work, we begin to walk in the life. When the word becomes flesh in us, we begin to walk in the life. We progress from 30 to 60 then to 100 fold of all God has for us as we embrace a journey mentality through the process God has for us.

SCRIPTURE READING: Job 23:10-12

PERSONAL APPLICATION: We need to embrace God's process in our lives even though process is not always comfortable. Going through it will release us into a greater dimension of what God has for us and who He would have us to be. Read through and meditate on the story of Joseph to see the process that God took him through—the pit, slavery, the prison and eventually prime minister of Egypt!

A PLACE OF SAFETY

"The Lord is your keeper;
The Lord is your shade at your right hand."
Psalm 121:5

The *Amplified Bible, Classic Edition* says, "live purposefully and worthily and accurately" (Ephesians 5:15). "All things work together for good to those who love God, to those who are the called according to His purpose" (Romans 8:28).
Find out what God is doing and plug yourself into it. The safest place to be is in the centre of God's will. Mordecai told Esther, "If you keep quiet at a time like this, deliverance and relief for the Jews will arise from some other place, but you and your relatives will die. Who knows if perhaps you were made queen for just such a time as this?" (Esther 4:14 *NLT*). Esther got the message and said, "If I perish, I perish". She took her life in her hands, as it were, and she approached the king. Esther didn't die! Why? She was right at the centre of the will of God. Many folks today are playing into the hands of Satan because they are out of the will of God. Don't let the fear of death, lack or rejection push you out of God's will and right into Satan's waiting claws! The will of God has the power to protect you from evil. The centre of His will is the place of protection, provision and promotion. "He that does the will of the Lord abides forever" (1 John 2:17). These days are so evil that you must ensure you stay where He wants you to be, go only where He wants you to go, do only what He wants you to do and say only what He wants you to say.

SCRIPTURE READING: Psalm 91:1-2, Psalm 121
PERSONAL APPLICATION: Ask yourself; 'how can I know if I am in the will of God or not?' If you notice that there are areas of your life where you are not in alignment to God's will, prayerfully submit those areas to God and receive the grace, strength, wisdom and willingness you need to get back to where you know you need to be.

THE CROSS OF DIVINE EXCHANGE

"Let us therefore come boldly to the throne of grace, that we may obtain mercy and find grace to help in time of need."
Hebrews 4:16

We all need to come to the cross and by faith receive what Jesus suffered to make available so we can live wholesome lives and glorify the Father God. We no longer have to suffer the rejection, failure, limitations and sickness of the past! In his writings, Apostle Paul calls us to take full advantage of our new position in Christ as seen in Ephesians 1-3 and challenges us to our responsibilities, relationships and thereafter warfare in Ephesians 4-6. We are accepted in the beloved (Ephesians 1:6) because He bore our rejection on the cross when He cried, "My God, My God, why have you forsaken me?" (Matthew 27:46). Through this we gained the acceptance due Him as a result of His sinless life! He suffered shame on the cross that we may share in His glory. He was perfected through suffering that He may bring many sons to glory. Isaiah 53 spells out the picture of our suffering Saviour; wounded for our transgressions, bruised for our iniquities and the chastisement of our peace was upon Him and by His stripes we are healed. He was rejected, smitten of God and afflicted. He bore the sins of mankind on Himself. Our Messiah fulfilled the justice requirement of God the Father and gained full redemption for the entire human race. Now we can and should proclaim salvation in no other name but the name of Jesus our Lord and Master. He became a curse on our behalf that we may be free from the effects and influence of the curse that befell the human race as a result of sin. He also took on our poverty so we can take on His riches. We now have the blessing of Abraham, God's covenant friend. He was blessed in everything.

SCRIPTURE REFERENCE: Isaiah 53:1-12
PERSONAL APPLICATION: Rise up today and begin to take full advantage of your new position in Christ.

TIME IN THE WORD

"Your word I have hidden in my heart,
That I might not sin against You."
Psalm 119:11

One of the ways we seek God's face is by spending time in His Word. His Word reveals His mind, His ways, His will and His plans for us. Jesus said, "If you abide in Me, and my words abide in you, you will ask what you desire and it shall be done for you" (John 15:7). God and His Word are one, so, if we have His Word abiding in us, when we pray, our prayers will be in alignment with His will. As we fellowship with His Word, His Word begins to shape even our desires and then when we ask what we desire, we get it! "Delight yourself also in the Lord, and He shall give you the desires of your heart" (Psalm 37:4). Psalm 1 talks about the man who delights in the law of the Lord and meditates in it day and night. God's Word is not only His will; it is also His covenant and His bond. We come to Him based on His Word - the provisions of His Word. There are matters that God has hidden in His Word; not from us, but for us, and it is our glory to search them out. The Bible says the things which are revealed to us belong to us and our children forever (Deuteronomy 29:29) but the responsibility is ours to dig them out. We must position ourselves in the study of, and meditation in the Word of God to reveal those things to us.

SCRIPTURE READING: 1 John 5:14-15, Psalm 1:1-6
PERSONAL APPLICATION: Why is it so vital to spend time in the Word of God? Make a fresh dedication today to realign your life and to spend quality time in the Word of God, seeking His face.

SETTING GODLY GOALS

"I have fought the good fight, I have finished the race,
I have kept the faith."
2 Timothy 4:7

To set a goal is to take the initiative that, given the perceived available resources and the given circumstances, one desires a particular outcome and one goes for it. Goal setting is the art of purposing in one's heart what exactly one wants to achieve or accomplish. It has many benefits as it helps us steward our time and possibly increase our potential. All through the Bible we see goals set and achieved, even though the word "goals" isn't written in the Bible. No great achievement was ever produced without it being set as a goal, even if it was not described as, or called, a goal. Goal setting can become a tool to help time management as well as inspire productivity and help accomplish great things in life. It can be used by an individual or any organisation and the results can be phenomenal when used properly. When written down, goals can become like a blueprint for the process we choose to go through to accomplish great projects. For us believers, some goals have been set for us in the Bible. They are character and service goals (read Romans 8:29-30). To be conformed to the image of the Son is to be transformed in character, having intimacy with the Father as well as in demonstrating God's power in our lives. Our Lord Jesus becomes the example by which we measure our progress in the things of God. He also gave us the mandate to go into all the world and make disciples of all nations. He promised us that signs will follow our ministries as we lay hands on the sick and cast out devils.

SCRIPTURE READING: Matthew 28:18-20, Mark 16:15-18, Romans 8:29-30
PERSONAL APPLICATION: We need action goals that will lead to the overall results we expect. For example, a goal such as reading the entire Bible in one year will bring us closer to God as we meditate on the scriptures we read and broaden our knowledge of the Word of God. May God help you from today to be a goal setter and achiever in Jesus' Name.

OVERCOMING THE IDENTITY CRISIS

"I will praise You, for I am fearfully and wonderfully made;
Marvellous are Your works, and that my soul knows very well."
Psalm 139:14

The greatest crisis in the world today is that of identity. Who are you really? Are you who the world says or thinks you are? On the other hand, are you who others say you are? You might even be assessing yourself by your own opinion of yourself; who do you say or think you are? When I was growing up, I realised how powerful the opinions of others (especially when verbalised) can be in forming my opinion of myself and in creating confusion in my mind about myself. Who am I really? I am definitely not who the world or others say I am. I'm not who I even think I am. I am who God says I am! No matter who the world says you are or what other people's or even your own assessment of yourself is, it is time to overcome that crisis by embracing the reality of who God says you are in His Word. "...but let God transform you into a new person by changing the way you think" (Romans 12:2 *NLT*). The way we think matters a great deal because, "as a man thinks in his heart, so is he" (Proverbs 23:7). We must let the Word of God mould our thoughts about ourselves. For you to do exploits in God, you must start seeing yourself the way He sees you. Fellowship with the Holy Spirit and you will begin to know God's thoughts towards you; that they are for good and not for evil (Jeremiah 29:11); that they are way higher than your thoughts about yourself (Isaiah 55:9); that they are precious and uncountable (Psalm 139:17-18). God is not thinking about how to punish you and get back at you for the wrong you did; He is looking forward to having you repent so He can enjoy good fellowship with you, just like the father of the prodigal son (Luke 15:11-32).

SCRIPTURE READING: Psalm 139:13-18, Ephesians 1:3-13
PERSONAL APPLICATION: Allow the Word of God to mould and challenge the way you see yourself. There is great power in knowing who you really are.

UNDERSTANDING THE GRACE OF GIVING

"Give, and it will be given to you. A good measure, pressed down, shaken together and running over, will be poured into your lap. For with the measure you use, it will be measured to you."
Luke 6:38 NIV

Apostle Paul refers to giving as a grace, and I have found out that giving is a major key to the operation of grace in our lives. The attitude and stance of being a giver activates grace in the life of a believer. I am talking about the giving that is motivated by the love of God (Agape). It is our privilege to give; it delivers us from selfishness. It increases our capacity to receive and develops our confidence in God's ability to sustain us. The condition for this is if we give as unto the Lord. To glorify God in our giving, He must be our focus as we do it. In 2 Corinthians 8 from verse 1, we see how the churches of Macedonia gave in response to some needs in other churches as Paul had informed them. This grace of giving was so prevalent amongst them that he said that despite the great trial of affliction, the riches of their liberality revealed the abundance of their joy and the depth of their poverty. I believe they gave because of their joy in spite of their poverty because of the grace of giving. They were freely willing and implored Paul to receive from them with urgency. They gave themselves to God first then to the apostles (2 Corinthians 8:5) by the will of God. Giving ourselves to the Lord is the first step in our flow of this grace. Many believe in Jesus but have not given themselves over to Him. When we give to others without first giving of ourselves to God, we tend to feel manipulated by others. The role God plays in our lives should be central in all we do. We are instructed in the Word to do all things as unto the Lord and in the Name of the Lord. Whatever good anyone does, he will receive the same from the Lord (Ephesians 6:8). Our reward is from the Lord, not from the ones who we give to.

SCRIPTURE READING: 2 Corinthians 8:1-15
PERSONAL APPLICATION: We've read that our motive for giving should be the love of God. Ask the Holy Spirit to search your heart and reveal any area where your giving is motivated by the wrong thing (read Psalm 139:23-24).

WALKING IN THE COUNSEL OF THE WISE

"There is a way that seems right to a man,
But its end is the way of death."
Proverbs 14:12

Psalm 1:1-3 says, "Blessed is the man who walks not in the counsel of the ungodly... But his delight is in the law of the LORD... He shall be like a tree planted by the rivers of water." The *Moffat Translation* says, "Happy is the man who never goes by the advice of the ungodly." We must however take note that a Christian isn't necessarily godly nor necessarily gives godly counsel. If not, Paul wouldn't admonish Christians to exercise themselves toward godliness (1 Timothy 4:7). The question is what the counsel is based on; is it in the Word or not? Jesus likened those who hear His words but don't do them to the foolish builder who built his house on the sand. He built a house quite all right but not on the rock; he built on sand - representing human and fleshly opinions and standards. Jesus said that great was the fall of that house when the storms came! It will take the storms of life to reveal what we and our lives are made of and built upon. Psalm 127:1 says, "Except the LORD builds the house, they labour in vain who build it". Note that the Bible did not say they didn't build, but it says their labour was in vain. How painful it is to find out at the end of the day that one's labour had only been in vain! But that is what is bound to happen if one doesn't build by the Word. There is a way that seems right to man but the end of it is destruction (Proverbs 14:12). Note that it is the end of it; not the start of it. Yet people have built marriages, families, ministries and even lives on every other thing but the Word. This is because it is easier to build on sand than on the rock. Did you notice that the man that built on the rock had to dig deep to get to the rock? Sand is superficial and the human nature loves superficiality. Sand is commonly found around and our nature likes to 'commonise'. The opposite of 'holy' is 'common'. You don't need much effort to build on sand and the human nature doesn't enjoy hardwork.

SCRIPTURE READING: Psalm 1:1-3, Matthew 7:24-27
PERSONAL APPLICATION: How can we discern whether the counsel we are receiving is godly or not?

LORD LIGHT MY CANDLE

"If one walks in the night, he stumbles because the light is not in him."
John 11:10

Our problem is not the darkness of our environment, but rather the absence of light on our inside. This is why the psalmist said, "Lord, you will light my candle" (Psalm 18:28). Do you know that it is possible to have a lamp or a candle that is not lit? When the Bible says, "the entrance of Your Word gives light", it is talking about the Word that has been quickened by the Spirit of God or the revealed knowledge of God's Word. The Bible says that the letter kills but the Spirit gives life. Many times we interpret the Bible with our natural mind but the strongholds and preconceptions in our minds hinder the Word from entering. What does it take to have the Word enter us? Our heart must be in a certain condition for the Word to shine in on us. We must remove offences and pride and we must have an attitude of reverence for the Word of God (Mark 4:24). The only way to respect the Word is to respect the God who gave the Word. When we do, the Word will begin to change our lives. Sometimes the Word of God comes to us and it doesn't sound like what we need, but the reality is that it has the ability and capacity to meet every need. Preconceptions do not allow us to receive the Word of God because we have already decided the kind of solution we want. When we begin to allow the Word of God to direct our lives, God will put thoughts in our minds that He'll establish as His will for our lives (Proverbs 16:3). How will He do it? When the light is inside us, our most dominant thoughts usually come from our spirits; not our minds. Through meditating in the Word we can begin to tell the difference between our carnal thoughts and desires and the Word of God.

SCRIPTURE READING: Psalm 18:28, John 11:10, Proverbs 16:3
PERSONAL APPLICATION: We need to prepare our hearts for the Word of God to enter into us. Let us pray this prayer together: *"Lord light my candle and give me the simplicity of heart so that your Word can enter and enlighten me. Let every stronghold that has been built up against your Word in my life come down in Jesus' name. Amen."*

THE KEY TO HAPPINESS

"Blessed (happy, fortunate, prosperous, and enviable) is the man who walks and lives not in the counsel of the ungodly [following their advice, their plans and purposes], nor stands [submissive and inactive] in the path where sinners walk, nor sits down [to relax and rest] where the scornful [and the mockers] gather."
Psalm 1:1 AMPC

Happiness is a choice you make in life. It isn't a decision somebody else makes or can make for you. Happiness is not a function of what somebody does or does not do for you; it is what you do for yourself. First and foremost, we must understand that there is a difference between godly happiness and worldly happiness. In the world, you are happy when everything is going your way, everyone is doing what you want, you are having all you want, doing all you want... And if you can't have it your way, you are not happy. The theme of worldly happiness is you, the focus is you—the 'world' must revolve around you if you are to be happy. "Practically everything that goes on in the world—wanting your own way, wanting everything for yourself, wanting to appear important—has nothing to do with the Father. It just isolates you from Him. The world and all its wanting, wanting, wanting is on the way out—but whoever does what God wants is set for eternity" (1 John 2:16-17 *MSG*).

In God's kingdom, it's a different ball game altogether. According to God's Word, another word for being happy is to be blessed. To be blessed means to be happy, to be prosperous, to be fortunate and to be enviable. Happiness is contentment and satisfaction. To know how to be happy in life, no matter your circumstances, you must therefore know what godly happiness is and what it isn't about. Happiness is a function of your internal condition and not your external condition. It is a function of living by the Word of God and not by worldly or human opinions or standards. Happiness is also agreeing with God and submitting to His plan and purpose for your life; being in total surrender to Him and His will. It is not struggling with God but yielding to Him.

SCRIPTURE READING: Matthew 5:1-12, Psalm 1:1-3 *AMPC*

PERSONAL APPLICATION: Determine today to say YES and to completely submit to the will of God. You will find happiness and contentment in the place of total surrender to Him no matter what your circumstances are.

HUMILITY, DILIGENCE AND SACRIFICE

"Humble yourselves, therefore, under God's mighty hand, that he may lift you up in due time.
1 Peter 5:6 NIV

Humility implies teachable-ness. God has so much to show, teach and enlighten us on but our disposition towards knowledge acquired can stop the process. Knowledge puffs up. Diligence implies going the second mile, doing what ought to be done, not just what is required of us. If we are going to pass our tests, sacrifices are involved. There are tests to pass for advancements in the journey to destiny to continue. How we interpret the circumstances in our lives will determine whether we understand our tests or not. Anything that will justify disobedience to God is a test failed.

Usually our attitudes are silently informed by our disposition to our circumstances in life. Through our nature, nurture and culture, we develop certain dispositions depending on what has informed our disposition, borne out of our interpretation of the things we have neem through or we are going through right then. Joseph's life exemplifies the attitudes found in 1 Peter 5. In Genesis 37, we see that He was diligent in obeying his father's instructions. He could have returned home saying, "I didn't see them where you said they were".

When David faced Goliath and said the Lord delivered him from the lion and the bear, what we don't see is that diligence and fearlessness were involved in going after a lion to deliver a sheep. Going home to tell his father about the lost sheep would have been good enough, given that the lion could kill him as well. David went beyond what was required of him. He now could use these experiences as a basis for his expectations from God.

SCRIPTURE READING: 1 Peter 5:5-10, Genesis 37:14-17, 1 Samuel 17:17-18, 32-37
PERSONAL APPLICATION: What is your disposition towards your circumstances? Do you see failure or hardship as a sign of God abandoning you, or training you? If Joseph had interpreted his experiences in life as God deserting him, or abandoning him to failure and suffering, he would not have had the attitude that we read about in the Bible.

GIVING THANKS

"And let the peace of God rule in your hearts, to which also you were called in one body; and be thankful."
Colossians 3:15

Thanksgiving is an expression of our faith; that we believe that God has heard us. At the tomb, Jesus prayed, saying, "Father, I thank You that You have heard Me" (John 11:41). When did God hear Jesus? When Jesus was told that Lazarus was sick He said, "This sickness is not unto death, but for the glory of God, that the Son of God may be glorified through it" (John 11:4). Jesus believed that the Father heard Him then; and Lazarus now being dead four days hadn't changed that! We must believe that we received what we prayed for when we prayed - even before we actually come into possession of it. After praying, we should have peace if we truly believe that God heard us. "Now this is the confidence that we have in Him, that if we ask anything according to His will, He hears us. And if we know that He hears us, whatever we ask, we know that we have the petitions that we have asked of Him" (1 John 5:14-15). Thanksgiving is also a form of prayer. Somebody said praise is the highest form of prayer! Jehoshaphat appointed those who should sing to the Lord and who should praise the beauty of holiness as they went out before the army, saying, "Praise the Lord, For His mercy endures forever". The Lord set ambushes against those who had come against Judah and they were defeated (2 Chronicles 20:21-23). To give thanks and rejoice is a commandment. We can do both based on God's Word and not based on our circumstances. The Bible says, "Rejoice in the Lord always. Again I will say, rejoice!" (Philippians 4:4). And in 1 Thessalonians 5:16, 18, "Rejoice always" and "In everything give thanks; for this is the will of God in Christ Jesus for you".

SCRIPTURE READING: Exodus 15:1-21
PERSONAL APPLICATION: You can start by giving thanks for and rejoicing over all God has done for you in Christ and all God says about you in His Word - despite your circumstances; and you will be surprised at the peace that will flood your heart.

SOME LESSONS ABOUT MOTIVES

"For the word of God is living and powerful, and sharper than any two-edged sword, piercing even to the division of soul and spirit, and of joints and marrow, and is a discerner of the thoughts and intents of the heart."
Hebrews 4:12

When our motives are inaccurate, we eventually stop doing what is right because whatever motivates us will determine our source of frustration and possible confusion. Motives do not usually become obvious until things go wrong and the real motives are exposed. The Bible says, "The heart of a man is deceitful above all things and desperately wicked: who can know it?" (Jeremiah 17:9 *KJV*). One of the unknown things about each heart is the inner motives. You cannot tell your heart's motives until conflicts expose them. Whenever you have a conflict, ask yourself this question, "Why am I feeling like this and why am I thinking these thoughts?" If you sincerely answer these questions, you will begin to know your true motives. If you let the truth of God's Word confront the true state of your heart, you are ready for the truth to set you free. Many can boast of their goodness but a faithful man who can find? Wrong motives affect the effectiveness of right deeds. Many lose their rewards simply because their motives were not pure. Ask yourself, "Why do I give or pray publicly?" The issue of motive was what Jesus was addressing in Matthew 6 when He talked about giving, praying and fasting. Our motives can also be revealed through the words of our mouth and our giving. Our motives reveal the content of our hearts. We are instructed to guard our hearts with all diligence in Proverbs 4. Do not stop doing a good thing if your reason for doing it is wrong; rather change your reason for doing it. Heart checks should form a major part of taking your spiritual inventory from time to time in life's journey. This is because the single most important element in a person's future is the content of the heart. What you continually focus your attention on will enter your heart. As the content of your heart changes, your motives will change. Change the focus of your attention and your motivation will change.

SCRIPTURE READING: Proverbs 4:23-27, Jeremiah 17:9-10
PERSONAL APPLICATION: How can we firstly discern wrong motives in our hearts? And secondly, how can we change them? Meditate on Hebrews 4:12 and allow God's Word to expose the intents of your heart.

READY FOR CHANGE

"Don't copy the behaviour and customs of this world, but let God transform you into a new person by changing the way you think. Then you will learn to know God's will for you, which is good and pleasing and perfect."
Romans 12:2 NLT

It is said that you can change without growing but you cannot grow or make progress without changing! Change is a necessary thing we must learn to love and embrace. Everyone who has broken through barriers embraced change. You need to change the way you think. "As a man thinks in his heart, so is he" (Proverbs 23:7). Confront and challenge your own thinking with the reality of the Word of God! Change what you believe! What do you believe about yourself? About your situation? The psalmist said, "I would have lost heart, unless I had believed that I would see the goodness of the Lord in the land of the living" (Psalm 27:13). Change the way you see your problems. Do you see a stumbling block or a stepping stone? What you see determines what you get. Change your speaking; Jesus said you shall have what you say (Mark 11:24). A lot of folks never speak to their problems but they speak to everyone about them. Your response to things, circumstances and even to people needs to change. You may not be able to choose or determine all the events in your life, but you can choose your response to them. Change your attitude, change your lifestyle, and change the things about your personality that are negative. Change, change, change! You are never too young or too old to change what needs to be changed!

SCRIPTURE READING: 2 Corinthians 3:16-18
PERSONAL APPLICATION: Have an internal assessment and pinpoint things in your life that need to change. Such as the way you see yourself; the way you respond to people or various circumstances. Then use the reality of the Word of God to help you make the necessary changes.

THE PLACE OF FAITH AND PATIENCE

"So then, faith cometh by hearing, and hearing by the Word of God."
Romans 10:17

Our participation is involved in bringing God's will to pass in our lives. Many will prefer for God to do it all for them. Since God does not impose His will on us, we need to understand the place of our reliance and active dependence on God. Hebrews 6:12 says we should imitate those who through faith and patience inherit the promises. Patience, endurance and long-suffering are three virtues that will enhance our walk with God. Patience is necessary in dealing with God, endurance in dealing with things and long-suffering when dealing with people. Faith has to do with our believing, receiving and acting on the Word of God. It is strengthened by our meditation in the Word (promises). Patience is the ability to stay consistently in faith until the promises become a reality. When you are ready to stand forever, you won't stand for long. When you believe, you receive. Patience (staying consistent) is necessary to have that which you believed you received. Faith demands a heart and mouth connection. Say God's Word until you believe it, then say it when you believe it until you actually build an inner-image of its reality on the canvas of your heart. That inner-image is the hope built by God's Word. It is the anchor of our soul in Hebrews. Faith is what opens the door; patience is what keeps it open until the promises are fulfilled here in this lifetime.

SCRIPTURE READING: Hebrews 10:35-39
PERSONAL APPLICATION: Let's make this faith confession together: *"I accept God's Word as final authority. I consciously believe it and I patiently dwell on it until the image of failure, death, sickness or poverty gets completely wiped out inside me."*

THE DECEITFULNESS OF SIN

"But exhort one another daily while it is called today, lest any of you be hardened through the deceitfulness of sin."
Hebrews 3:13

What does it mean to be hardened? It means to become insensitive. To be hardened is also to show no signs of shame or repentance. It also means to be rendered stubborn or unyielding. Eve was deceived and she became hardened enough to eat the forbidden fruit in disobedience to God. Saul was hardened through the deceitfulness of sin and he spared the king of Amalek and all the good things contrary to God's direct instruction. God called this act stubbornness (1 Samuel 15:23). Saul thought the end (i.e. sacrificing to the Lord) would justify the means (i.e. disobedience to God's instruction). What of Samson? He thought he could flirt around with Delilah without losing the anointing he had in God. He was very presumptuous of the presence and the anointing of God. He was deceived by this thought and he became hardened. The Bible says that he didn't know that God had left him. This is the reason why it looks like sin has stopped being sin. We see a lot of anointing without godly character and we think that God must have truly changed. The truth is that God has not changed, but we are the ones who have changed. We have become unfeeling and hardened through the deceitfulness of sin. Our hearts no longer prick us when we sin as they used to because our consciences have become seared with iron.

SCRIPTURE READING: Ezekiel 36:24-32
PERSONAL APPLICATION: Somebody said that the early church (in the book of Acts) was so sensitive and in tune to the Holy Spirit that if the Spirit left, 90 per cent of their activities would come to a halt. That is, they would know immediately that He had left. What about you? Are you in tune to and sensitive to the Holy Spirit? Would you know if He had left you? It's a sobering thought. Don't become presumptuous of the presence and anointing of God.

FINDING YOUR NICHE

"Ask, and it will be given to you; seek, and you will find; knock, and it will be opened to you."
Matthew 7:7

Have you noticed that those who are succeeding in what they do seem to have found their 'unique selling point'? They seem to have come to terms with who they are, what they have and how things work with them. They have found their niche. They may have built other things and relationships around their niche but they have a main thing (product or service) that they are known for and they deliver very effectively all the time. In the Bible, for Daniel, it was his consecration. For Joseph, it was his ability to interpret dreams. For Apostle Paul, it was his revelation of what God did for the human race in Christ. Check out almost every one who has made their mark and you can see their niche. How do you find yours? Some stumble on it, some labour to find it and some just 'have it'. Ask yourself the following questions: 'What is that one thing that I don't seem to be able to get out of the core of my being? What causes anger, pain and excitement all at the same time?' What are you willing to labour for even if you were not paid for the labour? What are you 'at home' with? What brings tears to your eyes? What is that thing that you will give anything to see happen for others? Nothing stands alone but working at this thing will bring such unspeakable fulfilment to your life. To be safe and sure, this 'thing' needs to be a God-thing; something God invested in you for His purpose. It will generate a lifestyle in you that is God-fearing and God-seeking. It will be the way God wants to 'manifest' Himself through you. You will usually find it as you commit to serving others; it activates certain hidden potentials in you. The more you do it, the more it grows inside you. Within it hides the place and possibility for you to take your promised land. It can be spiritual as well as physical, it can be an idea or a discovery, it can be a revelation or an insight, a method of doing something or a strength in doing it. It is destiny calling for discovery, development and adventure! It can be born in the place of intimacy with the Creator God. I challenge you to go for it! In all your getting, get understanding of this destiny call upon your life!

SCRIPTURE READING: Ephesians 2:10 *NLT*, Hebrews 13:20-21
PERSONAL APPLICATION: Spend time thinking about the questions and points raised in today's devotional. Ask God to reveal to you through prayer and your service in the kingdom the 'niche' that He has just for you.

KEYS OF THE KINGDOM

"The effective, fervent prayer of a righteous man avails much."
James 5:16

I believe that one of the keys God has given to us to operate in the Kingdom effectively, to lock and unlock, to bind and to loose, is the key of prayer. Jesus said whatever we bind on earth is bound in heaven, and whatever we loose on earth is loosed in heaven. Heaven responds when we pray on earth! Elijah prayed earnestly that it would not rain and it did not rain on the land for three years and six months. He prayed again, and heaven gave rain and the earth produced its fruit (James 5:17 -18). How powerful is the prayer of God's people? In the Book of Acts, Herod, when he saw that the killing of James pleased the people, then took Peter also to kill him. The truth is, when the devil gets away with something he gets bolder and stronger, except someone stops him! This time around, the Church woke up (Acts 12:5). God responded from heaven; He sent an angel who delivered Peter from the maximum security prison where he was being held to be killed. God delivered Peter from the hand of Herod and from all the expectation of the Jewish people because the Church prayed earnestly. Things will change if and when we pray. The enemy fears your prayer life so he seeks to attack it. In Babylon, a decree was written that whoever petitioned any god or man for thirty days except the King be cast into the den of lions (Daniel 6:7). This was aimed at Daniel; he knew it but he didn't allow that to stop him from praying. His praying momentarily got him into trouble but God delivered him. His test became a huge testimony to the king of Babylon.

SCRIPTURE READING: James 5:16-18
PERSONAL APPLICATION: You need to recognise the attacks of the enemy so that during your trials you can pump up and not tone down your prayer life!

VICTORY KEYS

"This book of the Law shall not depart from your mouth, but you shall meditate in it day and night, that you may observe to do according to all that is written in it. For then you will make your way prosperous, and then you will have good success."
Joshua 1:8

These prayers by Apostle Paul contain the keys to a future of victory and fulfilment in any Christian's life. Pray these prayers over yourself daily. I have just used the *Amplified Bible, Classic Edition* to write out the prayers below. Make them personal and you can use them to pray for others too! For eyes to be enlightened, to know the hope to which we are called and the inheritance we have in God and God has in us and the greatness of the power at work towards us who believe. Wow! May you function at levels higher than you have ever functioned before as you move up into more revelation in the knowledge of God and be filled with His fullness. Amen!

Ephesians 1:17-23 ***AMPC***
"[For I always pray to] the God of our Lord Jesus Christ, the Father of glory, that He may grant you a spirit of wisdom and revelation [of insight into mysteries and secrets] in the [deep and intimate] knowledge of Him, By having the eyes of your heart flooded with light, so that you can know and understand the hope to which He has called you, and how rich is His glorious inheritance in the saints (His set- apart ones), And [so that you can know and understand] what is the immeasurable and unlimited and surpassing greatness of His power in and for us who believe, as demonstrated in the working of His mighty strength, Which He exerted in Christ when He raised Him from the dead and seated Him at His [own] right hand in the heavenly [places], Far above all rule and authority and power and dominion and every name that is named [above every title that can be conferred], not only in this age and in this world, but also in the age and the world which are to come. And He has put all things under His feet and has appointed Him the universal and supreme Head of the church [a headship exercised throughout the church], Which is His body, the fullness of Him Who fills all in all [for in that body lives the full measure of Him Who makes everything complete, and Who fills everything everywhere with Himself]."

Ephesians 3:14-19 ***AMPC***

"For this reason [seeing the greatness of this plan by which you are built together in Christ], I bow my knees before the Father of our Lord Jesus Christ, For Whom every family in heaven and on earth is named [that Father from Whom all fatherhood takes its title and derives its name]. May He grant you out of the rich treasury of His glory to be strengthened and reinforced with mighty power in the inner man by the [Holy] Spirit [Himself indwelling your innermost being and personality]. May Christ through your faith [actually] dwell (settle down, abide, make His permanent home) in your hearts! May you be rooted deep in love and founded securely on love, That you may have the power and be strong to apprehend and grasp with all the saints [God's devoted people, the experience of that love] what is the breadth and length and height and depth [of it]; [That you may really come] to know [practically, through experience for yourselves] the love of Christ, which far surpasses mere knowledge [without experience]; that you may be filled [through all your being] unto all the fullness of God [may have the richest measure of the divine Presence, and become a body wholly filled and flooded with God Himself]"!

Be filled with all the fullness of God!

PERSONAL APPLICATION: Study and meditate on these scriptures regularly. Spend time praying these scriptures over yourself and others, and receive deeper revelations of what God has made available through His Word.

FULFILLING GOD'S PURPOSE

"But rise and stand on your feet; for I have appeared to you for this purpose, to make you a minister and a witness both of the things which you have seen and of the things which I will yet reveal to you."
Acts 26:16

The purpose of anything manufactured is found in the mind of the manufacturer. The creator knows the purpose of his creation. It takes reading the manual prepared by the manufacturer of a car to know how best to use the car and all the benefits built into the car. Purpose can be said to be the original intent of the manufacturer or creator. The subject of purpose (when it comes to God) has been made mysterious as we hear it, especially when we cannot explain why things happen. God has expressed many of His purposes in His Word and by His Spirit. He still expresses many more. Everything God created was designed to fulfil His purpose and when purpose is unknown, abnormal use (abuse) is inevitable. In all matters, when we do not check with the Word of God and we use our experience or observation to determine the purpose of the thing, we are usually not accurate. What is God's purpose for marriage? His purpose for the church? His purpose for your life? His purpose for your work? His purpose for your family? Everything God created is loaded with potential to become greater than its obvious or perceived ability or capability. It takes us having a mind of stewardship to help unravel the potential and eventually fulfil His purpose for the thing or subject in question. It is easy to assume that things happen accidentally. When we are connected to God for His purpose to be fulfilled, there are no accidents. He works out His purpose in every occasion. Our hunger for Him to carry out His purpose positions us to experience His power and enjoy the fullness of His purpose in our lives!

SCRIPTURE READING: Ephesians 1:11-12, Acts 26:16-18
PERSONAL APPLICATION: Decide today to rise up in your personal life in study, staying hungry and acting on God's Word for His purpose to be fulfilled in your life. Dig deep to discover the unique purpose for your life, family, marriage and work.

FLOWING WITH THE GRACE OF GOD

"For the grace of God that brings salvation has appeared to all men"
Titus 2:11

God's grace is the energy of God at work in us humans, bringing us to terms with God's plans and purposes in the earth. It starts with a saving grace to get us into salvation brought about by Jesus' work on the cross. On our journey into the purposes of God, which will end up in the very presence of God at the Throne of Grace, we need grace all the way. In the book of Titus we are told, "For the grace of God that brings salvation has appeared to all men, teaching us that, denying ungodliness and worldly lusts, we should live soberly, righteously, and godly in the present age" (Titus 2:12). Grace teaches us how to live in this ungodly world. Grace has a process involved in it and is visible. As can be seen in the book of Acts 11:23, Barnabas saw the outworking of grace on the lives of the people of God in Antioch. Grace comes from the love heart of God. The book of Ephesians chapter 1, like many chapters from the pen of Apostle Paul, starts with the grace greetings. Grace and peace comes from the knowledge of our Lord Jesus Christ. Our redemption, forgiveness of sin and all spiritual blessings come from the grace of God. Our love for God and desire to stay humble before God are the prerequisites to receiving more grace. We have access to all grace by faith in Christ Jesus. All of God's purposes can only be fulfilled when we yield to His grace to effectually work in us. No wonder Jesus the child grew and the grace of God was on him. Apostle Peter encourages us to grow in grace and in the knowledge of our Lord Jesus Christ.

SCRIPTURE READING: Titus 2:11-14
PERSONAL APPLICATION: God's grace has been made available to you. Think about how you can access and experience the grace of God in your life.

THE WONDERFUL CROSS

"In Him we have redemption through His blood, the forgiveness of sins, according to the riches of His grace"
Ephesians 1:7

We all need to come to the cross and by faith receive what Jesus suffered to make available so we can live wholesome lives and glorify the Father God. In his writings, Apostle Paul calls us to take full advantage of our new position in Christ as seen in Ephesians 1-3 and challenges us to our responsibilities, relationships and thereafter warfare in Ephesians 4-6. We are accepted in the beloved (Ephesians 1:6) because He bore our rejection on the cross (when He cried, "My God, My God, why have you forsaken me?" in Matthew 27:46) and we gained the acceptance due Him as a result of a sinless life! He suffered shame on the cross that we may share in His glory. He was perfected through suffering that He may bring many sons to glory. Isaiah 53 spells out the picture of our suffering Saviour. Wounded for our transgressions, bruised for our iniquity and the chastisement of our peace was upon Him and with His stripes we are healed. He was rejected, smitten of God and afflicted. He bore the sins of mankind on Himself. Our Messiah fulfilled the justice requirement of God the Father, and gained full redemption for the entire human race. Now we can and should proclaim salvation in no other name but the name of Jesus our Lord and Master. He became a curse on our behalf that we may be free from the effects and influence of the curse that befell the human race as a result of sin. He also took on our poverty so we can take on His riches. We now have the blessing of Abraham, God's covenant friend.

SCRIPTURE READING: Isaiah 53:4-5, Ephesians 1:7
PERSONAL APPLICATION: Think about this for a minute... without the Cross of Jesus, where would you be? We need to pray that God will grant us a revelation of the reality of what took place on the Cross for the entire human race; not just for us believers.

UNDER COVER

"For I myself am a man under authority, with soldiers under me. I tell this one, 'Go,' and he goes; and that one, 'Come,' and he comes. I say to my servant, 'Do this,' and he does it."
Matthew 8:9 NIV

At the baptism of Jesus, when He came out of the water, the Holy Spirit descended on Him and being filled with the Spirit, He was led by the Spirit into the wilderness. He was in the wilderness for forty days. Jesus passed His tests and the Bible says He returned, "in the power of the Spirit to Galilee and news of Him went out through all the surrounding region" (Luke 4:1-14). One could see the development of character even in Christ as the pattern Son. Jesus submitted to John's baptism. He submitted Himself to His earthly parents. He was even called, "the carpenter's son" (Matthew 13:55) and sometimes "the carpenter" (Mark 6:3). Jesus submitted Himself absolutely to the Father's will. The Bible says that He was faithful as a Son over His own house (Hebrews 3:6) and though He was a Son, He learnt obedience by the things which He suffered (Hebrews 5:8). He made Himself of no reputation, took the form of a servant and came in the likeness of men. He humbled Himself and became obedient even to the point of death. "Therefore God also has highly exalted Him and given Him a name which is above every name" (Philippians 2:7-9). Jesus walked in unparalleled authority in His earthly ministry. The centurion recognised this authority; he said to Jesus, "Lord, I am not worthy that You should come under my roof. But only speak a word, and my servant will be healed" (Matthew 8:8). The secret of that authority was in Jesus being a Man under authority Himself. The centurion said, "I also am a man under authority, having soldiers under me. And I say to this one 'Go,' and he goes; and to another, 'Come,' and he comes; and to my servant, 'Do this,' and he does it" (Matthew 8:9). You can't exercise authority effectively if you are not under authority yourself. You must therefore put yourself under the authority of God through His Holy Spirit and the Word and under every authority God has placed in your life.

SCRIPTURE READING: Matthew 8:5-10
PERSONAL APPLICATION: Why is it vital for us believers to ensure that our lives are subjected to the authority of God, His Word and the authorities He has placed in our lives? What is the connection between being under authority and faith?

GOD'S PURPOSE FOR MARRIAGE

"Therefore a man shall leave his father and mother and be joined to his wife, and they shall become one flesh."
Genesis 2:24

On the surface, marriage is about two people loving one another, getting married, starting a family and then trying to raise the children well, whilst trying to earn money to keep the family, etc. All these things are important but we can do these without fulfilling God's entire purpose for marriage. God's purpose is higher than that. He wants to create a picture of the love relationship between Christ and the church as His bride. Hence the instructions for the husband to love his wife as Christ loved the church, etc. Christ is the example of headship as well as submission, for the husband and the wife respectively. He is the head of His church and He is in submission to the Father. The love of God within the context of marriage has to do with submission and headship in the home. The focus is Christ being in the centre as an example of submission as well as headship. A Christ-centred home will reflect the love of God to all in the family, enabling God's will to be done in everyone's life in the family. The purpose of God for marriage includes the fulfilling of God's plans in each member's life, their growth, maturity and encouragement as well as healing from the past. The home is meant to be a place for the building of lives to fulfil destiny.

SCRIPTURE READING: Ephesians 5:22-33
PERSONAL APPLICATION: Does your marriage reflect the picture painted in today's devotional of submission and headship? Spend time reading through and meditating on today's scripture reading. Wives, what does it mean to submit to your own husbands? Husbands, what does it mean to love your wives just as Christ loved the church? How can that be reflected in your everyday life? What adjustments need to be made on both sides in your attitude towards each other?

FROM BONDAGE TO THE PROMISED LAND

"To Him who led His people through the wilderness,
For His mercy endures forever;"
Psalm 136:16

'Wilderness' literally means a desert and it implies a place of solitude, lonesomeness, waste and desolation. Spiritually speaking, I like to define 'wilderness' as the place between the land of bondage and the Promised Land. It is the passage to the Promised Land from the land of bondage. The wilderness is the place between being called and being empowered. Contrary to the belief or mentality of many Christians, the wilderness is not a curse. It is part and parcel of God's plan for His children. The wilderness is not a result of disobedience. God took the Israelites out of Egypt to take them into a land flowing with milk and honey, but they had to go through the wilderness to get there (Exodus 13:17-18). It was God himself who led them by way of the wilderness; and he had a purpose for doing that. What of Jesus Christ our Lord? Luke 4:1 says, "Then Jesus, being filled with the Holy Spirit, returned from the Jordan and was led by the Spirit into the wilderness." Jesus was in the perfect will of God. He never disobeyed God; the Bible says he was tempted in every way, yet without sin. Like the Israelites, he too was led into the wilderness by God! What of Apostle Paul? He said, "...I did not immediately confer with flesh and blood, nor did I go up to Jerusalem to those who were Apostles before me, but I went to Arabia..." (Galatians 1:16-17). Arabia was a desert. The children of Israel could not enter the Promised Land until they had passed through the wilderness. In Luke 4:1, Jesus went into the wilderness 'filled' with the Holy Spirit; in verse 14, He returned in the "power" of the spirit to Galilee. It was after the wilderness experience that Jesus stood up in the synagogue to declare, "The Spirit of the LORD is upon me, because he has anointed me..." (Luke 4:18-19). Paul said he did not rush into ministry even after he was called until he had been through the wilderness. From these three case studies, we can establish that the wilderness prepares us. It's God's pattern for us to come into the fullness of His promises, plans and purposes.

SCRIPTURE READING: Luke 4:1-15
PERSONAL APPLICATION: When you find yourself in the wilderness season, don't waste it. Create a routine for devotion and prayer—spend time in God's Word and learn to hear from Him. Avoid negativity, complaining and speaking evil. Don't spend longer in the wilderness than you need to.

KINGDOM GIVING

"Give, and it will be given to you: good measure, pressed down, shaken together, and running over will be put into your bosom. For with the same measure that you use, it will be measured back to you."
Luke 6:38

Giving is one of the keys of the Kingdom of God. The account of Matthew showing the teaching of Christ shows how He discussed giving, along with praying and fasting in Chapter 6. He was teaching these subjects and revealing the right attitude and heart-position we should have to do these things to get the results God wants us to get. So many realise the importance of praying and fasting especially in dire circumstances but fail to see the role of giving in such circumstances. In Luke 6:38 we read, "Give, and it shall be given unto you; good measure, pressed down, and shaken together, and running over, shall men give into your bosom." This giving includes forgiving, not judging, not speaking evil of others, etc. Whatever you give will be given back to you. Seedtime and harvest shall not cease says God Himself in Genesis 8:22. As I grew in my understanding of God's ways, purposes and plans, I realised that the goal of our Christian faith is not just to be blessed, important as that is, but that it also includes being conformed to the image of the Son as recorded in Romans 8:29. We please the Father when we allow His Son's image to be formed in us. We were made in His image and the Son is the express image as recorded in Hebrews 1:3. This talks of character and power as the Son manifested. At the water of baptism, the Father was pleased before the Son had done any miracle. So character is premium with God. Apostle Paul told Timothy to commit to faithful men who will be able to teach others also (2 Timothy 2:2). Faithfulness is the cornerstone of character. If giving runs through the Bible, and faithfulness is a cornerstone for our development, then giving has something to do with our character development.

SCRIPTURE READING: Luke 6:37-38, Romans 8:28-30
PERSONAL APPLICATION: Giving is a Kingdom principle; not just giving of our substance, but of our time and our talents. As Christians, it is vital for us to give; not just when things are going well for us but through every circumstance and situation we face. Remember, whatever measure we deal out is what is going to be measured back to us.

BE SOBER & VIGILANT

"And the Lord said, 'Simon, Simon! Indeed, Satan has asked for you, that he may sift you as wheat. But I have prayed for you, that your faith should not fail; and when you have returned to Me, strengthen your brethren.'"
Luke 22:31-32

Ephesians 5:14 says, "Awake, you who sleep, Arise from the dead, And Christ will give you light." Sleeping connotes a lack of watchfulness and prayerlessness. In the parable of the wheat and the tares, Jesus said that while men slept, the enemy came and sowed tares among the wheat and went his way (read Matthew 13:24-30). Note that firstly, the man sowed good seed in his field. Secondly, the tares were sowed among the wheat. Thirdly, the tares weren't detected until they sprung up. We cannot afford to be spiritually careless. Peter admonishes us, "Be sober, be vigilant; because your adversary the devil walks about like a roaring lion, seeking whom he may devour" (1 Peter 5:8). Praise God! Satan cannot pounce on us. Jesus has stripped him of all his authority and given us authority over all his ability. The Bible says that we should give him no room. That is why Satan has to go about "seeking whom he may devour". Beloved, you cannot afford to be careless in any area of your life. It is like leaving your door wide open while living in a rough neighbourhood! Don't give Satan room in your thought life, in your utterances, in your emotions, in your marriage, and so forth. Keep him out by being sober and vigilant!

SCRIPTURE READING: Matthew 13:24-30
PERSONAL APPLICATION: Think about what it means in practical terms to "give Satan no room" in your thought life, utterances and emotions.

A WINNING ATTITUDE

"I have strength for all things in Christ Who empowers me [I am ready for anything and equal to anything through Him Who infuses inner strength into me; I am self-sufficient in Christ's sufficiency]."
Philippians 4:13 AMPC

Your attitude is a function of your knowledge, thoughts and expectations in life. Paul said he had learned to abase and abound and could do all things through Christ who strengthened him. His attitude was, "no matter my financial state, I will not let the natural control me. I am regulated internally by the presence of the Greater One in me". A winning attitude seeks to develop, improve and be the best one can be in life. No excuses are allowed and no one is to receive the blame for any circumstance in one's life. You are a victor not a victim. This winning attitude is essential if we want to undo the past and prevent the mistakes of the past from affecting our destiny in the future. Determine this as your new attitude today; I will give my best, I will learn my lessons, I can do all things through Christ who strengthens me!

SCRIPTURE READING: Philippians 4:12-13 *AMPC*
PERSONAL APPLICATION: Spend time thinking about ways in which you could develop a winning attitude that could infiltrate every area of your life. What changes to your thoughts and belief system would you have to make?

DIVINE REVELATION

"Call to Me, and I will answer you, and show you great and mighty things, which you do not know."
Jeremiah 33:3

There are many things that we ought to know, but do not know. For instance, we do not know what to pray as we ought to! And it isn't automatic for God to show us those things; He said we should call to Him. The psalmist said that his desire is to dwell in God's house; to behold His beauty and to inquire in His temple (Psalm 27:4). There are things we couldn't have figured out, and still can't figure out on our own, but can only be revealed to us supernaturally. There are things our natural eyes cannot see or conceive in our minds, but can only be revealed to us by the Spirit of God. The Bible says that we have received the Spirit who is from God, that we might know the things that have been freely given to us by God (1 Corinthians 2:9-12). Jesus asked His disciples who they said He was and Peter said He was the Christ. Jesus said, "Blessed are you, Simon Bar-Jonah, for flesh and blood has not revealed this to you, but My Father who is in heaven" (Matthew 16:15-17). Jesus told His disciples that when the Holy Spirit, the Spirit of truth, comes, He will guide them into all truth, tell them things to come and will reveal to them the things of God (John 16:12-15). God wants to reveal His plans and purposes to us so we can participate with Him. The revelation of God's will gives purpose and direction to our lives. "If people can't see what God is doing, they stumble all over themselves; but when they attend to what he reveals, they are most blessed" (Proverbs 29:18 *MSG*).

SCRIPTURE READING: 1 Corinthians 2:9-12, John 16:12-15
PERSONAL APPLICATION: God is willing to share His secrets with us but it seems that we are the ones to determine how much of those secrets will be revealed to us. Decide today to seek God and to call on Him and expect Him to answer you.

THE FEAR OF GOD

"The fear of the Lord is the beginning of wisdom,
And the knowledge of the Holy One is understanding."
Proverbs 9:10

If there is one virtue that ranks high in God's agenda, it is the fear of God. This is the true foundation for a lasting and genuine walk with God. The one quality that will cause the Word of God to remain a final authority in our lives is the fear of God. Walking in the fear of God is to have a healthy reverence for Him. It is the beginning of wisdom. Little wonder why wisdom is a scarce commodity amongst many today. The fear of God causes us to esteem God's Word as precious, worthy of our submission and deserving of our surrender to the demands in His Word. The Word carries the ability to overrule our human feelings as we subject all things in us to His expectations of us. We are not robots and He is not asking for a mindless, thoughtless obedience but an intelligent and willing acceptance of His authority to rule over us as Lord. Without the fear of the Lord, the presence of the Lord will not be a regular occurrence in our lives. Joseph had the fear of the Lord, experienced the presence of the Lord and he knew his boundaries. He avoided sinning against God when he was given opportunity to have an affair with Potiphar's wife. His intimacy with God and his understanding of boundaries produced in the young man a strength that could carry him through the falsehood he had to face.

SCRIPTURE READING: Proverbs 9:10 *AMPC*, Ecclesiastes 12:13, Psalm 33:8
PERSONAL APPLICATION: What does it mean to truly walk in the fear of the Lord? For example, if we truly walked in the fear of God, what things in our lives would we change? How can we develop a deep and reverential fear of God in our lives?

THE ANCHOR OF YOUR SOUL

"May the God of hope fill you with all joy and peace as you trust in him, so that you may overflow with hope by the power of the Holy Spirit."
Romans 15:13 NIV

Hope means a favourable and confident expectation. It has to do with the unseen and the future - "But hope that is seen is not hope; for why does one still hope for what he sees? But if we hope for what we do not see, we eagerly wait for it with perseverance" (Romans 8:24-25). Hope describes the happy anticipation of God, the ground upon which hope is based, "Christ in you, the hope of glory" (Colossians 1:27) and the object upon which hope is fixed (i.e. the Lord Jesus Christ Himself, 1 Timothy 1:1). The Bible says Abraham hoped against hope so he became the father of many nations (Romans 4:18 *KJV*). That is, he hoped against natural hope. There is natural hope and there is supernatural hope! As you focus on God's Word, the Holy Spirit injects you with hope. "May the God of hope fill you with all joy and peace as you trust in him, so that you may overflow with hope by the power of the Holy Spirit" (Romans 15:13) That hope becomes an anchor for your soul (Hebrews 6:19) in the storms of life and in the face of contradictory evidence. The Bible says that we should rejoice in hope of the glory of God and hope does not disappoint us because of the love of God (Romans 5:2-5). God is truly a God of hope. Even in the gloomiest and darkest hour, God's Word still brings hope to us. When Adam and Eve fell and right in the midst of the curse, God still brought a message of hope to them – the seed of the woman was going to come and bruise the head of Satan (Genesis 3:15).

SCRIPTURE READING: Romans 5:1-5, Romans 8:24-25
PERSONAL APPLICATION: Hope truly is the anchor of our souls. Be encouraged to really place your hope in God and on His Word. Remember, hope does not disappoint.

THE POWER OF PERSONAL INTEGRITY

"Let Integrity and uprightness preserve me, for I wait for You"
Psalm 25:21

Integrity has to do with walking in the truth or in principles of rightness of behaviour (based on the Bible) and doing so with harmony between our hearts and mouths. Since the fall of man, sin has made it difficult, if not impossible, to walk in integrity without divine help from God. The word integrity is from the word "integer" which means a whole number. Being whole implies being able to let the mouth and the heart say the same thing. The nature inherited in Adam and our cultures alongside with our upbringing, all puts in us a disposition that is contrary to integrity. Unhealthy comparisons, competitive jealousy and selfish ambitions all lodged into our hearts are hard to deal with if we are to maintain "truth in the inward parts" according to Psalm 51:6. Truth here means rightness and trustworthiness. It derives from the verb meaning to be firm, permanent and established, conveying the sense of dependability, firmness and reliability. Truth is therefore something upon which a person may confidently stake his life. Truth also means reality. The reality of anything is the truth of it. God's truth is His reality. Our hearts need to be true to the ever present seeing eyes of God and attempt to stay true to a Holy God.

SCRIPTURE READING: Psalm 15:1-5
PERSONAL APPLICATION: How can you come to a place where your heart and your mouth are in alignment with each other? Why is it important to be a person of integrity?

PULLING DOWN STRONGHOLDS

"For the weapons of our warfare are not carnal but mighty in God for pulling down strongholds"
2 Corinthians 10:4

What are strongholds? They are fortresses of demonic activities that constitute a hold on us bringing us into subjection to the dictates of demonic lifestyles. They constitute hideouts for demonic activities from where many lives are controlled, manipulated and kept in bondage. They operate through the mind and emotions and affect the wills of people. They come in through various avenues into the soulish arena of mankind. They can start as thoughts, translate to words, influence actions and then constitute themselves as forces to be reckoned with. Every known sin that one deliberately gets into gives rise to a stronghold in the life of the person. Every addiction is a sign of a stronghold. Our salvation makes the provision available to be delivered totally from these things but we need to apply ourselves to experience the provision. We are encouraged to guard the loins of our minds and put on our waist the belt of truth. The thoughts that we permit and the activities we engage in have everything to do with the nature of strongholds we welcome into our lives. When our spirits get recreated we have the seed of God inside our spirits. The nature of God is there but our souls and bodies need education and discipline to come in line.

SCRIPTURE READING: 2 Corinthians 10:4-6
PERSONAL APPLICATION: Spend time thinking about these two questions: Why is it vital for us to identify and pull down strongholds? In what ways can we practically pull down the strongholds in our minds?

MERCY IN OUR WEAKNESS

"Remember, O Lord, Your tender mercies and Your lovingkindnesses, For they are from of old."
Psalm 25:6

God shows us His mercy in our weaknesses. Though saved, we all have areas in which we are weak; areas where we tend to fail and to fall, i.e. our faults and shortcomings. "For we do not yet have a High Priest who cannot sympathise with our weaknesses, but was in all points tempted as we are, yet without sin. Let us therefore come boldly to the throne of grace, that we may obtain mercy and find grace to help in time of need" (Hebrews 4:15-16). Jesus came to help the seed of Abraham and because He Himself was tempted in all things (yet without sin), He is able to help those who are tempted (Hebrews 2:16-18). Jesus told Peter that Satan had asked to sift him (Peter) as wheat but He had prayed for him that Peter's faith should not fail (Luke 22:31-32). "As a father pities his children, so the Lord pities those who fear Him. For He knows our frame; He remembers that we are dust" (Psalm 103:13-14). The Bible says that God is faithful. Not only will He not allow us to be tempted beyond what we are able to bear, He will also make the way of escape for us with every temptation we face (1 Corinthians 10:13). What a merciful God we serve! He is always looking out for us; not to 'get' us, but to help us out!

SCRIPTURE READING: Hebrews 4:15-16

PERSONAL APPLICATION: Jesus understands our weaknesses. He walked on this earth and like us, He faced temptations, yet He never sinned. Rather than trying to hide your weaknesses and failures from God, come to Him and receive the grace, the wisdom and the strength you need to overcome every challenge, every test and every temptation.

SUSTAINED GROWTH

"When He had stopped speaking, He said to Simon,
'Launch out into the deep and let down your nets for a catch.'"
Luke 5:4

Growth or increase that will last is usually preceded by change. Changes have to take place if you are to be all that God wants you to be. The scripture in Luke 5:1-11 tells us of the experience that Peter had with Jesus. Read the passage to refresh your mind with its contents. Peter said, "Nevertheless at thy word", and went on to do what Jesus said and had a miracle that he had toiled for without results. Sometimes it is not a lack of knowledge about what to do that produces a lack of results; though sometimes that is the case. Always doing what Jesus says produces. It is the demand that doing what He says places on us that causes us to do otherwise. This is because doing what He says demands change in us that is sometimes contrary to our preconceptions or ideas. It demands our faith and dependence on Him. That kills our pride and independence. The flesh doesn't like that. Remember the man who built his house on the rock had to dig deep through the flesh to remove pride to build on the rock. This is especially serious when we think we know what to do and when what we know is not what He would want us to do at the time. We are too busy to fellowship with Him in His Word and Spirit so we just do what seems right to us and wonder why we don't get the results we expect to get. What I have discovered is that if you don't give yourself to the right changes, you leave yourself open for experiences to force changes on you. Joseph went through changes that brought him into the state of preparedness for his destiny. Some of the things you are going through have the potential of preparing you if you embrace change and allow the process to fulfil its purpose.

SCRIPTURE READING: 2 Kings 5:1-14, Luke 5:1-11
PERSONAL APPLICATION: Are there any areas in your life where you are toiling and seeing no results? Bring these areas before God in prayer. What does He have to say to you concerning those areas? What changes to your actions or mindset might you need to make?

SEEING THE INVISIBLE

"For we walk by faith not by sight."
2 Corinthians 5:7

Faith is a supernatural force. When things don't make sense, they can make 'faith'. The Bible says, "faith is the substance of things hoped for, the evidence of things not seen" (Hebrews 11:1). We don't see them with our physical eyes because they exist in another realm – a realm that can't be accessed by the natural or physical senses. The Bible talks about the mature, who have their senses trained to discern both good and evil (Hebrews 5:14). It seems to me that every one of our five physical senses (i.e. sight, taste, touch, smell and hearing) has its spiritual equivalent. The Bible says that Moses endured or persevered because he saw Him who is invisible (Hebrews 11:27). You can't see something which is invisible with your physical eyes, can you? Remember when Elisha asked God to open the 'eyes' of his servant to see that those who were with them were more than those who were against them (2 Kings 6:17)? The Bible says that God will give His angels charge over us to keep us in all our ways (Psalm 91:11). We might not see them but they are there. Praise God! Moses endured because he saw Him who is invisible. Jesus endured the cross, despising the shame, because He saw the joy set before Him (Hebrews 12:2). Abraham didn't waver at the promise of God through unbelief because he did not consider his dead body and the deadness of Sarah's womb (Romans 4:19-21). He kept his eyes on the promise and on the One who had promised. Focus produces strength. What are you focused on? You cannot possess beyond what you can see or envision with your spiritual eyes. There is a limit to what you can see with your physical eyes and that can limit you in your walk with God. Also, more often than not, what we see with our physical eyes can be so discouraging or daunting, that we need to switch to the invisible realm. In the physical, Abraham could only see his dead body and Sarah's dead womb; Elisha's servant could only see the Syrian army and he knew that he and his master were no match for them. How much do we need our spiritual glasses!

SCRIPTURE READING: 2 Kings 6:8-17, Hebrews 11:1-12
PERSONAL APPLICATION: How can we train ourselves to not see things merely from a natural perspective, but rather to make the switch to the invisible realm and see things from a faith perspective with our spiritual glasses?

THE POWER OF CONSISTENCY

"Also I heard the voice of the Lord, saying:
'Whom shall I send,
And who will go for Us?'
Then I said, 'Here am I! Send me.'"
Isaiah 6:8

The Father has been waiting for us to bring our lives to the place where He can pour out His power on and through us to this dying world. His Son has paid the price to release it from heaven. Someone needs to pay the price to release it on earth for others to enjoy. Will you be the one? Intimacy with God cannot be accomplished without the power of the Holy Spirit; but the decision is ours to start with. The determination is also ours. To be consistent, we must take responsibility for where we are, where we are going and what we are becoming. Being consistent is the key to the flow of life and power. God must be our priority over our feelings, comfort or convenience. The authority that we carry as a result of our yieldedness to God positions us to do things in His name and He in turn backs us up as it is done according to His will. This is when prayer takes a new turn. The praying man has power with God as a result of the lifestyle cultivated. This stance or position is further enhanced by our readiness to obey instructions from God and His Word.

SCRIPTURE READING: Deuteronomy 28:13-14, Psalm 51:10
PERSONAL APPLICATION: Spend time giving thought to these questions: Why is consistency so important in your walk with God? How can you develop consistency in your life?

PURSUE, OVERTAKE AND RECOVER ALL

"So David inquired of the Lord, saying, 'Shall I pursue this troop? Shall I overtake them?' And He answered him, 'Pursue, for you shall surely overtake them and without fail recover all.'"
1 Samuel 30:8

If the thief is caught, he must pay back sevenfold what he has stolen (Proverbs 6:31). But he must first of all be caught! That is why it is important for us to accurately identify who the enemy is. In the parable of the sower, the farmer identified who sowed the weeds among the wheat, he said, "An enemy has done this" (Matthew 13:28). Remember, God isn't your enemy, neither are human beings; "we are not fighting against flesh and blood enemies, but against evil rulers and authorities of the unseen world, against mighty powers in this dark world, and against evil spirits in the heavenly places" (Ephesians 6:12). After identifying who the enemy is, the next thing to do is to "pursue, overtake, and without fail, recover all" that Satan has stolen from you. Command Satan and those wicked spirits to take their hands off what he has stolen from you e.g. your finances, your health, etc. Declare what God says about your finances, your health, etc. Start sowing the right seeds, even where you are. Don't wait until you are out of the woods. "Bring back our captivity, O Lord, as the streams in the South. Those who sow in tears shall reap in joy. He who continually goes forth weeping, bearing seed for sowing, shall doubtless come again with rejoicing, bringing his sheaves with him" (Psalm 126:4-6). Keep standing on God's Word and don't back down. Remember, your victory has already been settled in Christ Jesus.

SCRIPTURE READING: 1 Samuel 30:1-19
PERSONAL APPLICATION: Whatever you are doing or you need to do to recover all from the enemy, don't stop! Don't stop praying, don't stop confessing the Word, don't stop praising God and don't stop sowing the right seeds.

DEATH AND LIFE

"For the law of the Spirit of life in Christ Jesus has made me free from the law of sin and death"
Romans 8:2

Wherever God is, life is there. God is life, love and light, the Bible says. The absence of His presence means the absence of His life, love and light. Death on the other hand is the absence of His presence, person and purpose. Death reigns in the lives of those who live in sin. Through Jesus, we have access to the life of God (John 10:10). This life was manifested even in the lives of the saints of old. The Daniel story shows that, as he put God first in his life, he developed mentally. He interpreted dreams, was saved from death, and with his covenant friends, stayed relevant to the purpose of God in their time. The same can be said of Joseph who refused bitterness and hence allowed God's purpose to be fulfilled. We will always fail the tests of God if we don't give God first place in our lives. We usually complain because it is natural to do so when things are not going the way we want them to go. Our ways are not His ways. It takes faith in Him to follow Him, learn of Him and not complain. Remember, you release the dynamics of death into your life by your words. Death and life are in the power of the tongue (Proverbs 18:21). The same is with life. We engage the law of the spirit of life in Christ Jesus by exercising faith in God's Word and that involves the speaking of faith-filled words. Fear, unbelief and evil speaking are involved in engaging the law of life and death. The choice is OURS. Our heart condition plays a major role in what dynamics we release into our lives. Choose life and you shall live!

SCRIPTURE READING: Proverbs 18:21, Psalm 19
PERSONAL APPLICATION: The Bible tells us that death and life are in the power of the tongue. It is vital therefore that we watch the words that we allow to come out of our mouths because they are seeds that will bring to us a harvest, whether good or bad.

BROKENNESS

"And whoever falls on this stone will be broken;
but on whomever it falls, it will grind him to powder."
Matthew 21:44

Brokenness is the state wherein we can be corrected and still bounce back with joy and continue to serve without bitterness. This is an achievable state as we go through our process of receiving correction and moving on from one level of excellence to another. Many get stuck because of the subtle pride that hides behind our gifts from God. Gifted people can sometimes be the most difficult to disciple. Behind our gifts is the self-confident boasting that says, 'I can do it too', 'I have what it takes'. We all go through this. God gives gifts and we get proud as if it was by our efforts we got them. We claim we want to use the gifts for God but really it is to boost our poor self-image. When we are corrected, the 'monster' behind the gifts shows up. God gives and chooses how He wants to use the gifts. He does want us to employ our gifts for His purposes but how will He deal with what has attached itself to what He gave? Process is the sifting of the old inhabitants from the new. The new creation battles with the carnal nature for expression in us. Process takes us through the fire of purification where the dross surfaces so it can be dealt with. Unfortunately when the dross surfaces like anger, hatred and bitterness, instead of recognising and removing them, we allow these things to remove us from the beauty of the cleansing process. We take the offence and leave the environment where correction can take place. How tragic. "Every plant, which my heavenly Father has not planted, shall be rooted out" (Matthew 15:13). Offences can root us out of the path to our destiny if we hold on to them, or, we can let God root them out of our hearts through repentance and forgiveness. Rather than become better, bitterness takes us away and our hearts become polluted; hence our destiny is no longer what He meant for it to be. How we need those who help interpret our experiences correctly so that Christ can be formed in us.

SCRIPTURE READING: Matthew 15:13, Job 23:10, Luke 17:1-4
PERSONAL APPLICATION: Offence is a matter not to be taken lightly. Ask God to help you identify any and every offence in your heart. It's time to let them go and allow God to take you through process.

IT'S A NEW SEASON

"I will instruct you and teach you in the way you should go;
I will guide you with My eye."
Psalm 32:8

Obedience to heaven's instructions is the key to flowing with God's times and seasons. The life that stays connected to heaven to hear the next instruction is the life that will not miss out on God's will in His times and seasons. When competition, comparisons and copying everyone else goes on, specific instructions are lost and specific purposes never achieved. The will of God unfolds in times and seasons. God's ultimate purpose is that we be conformed to the image of His Son, Jesus Christ. He will build character, faith, selfless service and total dependence on God into our souls through all that we experience in His will. Even in our disappointments, He can still work out something good if we let Him. Our promptness in obedience is also a sterling quality if we are to understand times and seasons. We cannot harbour sin, offence, bitterness and any such vice if we are to 'navigate' accurately during the times and seasons that come upon us in our pursuit of God's will. Biblical characters all went through their various times and seasons and the effect of their seasons can be seen in the outcomes they had in their lives. God prepares us for what He has prepared for us. His preparation will take you through various seasons in your life. The lessons you learn and the tests you pass will determine your readiness for the next phase of His will for your life. Failed tests lead to a repetition of phases and delayed progress. As we deepen our intimacy with God we will see more clearly the intentions of His heart for us. Whatever we go through, His intention is to do away with anything in us that is not in harmony with His nature. When we recognise in ourselves any such thing, we cooperate with Him by our repentance to deal with such traits in us. Let us learn to cooperate with God in all we go through in life.

SCRIPTURE READING: 1 Samuel 15:1-26
PERSONAL APPLICATION: Why is prompt obedience such a critical aspect in our walk with God?

WHEN THE RIGHTEOUS ARE IN AUTHORITY

"If that is the case, our God whom we serve is able to deliver us from the burning fiery furnace, and He will deliver us from your hand, O king."
Daniel 3:17

God is looking for more righteous people who will be bold enough to step out in authority and He will show Himself strong in the earth. God is looking for the Esthers who will say, "...if I perish, I perish" (Esther 4:16). God is looking for the Shadrachs, Meshachs and Abednegos, who will refuse to bow down to the image of gold (Daniel 3:18). God is looking for the Mordecais who will not bow to Haman, even when everyone around them is bowing (Esther 3:2). God is looking for the Daniels who cannot be stopped from praying by the decree of man or king (Daniel 6:10). The major thing that will stop us from being such people is fear! The fear of man, the fear of losing face or our reputation before people, the fear of losing our position, the fear of lack, the fear of death and so forth. Fear is very much part of the fallen human nature. Fear could be very real and legitimate. Fear is part and parcel of our human nature but very foreign to our recreated spirit. The antidote to fear is trust. God is truly a very present help in trouble. His help is always timely. God was a very present help for Esther; she found favour with the king. God came through for the three Hebrew men in the fiery furnace. The list is endless about God's timely intervention in the lives of those who trusted in Him. We must therefore learn to walk in and exercise our God-given, blood-bought authority.

SCRIPTURE READING: Psalm 46, Daniel 3
PERSONAL APPLICATION: How can you overcome any fear that holds you back and begin to exercise and step out in your God-given, blood-bought authority?

PURITY OF HEART

"For the word of God is alive and active. Sharper than any double-edged sword, it penetrates even to dividing soul and spirit, joints and marrow; it judges the thoughts and attitudes of the heart."
Hebrews 4:12 NIV

God sees the heart while men look on our outward appearance. What God sees are our motives and focus. He actually judges us based on these. Part of the purpose of the process we go through in God is to allow us to see our motives so we can allow the purifying power of repentance from dead works to have its effect in us.

In Hebrews 12:1-2, we see three aspects of God's will.

1. The race is already marked out for us. We do not get to define our race or the path we run on.
2. We are to look unto Jesus as our pattern and inspiration.
3. He who started is also able to finish what He started in us. He is the author and finisher of our faith. As we look to Him we see that His motivation was to do the will of the Father-God.

Hebrews 10:5-10 clearly shows that Jesus was motivated by a desire to please the Father by doing His will. Again we see that the path He took was discovered in the Scriptures and the final deal involved the laying down or sacrifice of His body. Being the pattern Son, our focus should be on Him and our motive should be like His. He loved, obeyed and was sold out on pleasing the Father.

SCRIPTURE READING: Hebrews 10:5-10, 12:1-2

PERSONAL APPLICATION: Like Jesus, we need to be motivated by a desire to please the Father by doing His will. How can we practically cultivate the desire to do the will of God?

EXPOSE THE WORKS OF DARKNESS!

"I will no longer talk much with you, for the ruler of this world is coming, and he has nothing in Me."
John 14:30

We must learn how to live carefully in these evil times to appropriate the victory that is already ours in Christ Jesus. We need the wisdom of God to be able to navigate through life. Satan is the ruler of darkness. He loves secrecy; that is his domain. Expose lust, pride, rebellion, sexual immorality, sin and so on. Bring them out in the open. It is whatever he has in you that he will place a demand upon, either now or in the future! Satan won't use what is outside you to get you; he'll use what is inside of you. So expose it or it will explode one day on your inside like a time bomb that's been ticking away unnoticed. The truth is that whenever we are ready to deal with issues in our lives, then we will be ready to expose them. When you are truly ready to be delivered from the sinful habit of addiction, bring it out into the light. That breaks Satan's control over you. If we are going to be free and not come under bondage to Satan and sin, we must expose the unfruitful works of darkness in our lives.

SCRIPTURE READING: Ephesians 5:2-20
PERSONAL APPLICATION: Spend time thinking about your life. What (if any) areas need to come to light so that, just like Jesus, you can also boldly say that Satan has nothing in you?

THE GOAL OF OUR FAITH

"For whom He foreknew, He also predestined to be conformed to the image of His Son, that He might be the firstborn among many brethren."
Romans 8:29

Many of us think that whatever spiritual activity we have is meant to lead to another end, i.e. healing or deliverance. No. The ultimate purpose of every spiritual activity is to bring us to Christlikeness. Satan is not going to sit down and fold his hands and see Christlikeness being manifested, because the only person who manifested the fullness of Christ made an open show of Satan. He knows that if he can stop someone from coming into Christlikeness he can mess them up. There is a war out there. There is nothing as bad as a whole army thinking everything is fine when everything is going wrong. The church has become meeting centred and meeting minded instead of lifestyle orientated. So we wait until church service to worship, read the Bible and pray. We should be praying, worshipping, and winning souls 24/7! Church should be a time when we get reinforced to go out and live the life. But what happens is that people come to church with the mind of fulfilling their religious obligations. True Christianity is translating the principles of the kingdom into daily living. If you don't do that then you don't have the true Christian faith; what you have is a religious faith. Until you translate Christianity to become a lifestyle, people cannot see the difference between religious Christianity and true Christianity.

SCRIPTURE READING: Romans 8:28-29
PERSONAL APPLICATION: The goal of our faith is Christlikeness, for you and I to be conformed to the image of the Son. What does it mean to become truly transformed into the image of the Son? How will this affect your daily life and activities?

A PLACE OF TESTING

"Know then in your heart that as a man disciplines his son, so the Lord your God disciplines you."
Deuteronomy 8:5 NIV

In the wilderness you are trained or disciplined to live on just enough, so that when you come into the land of abundance you will know how to manage wealth. The purpose of the wilderness is to prepare us for the Promised Land. In Deuteronomy 8:11, the Israelites were warned, "Beware that you do not forget the LORD your God..." It is very easy to forget the Lord when you get into the Promised Land. It is easy to disobey God then and live carelessly. It is easier to pay your tithe or give when you don't have much than when you have much. It is easier to fast when there is no food than to fast in the midst of abundance. Freedom is more difficult to handle than bondage. When I was in boarding school, our lives were regulated externally. The bell was rung to wake us up, the attendance register was taken in the classes, roll calls were made at assembly; so it was difficult not to keep in line. It was a different story at university. We were regulated from within and your exam results were the only check you had. I thank God for the wilderness. I thank God I went through it. I thank God I learnt to pass my tests. The wilderness is what prepared us for what we are doing today. By way of concluding this exhortation, I want to emphasise the fact that it is not enough to go through the wilderness, you must let the purpose of the wilderness be fulfilled in your life. You must come out humble, you must pass your tests, you must be trained and disciplined, you must learn to absolutely depend on God. Don't stay in your wilderness longer than necessary. And a word of advice, now that you know you must go through wilderness, don't wait for it to be thrust upon you. Decide to go into the wilderness yourself! Don't wait to be humbled; humble yourself under God's mighty hand. Discipline yourself, train your senses to discern between good and evil.

SCRIPTURE READING: Exodus 13:17-18, Deuteronomy 8
PERSONAL APPLICATION: Ask yourself: 'Am I passing my tests as I go through the wilderness or do I find myself re-taking them?'
If you do not pass your tests, you can be certain that you will remain in the wilderness longer than necessary or planned by God. Learn to pass your tests and learn the right lessons. Read Deuteronomy 8:2.

CHANGING SEASONS

" of the sons of Issachar who had understanding of the times, to know what Israel ought to do..."
1 Chronicles 12:32

When we connect with God through His Word and reach out in faith to lay hold on His Word, we can see the change of seasons within the context of His will. When we are in the season of preparation, for example, and we want to jump into the manifestation season, then we may miss out on the purpose of the preparation season and never be fully prepared. David killed Goliath to put an end to a season of defeat for God's people but he was still in a season of hiding in his personal life where the process of him becoming king was concerned. He was not quite ready for that phase in God's timetable. So into hiding he went when Saul was after him. David's Adullam cave experience was within his 'hiding season'. He helped many who were distressed and discouraged. I see a pattern that whenever a new church starts in an area, it attracts the needy people first. The pastor may want stardom but his faithfulness over the few distressed ones is what prepares him for the next season of the process in God. Many get stuck here with discouragement as they compare themselves with others who may have gone past that equivalent season in their lives. The reason for every season needs to be maximised. The ability to recognise indications for the future and not jump as if the sign has been given to move into a new season is one of the graces needed in these last days. The phases of birthing a child show seasons. We have intimacy, conception, gestation, labour and birth. Each phase represents a season and there are events that describe each season. Let us recognise the season we are in as we walk with God and also recognise the season the Body of Christ is in around the world. The interplay between the two is where God's wisdom helps us in decision making.

SCRIPTURE READING: Ecclesiastes 3:1-8
PERSONAL APPLICATION: How can you recognise the seasons that we you in? Why is it so vital that you understand what season you are in?

FORGET THE THINGS BEHIND

"forgetting those things which are behind and reaching forwards to those things which are ahead, I press towards the goal"
Philippians 3:13-14

Your past can be your greatest hindrance and your worst enemy. Good could stop you from accomplishing best - an enemy called 'average'. Average means, the generally prevailing rate, degree or amount. For example, most people from average homes, background, etc. never strive for excellence; they are always satisfied with just being 'comfortable'. Don't let the past hold you down or limit you. Your past can be your worst enemy and greatest hindrance; you can learn the right lessons but you must move on. Don't let your past be the graveyard for your future. Joseph had two sons in Egypt. He named his first son, Manasseh, "For God has made me forget all my toil and all my father's house" and his second, Ephraim, "For God has caused me to be fruitful in the land of my affliction" (Genesis 41:51-52). It seems you can't be fruitful until you let go of the pains of the past. "For our present troubles are small and won't last very long. Yet they produce for us a glory that vastly outweighs them and will last forever! So we don't look at the troubles we can see now; rather, we fix our gaze on things that cannot be seen. For the things we see now will soon be gone, but the things we cannot see will last forever" (2 Corinthians 4:17-18 *NLT*).

SCRIPTURE READING: Philippians 3:1-14, Isaiah 43:18-19
PERSONAL APPLICATION: In forgetting the things behind, applying these three practical things will greatly help you:
i. Don't be discouraged by the past.
ii. Don't be afraid of failing.
iii. Don't be complacent.

AN ATTITUDE OF GRATITUDE

"In everything give thanks; for this is the will of God in Christ Jesus for you."
1 Thessalonians 5:18

The quality of your life, whether good or bad, is based upon how thankful you are towards God. It is one attitude that determines whether life unfolds into a place of blessedness or wretchedness. To find joy in life, find thankfulness. One who is thankful for a little enjoys much but the unappreciative soul is always miserable, always complaining. In the book of Philippians, the apostle Paul admonishes us to, "rejoice and again I say rejoice" (Philippians 4:4). We are told to "be careful for nothing but in everything by prayer and supplication with thanksgiving, let our requests be made known to God" (Philippians 4:6). Many scriptures encourage us to praise God and be thankful. In Mathew 6:34 we are admonished to not allow ourselves to worry about anything. Gratitude is the healthiest human emotion.
These are things we can put into practise as we enjoy the power of gratitude:
1. Become one with an attitude of gratitude no matter what circumstances you face.
2. Think about the right things (Philippians 4:6-9).
3. Change the way you are thinking if you want to reduce the level of stress in your life.
4. Let the peace of God rule your heart (Colossians 3:15-17). Giving thanks is one way to let the peace of God rule in your heart.
5. Constantly offer praise to God and be grateful (Hebrews 13:15). Magnify God in your heart through regular praises.
6. The earth yields her increase when we praise God (Psalm 67:3-7).

SCRIPTURE READING: Philippians 4:4-9, Colossians 3:15-17, Hebrews 13:15, Psalm 67:3-7
PERSONAL APPLICATION: How can we maintain an attitude of gratitude even in the face of life's hardships and challenges? How can we change and control the direction of our thoughts?

RAISING GODLY CHILDREN

"And that from childhood you have known the Holy Scriptures, which are able to make you wise for salvation through faith which is in Christ Jesus."
2 Timothy 3:15

Parenting is one of the greatest challenges in the 21st century in view of changes in society, the law, etc. - all in the name of civilisation and modernisation. For instance, children are put under severe peer pressure to be or have what they are not quite ready for. One of the activities of the anti-Christ is to "intend to change times and law" (Daniel 7:25). Have you noticed that children grow up so quickly now? Waiting is no more a virtue; they want everything now! Yet maturity is said to be the ability to delay gratification. Paul wrote in 2 Timothy 3:1-3 that there will be very difficult times in the last days, because among other things, people will be disobedient to their parents and ungrateful. They will consider nothing sacred (e.g. marriage, sex, etc.), they will have no self control, have no interest in what is good, they will be puffed up with pride and love pleasure rather than God. Yet the challenge is, "don't copy the behaviour and customs of this world, but let God transform you into a new person by changing the way you think" (Romans 12:2 *NLT*). We are to be in this world but not of this world. The enemy is bombarding the minds of children from every angle with all kinds of vices - through friends, ideologies and theories being taught in schools, the media, literature, etc. The entertainment industry today is a major tool in the hand of the enemy. Someone said, "what entertains you, enters you". Nebuchadnezzar, King of Babylon took young men in whom there was no blemish, but good looking, gifted in all wisdom, possessing knowledge and quick to understand, who had ability to serve in the King's palace and whom they might teach the language and literature of the Chaldeans (Daniel 1:4). Note that the world catches them young and goes for the gifted and talented ones. Satan preys on precious souls.

SCRIPTURE READING: 2 Timothy 3:1-15
PERSONAL APPLICATION: You do not have to lose your children to the devil or the world. You can still win with your children. Ask God today to give you the wisdom to know how to raise godly children in this ungodly world.

SANCTIFICATION & CONSECRATION

"Sanctify them by Your truth, Your Word is truth."
John 17:17

A sanctified and consecrated life is one of the secret treasures of the people of old who walked with God in their times and had very successful outcomes in their obedience and response to God's dealings in their lives. The enemy has taken advantage of our humanity's tendency to laziness, entertainment, carelessness and generally pandering towards ease. He (Satan) has combined this well with disappointment and hurts to breed strife and disconnections among the saints of God. All of these were designed to stop the advancement of God's kingdom, influence and purpose, in the lives of individuals, then corporately in the Body of Christ. What is needed is for every believer to realise these things and to learn to cultivate lifestyles that are contrary to Satan's plans and in alignment with God's ways of doing things: consistency in obeying God's Word, deepening our intimacy with God, being quick to forgive one another and being battle ready against the schemes of the devil. God's plans are great and exciting but sometimes the trials we go through make them look dull and unexciting. There are different phases in God's plans for our lives, so let us develop the necessary disciplines to go through every phase to the final outcomes God has for us. Such disciplines will include time in the Word of God, in study, meditation and confession, and prayer of all kinds. Once your heart is set to establish godly standards, the Holy Spirit will help you. God will help us when we make the decision to step up our walk with Him. May the Lord grant us grace to be doers of these things.

SCRIPTURE READING: John 17:17-21 *AMPC*
PERSONAL APPLICATION: There should be no area of your life where you are not open to God's input. What does the Word say about it? And what is God telling you? The Holy Spirit will help you so that you are ready to respond to and obey God.

BE A DIFFERENCE MAKER

"Those who do wickedly against the covenant he shall corrupt with flattery; but the people who know their God shall be strong, and carry out great exploits."
Daniel 11:32

God's will for each and every one of us is to make a difference on earth. Whoever you are, wherever you are and whatever you do - you can make a difference. To be different is to differ or to be unlike somebody or something else. It also means to disagree in opinion, to be distinguishable, to be significant, to be important and to be noteworthy. God created us to be different from one another – to see things differently, to think differently, to respond differently, etc. and that is designed for the good of all. "For as we have many members in one body, but all the members do not have the same function, so we, being many, are one body in Christ, and individually members of one another. Having then gifts differing according to the grace that is given to us, let us use them" (Romans 12:4-6). However, it is one thing to be different but it is a totally different thing to make a difference! The Bible says Daniel distinguished himself above the governors and satraps because an excellent spirit was in him and he was therefore set over the whole realm (Daniel 6:3). Everyone is different but not everyone will make a difference! Everyone has a purpose, but not everyone will fulfil their purpose. Everyone has potential, but not everyone will fulfil their potential. Everyone has a destiny, but not everyone will fulfil their destiny. That would be a sad thing though, because it is God's will that we all should make a difference, that we all should fulfil our purpose on earth, fulfil our potential and fulfil our destiny so that, like the Apostle Paul, we can say, "I have fought the good fight, I have finished the race, I have kept the faith" (2 Timothy 4:7). We will only be able to make a difference if and when we are willing and ready to pay the price.

SCRIPTURE READING: 1 Corinthians 12:12-31
PERSONAL APPLICATION: What could you do differently to make a positive impact in someone's life today? Ask God to help sensitise you to the needs of others around you. It may require from you selflessness, breaking through barriers of race, colour, gender, culture and so forth in order to make a difference. Whatever it is, God will help you and give you the grace and strength you need.

THE ART OF SUCCESSFUL LIVING

"And God sent me before you to preserve a posterity for you in the earth, and to save your lives by a great deliverance. So now it was not you who sent me here, but God; and He has made me a father to Pharaoh, and lord of all his house, and a ruler throughout all the land of Egypt."
Genesis 45:7-8

Life is filled with problems. In fact, overcoming problems is a way to describe a successful life. What are your problems? A way to look at them is to consider them as doors of greatness that await your entry. They are a revelation of the size of your potential and they are the opportunities for growth that life presents you. They represent areas of your life where growth, development and discoveries lie. The Bible says seek, knock and ask. Some problems are solved by seeking the truth of the matter or by confronting some issues in your heart. Problems represent areas of your life that need adjusting, investigating and examination. The longer the problem persists, the more you can learn from it. Please take the pains to learn the right lessons from your problems. You can allow your problems to enlarge you - experience in life is not measured by what happens to us, but what we do with what happens to us. All the greats in the Bible are known to solve problems through the power of the Almighty God. David killed Goliath by the power of God. Daniel interpreted the king's dream. Joseph preserved the posterity of Israel. The additional key here is that these guys cultivated a relationship with God before they faced the problems and the power of God was released through their lifestyle of faith and obedience to God. When we master the art of solving problems, letting problems work for us and allowing our problems to grow us, we have mastered the art of successful living.

SCRIPTURE READING: Genesis 41:1-40
PERSONAL APPLICATION: Case study - read through the story of Daniel. See how he continually solved humanly impossible problems and situations through the power and wisdom of Almighty God. Remember, the key here is that he had cultivated a relationship with God before the problems arose. Let's spend time cultivating our relationship with God so that through Him, we will have what it takes to rise up to and solve the problems that life throws at us.

DEVELOPING CONFIDENCE IN GOD

"By faith Abraham, when he was tested, offered up Isaac,
and he who had received the promises offered up his only begotten son,
of whom it was said, "In Isaac your seed shall be called,"
concluding that God was able to raise him up, even from the dead,
from which he also received him in a figurative sense."
Hebrews 11:17-19

Confidence means: firm trust, a feeling of certainty, boldness, etc. Confidence comes from knowing who you are – "You are of God, little children, and have overcome them, because He who is in you is greater than he who is in the world" (1 John 4:4). Confidence comes from knowing whose you are and whom you serve. Paul was confident that there would be no loss of life among those on the ship. He said, "For there stood by me tonight an angel of the God to whom I belong and whom I serve" (Acts 27:23). Confidence comes from knowing what you have. Peter said to the lame man at Gate Beautiful, "silver and gold I do not have, but what I do have, I give you" (Acts 3:6). Confidence is in knowing who your source is! "I will lift up my eyes to the hills – from whence comes my help? My help comes from the LORD, who made heaven and earth" (Psalm 121:1-2). Daniel said the people who know their God shall be strong and carry out great exploits (Daniel 11:32). "And we have such trust through Christ toward God. Not that we are sufficient of ourselves to think of anything as being from ourselves, but our sufficiency is from God, who also made us sufficient as ministers of the new covenant" (2 Corinthians 3:4-6). Confidence comes from knowledge - what you know and who you know. Do you have such confident assurance in God? Do you know the God you serve? If not, it is time to build up your knowledge, faith and confidence in the Lord God Almighty, the Creator of the heavens and the earth.

SCRIPTURE READING: Psalm 46
PERSONAL APPLICATION: You can develop this kind of confidence and assurance in God in every area of your life. Spend time getting to intimately know God. He is an ever present help in trouble.

THE POWER OF DECISION

"Then Mary said, "Behold the maidservant of the Lord!
Let it be to me according to your word.""
Luke 1:38

In Luke 1:38 we see in Mary the power of decision when she said to the angel, "Let it be to me according to your word". Mary believed and was willing to obey, then she voiced her decision. Too many of us do not know the power of a decision that is backed by determination, discipline and diligence. The decision settles a lot of things in the realm of the spirit. Whatever has been made available to us in Christ needs our decision for there to be a manifestation in our lives. "Blessed is she who believed for there shall be a manifestation of what was spoken to her because she believed". This was said by Elizabeth to Mary when the latter visited her in Luke 1:45. Do you know that the decisions you make with your life determine many of the things you allow or disallow in your life? A decision to be in health does not wait for sickness to hit before meditating in the Word concerning health. The decision affects your present choices and determines the outcome in your life. Same is true with God's blessings in your life. They won't just fall on you like ripe mangoes; you need to make decisions and do what the Word says so you can be positioned for the harvest that the Word promises. Salvation has been made available to all. Those who believe make the decision to receive and they become possessors of the salvation of God in Christ; same with receiving the in-filling of the Holy Spirit. Do not wait for the tests to come before trying to make the decision to stay holy or avoid sin. Make the decision as soon as possible so the day of testing will not meet you unawares.

SCRIPTURE READING: Genesis 32:24-32
PERSONAL APPLICATION: The Bible is full of God's promises to His people - health, divine protection, provision, salvation and so much more. Let us make a quality decision today to meditate in the Word of God (before challenges arise) to see those promises come to pass in our lives.

RESTORING FELLOWSHIP WITH GOD

"This is the message which we have heard from Him and declare to you, that God is light and in Him is no darkness at all."
1 John 1:5

Sin is the main reason for broken fellowship with God and I dare say, with our fellow men also. The Bible says that the rebellious dwell in a dry land (Psalm 68:6). Perhaps the dryness you are facing now in your prayer life, finances, relationships with others and so forth, is traceable to sin? The truth is that the dryness, if caused by sin, cannot be cured by a change of geographical location. I see people change geographical locations because things are tough. God is not limited to a particular place. He is omnipresent. He is the God of the land, sea and sky; the God of all the earth. What matters is obedience to God. My husband often says that the right person is not a rich or influential person but whoever God connects you to! The right place is therefore where God leads you to. It is not necessarily a comfortable or convenient place. Therefore, instead of running away from, or covering up your sin, please confront and deal with it. How? The Bible says anyone who covers up his sin shall not prosper but whoever confesses and forsakes his sin shall obtain mercy (Proverbs 28:13). Before the appearing of Jesus Christ, John the Baptist was sent ahead to prepare the way of the Lord. What was it that preceded His appearing? The Bible says that multitudes went to John in the wilderness, confessing their sins (Matthew 3:5-6). The truth is that before we see Jesus come again, there shall be a divine move of God that will lead folks into the 'wilderness' to confess their sins with a decision to forsake them. Jesus is coming for a glorious church, a church without spot or wrinkle. Moreover, I know it won't be by might or by power, it shall be by the Spirit of the Lord, Hallelujah!

SCRIPTURE READING: James 5:13-18, 1 John 1:5-10
PERSONAL APPLICATION: The Bible says in 1 John 1:9 that if we confess our sins God is faithful and just not only to forgive us, but also to cleanse us from all unrighteousness. When sin is confessed, the blood of Jesus goes straight to work, cleansing the believer. The believer is justified, just as if he never sinned. Don't allow sin to separate you from God. Go before the mercy seat of God, confess your sins and receive cleansing and justification.

UNDERSTANDING SUBMISSION

"Giving thanks always for all things to God the Father in the name of our Lord Jesus Christ, submitting to one another in the fear of God."
Ephesians 5:20-21

To submit implies 'to surrender'. God in His wisdom has chosen that the key to winning is surrendering! This is why submission is so difficult for many of us. We often surrender only when we can no longer fight or resist it. Very rarely do we surrender by choice. Yet to be victorious, God says that we must surrender. Submission is one of the key principles that will enable us to live victoriously and overcome in the times in which we live. It is important to remember that submission is, first of all, an attitude. Submission is primarily revealed in the attitude of our hearts towards those God has placed over us. "Everyone must submit himself to the governing authorities for there is no authority except that which God has established. The authorities that exist have been established by God. Consequently, he who rebels against the authority is rebelling against what God has instituted, and those who do so will bring judgement on themselves" (Romans 13:1-2 *NIV*). As believers we must understand a right attitude towards those in authority is not optional behaviour.

SCRIPTURE READING: 1 Peter 2:13-25
PERSONAL APPLICATION: Our ability to embrace the principle of submission may make the difference in whether we fulfil our destiny in God or not. We must remember that, even though we are not of the world, we are in the world and there are principles that God has given to us which are specifically designed to help us with our relationships with those in authority.

POSITIONING OURSELVES FOR FRUITFULNESS

"But these are the ones sown on good ground, those who hear the word, accept it, and bear fruit: some thirtyfold, some sixty, and some a hundred."
Mark 4:20

The condition of our hearts can influence how fruitful the Word of God is in our lives. God expects us to deal with the condition of our hearts—to address all internal issues that have the ability to affect the productivity of God's Word in us. Regarding the heart, the Bible clearly states that, "out of it spring the issues of life" (Proverbs 4:23). The condition of our hearts will to a large extent determine whether or not we will be able to bear the fruit of the Word we have received. There are many issues that if not dealt with can affect our productivity. Cares, distractions, bitterness and unforgiveness are just a few. Such issues, unbeknown to many of us, create a climate that is not conducive to nurturing God's Word. If these internal issues are not dealt with, we will be frustrated and keep wondering why it seems the Word of God is not doing much in our lives. God's Word is a seed that comes into our hearts and that seed is meant to produce fruit. We are the ones with the responsibility of bearing fruit. In essence, we must apply our faith and love to ensure that what we have received is producing results in us. Bearing fruit is not a passive activity. We must be actively involved. Our faith and love must be engaged. We must put the Word in our mouth as our confession and carry an attitude that creates a climate for God's Word to produce. Many times we wait on God expecting God to do the work, but God is waiting on us.

SCRIPTURE READING: Mark 4:3-20
PERSONAL APPLICATION: We have the responsibility of bearing fruit, not God. Once the Word is sown, the fruitfulness of that Word is no longer determined by the sower; it is the determined by the soil. May God help us all to become good soil in Jesus' name!

THE BATTLE BELONGS TO GOD

"And he said, Hearken ye, all Judah, and ye inhabitants of Jerusalem, and thou king Jehoshaphat, Thus saith the Lord unto you, Be not afraid nor dismayed by reason of this great multitude; for the battle is not yours, but God's."
2 Chronicles 20:15 KJV

I want to say something to you today and I believe that God will grant you the revelation of it. The battle is not between you and the devil! Do you know why some of us are battle weary? Do you know why some of us are tired? We are trying to take on the devil. God says, "your warfare is accomplished" (Isaiah 40:2). The Lord dropped that into my heart. The battle is not between you and the devil. The battle was between the Lord and the devil. Praise God! That is why faith is the victory. If you try to take on the devil, you are going to be whipped. You must come to the place where you know you already have the victory. Jesus defeated him for us. He won the victor's crown. He won it all for us: the battle over sin, the battle over poverty, the battle over sickness and disease. Whatever the devil is doing is not between you and him. A lot of times we forget about that and we take on a battle that is not ours.

Today, step into the reality of the victory that Christ has already won for us. Know this, that He who knew no sin became sin for you, that you might become His righteousness. Stand in God's righteousness and remember the battle is not yours but God's.

SCRIPTURE READING: Hebrews 2:14-16, 1 John 3:8, Revelation 12:10-12

PERSONAL APPLICATION: It's time to stop struggling and trying to defeat the devil in your own strength. Find scriptures that talk about the victory that we already have in Christ. Remember, the devil is a defeated foe! Jesus defeated him on the cross and we share in that same victory.

STALE MANNA

"But be doers of the word, and not hearers only, deceiving yourselves."
James 1:22

The Bible says, "Be not deceived, God is not mocked, whatever a man sows that he will reap" (Galatians 6:7). It does not matter who that man is or even if he thinks otherwise; he will reap whatever he sows. In fact, the height of deception is when we think that we will not reap what we sow or, that we will reap what we have not sown. Sowing God's Word into our hearts through the study, meditation and doing of the Word must be a daily affair if we are going to be free of the deceitfulness of sin. You can't fight the devil's lies with the residual knowledge of the Word of God. The new man is being renewed 'daily' in the knowledge of Him who created him. You can't afford to take a break from being a doer of the Word or else you move into the trap of deception. I have discovered that living on stale manna makes you a moving target of the spirit of deception!

SCRIPTURE READING: James 1:21-26
PERSONAL APPLICATION: Be committed to doing what God says in His Word. It is your own strict obedience and commitment to the Word of God that will deliver you from deception. God's Word has an answer to every lie of the devil.

THE CHRISTIAN SOLDIER

"You therefore must endure hardship as a good soldier of Jesus Christ."
2 Timothy 2:3

A soldier is a person who has been deprogrammed from thinking like a civilian. He is trained to know that he has been enlisted for a definite purpose. He goes through a lot of rigours just to maintain a life of discipline. He sets a standard to be not just a good soldier but also an extraordinary one. When there is no war, he still trains so that when there is war, he is already fit and prepared. He does not just then begin training for fitness. He is always battle ready.

The Christian life demands that we are ready like soldiers at all times. The secret is not in trying to look for a fight, it is in being disciplined so as to be ready for a fight at any time. This calls for focus, discipline and determination. Life is no holiday; you must always be prepared for war.

Set goals that will keep you spiritually alert, disciplined and on your tippy toes because you are a soldier of Jesus Christ.

SCRIPTURE READING: 2 Timothy 2:1-6

PERSONAL APPLICATION: Your mentality must be that of warfare and you must train yourself to be ready for it. Establish a warfare lifestyle. This will help you discipline yourself and become spiritually fit.

SEEKING GOD WHOLEHEARTEDLY

"And you will seek Me and find Me, when you search for Me with all your heart."
Jeremiah 29:13

Hannah was an example of someone who sought God with all her heart. The Bible says she was in deep anguish, crying bitterly as she prayed to the Lord. She made a vow that if the Lord would give her a son she would give him back to the Lord (1 Samuel 1:10-11). When Hezekiah became terminally ill and was told by the prophet that he was going to die, the Bible says he turned his face towards the wall and prayed to the Lord. He pleaded his case with Him and wept bitterly. God responded to Hezekiah. He sent the prophet back to him with these words, "I have heard your prayer, I have seen your tears; surely I will add to your days fifteen years" (Isaiah 38:5). Some of us give up too soon and some don't put up any fight at all. Like Eli, they say, "It is the Lord. Let Him do what seems good to Him" (1 Samuel 3:18c). That is the most defeatist, though very religious, stance to take. God Himself has invited us to plead our case with Him, bringing forward our strong reasons (Isaiah 41:21)! Jacob wrestled with the angel throughout the night. He said to the angel, "I will not let You go unless You bless me" (Genesis 32:26). Jacob was blessed. His name was changed from Jacob (supplanter/deceiver) to Israel (triumphant with God). It is such tenacity that gets results. Jesus said people ought to pray and not give up or lose heart. Faith pleases God and it is also the victory. The woman with the issue of blood, the Syro-Phoenician woman and Blind Bartimaeus are also examples of those who sought God with all their heart and they found Him in their different situations.

SCRIPTURE READING: Psalm 63

PERSONAL APPLICATION: You must mean business with God to get the kind of results you desire to see in your life. You will find Him and be found by Him if you seek Him with all your heart (Jeremiah 29:13).

TOOLS FOR SHARING JESUS EFFECTIVELY

"For we cannot but speak the things which we have seen and heard."
Acts 4:20

We need to have compassion for people. Many are perishing for lack of the knowledge of the truth. Many are scattered like sheep without a shepherd and there are not many labourers labouring with the Father's heart to see to it that the harvest comes into the storehouse of God. Two necessary keys in evangelism are compassion and the power of the Holy Spirit! Read Acts 1:8 about receiving power through the Holy Spirit. Compassion is when we identify with the needy but allow the love of God within us to reach out with the power of God to meet the need. Jesus was always moved with compassion. When we consider the many who have not heard or who have not had the opportunity to hear correctly about what God has done for them in Christ, we let God's love in us rise up to meet their need for the Gospel. The greatest demonstration of love you can have to humanity is to give God to them. You can be sure of God's wisdom and favour on your life as you step out in obedience.

SCRIPTURE READING: Acts 1:8, Romans 10:13-17
PERSONAL APPLICATION: Ask Jesus today to give you a heart for the lost and a passion for souls. Receive His grace, wisdom, compassion and dunamis power to go out and be an effective witness for Him.

RUN YOUR OWN RACE

"If I will that he tarry till I come,
what is that to thee, follow thou me."
John 21:22 KJV

God has a plan for your finances, your marriage, your ministry/vocation, etc. There is a general plan for marriage but there is a specific plan for your own marriage. There is a general plan for financial prosperity, but God has a specific plan about how He wants to prosper you financially. God's plan for your life is unique. Mary said to the people who needed wine at the wedding, "whatever He says to you, do it" (John 2:5). There is a particular race that is set before you. Don't run another man's race. Know the race that is set before you (Hebrews 12:1). Discover the works you've been called to do. God says different things to different people. He requires different things from different people. The level of consecration God demands of you, for instance, might be different from what He demands of another person. He won't hold you responsible for what He told others to do. You will be held accountable for what you were told to do. Apostle Paul said the same grace that was at work in Peter to the Jews was also at work in him to the Gentiles because he had been entrusted with the task of preaching to the Gentiles as Peter had been to the Jews (Galatians 2:7-8). He says he did not receive God's grace in vain, neither did he frustrate it.

SCRIPTURE READING: John 21:17-23
PERSONAL APPLICATION: You must interact with God to know His unique plan for your life. You must ask Him questions (Jeremiah 33:3). You need to follow God's pattern of dealing with you. You need to live by every word that comes out of His mouth (Matthew 4:4). That is how to run your own race.

UNDERSTANDING AUTHORITY AND SUBMISSION

"Jesus saith unto them, My meat is to do the will of him that sent me, and to finish his work."
John 4:34 KJV

The subject of authority has been the unspoken reason for many unexplainable yet undeniable occurrences in many lives. It is so vital that many have run into dead ends and some have experienced certain levels of power and victory that do not compute with other things in their lives. In this brief study, we want to look at the heart of the issues involved in authority and submission. There are similarities in the principles that govern authority in the natural and the spiritual. The basic difference lies in the receiving of authority and the heart of submission and also the source of the power. Most of the conflicts we face are just manifestations of the battle for our souls between the kingdom of light and the kingdom of darkness. Our decisions and choices determine who wins the battle. The kingdom of darkness wants to be in authority over as many lives as possible. Deception, lust, wiles and schemes are all designed to bring humanity under the authority of the prince of darkness. We need a higher authority to deal with the authority of darkness. Authority is designed by God to bring protection, give direction and cause all those in subjection to progress in the specific process that produces fulfilment. Submission, on the other hand, is also a kingdom principle that allows God's will to be done. It implies a yieldedness that frees ourselves and others to be and do all that please the King of the kingdom, Jesus. The focus in both cases is, "Thy will be done, Thy kingdom come". The ones in authority have the purpose of seeing the will of God done in the lives of those in submission. Jesus submitted to God the Father to fulfil His task on earth. We need to as well. Jesus also submitted to Joseph and Mary before age 30. This defines God's plan for the family structure. He submitted to man's ordinance and practices while he was a baby. He submitted to John's baptismal ministry. He eventually submitted to God's will on the cross by dying. Today His name carries authority in all worlds. Every knee bows in His Name. If you are not under authority you cannot exercise authority.

SCRIPTURE READING: Ephesians 5:15-6:9
PERSONAL APPLICATION: How can we rise above our limited human understanding and embrace God's pattern for authority and submission.

GOD HAS A PLAN

"If men who are evil know how to give good things to their Children, how much more shall your Father which is in Heaven give good things to them that ask Him?"
Matthew 7:11 KJV

There is definitely no doubt about it that God has plans for your life. To doubt it is to doubt the fatherhood of God because it is difficult to imagine that a responsible father would not have plans for his own children. Our Lord Jesus Christ many times referred to God as our heavenly father. When asked to teach them how to pray, He taught His disciples to start praying by saying "Our Father, which art in heaven" (Matthew 6:9). Take note of the word 'family'. God has only one family and no matter where the members are located, He cares for them in the same way. God is the pattern for fatherhood; all fathers derive their fatherhood from Him!
God's plans for His people are multifaceted. God had plans for Abraham when He called him to get out of his country and to leave his family. In the time of famine, God had plans as to how His servant Elijah would be sustained (1 Kings 17). God had plans for Joseph. He had plans for David and for all His people. God has plans of sure victory and success for the Church. Jesus said the gates of hell shall not prevail against the Church.

SCRIPTURE READING: Proverbs 25:2-3
PERSONAL APPLICATION: God's plans and purposes are unchanging. They have been settled before the foundations of the earth, even before you and I were conceived in the womb. May you be stirred up with a desire and determination to find out and follow God's plans for your life.

THY KINGDOM COME

"Our Father which art in heaven, Hallowed be Thy name.
Thy kingdom come, Thy will be done..."
Matthew 6:9-10 KJV

Lately the phrase, "Thy kingdom come" has really stayed with me in my thoughts. God's kingdom: His government coming on the earth through our spirits, souls and bodies is what releases His will to be done on earth. Many times we think of God's will in terms of external activities like location and vocation. I perceive that God's will is a product of His government being established in our lives first of all. The coming of His kingdom on earth is only possible when we yield in our minds and wills to the principles, practices and attitudes of God's kingdom. The expression of the kingdom in us will be the expression of His will on earth. Before we think of the earth being filled with His kingdom, let us start with our own lives. Our birth into the kingdom is similar to the birth of Jesus in that the Word produces us. A new nature was released into our spiritual wombs. We need to allow the new nature to grow in us to the point that we begin to reflect the character of Christ. When we pass our tests we are empowered by the Holy Spirit like He was. When we submit to the will of the Father like Jesus did, we overcome like He did. The constancy of the fellowship and intimacy with the Spirit of God (which is only possible as we yield our spirit, soul and body to the government of God) will release the will of God into manifestation in our lives.

SCRIPTURE READING: Matthew 5-7

PERSONAL APPLICATION: Can you identify any hindrances to God's will and kingdom being established in your life? Ask the Holy Spirit today to help you to truly submit to and embrace the will of the Father just as Christ did when He was on earth.

RELIABLE, DEPENDABLE AND CONSTANT

"Most men will proclaim every one his own goodness: but a faithful man who can find?"
Proverbs 20:6 KJV

We must be faithful to do what God has called us to do. We must be faithful to walk in all the light that we have. We must be faithful to serve others with the gifts God has given to us. Faithfulness is a vital currency in God's kingdom. The Bible says that a man who is faithful in little is already faithful in much (Luke 16:10) because what matters is faithfulness and not the size of what you are doing. The ones who faithfully used the talents they received, faithfully were given more (Matthew 25:21-23). God does not give us more if we are not faithful in what we have now.
We must also be faithful in what belongs to others. The Bible says if we are not faithful in another man's who will give us our own? (Luke 16:12). We often discover God's plans and purposes for our lives while we are faithfully serving others. David faithfully kept his father's sheep. The sheep were not many, but he faithfully kept them. He risked his life for the sheep. He ran after the bear and lion that came after some of them. His experiences with the lion and the bear as a faithful shepherd became his confidence and qualification to take on Goliath. The Bible talks about the man who ran from a bear and a lion only to be bitten by a snake as he rested on a pillar in his house (Amos 5:19). We are not to run away from our challenges, we are to face them and overcome them!

SCRIPTURE READING: 1 Samuel 17:32-37
PERSONAL APPLICATION: Whatever you run away from today i.e. a difficult boss, a humble job, an unappreciative or unreceptive congregation, poverty, etc. will stare you in the face in the future in an even more intense proportion. Paul said, "I have learnt how to handle abundance and lack; I can do all things through Christ who strengthens me" (Philippians 4:12-13). Drop all your excuses for being unfaithful, they won't help you.

LIVING BY THE WORD

"Take My yoke upon you and learn from Me, for I am gentle and lowly in heart, and you will find rest for your souls. For My yoke is easy and My burden is light."
Matthew 11:29-30

God wants us to be able to live by His Word. He does not want the demands of His Word to be an external imposition but an internal delight. He wants sons and daughters who rejoice at His Word.

Grace is God's influence on the heart of a man or woman and it is reflected in that person's life. When we are living by His grace, we have the strength to live by the Word of God and say 'No!' to sin. The Bible says, "For the grace of God that bringeth salvation hath appeared to all men, teaching us..." (Titus 2:11-12 *KJV*).

God is bringing truth to us, but the truth is accompanied by grace. There is no need for despair or discouragement when we know that the same One who places a demand on us by His Word, supplies the grace to do what His Word demands. God is for us, not against us. His love and mercy have made a provision for us to live in victory. As He did not withhold His only begotten Son, we should be confident that God will not withhold anything we need to live a victorious Christian life.

SCRIPTURE READING: Titus 2:11-14

PERSONAL APPLICATION: Let us be strong in the grace of God. Let us be confident in the assurance of the Father's love for us and let us step out in faith as bold doers, not just readers, of the Word of God.

LOOK OUT FOR OTHERS

"And many people shall come and say, Come, let us go up to the mountain of the Lord, to the house of the God of Jacob, that He may teach us His ways and that we may walk in His paths. For out of Zion shall go forth the law and instruction, and the word of the Lord from Jerusalem."
Isaiah 2:3 AMPC

We must raise kids not only to think of what people can do for them, but also of what they can do for people; not just of what they can get, but what they can give! We must remember that whatever anyone becomes today is not just a product of their nature (which is inherent), but also, largely, a product of their nurture and culture. To produce adults who will give back more to society, we must start by raising such children because an adult was once a child. Jethro told Moses to appoint among the people able men who will judge small matters and will bear the burden with him. We must raise kids who will not only enjoy privileges, but who will also share responsibilities. When you have taught them, trained them, modelled things before them and invested in them, it is only appropriate for you to let them do things. You must train them to be responsible people. Children must not be raised to be selfish, but to look out for others - "Share each other's troubles and problems, and in this way obey the law of Christ" (Galatians 6:2 *NLT*).

SCRIPTURE READING: 1 Samuel 12:23, Proverbs 22:6 *AMPC*, 2 Timothy 3:15 *AMPC*
PERSONAL APPLICATION: A practical way to teach your children to be responsible people is to simply let them share in family responsibilities and values. Give them those responsibilities proportional to their age and ability e.g. household chores. Though, as parents, note that it is very important that we ourselves model the values and responsibilities we teach our children.

LOVE THAT COMPELS

"He said to him the third time,
'Simon, son of Jonah, do you love Me?'"
John 21:17

Jesus said, "If ye love Me, keep my commandments" (John 14:15). This scripture has often been interpreted to mean that keeping God's commands is proof of our love for Him. I do believe there is validity in this interpretation because truly one of the ways we prove our love for God is by keeping His commands. But I want us to look at this scripture from another perspective.

Those of you who are married or who have been in love with someone will understand this perspective. When you fall in love with someone, you are willing to do so much for that person. You listen carefully to find out what that person likes or dislikes, you find out the person's interests and you willingly and ungrudgingly do things for that person. When most men meet a woman and fall in love, they are ready to do almost anything (within godly boundaries) that they know the woman likes or wants them to do. Do they do these things to prove they love the woman? Yes, but more than to just prove their love, they do such things because they are in love! I am simply saying, when we truly love a person, the love in our hearts makes us do what will please the one we love. We do not want to offend and we conduct ourselves in a manner that will foster the relationship with that person. When we love God, we will obey His commandments. Our love for Him will compel us to obey Him. That love will drive us to a life of consecration, a life where we are fit for intimacy with Him. Let us draw ever closer to our King!

SCRIPTURE READING: John 21:15-22

PERSONAL APPLICATION: We need to note that our love for God should be balanced with the reverential fear of God. Many people claim to love God but their actions demonstrate a lack of the fear of the Lord. May we never depart from the fear of God.

THE PRINCIPLE OF OBEDIENCE

"Confident of your obedience, I write to you, knowing that you will do even more than I ask."
Philemon 1:21 NIV

Jesus likens the man who comes to Him and hears and obeys His saying to a wise man who builds his house on the rock. The house remained standing even after the storms, winds and rains had come and gone (Luke 6:46-49). God told Isaac not to go to Egypt but to dwell in the land of the Philistines in spite of the famine and Isaac obeyed. He sowed in the same land and reaped a hundredfold in the same year! The widow of Zarephath obeyed the word of the LORD through Elijah and she was sustained throughout the famine (1 Kings 17). Isaiah 1:19 says, "if you are willing and obedient, you will eat the good of the land". Obey, even if it doesn't make sense or when it isn't convenient. "He who observes the wind will not sow, And he who regards the clouds will not reap" (Ecclesiastes 11:4). Let the Lord lead you. He knows where the provision is. "The Lord is my shepherd; I shall not want. He makes me to lie down in green pastures; He leads me beside the still waters" (Psalm 23:1-2).

SCRIPTURE READING: 1 Samuel 15:22, Romans 5:19
PERSONAL APPLICATION: Obedience is hard at times as the flesh has other ideas, but we must remember we are a new creation in Christ (2 Corinthians 5:17). We must not try to achieve things merely by our human efforts; that always leads to trouble. Instead, listen out for the voice and instruction of God, then willingly obey Him—even if it doesn't make sense!

INCREASE IN STRENGTH

"Finally, my brethren, be strong in the Lord and in the power of His might."
Ephesians 6:10

Don't ever be afraid of warfare. When anything that is contrary to God's will comes up, you should rise up like a soldier and war against it because you are battle ready. Soldiers believe that there are enemies and they always want to be battle ready. That is why they train to a high level of fitness. You must not let your battle determine your level of fitness. A good, well disciplined soldier keeps himself fit and strong and increases in strength by constant and thorough training. A Christian will increase in strength by fasting, praying and meditating in the Word habitually. Consistency and focus can only lead to the top. One of the reasons why we cannot afford to live as civilians do is because no soldier goes to war without being armed. If he does, he will be a casualty. As Christians we must always put on the whole armour of God to be able to stand against the wiles of the devil. God has provided all we need to wage a good warfare; all we need to do is position ourselves. Everything must be in place so that we can withstand in the evil day. As a soldier, every bit of your armour must be on and fit comfortably. As a Christian therefore, you must be mentally and spiritually alert at all times. In the army, the soldiers are taught and trained to be ready at a moment's notice and sometimes, at no notice at all—yet be ready to fight—and win. It is not enough to fight; the desire to win must totally fill the soldier's mind. Christian, you must not be caught unawares! If you are to be empowered for destiny, learn how a soldier in the army stays fit for battle. Use your training manual, the Bible. Be a doer of what it says not just a hearer.

SCRIPTURE READING: Ephesians 6:10-18

PERSONAL APPLICATION: There are times where some very difficult situations of life come knocking on your door. If you don't possess a warfare mentality as a soldier, you may find yourself begging the situation. Guess what? The situation will not change. But when you rise up on your inside because you know you've been empowered, then change happens!

PEACE LIKE A RIVER

"Let all those who seek You rejoice and be glad in You;
Let such as love Your salvation say continually,
"The Lord be magnified!"
Psalm 40:16

God's promises are meant to bring us into the rest God wants for us, if we would believe them. For every concern, worry or anxiety, there is at least a promise of God to counter it, but unfortunately a lot of believers don't believe! Just like the Bible says, "but the word which they heard did not profit them, not being mixed with faith in those who heard it. For we who have believed do enter that rest" (Hebrews 4:2-3). God keeps us in perfect peace when our minds are fixed on Him and trust in Him (Isaiah 26:3). Sometimes, when you're agitated or you sense the anxiety coming over your soul, you may just need to spend some time praying in the Spirit. "For with stammering lips and another tongue He will speak to this people, To whom He said, 'This is the rest with which You may cause the weary to rest,' And, 'This is the refreshing'" (Isaiah 28:11-12). The Bible also says the one who prays in the Spirit edifies, that is, builds up himself (1 Corinthians 14:4). When we pray in the Spirit, rather than give in to anxieties, we can build up our faith, "[make progress, rise like an edifice higher and higher]", above the situation (Jude 1:20 *AMPC*). God wants to give us rest—peace and quiet, in spite of the troubles, pressures, anxieties, fears, uncertainties and worries that we have around us in the world. But that peace doesn't happen automatically; we must allow Him to lead us. "The Lord is my shepherd; I have all that I need. He lets me rest in green meadows; He leads me beside peaceful streams" (Psalm 23:1-2 *NLT*). God told the Israelites, "I am the Lord your God, Who teaches you to profit, Who leads you by the way you should go. Oh, that you had heeded My commandments! Then your peace would have been like a river" (Isaiah 48:17-18).

SCRIPTURE READING: Psalm 119:165, Matthew 11:27-30
PERSONAL APPLICATION: God says do not fret or worry (Matthew 6:25-34). Why? Because it is unproductive and contrary to His will. We must cast all our cares on Him for He cares for us. Spend time praying in the Spirit. This is not always easy, but it is worth it. Give it up and trust in God.

POWER IN HIS WORD

"Heaven and earth shall pass away, but my words shall not pass away."
Matthew 24:35 KJV

When God wanted to deliver the Israelites from Egypt, He said in Exodus 3:8, "And I am come down to deliver them out of the hand of the Egyptians..." He didn't come physically but when He sent His Word through Moses, it meant that He came. If the Word of God comes to you, and you value it, God's nature, wisdom, grace and anointing will be made manifest as a result of that Word. Everything that God is has been encapsulated in His Word and anyone that receives His Word can begin to decipher, discern and live it as long as he lives because God's Word is eternal. The Bible says in Mark 13:31 that, "Heaven and earth shall pass away, but my words shall not pass away". If God said it, you can depend on it! The reason why the Word doesn't produce for many people is because they treat it with levity. They do not recognise that there is power, strong enough to bring solutions to their predicaments, in the Word. You must feed your inner man with the Word of God because that is where life is, for in Him was life and the life was the light of men. Everything from God has the potential to multiply itself if it is highly valued. If you don't value it, nothing happens. For instance, a man that is prospering in God today has simply laid hold on the power of God in His Word. It is always better when your need is met by the Word of God. Fellowship with the Word - if you find it out in the Word and you lay hold on it, you've got it. The Word has an inherent power to fulfill itself.

SCRIPTURE READING: John 1:1-5, 14-18
PERSONAL APPLICATION: There are times when you come across something in the Word that your faith cannot sustain. What you need to do when this happens is to feed your eyes and mind on the Word. As faith comes by hearing the Word, your faith will grow and consequently be able to sustain that Word. Thus, your spiritual capacity enlarges. It will seem like all those issues in your life that seemed to evade solutions will be solved.

LIVING AN OBEDIENT LIFE

"The Lord said to Moses, "Send some men to explore the land of Canaan, which I am giving to the Israelites. From each ancestral tribe send one of its leaders."
Numbers 13:1-2 NIV

God does not usually reveal to us at one go the steps we should take or the things we will face in reaching the fullness of His plan for our lives. But as He reveals each step to us, we are expected to obey Him in taking that step and also to do what He says as we face challenges. Joseph didn't know he would be sold as a slave and later put in prison when he was having dreams about his brothers bowing down to him, but thank God he yielded to God's dealings all the way to destiny. God had plans to keep Elijah during the famine but Elijah had to obey God's Word to go to the brook of Cherith to be fed by ravens and then to the widow of Zarephath to be sustained by her when the brook dried up. Abraham didn't know that God would ask him to sacrifice his son Isaac when he received the call and the promise that he would be the father of many nations, but thank God he didn't withhold Isaac from God when asked to offer him. A life of obedience to God will bring us into the fullness of God's good plans for our lives, whereas, disobedience will prevent us from experiencing all God has in store for us. There is a place called "there" in God's program where God guarantees your provision, promotion and fulfilment. It takes obedience for you to be there. It may not be a good or a comfortable place but it is the right place. Abraham had to leave his father's house to go to a land God would show him. Some of the things that hinder our complete obedience are: preconception, unbelief, doubt, fear, insecurity and the opinion of others. We must break out of such things and be like Joshua and Caleb who followed the Lord fully because they had a different spirit.

SCRIPTURE READING: Numbers 13:1-30
PERSONAL APPLICATION: You can't obey God by doing what others are doing. What God demands from you is different from what He expects from others. You must have a spirit different from the prevailing spirit of the age to follow through on God's plans for your life.

WAITING FOR GOD

"Be still in the presence of the Lord, and wait patiently for him to act.
Don't worry about evil people who prosper
or fret about their wicked schemes."
Psalm 37:7 NLT

God is calling His people aside, separating them from the world and creating a covenant mindset in them for kingdom exploits. God wants to elevate and promote us and He has to prepare us for that season of promotion. Watch out though. The enemy may try to force us into that promotion before we are ready! If he succeeds, we will not be qualified as far as heaven is concerned. Then instead of bringing a blessing, it will bring a curse because we did not take our place in God's timing, waiting for Him.

We are being prepared for a future in God. Meanwhile, we should not be enticed in the present to be like others, to copy others and to risk losing out on our destiny. My prayer is that God will show you His dream for you. Daniel served God's purpose through the reign of at least four kings. Even when the reign of some of them came to an end, Daniel continued to function as God's man in the kingdom. God gave him his rightful place. Do not seek a position you are not internally prepared for. If you want to succeed over the long haul, wait for God and do it God's way.

SCRIPTURE READING: Psalm 40:1-8

PERSONAL APPLICATION: God wants you to go through process so that you will be properly equipped for what He has prepared for you. Shortcuts do not exist in spiritual matters. What looks like a shortcut may end up being a detour that gets you sidetracked. Stay on the straight and narrow way.

THE SACRIFICE OF COVENANT

"But the king replied to Araunah, 'No, I insist on buying it, for I will not present burnt offerings to the Lord my God that have cost me nothing.' So David paid him fifty pieces of silver for the threshing floor and the oxen."
2 Samuel 24:24 NLT

In covenant, sacrifices are involved. The Bible says we should present our bodies to God as a living sacrifice, holy and acceptable to Him (Romans 12:1). And in Psalm 50:5, God said, "Gather My saints together to Me, Those who have made a covenant with Me by sacrifice." We can't talk about covenant without sacrifice. That is why husbands are to love their wives as Christ loved the Church and gave Himself for her and wives are also to submit themselves to their own husbands, as to the Lord (Ephesians 5:22-25). I believe that one major reason for divorces and breakdowns in marriages today is the unwillingness of people to make sacrifices. No marriage can work without sacrifices. You have to be willing to sacrifice your time, your dreams, your talents, your will, etc. for your marriage to work. Don't forget that marriage is between two people who are on their way to becoming one. You are not going to become one if you are not willing to leave so you can cleave! There are things you must be willing to leave; that is where sacrifice comes in. Sometimes you give up your favourite TV shows, your hobbies, etc. just to make time to bond together. However, in making the necessary sacrifices, your motive and attitude must be right! "And whatever you do, do it heartily, as to the Lord and not to men, knowing that from the Lord you will receive the reward of the inheritance; for you serve the Lord Christ" (Colossians 3:23-24). The Bible says we should let the same attitude that was in Christ, be in us. Jesus did not hold on to his right as being equal with God, but made Himself of no reputation, took the form of a bondservant, coming in the likeness of man and humbled Himself and became obedient even to the shameful death of the cross (Philippians 2:5-8). Though husbands and wives are heirs together of the grace of life, they will need to learn to humble themselves in order to make their marriage work.

SCRIPTURE READING: Colossians 3:23-24, Genesis 2:22-24
PERSONAL APPLICATION: Commitment to a relationship will draw on our resources. In order to find time to invest, some things must give way. Whatever God gave us is a valuable commodity and must be invested in others and not only ourselves.

TAKING A STAND

"When you pass through the waters, I will be with you;
and when you pass through the rivers, they will not sweep over you.
When you walk through the fire, you will not be burned;
the flames will not set you ablaze."
Isaiah 43:2 NIV

Whenever we decide to take a stand against the devil, whenever we decide we will not bow, the enemy may bombard our minds with negative thoughts. The devil might tell us that if we don't lie, if we don't cheat or if we don't pretend to be who we are not, we will never make it. The devil is trying to tell us at such times, "I will sentence you to the fire of misery, mediocrity and poverty." We must know how to reply the devil. We must be able to tell him, "I am not slow to answer you... I will not bow" (Daniel 3:16-18).

When we take a stand for righteousness, integrity and truth, we cannot lose. The very things we refuse to bow to, will bow to us when we come out of the fire. The Hebrew children had made their decision before the question was asked.

This is the secret: when we do not bow, what we refuse to bow to will bow to us. When we bow, we lose it. We lose it because what we bow to will control us. We will not use it for what God wants. It will use us for what it wants. This is why many people today lack proper direction for their lives. Instead of responding to God and His purposes, they respond to money and its demands. Jesus was very clear when He said, "You cannot serve both God and money" (Matthew 6:24 *NLT*). In bowing to money and to the things of the world, we lose our freedom. People often ask me why I look so calm and free. It is simple really; I do not bow because I am ready to go through the fire. How about you, are you ready to go through the fire?

On a side note, we should not expect to be celebrated by our brothers and sisters in church when we refuse to bow. Do you think the other Jews celebrated when Shadrach, Meshach and Abednego refused to bow? Do you think their eventual promotion was celebrated? I believe that the other Jews envied them and hated them because they (the other Jews) had already bowed. So, don't expect accolades or applause; all the same, we should not bow!

SCRIPTURE READING: Isaiah 43:1-7, Daniel 3:1-30

PERSONAL APPLICATION: What can you take a stand on today? Ask God for the strength to stand for righteousness integrity and truth, no matter the circumstance!

OUR EXAMPLE

"Looking unto Jesus the author and finisher of our faith; who for the joy that was set before him endured the cross, despising the shame, and is set down at the right hand of the throne of God."
Hebrews 12:2 KJV

Jesus is our example in overcoming Satan's temptations and in passing our tests so that we can be promoted to the next level. The Bible says God highly exalted Jesus and gave Him the name that is higher than any other name, because He became obedient even to death on the cross (Philippians 2:8-9). Jesus endured the cross, despising its shame because of the joy that was set before Him (Hebrews 12:2). I believe that the secret of His success is found in Gethsemane, where Jesus prayed till His sweat became like drops of blood falling on the earth (Luke 22:44). Jesus prayed, "Father, if thou be willing, remove this cup from me: nevertheless not my will, but thine be done" (Luke 22:42 *KJV*). The Bible says an angel appeared from heaven strengthening Him (Luke 22:43).

We can learn many secrets from Jesus' prayer. It shows us firstly that Satan's strategies and plans are uncovered and can therefore be forestalled in prayer. It shows us that we can establish future victories whilst in the present. There is no time or distance in the spirit realm. It shows us that the spiritual controls and conditions the physical. We can operate in the spirit realm in prayer. It also shows us that prayer is a place of exchange, where we exchange our weakness for His strength (Isaiah 40:31). The strength to overcome Satan, the flesh and sin as well as the strength to do God's will in the face of fierce opposition and temptations come in prayer.

SCRIPTURE READING: Luke 22:39-46

PERSONAL APPLICATION: Many battles are won in the place of prayer. The enemy tries his hardest to stop us from effective praying by distraction and discouragement. Make up your mind today not to allow him to rob you of your future victories.

LIGHT OF THE WORD

"Then you shall again discern
Between the righteous and the wicked,
Between one who serves God
And one who does not serve Him."
Malachi 3:18

In Matthew chapter 5, Jesus says that as believers, we are to be the salt of the earth and light of the world (see Matthew 5:13-14). One thing about light and darkness is that they do not mix. Jesus specifically used light when referring to our relationship with the world. 'World' here is the translation of the Greek word 'kosmos', which is the word used when referring to the systems or arrangements of the world. As far as the systems of the world are concerned, we are to see ourselves as light—distinct and separate from the world.

Today many Christians have one foot in the church and one foot outside in the world. We are not separate. In order for us to be able to overcome the Babylonian (worldly) systems, we must have the mind-set of a people separated from the world. There is definitely a place for us to reach out to people bound by the world—just like Jesus did, but we must not allow the systems governing such people to influence our thoughts, attitudes or actions. This is why Jesus also refers to believers as salt. Even though salt seems to mix with the environment in which it is placed, the mixing allows the salt to influence its environment, not vice versa.

SCRIPTURE READING: Matthew 5:13-16

PERSONAL APPLICATION: You are the light that shines in the darkness, you are the salt that gives flavour! Pray according to Matthew 5:16, "Lord, I want my light to shine before others, so that they may see You through me, and that I may glorify you!".

BRINGING DOWN THE WALL

"Now I will tell you
what I am going to do to my vineyard:
I will take away its hedge,
and it will be destroyed;
I will break down its wall,
and it will be trampled."
Isaiah 5:5 NIV

Confrontation is not necessarily negative or hostile, so we don't need to be afraid of it or run away from it. To confront simply means, to bring (a person) face to face with something. Jesus said, "If your brother sins against you, go and tell him his fault between you and him alone" (Matthew 18:15). Unfortunately, oftentimes we reverse the whole order: we tell others first, and the offending party is the last to know about what he or she has done wrong! We spread stories we've not verified from the person concerned. We have too many phoney and hypocritical relationships because we all run away from confronting issues with one another. Also, in Matthew 5:23, Jesus said if we bring our gift to the altar and there remember that our brother has something against us, we should leave the gift there and go and first be reconciled to him and then come back to offer our gift. When we notice there is an unseen wall between us and another, Jesus expects us to take the initiative in restoring the relationship. "Let all bitterness, wrath, anger, clamour and evil speaking be put away from you, with all malice. And be kind to one another, tender-hearted, forgiving one another, even as God in Christ forgave you" (Ephesians 4:31-32).

SCRIPTURE READING: Ephesians 2:14, Galatians 2:11-16
PERSONAL APPLICATION: Confrontation is a challenge. It takes courage. It should not be done without careful and prayerful consideration. However, we must not allow fear to hinder us from doing what is right. We must ask God for grace.

DEVELOPING BACKBONE

"For the grace of God that brings salvation has appeared to all men, teaching us that, denying ungodliness and worldly lusts, we should live soberly, righteously, and godly in the present age"
Titus 2:11-12

For most believers, grace is a big cover-up. We live a life of sin and say, "thank God for His grace". Grace is not a cover-up for sin. Grace is not an excuse for our weakness. God's grace imparts a dimension into our spirit that enables us to say no to sin. The book of Titus says, "For the grace of God that brings salvation has appeared to all men" (Titus 2:11 *KJV*). Grace is taking a position, a permanent position of having said no to sin. Then when we are presented with an opportunity to sin, when sin is offered on a platter of gold, we must remember that grace has taught us to say no! Sin will no longer be an option. Grace enables us to see sin for what it really is. No matter how well packaged or dressed sin may be, it was not meant for us and will definitely have negative effects on our spirit, soul and body. How about the people who offer us sin? Why do we still sometimes find it so easy to commune with people who are offering us a deadly substance? Surely, such people, no matter who or what they are to us naturally are not our friends. Grace will give us the backbone to say no to sin. It will no longer be a debate; it will no longer be an issue. We must enter this dimension of grace. The three Hebrew children were operating in this dimension, which is why they could boldly say, "We do not need to defend ourselves before you in this matter" (Daniel 3:16 *NIV*). They had taken a stand; they had made their decision. I think it should be very clear to us now that it takes grace to live a consecrated life. Living a consecrated life is not a life of following rules and regulations. It is a life of having received grace. The grace of God is available to all who are saved.

SCRIPTURE READING: Titus 2:11-14, Romans 6:1-18
PERSONAL APPLICATION: Make it your prayer today for God to bring you into this level of grace; where you take a permanent position of saying 'no' to sin.

GOD'S WORD AND PROMISES

"You are my hiding place and my shield; I hope in Your Word."
Psalm 119:114

The expectation of a brighter tomorrow, of good health and of a long and prosperous life is based on God's precious promises. And through those promises, we have become partakers of His divine nature and have escaped the corruption that is in the world (2 Peter 1:3-4). We expect answers to our prayers because they are based on the Word of God. Jesus said, "If you abide in Me, and My words abide in you, you will ask what you desire, and it shall be done for you" (John 15:7). The Word of God reveals His will to us and we have the confidence in Him that if we ask anything according to His will, He hears us and we know that we have the petitions that we have asked of Him (1 John 5:14-15). Note that it didn't say, 'we think' or 'wish'; rather it says, 'we know'! The Word of God moves us from the realm of uncertainty, insecurity, doubt and fear into the realm of certainty, assurance, security and faith. Abraham was fully convinced that God was able to perform what He had promised (Romans 4:21). God did not only promise but also bound Himself with an oath, so that those who received the promise could be perfectly sure that He would never change His mind. "These two things are unchangeable because it is impossible for God to lie. Therefore, we who have fled to Him for refuge can have great confidence as we hold to the hope that lies before us. This hope is a strong and trustworthy anchor for our souls" (Hebrews 6:17-19 *NLT*). The hope we derive from God's promises and oath to us can be relied on for support, stability, security and mainstay, in times of trouble or contrary circumstances. Jesus said we will have troubles in the world; but we should be of good cheer, because He has overcome the world (John 16:33).

SCRIPTURE READING: 1 John 5:14-15
PERSONAL APPLICATION: God always keeps His Word and his promises (Jeremiah 29:11, Isaiah 54:17, Joshua 1:9, Isaiah 45:19, Genesis 15:1). Spend time reading God's Word and promises. Allow God's Word to fill you, strengthen you and enlarge you.

DEFEATING THE ENEMY

"And He came to the disciples and found them sleeping, and He said to Peter, What! Are you so utterly unable to stay awake and keep watch with Me for one hour?"
Matthew 26:40 AMPC

Prayer is the channel through which we maintain contact with our King and through which He releases Kingdom resources to us. In warfare, two of the primary targets are always the communication centre and transport routes. Airports, bridges, boats and supply convoys are identified as prime targets. The mindset of an army is, 'if we can break communication and stop supplies, the enemy will be cut off and will be easy to destroy!' How true! An army that is cut off from its source is an isolated army, easy to defeat. Natural armies recognise this and take extreme measures to guard communication centres and supply routes. Unfortunately, many in the Body of Christ have failed to understand the strategic importance of prayer, and unfortunately for them, the devil does! The Christian's prayer life is one of the first things the devil attacks, and he never stops attacking. The devil's mind-set is simple: separate the Christian from the Kingdom they represent and they can be easily destroyed! We must wake up and realise that we are surrounded by the enemy. We are in a war zone. Our King has sent us behind enemy lines to launch an attack from within the enemy's territory and take over (see Mark 16:15). The only way we can defeat the enemy in his own territory is by maintaining contact with our Commander. Through prayer, we establish a communication centre and open a supply route between ourselves and our Kingdom. It is not enough to pray when we are in trouble or when we have needs. We must have a disciplined pattern of regular prayer.

SCRIPTURE READING: Daniel 6:3-10
PERSONAL APPLICATION: To win in life, not only must you pray, you must develop a habit of prayer. You need to have a disciplined pattern of regular prayer or else you will short change yourself.

SUBMISSION TO HIS WILL AND WAY

"Submit to God and you will have peace;
then things will go well for you."
Job 22:21 NLT

God has a will and a purpose for our lives. He created us; we didn't create ourselves. We are here for a reason; and it's our responsibility to discover it and yield to it. "Submit to God, and you will have peace; then things will go well for you" (Job 22:21 *NLT*). A lot of folks live their lives resisting God's will for their lives, and that is why they don't have peace and the devil seems to be having the upper hand in their lives. The Bible says, "Therefore submit to God. Resist the devil and he will flee from you" (James 4:7). God didn't intend for us to be defeated by the enemy, He made us to be more than conquerors through Christ Jesus. He is with us even to work out all things for the good of those who love Him, and are called according to His purpose for them (Romans 8:28). God has His ways of doing things; and His ways are not our ways. The Bible says they are higher (Isaiah 55:8-9)! Two cannot walk together, except they are in agreement; we are the ones to forsake our own ways and embrace His ways, if we are to experience His peace in our lives. "But seek (aim at and strive after) first of all His kingdom and His righteousness (His way of doing and being right), and then all these things taken together will be given you besides" (Matthew 6:33 *AMPC*). God's ways are the ways of humility, giving, service, forgiveness and so forth.

SCRIPTURE READING: 1 Samuel 24:3-10, Job 22:21 *AMP*
PERSONAL APPLICATION: We can be deceived into believing that God's will is easy or painless, but we only have to look at the cross to see sometimes there is pain in the offering. Although we may not have nails through our hands, it can be painful when we choose not to take revenge on someone who has hurt us, or forgive someone who isn't sorry.

THE LIFE AND THE LIGHT

"In him was life, and that life was the light of all mankind."
John 1:4 NIV

Anything that is built to last and stand the test of time must be built on a secure foundation. For the Christian, the most secure foundation to build anything on is the Word of God. "The same was in the beginning with God. All things were made by Him; and without Him was not anything made that was made. In Him was life; and the life was the light of men. And the light shineth in darkness; and the darkness comprehended it not" (John 1:2-5). If you are walking in darkness, it is not because there is darkness outside; it is because there is no light inside you. In other words, until the light shines in you, you won't see the possibilities around you. That light is the Word. 1 John 1:4 says, "In Him was life", in other words, in the Word was life and the life was the light of men. If there is light in you, the darkness around will not overcome you. Darkness can be likened to ignorance. If you have light in you, no situation will be a mystery and you will not be ignorant of what to do when an adverse situation arises. What you need in order to have a breakthrough in any area of your life is already within you. The light in you needs to be turned on through faith, so that you can see the possibilities God has placed around you.

SCRIPTURE READING: John 1:1-5
PERSONAL APPLICATION: Learn to cultivate a deep walk with God, it will develop your faith in God. Know this, it is not necessary for you to have anything physically or naturally speaking for you to become a victor in any situation! All you need is God. Let the light come on in you and watch yourself face and defeat any situation in the strength of God.

USING WHAT YOU HAVE

"There is one who scatters, yet increases more; and there is one who withholds more than is right, but it leads to poverty."
Proverbs 11:24

When the widow went to Elisha in distress because the creditors had threatened to take her children, Elisha asked her, "What do you have in the house?" (2 Kings 4:2). She said, "Nothing, but a jar of oil". It is what you have in your house, in your possession and at your disposal that God will use to turn your situation around! Some of us have things that we could sell - things that we bought but have no use for; things we could do absolutely fine without. We could organise garage or car boot sales; we could sell on the internet; etc. It is not a sign of poverty to dispose of what you don't need; rather it is when you keep what you don't need. We need a paradigm shift! You might also need to free your money, by cancelling some direct debits you set up on your accounts for services you don't really need. The list is endless, but the point is - cut out wastage! Contentment looks inward, while covetousness looks outward. God will not use what you don't have to meet your needs. He will use the talent, the gift, the resources (physical, spiritual and mental) within your reach to bless you. You must reckon with what you have. Begin to value what you have. David used his stones and sling to kill Goliath. God used the staff in Moses' hand to part the Red Sea. Elisha used the pot of oil the woman had to perform the miracle. He said to her, after all the vessels had been filled with oil, "Go, sell the oil and pay your debt, and you and your sons live on the rest" (2 Kings 4:7). Jesus blessed the five loaves and two fish, and after feeding five thousand men, they gathered up twelve baskets of leftovers! Convert what you have into a seed, so it can meet your need. When the widow of Zarephath baked for Elijah first, her need was met for the duration of the famine.

SCRIPTURE READING: 2 Kings 4:1-7, Mark 12:41-44, Luke 6:38
PERSONAL APPLICATION: Instead of thinking about all the things you do not have, ask God to open your eyes to see and value all the things you do have! Start looking inwards and trust God to use the things you have to meet your needs. You'll be amazed at the divine ideas He will give to you.

THE SECRET TO VICTORY

"Obey those who rule over you, and be submissive, for they watch out for your souls, as those who must give account. Let them do so with joy and not with grief, for that would be unprofitable for you."
Hebrews 13:17

In Revelation chapters 2 and 3, God had messages that He wanted to pass on to the churches. But in speaking to the churches, He did not call everyone that was a member and talk to them all. He identified the leader—the angel or messenger—and gave the message to that angel (see Revelation 2:1).
Only those who are submitted to their leader will be able to hear the voice of God in the voice of their leader. This is why submission is so important! Often, God speaks to us through the leaders whom He has set in authority over us. If we choose to despise and disregard them, we will never hear the voice of God through them. God must be first in our lives, no doubt about that at all, but the godly authority placed over us must be respected. A humble person will be taught by the anointing and will get the balance. Godly authority is always confirmed in the hearts of godly people. If a person who is under God's authority speaks God's Word to you, there will be a witness in your heart that the Word is of God. We must understand that God ordained the principle of submission to authority, and He will not break it. We must allow God to be placed first in our lives and respect everything He has put in place. We must strive to follow God's order and not our own way. It is only when we do things His way that we can be sure of always walking in victory.

SCRIPTURE READING: Romans 13:1-7, 2 Kings 5:15-27
PERSONAL APPLICATION: Once we are in a church, God expects us to submit to the authority He has placed over that church. It is as we submit and are faithful, that we will see manifestations of the fulfillment of destiny and purpose.

TEMPTED, YET WITHOUT SIN

"For we do not have a High Priest who cannot sympathize with our weaknesses, but was in all points tempted as we are, yet without sin."
Hebrews 4:15

We are living in a time when it seems as though in order to make it in life, you must lie or cheat or defraud, or even commit sexual immorality. That is what Satan has made us believe, but God still has a way out of all that. Jesus says, "I am the Way, the Truth and the Life". He is the way out. The way of righteousness wins out any day. Sin is a reproach to any nation and to anybody; it is righteousness that exalts. The Bible says that God leads us in the path of righteousness for His name's sake (Psalm 23:3). Whatever you compromise to get, you will eventually lose. The devil always has a string attached to whatever he offers. He told Jesus, "I will give you all the glories of the world, you just bow down to me in worship". Thank God Jesus didn't bow, thereby leaving us an example to follow. God says all the things the heathens seek after will be added to us if we will seek first His Kingdom and His righteousness. Righteousness means, among other things, God's own way of doing things! God has His own way of prospering you; promoting you; keeping you in good health and so forth. God can give you your own husband without having to sleep around with men just because they promised to marry you. Don't jeopardise your future peace and joy. Don't jeopardise your eternal bliss in Heaven. Don't be like Esau, who for a single meal sold his inheritance rights as the first born (Hebrews 12:16-17).

SCRIPTURE READING: Hebrews 4:12-16
PERSONAL APPLICATION: The devil will make it look as if you have no other choice but to sin. You do have a choice! Choose God's way of doing things. Seek first His Kingdom and His righteousness. Wait on God and wait for Him. Don't do things without Him.

FACING GOLIATH

"Today the Lord will conquer you, and I will kill you and cut off your head. And then I will give the dead bodies of your men to the birds and wild animals, and the whole world will know that there is a God in Israel!"
1 Samuel 17:46 NLT

Let's look at the story of David and Goliath. Goliath had challenged Saul and his soldiers; everyone (on both sides) thought that Goliath was too tall and too big to be defeated. All the training the Israelites had undergone in military school had not prepared them for someone of Goliath's size. They were faced with a situation bigger than their knowledge could handle. But then, there was David. David had no military training, no knowledge of warfare tactics or strategy. He had never been in the army nor commanded men. All he had been in charge of during his life was a few sheep. But he knew God! In these days, what you know may fail you, but who you know will sustain you. It was not what David knew, but who he knew. David had cultivated a relationship with God in the quiet of the wilderness. He had enjoyed close communion and fellowship with the Most High. He had known and experienced the love and faithfulness of God. This is why, even when facing a giant like Goliath, David knew that before the God whom he served, Goliath was no better than an animal, an uncircumcised Philistine (see 1 Samuel 17:36). This was the knowledge that propelled David to act; it caused him to run toward a giant that every trained soldier had been running from. He ran toward Goliath in the Name of the Lord, and the victory was given to him (see 1 Samuel 17:48-49). One man with the knowledge of God was able to defeat what had caused a king and an army of trained soldiers to be terrified, dismayed, and run away in great fear.

SCRIPTURE READING: 1 Samuel 17:1-51
PERSONAL APPLICATION: What are the Goliaths in your own life? Have you been coming against Goliath based on what you know or based on Who you know? God will allow Goliaths to arise. Why? Because He wants the Daniels and Davids to walk in victory. Daniels, Davids and Josephs are those who have cultivated a lifestyle of intimacy, a deep walk with God that has produced knowledge of Him who knows all things. Determine today to cultivate that same level and depth of intimacy with God.

THE POWER OF FORGIVENESS

"If you forgive the sins of any, they are forgiven them; if you retain the sins of any, they are retained."
John 20:23

When we don't forgive, we make it hard (if not impossible) for people to turn around. The unforgiving servant threw his fellow servant into the prison because he was owing him, and he wouldn't forgive the debt. When the master heard about it, he commanded that the unforgiving servant be also imprisoned, because he too was owing his master. And Jesus said, "So My heavenly Father also will do to you if each of you, from his heart, does not forgive his brother his trespasses" (Matthew 18:35). We would notice that the fellow servant wasn't released from the prison, because he was actually owing; so we now have two people legitimately in prison. How much liberty, peace, joy, etc. do you have in prison? How much can you accomplish in prison? The unforgiving servant was handed over to the torturers and tormentors, until he should pay all that was due to the master. Jesus stated very clearly how important forgiving others is, to our prayers. "And whenever you stand praying, if you have anything against anyone, forgive him, that your Father in heaven may also forgive you your trespasses. But if you do not forgive, neither will your Father in heaven forgive your trespasses" (Mark 11:25-26). Jesus taught us to pray, asking our heavenly Father to "forgive us our debts, as we forgive our debtors" (Matthew 6:12). Offences and wrongs done against us are like debts people owe us, and if we don't forgive them, they will be held in prison by us until they can pay us back. We often complain about people, and never stop talking about what they did or do. It actually shows we have not forgiven them. When we forgive, we give people a chance to change; because they are released to change. To forgive means to drop it, and let it go.

SCRIPTURE READING: Matthew 18:21-35, 1 Corinthians 13:1-8 *AMPC*
PERSONAL APPLICATION: Receive the grace and strength you need from God to forgive those who have hurt you in any shape or form. There is no wrong done to you, no matter how great that wrong is, that justifies harbouring unforgiveness.

HEEDING HIS CALL

"But we are not like those who turn away from God to their own destruction. We are the faithful ones, whose souls will be saved."
Hebrews 10:39 NLT

In both the Old and New Testaments, we see how believers handled their challenges and prevailed. The Bible says that the love of many will wax cold because iniquity shall abound (Matthew 24:12). We should not be those whose love will wax cold. We can have the testimony that when sin abounds, grace does much more abound. Defeat is not part of our inheritance, "we are not of them who draw back... but of them that believe to the saving of the soul" (Hebrews 10:39 *KJV*). By His grace and mercy, coupled with our desire to love and obey, we shall be part of the glorious Church, without spot or wrinkle. Our prayer is that you will not just learn but be imparted with grace to win. From the examples we see in the Bible, we know that those who overcome may be few in number. Consider Esther and Mordecai, consider Daniel and his friends, consider Joseph... Even though they had to stand alone at times, their obedience usually brought great benefit and blessings not only for themselves but to others as well. All these people were instruments in the hands of God, who were used to bring about something greater that benefited God's people. Who knows, perhaps you are an Esther or Daniel. I believe God is waiting for each of us to take our place so that His Kingdom can come on the earth. What are you waiting for? Let's hear His call and begin to dance to the music flowing from heavenly realms. God bless you as you heed His call.

SCRIPTURE READING: Hebrews 10:19-39
PERSONAL APPLICATION: Let us pray. *"Father, we thank You for Your plans and purposes for our lives. We ask that we will come into the understanding of Your ways and be strengthened by Your grace to walk in obedience to You in all areas of our lives. May the spirit of truth breathe into us the wisdom and spiritual understanding needed for us to rise up and win over every situation we face in life. Help us to be all You want us to be by Your Word and your Spirit. We pray this in the Name of our Lord Jesus Christ. Amen."*

RUNNING THE RACE

"I have fought the good fight, I have finished the race, I have kept the faith."
2 Timothy 4:7

The Bible says we should run the race that is set before us with perseverance (Hebrews 12:1). We are to emulate those who through faith and patience (endurance) inherited the promise (Hebrews 6:12). Jesus, for the joy that was set before Him, endured the cross, despising its shame (Hebrews 12:2). Don't be tempted to take the easy way out! Jesus could have chosen to get the world back by bowing to Satan, the god of this world, but He chose to go the painful and shameful way of the cross. God might have called you to go on an unpopular, painful and less travelled route. He Himself will encourage you as you stick to it. In spite of the Spirit's warning to Paul about bonds and afflictions in every city, Paul said, "But none of these things move me, neither count I my life dear unto myself, so that I may finish my course with joy and the ministry which I have received of the Lord Jesus..." (Acts 20:24).

To finish our course and our ministry with joy, we must not allow any of these things (fame, popularity, pain, bonds, etc.) to move us! We must persevere and not yield to distractions, which could come in the form of rumours, false accusations, suspicion and so forth. We have a lot to learn from people like Nehemiah who allowed nothing to take him away from the great work he was doing (Nehemiah 6:3).

SCRIPTURE READING: Nehemiah 6:1-4, Hebrews 12:1-2 *AMPC*

PERSONAL APPLICATION: An Olympic athlete will train to run a race at their own individual pace to ensure they hit a personal best and ultimately win. If during the race they judge their own success on where they are compared to others in the field, they run the risk of losing. Let God show you your own race so that you don't judge your progress by others around you, but rather by the tests you are overcoming in your own personal walk.

BECOMING A LOVER OF GOD

"Gather to me this consecrated people,
who made a covenant with me by sacrifice."
Psalm 50:5 NIV

Worship involves more than singing songs. It is our heart expression of how much God is worth to us, manifested in our daily lives through our thoughts, attitudes and actions. It includes a value system that values God above all else. It is also a measure of our response to His goodness and mercy toward us. In John chapter 4, Jesus said the Father seeks worshippers who will worship Him in spirit and truth (see John 4:23-24). The first mention of the word 'worship' in Scripture was when Abraham was going to offer Isaac, his son, in response to God's instruction. In Genesis 22, God instructs and Abraham obeys promptly, trusting in God to raise his son back according to Hebrews 11:17-19. The elements of worship are found in this account. It is initiated by God and involves: a heart of truth (placing more value on God than His gifts), a willingness to obey (whatever the cost), and a willingness to sacrifice what is so dear to us in response to God's demands on us. Even while going through such a test as this, Abraham passed his tests and came into fulfillment of the promises of God. Becoming a worshipper of God is to become a lover of God irrespective of any provision of material comfort. It attracts the presence of God. Worshippers will know God in a way that others may not. They will respond to Him in a different way and get results in a new dimension. When you have a group of worshippers, expect God's grace and power to be in ready manifestation.

SCRIPTURE READING: Psalm 50:1-14, John 4:23-24
PERSONAL APPLICATION: May God help us to become true worshippers, seeking His heart and not just His hand.

TRAINING YOUR CHILDREN

"Train up a child in the way he should go and when he is old, he will not turn from it."
Proverbs 22:6

According to the Oxford English Dictionary, to train is to bring to a desired standard of performance or behaviour by instruction and practice; to teach or accustom a person to do something; and also to cause to grow in the required direction. "Train up a child in the way he should go and when he is old, he will not turn from it" (Proverbs 22:6). Don't train your children in the way you want them to go, but in the way they should go. A lot of parents try to force-fit their kids into their own dreams, instead of helping them discover and develop what is inside them. The Bible says we are God's workmanship created in Christ Jesus for good works, which God prepared beforehand that we should walk in them (Ephesians 2:10). God knows our children more than we do - He created them in the first place. God told Jeremiah, "I knew you before I formed you in your mother's womb. Before you were born I set you apart and appointed you as a prophet to the nations" (Jeremiah 1:5). Find out the way your child should go and train them in that way - it is your responsibility. And remember that your children differ from one another (with different gifts and talents, different purposes, different temperaments and personalities) so deal with them knowledgeably and as individuals. In addition, don't wait for your children to be old before you start to train them in the way they should go. No, you start training and directing them, from when they are young. The 'formative years' of a child is that period of their lives when their character, values, behaviour and so forth are still being formed; so that is the time to start training them.

SCRIPTURE READING: Psalm 127:3-5
PERSONAL APPLICATION: The Bible says that great will be the peace of our children because they will be taught by the Lord - what a promise! Ultimately all training for children should lead to that goal so that they develop their own relationship with God their Father and enjoy a lifetime of learning God's ways.

VALUE AND REWARD

"And He said to them, Be careful what you are hearing. The measure [of thought and study] you give [to the truth you hear] will be the measure [of virtue and knowledge] that comes back to you—and more [besides] will be given to you who hear."
Mark 4:24 AMPC

Read Mark 4:24-25. God showed me a principle from this verse. The principle God showed me here, is that it is the value I place on what God has said that determines what I enjoy in my life. The problem with most Christians is that they do not place a value on anything, let alone the Word of God, and so it does not produce anything for them. It looks to them as if the Word is powerless, whereas it is as powerful as ever because the Word is God Himself, the only problem is the value people measure to it.

The more we value the Word of God, the more we will value His presence. We do not know how to measure value to the presence of God around us, so we miss out on a lot of things we would have experienced in His presence.

The reason why the devil is trying to force the Church into the natural realm is to limit the Church. But you must recognise what the enemy is trying to do and begin to measure value to everything of God that you know. You should measure great value to your God connection. You must learn how to operate in the realm of the supernatural because a time comes in many situations where there will be no answer in the natural realm, and if you have embedded yourself in the supernatural, you will be able to find the answer you need. You must break off the limitations of the enemy from your mind. Deal with them by dealing with the thoughts you allow into your mind.

SCRIPTURE READING: Matthew 25:14-30, Mark 4:24-25

PERSONAL APPLICATION: The principle that what one values will appreciate, is applicable in any area of your life. If you minister value to anything, it will appreciate and likewise, if you do not minister value to something, it will depreciate. Decide today to measure value to the Word and of anything that is of God, and watch it appreciate in your life.

GODLY GOALS FOR GODLY RESULTS

"For she said to herself, 'If only I may touch His garment, I shall be made well.'"
Matthew 9:21

Many of those, who demonstrated their faith in Jesus' ability to heal them, can be seen as setting faith goals. Actually, goals are faith statements and faith needs goals for effectiveness. Their faith needed the goals they had set for God's power to move in on their needs. For example, in Luke 18:41 Jesus asked the blind man, "What would you have me do?" The blind man replied, "That I may receive my sight". He needed to be clear as to what he wanted accomplished and he needed to speak it out in faith. The principles of faith include believing in your heart, speaking with your mouth, as well as acting like the Word is true. Wrong beliefs also affect the operation of faith. Believing in the Word of God is a choice we make.
"We having the same spirit of faith, according as it is written, 'I believed, and therefore have I spoken'; we also believe, and therefore speak" (2 Corinthians 4:13 *KJV*).
So we can see that our choices affect how and what we believe. Our beliefs affect our thoughts, decisions and actions. Our actions eventually affect the outcomes of our lives. See what the Bible says and make a commitment to speak, do and act on the Word. Set goals and commit yourself to do these things; then watch the outcome of your life begin to change.

SCRIPTURE READING: Matthew 9:20-22, Luke 18:35-43
PERSONAL APPLICATION: Godly goals bring about godly results. They stretch your faith and bring glory and honour to God. Godly goals should be birthed in prayer so that God's will is established. It is crucial that we align our lives with God's purposes for our lives. God reveals His purposes through His Word and by His Spirit and also by the godly desires He plants in our hearts.

DO NOT BE ANXIOUS

" Be anxious for nothing, but in everything by prayer and supplication, with thanksgiving, let your requests be made known to God"
Philippians 4:6

When things go wrong or we find ourselves in bad situations, the most natural thing the enemy wants us to do is worry. Well, that lets it out of the bag, doesn't it? The enemy wants you to do the natural thing—don't do it! He bombards your mind with all sorts of negative outcomes that drive you into worry and anxiety, and you begin to meditate on worst possible results that can occur. Don't do it, do the supernatural thing. You always have a choice, either to worry yourself into a state of insanity or to roll over your cares upon the Lord and be in a position of faith to receive the wisdom from God and to know what to do in that situation. And when you think about it, worry has never made a situation better; it has only given the 'worrier' a very bad case of nerves. And what does that solve?

When a bad situation creeps into your life, you must learn to retrain your spiritual reflexes to respond to the Word of God first, rather than react to the situation. But this is possible only if your heart is filled to overflowing with the Word of God. Then you will almost by reflex respond to any bad situation in the 'Word of God' way.

SCRIPTURE READING: Philippians 4:4-9, Matthew 6:25-34

PERSONAL APPLICATION: If you are so busy caring and worrying about things you cannot change, you will not be able to think straight. The wisdom to do what is right is possible only when you have completely rolled your cares upon God.

OUR FELLOWSHIP WITH THE FATHER

"Now may the God of patience and comfort grant you to be like-minded toward one another, according to Christ Jesus, that you may with one mind and one mouth glorify the God and Father of our Lord Jesus Christ."
Romans 15:5-6

Jesus, throughout His earthly Ministry was in perfect fellowship with the Father. He Himself often withdrew into the wilderness (or lonely places) to pray (Luke 5:16). It was after one of such times in prayer, that His disciples asked Him to teach them to pray (Luke 11:1-5). In another instance, the Bible says, "Very early in the morning, while it was still dark, Jesus got up, left the house and went off to a solitary place, where He prayed" (Mark 1:35 *NIV*). Jesus spent the night praying to God, and in the morning He chose His twelve apostles from His many disciples (Luke 6:12-13). Truly, Jesus did nothing of Himself; His works and words flowed from His fellowship with the Father!

In addition to knowing that our fellowship is with the Father, we also need to note that the word 'our' is not singular, it is plural. God is the Father of a family; it isn't therefore just about an individual's fellowship with Him, but our fellowship with one another also. For instance, the Bible doesn't just talk about us confessing our sins to God, but to one another also - "Confess your trespasses to one another, and pray for one another, that you may be healed. The effective, fervent prayer of a righteous man avails much" (James 5:16). God's blessing is commanded where His people live in harmony or unity (Psalm 133). When they were all with one accord in the upper room, the promise of the Father - the Holy Spirit - came in like a mighty rushing wind (Acts 2:14). As the people lifted up their voice (not 'voices') in unity, the prayer room was shaken, and they were all filled with the Holy Spirit (Acts 4:24-31).

SCRIPTURE READING: Romans 12:9-21, 2 Chronicles 5:2-14

PERSONAL APPLICATION: We need to make sure that we are people of prayer. But as we have learned today, our fellowship with the Father is not just singular but plural. When we as believers stand united, so much more can be done and accomplished. Put away envying and strife. The Bible says faith works (i.e. is activated, energized and expressed) through love (Galatians 5:6).

HAVE FAITH IN GOD

"So Jesus answered and said to them, "Have faith in God."
Mark 11:22

There is a place in prayer when you go to God based on the provision He has made available in His Word. The Bible says, "whatsoever things ye desire, when ye pray, believe that ye receive them" (Mark 11:24 *KJV*). The place of prayer is the place of power and faith, when you receive answers to your prayers without having seen them. I have a prayer principle that says, 'don't go to the place of prayer filled with worry'. Roll your cares, then you can be clear minded to pray. If you do go into the place of prayer with worry on your mind, do so only to repent of worrying then drop it at Jesus' feet. The enemy knows that if you do not cast your cares on the Lord, your prayers will be hindered, because you cannot have faith and worry in your mind at the same time. In other words, if God cannot do it, then why are you praying that He should? The devil will make it look like you are unreasonable and irresponsible not to worry.

You must know how to put the Word in your heart and refuse to be burdened with the cares of this world. What we need to solve our problems is wisdom; so ask for wisdom in the place of prayer. Divine wisdom is stress free while worry is stressful. Think about it. I know which I'd choose.

SCRIPTURE READING: Matthew 6:25-34

PERSONAL APPLICATION: Your faith works best when your head is at rest. Peace in your heart will guarantee rest in your mind. Be aware that the devil will make sure you stay away from your Bible, he will make sure you worry instead of praying. You must be alert spiritually and do exactly opposite of what the devil wants you to do. "Be anxious for nothing, but in everything by prayer and supplication, with thanksgiving, make your requests known unto God..." (Philippians 4:6-7).

STAYING FAITHFUL

"Whatever you do, work heartily, as for the Lord and not for men, knowing that from the Lord you will receive the inheritance as your reward. You are serving the Lord Christ."
Colossians 3:23-24 ESV

Many people don't give their all and their best except when they are serving themselves. Some people "reserve" their energy and skill to the time they have their own company or their own ministry. That is gross deception. In the first place, your own cannot be given to you by God (of course you may get it by yourself) if you are not faithful in another man's, and secondly, by the time you now have yours, you won't be able to do better than what you did to others, because your spiritual muscles would have become atrophied.

Some people also believe that they cannot serve God if they are in another man's company or employment. That is error. The Bible is full of people who had the mentality of serving God though they had human masters. Are we not told to do heartily as unto the Lord whatever we do, and that it is from the Lord that we shall receive our reward? Women are told to submit themselves to their own husbands as unto the Lord, or as a service to the Lord (Ephesians 5:22). The Bible says, "The boy Samuel ministered before the Lord under Eli" (1 Samuel 3:1 *NIV*).

David was in the service of Saul as his armour bearer and he behaved himself wisely, the Bible says. Joseph faithfully served a heathen King, Pharaoh. All the land he got from the Egyptians in exchange for grain were gotten in Pharaoh's name. Joseph didn't do anything in his own name when he was serving Pharaoh. That was faithfulness.

SCRIPTURE READING: Colossians 3:17-25

PERSONAL APPLICATION: Don't allow any man to be your focus when you are serving or else you will not be faithful. Anything you do for God, will be deposited in your own account with God, so stay faithful.

GOD IS STILL THE SAME

"For I am the Lord, I do not change;
Therefore you are not consumed, O sons of Jacob."
Malachi 3:6

In this time and age the forces of hell are more aggressive in their operations of lies and deception. We, as believers must be on our 'tippy toes', making sure we don't fall for any of their lies and deception. They bombard our minds with all sorts of negative thoughts, their intention is to tempt us to treat the Word of God with disrespect and disregard and lose out on the promises God has given to us.

The Bible says in Hebrews 13:8, "Jesus Christ the same yesterday, and today and forever." God has not changed and He is not about to change either; we are the ones always changing. His Word is 'Yes and Amen'. What He has promised in His Word, He is able to do. We need to break off every limitation in our minds because only then can we experience Him in His fullness. We must live a life of faith and this can only be possible when we fellowship with God and His Word. We must believe that every Word of God is God-breathed; God is powerful so we should measure value to His Word.

SCRIPTURE READING: Isaiah 55:8-11

PERSONAL APPLICATION: It is only when we measure value to the Word of God that it can produce for us. When His Word is hidden in our hearts, we will respond to His Word rather than responding to the fearful thoughts the enemy flings at us.

VALUE WHAT YOU HAVE

"As surely as the Lord your God lives," she replied, "I don't have any bread—only a handful of flour in a jar and a little olive oil in a jug..."
1 Kings 17:12 NIV

The value of a thing is its desirability, usefulness and importance. To value what you have is therefore, to put a price on it, to have a high opinion of it, and to attach importance to it. You must value what you have. The Apostle Paul said, "inasmuch as I am an apostle to the Gentiles, I magnify my ministry" (Romans 11:13); that is, "I make as much of this as I can." People won't value what you have, if you don't value it yourself. You must consider what you have and what you are doing important enough to make people value it. Tobiah and Sanballat didn't think much about the wall Nehemiah and the Jews were building; they ridiculed them. They invited Nehemiah to a meeting with them, but he sent messengers back to them, saying, "I am doing a great work, so that I cannot come down. Why should the work cease while I leave it and go down to you?" Nehemiah valued what he was doing. Paul told Timothy, "Let no one despise you because you are young..." (1 Timothy 4:12). 'Let' means, allow; so it was up to Timothy, at the end of the day, to determine what he would allow or disallow. Nehemiah surely didn't allow anyone to despise the great work he was doing. Be careful not to cast your pearls before swine, or else, they will rubbish them and then turn on you. Don't be too excited to throw out what you've got; let people show they value it enough to want it. Why would Jesus ask people before performing a miracle, "Do you believe I am able to do this?" (Matthew 9:28).

SCRIPTURE READING: 2 Kings 4:1-7
PERSONAL APPLICATION: The way people treat you or something of yours is a reflection of the value you place on yourself and the things you have. Determine today to start to place a higher value on yourself, your ministry, your work, your family, your skills, your gifts and so forth. Don't despise them and don't let anyone else despise them either.

FOLLOWING JESUS' EXAMPLE

"Very early in the morning, while it was still dark, Jesus got up, left the house and went off to a solitary place, where He prayed."
Mark 1:35 NIV

Defilement can give the enemy a place in us, but we must follow Jesus' example. Jesus said in John chapter 14, "Hereafter I will not talk much with you: for the prince of this world cometh, and hath nothing in Me" (John 14:30 *KJV*). This verse says that the prince of this world had nothing in Jesus. Jesus was not defiled or soiled in any way at all. This is one of the reasons He was totally effective in everything he did. Jesus invaded an atmosphere laden with sin, a place under the influence of Satan, yet He was victorious in all He did. Not for a moment do we see Jesus defeated. Jesus knew His Father's will! He spent much time in prayer. I also believe that by staying in the Father's presence, Jesus was able to stay free from the things that could have been a drag on His soul and a limitation to the call of God on His life. We must learn from the Master. A life of prayer is not an option!

SCRIPTURE READING: John 13:1-17

PERSONAL APPLICATION: Our daily exposure to the world allows deposits to be made on our souls which need to be cleaned and washed away regularly through prayer. What Jesus did for His disciples in John 13:1-17 is symbolic. Jesus, the Living Word, washed the feet of His disciples. Likewise, we are cleansed with the washing of the water by the Word (see Ephesians 5:26).

TIME TO SEEK THE LORD

"Sow for yourselves righteousness;
Reap in mercy;
Break up your fallow ground,
For it is time to seek the Lord,
Till He comes and rains righteousness on you."
Hosea 10:12

Most people can relate to the fact that there are things they have asked God for, that they have not yet received - though they have done all they know to do! Could it be that it's time to seek the Lord concerning those things? God wants us to seek Him, "When You said, 'Seek My face,' My heart said to You, 'Your face, Lord, I will seek'" (Psalm 27:8). To seek the Lord also means to inquire of, the Lord. After David became king over Israel, the Philistines came against him, so David inquired from God if he should go up against them, and if the Lord would give him the victory over them. God gave him a go-ahead, and the victory. When they came against him once again, David inquired from God again and God gave him the strategy for the war and he got the victory again (2 Samuel 5:17-25)! When Jehoshaphat was told that a great multitude was coming against him, he set himself to seek the Lord - he proclaimed a fast throughout all Judah (2 Chronicles 20:4). And as they prayed, they heard from God, and they got the victory; they spent 3 days gathering the spoil of war, and God also gave them rest all around from their enemies. After the Amalekites had raided David and his men, David inquired of the Lord, saying, "Shall I pursue this troop? Shall I overtake them?" And the Lord gave him a go- ahead; so David pursued and overtook the Amalekites, and he recovered all they had carried away (1 Samuel 30: 18-19). Notice that every time they sought God, He spoke to them; and whatever He said to them always brought about victory in their situations!

SCRIPTURE READING: Jeremiah 33:2-3, Lamentations 3:24-26
PERSONAL APPLICATION: One of the secrets to living a life of victory is to stay connected to God in prayer and hear what He has to say. He has given many examples of His responses when we seek Him. Today, make a fresh dedication to seek the Lord in all you do.

AMBASSADORS FOR GOD

"Now then, we are ambassadors for Christ, as though God were pleading through us: we implore you on Christ's behalf, be reconciled to God."
2 Corinthians 5:20

We always need to remember that though we live in the world, we are not of the world. We are citizens of the Kingdom of God, released into the world to overcome and to bring the kingdoms of the world under the Lordship of Jesus Christ. Just like Daniel, we are citizens of another land, operating as it were, in our own Babylon. We have been placed in enemy territory to take over. God's plan is not for us to merely survive. God does not want His people hiding in caves! From the beginning, God's plan has been world dominion (see Genesis 1:26-28). Man is the agent God intends to use to bring His dominion on earth. For this to happen, our purpose and identity must be very clear to us. God created us in His image and likeness and released us on earth to express His will, person, and power as His representatives here on earth. It is only when we have a clear understanding that we are representing the Kingdom of God on earth that the absolute importance of prayer becomes evident. Prayer is the means by which we stay in touch with our home base, understand the mind and will of the government we represent and receive the grace and wisdom to execute the will of our government on earth. We are life ambassadors representing the Kingdom of God on the earth. Just like any ambassador who knows what he or she is doing, we must maintain contact with our home government to know and understand the will and the policies of the government we represent. In addition, we must maintain open channels of communication so that resources can be sent to us when needed. This, among other things, is the role prayer plays in the life of a Christian.

SCRIPTURE READING: Genesis 1:26-31, Hebrews 11:13-16
PERSONAL APPLICATION: Our ability to overcome the challenges of the day and beat the systems of the world, is dependent on a strong prayer life.

BUILDING AN ARK FOR YOUR FAMILY

"So make yourself an ark of cypress wood; make rooms in it and coat it with pitch inside and out."
Genesis 6:14 NIV

Somebody said, "delegation without supervision is abandonment"! Don't abandon your children - don't leave them to themselves, don't leave them to the government or the schools or the Society or even the Church to raise them. You raise kids yourself; of course with help and input from others! Commitment breeds commitment. Whatever you would require of them, make sure you first invest it into them; 'No deposit, no withdrawal'. Jesus first loved us, before we could love Him. Sometimes parents want to reap from their children what they haven't sown into them. We expect from them what we never gave them in the first place! Invest time, love, understanding, finances, and yourself into your children. Bond with them when they are little and as they grow up. Give them good memories - someone said that a happy childhood is one of the best gifts that parents have in their power to bestow. Someone else said that the best thing you can give children, next to good habits, are good memories. Eat out with them, shop with them, have family fun times together, remember their birthdays, pray with them; do things, not only for them but also with them. God ordained the family to provide a safety net for children. A lot of children involved in crimes, prostitution, drugs, gangs, suicide, and so forth are from troubled homes. Such kids are usually very vulnerable, and they fall into the wrong hands most of the time in a bid to get from outsiders what they did not get from their family. A healthy, strong and loving family is God's answer to the decadence in the world today. "Didn't the LORD make you one with your wife? In body and spirit you are His. And what does He want? Godly children from your union. So guard your heart; remain loyal to the wife of your youth" (Malachi 2:15 *NLT*).

SCRIPTURE READING: Colossians 3:18-25, Isaiah 8:18, 1 Thessalonians 2:5-13, Psalm 127:1-5

PERSONAL APPLICATION: Children are our heritage from the Lord (Psalm 127:3). They must be treated with love. Honesty and wisdom are the greatest principles in raising children. Therefore ask the Father, who withholds no good thing, to help you in raising your kids.

WAIT, WATCH AND LISTEN

"Be still, and know that I am God;
I will be exalted among the nations,
I will be exalted in the earth!"
Psalm 46:10

Waiting is one of the things the flesh finds most difficult to do. God has a lot to say to us, but we must learn to wait, watch and listen. After Jehoshaphat and all of Judah fasted and prayed, they waited to hear what God would say to them. Moses said to the children of Israel, with the Red Sea in front of them and the host of Pharaoh behind them, "Do not be afraid. Stand still and see the salvation of the Lord, which He will accomplish for you today. For the Egyptians whom you see today, you shall see them no more forever. The Lord will fight for you and you shall hold your peace" (Exodus 14:13-14).

In seeking the face of God, don't jump ahead of God; wait on Him and wait for Him. Have you noticed that because we are under so much pressure, taking out a day or two to seek God's face and hear His counsel, before making a decision, seems unaffordable; we fear all hell may break loose on us if we did. The swifter and faster we run, the swifter and faster our problems are catching up with us. One day spent with God can save us a lot of chaos and crises. Jesus said the cares of this age, the deceitfulness of riches and desires for other things come in and choke the Word and we (not the Word!) become unfruitful (Matthew 13:22). Someone actually said, you are too busy not to pray! Life is fragile, handle with prayer. God wants to be God in our lives and in our situations; but we must let Him.

SCRIPTURE READING: 2 Chronicles 20:1-15

PERSONAL APPLICATION: What are the main challenges or battles facing you right now? Are you trying to solve them yourself or are you running to God? It is time to turn around and look up! Nothing you are facing today is too big for God. Let Him in and let Him fight for you.

THE ROLE OF FAITH

"By faith Abraham obeyed when he was called to go out to the place which he would receive as an inheritance. And he went out, not knowing where he was going."
Hebrews 11:8

Faith is an inward conviction about God and His Word, and His willingness to demonstrate His power on our behalf. Faith is the spiritual substance poured into our hearts when we believe God's Word. It comes by hearing, affects our convictions and fills us with assurance. Faith in our hearts is what influences our words, actions and expectations. When faith is present, the power flows. When faith is reduced, the power is reduced. Let us rise up today to live a life of faith and to trust Him to perform His Word in our lives.

SCRIPTURE READING: Mark 11:23-26 *AMPC,* Romans 4:18-22, Hebrews 11
PERSONAL APPLICATION: Set aside some time on a regular basis to feed on scriptures that build up your faith. Substitute time spent on other things. Engage with God's Word—speak it out, meditate on it, let it consume you more than anything else. Whatever you are trusting God for, spend time building up your faith until you know beyond any shadow of doubt that, "He who promised is faithful" (Hebrews 10:23).

MAINTAINING A PURE HEART

"Above all else, guard your heart,
for everything you do flows from it."
Proverbs 4:23 NIV

Too many hearts have become calloused because they have been exposed to so many things for too long. We can expose our hearts to something for so long that after a while that thing no longer moves us. For example, if we expose our hearts to violence in movies, after a while our hearts will get hardened so that when we see violence it no longer moves us. Maintaining a pure heart takes a lot of effort. We must not allow anything to bring impurities into our hearts. What we watch will sow seeds into our hearts. What we listen to will sow seeds into our hearts. Every experience we go through in life will make a deposit in our hearts. Our heart is something we need to be aware of and maintain as a matter of practice, because the things we hear and keep hearing will make deposits in our hearts. The things we encounter and the experiences we go through will make deposits in our hearts. It may look subtle, it make look ordinary but whatever entertains us, enters us; for example, the Jezebel spirit on earth today is entering people through entertainment. So, maintaining a pure heart is something we need to keep on the front burner of our thought life. We need to ask ourselves, 'what deposits will certain things make in my heart'? Can we keep a tender heart? Sometimes the goal of a fast is just to make our heart tender before God so that God can keep it sensitive. We need to work at keeping our hearts tender.

SCRIPTURE READING: Proverbs 4:20-27, Jeremiah 17:7-10, Psalm 139:23-24
PERSONAL APPLICATION: How can you live in the world and guard your heart at the same time? What things in your life can you decide to do without for the health of your heart? Spend some time examining the things that grab your attention, or that you do for fun and relaxation. How do these things affect how you respond to the things of God?

VALUING YOURSELF

"For You formed my inward parts;
You covered me in my mother's womb.
I will praise You, for I am fearfully and wonderfully made;
Marvellous are Your works,
And that my soul knows very well."
Psalm 139:13-14

Don't be intimidated by what others have, but value what you have. There is something in you, that is waiting to be stirred up; and the challenges you face might just be what is needed to stir it up. Goliath's challenge to the army of Israel was all that David needed to stir up his potential; he just got 'mad' when he heard Goliath. David wasn't intimidated by the stature of Goliath, or the fact that he was a champion or even the sophistication of his weapons; he told Goliath, "You come to me with a sword, with a spear, and with a javelin. But I come to you in the name of the Lord of hosts, the God of the armies of Israel, whom you have defied. This day the Lord will deliver you into my hand, and I will strike you and take your head from you" (1 Samuel 17:45-46). David brought down Goliath with his sling and five smooth stones! Stop comparing yourself with others. You may not have what they have, but you have something; and if you would value what you have enough to develop it, others will come to see the importance of it too. The grass isn't greener on the other side; and if it is, it's because they mowed their lawn - so you get busy with yours too.

SCRIPTURE READING: 1 Samuel 17:1-51, Mark 6:30-44
PERSONAL APPLICATION: What has God put in your hand? Perhaps you have the gift of encouragement, or extra time to be of service to others in your church? Take out some time to acknowledge and thank God for every good thing you have, and then ask Him to multiply it for the furtherance of His Kingdom.

RELATIONSHIPS WITH THOSE IN AUTHORITY

"And he said to his men, "The Lord forbid that I should do this thing to my master, the Lord's anointed, to stretch out my hand against him, seeing he is the anointed of the Lord."
1 Samuel 24:6

From the story of David in 1 Samuel, we learn that there is a way we ought to conduct ourselves in submission and in humility to authority. We clearly see that to submit to and respect those in authority over us, is honouring to God. We accord heart respect to them because of their God-given authority.

We need to maintain a heart of honour and respect for those in authority over us, even when they have missed God. There are the stories of Samuel and Eli in 1 Samuel 3; of Daniel in Daniel 6, when the king ordered the people to pray to no other god; and of the three young Hebrew men who were commanded to bow to the golden image in Daniel 3. Our hearts should first be in submission to God. He is the ultimate authority, and all authority flows from Him; we then should also submit to His authority-delegate in our lives. Whether it be parents, church leaders or civil leaders, they all deserve our heart submission, where seeds of pride can never be allowed to take root. Our attitude of submission then determines the response of God to our situations.

SCRIPTURE READING: Romans 13:1-5, Daniel 3:16-18, 1 Samuel 24:1-13, 1 Samuel 26:1-11

PERSONAL APPLICATION: To submit to those in authority over us is to honour God by respecting the authority He has given over us. Set time aside to pray for those put in authority over you, that God will fill them with all wisdom and understanding. Receive His grace to walk in true submission.

BELIEVING WHAT GOD SAYS TO YOU

"As soon as Jesus heard the word that was spoken, He said to the ruler of the synagogue, "Do not be afraid; only believe."
Mark 5:36

Ordinarily, to believe simply means to accept as true or conveying truth. God said to Abraham that his descendants would be too many to count, when as yet he had no child. The Bible says he believed God and God counted it to him for righteousness (Genesis 15:6). To believe God means to accept His Word as true – whatever He says to you or about you – and to be persuaded that God's Word is true. It also means to agree with God and His Word. When Mary was told by angel Gabriel that she was going to be the mother of the Lord, she answered the angel, "Behold the maidservant of the Lord! Let it be to me according to your word" (Luke 1:38). "Stop quarrelling with God! If you agree with Him, you will have peace at last and all will go well for you" (Job. 22:21 *NLT*). Jesus would ask someone in need of a miracle, "Do you believe I am able to do this?" (Matthew 9:28). He said to Jairus, "Don't be afraid, only believe" when they told Jairus that his daughter was already dead (Mark 5:36). Elizabeth, filled with the Holy Spirit said, "Blessed is she who believed, for there will be a fulfilment of those things which were told her" (Luke 1:45). Jesus said, "If you can believe, all things are possible to him who believes" (Mark 9:23). He also said certain signs would follow those who believe the Word of the Gospel (Mark 16:17-18).

SCRIPTURE READING: Romans 4:18-25
PERSONAL APPLICATION: What are you believing God for today? Take one or two promises concerning your situation and allow the Word of God to change the way you see and talk about your situation. Go to God in prayer and be sincere with Him about any areas of fear and unbelief, and declare that you believe all He has spoken.

THE POWER TO FINISH

"I have fought a good fight, I have finished my course, I have kept the faith."
2 Timothy 4:7 KJV

The ability to bring things to conclusion needs the power to finish. Bringing the sin age to a conclusion, or as it is called coming into perfection, must be seen as a correct conclusion for the sacrifice of Christ. The fullness of Christ and the ultimate purpose of God demand that we have a mind not only to work, but to finish the work of Him who sent us. Finishing strong is a 'must' for those who will win in these end times. Many times, short range effect and efforts affect how strong we finish what we are about. God is willing to give us the power to finish strong. Let us go for it. When the foundations of our lives are set on the solid rock - the Word of God - and we cultivate intimacy with our Father God, we can expect Him to supply all that we need to run the race set before us as we keep our eyes on the Lord Jesus Christ. He finished strong, and by His grace we will as well. Amen!

SCRIPTURE READING: Hebrews 12:1-4, 2 Corinthians 12:9

PERSONAL APPLICATION: Everyday is an opportunity to receive strength from God to keep going. We must constantly keep our eyes on Jesus—through regularly spending time with Him and His Word. Spend time considering resolutions you have made. How many of these have you followed to their conclusion? What do you need to adjust in order to stick with and complete the course Christ has set before you? God is ready to provide the help that you need.

DARE TO BE DIFFERENT

"Let your speech always be with grace, seasoned with salt, that you may know how you ought to answer each one."
Colossians 4:6

People actually don't care about what you know until they know you care. The Bible says knowledge puffs up (our heads) but love builds up! "Let all things be done for edification" (1 Corinthians 14:26). Our goal must not be to display ourselves or what we know, but to build up others. I believe one reason why Jesus was and is still such a great influence was because He gave His life for all. He said, "Greater love has no man than this, than to lay down one's life for his friends" (John 15:13). Have you noticed that people don't change in an atmosphere of criticism and hatred? Rather they change when they know they are loved and accepted. I believe God is calling all believers to become people of positive influence. People who will dare to be different in these times so as to make the difference not only in their generation but in the next.

SCRIPTURE READING: 1 Corinthians 13, James 3:3-12

PERSONAL APPLICATION: It's time to drastically change what you say and do! Your words carry life or death. You can decide to spread life and encouragement wherever you go. Take on the challenge to respond in love, care and understanding whenever the opportunity presents itself.

WALKING IN SUSTAINABLE VICTORY

"Trust in the Lord with all your heart, And lean not on your own understanding; In all your ways acknowledge Him, And He shall direct your paths."
Proverbs 3:5-6

Many factors contribute to our walking in sustainable victory in our lives in Christ Jesus. Whether we stand the test of time, fulfil God's purposes and experience victory in our lives, all depends on how much of God's grace we allow ourselves to walk in. Our faith in His Word, a life of obedience, as well as our motives and focus, all have something to do with whether we walk in His grace or not. We know He gives grace to the humble, so if we humble ourselves under His mighty hand, He will exalt us in due time (1 Peter 5:6). There are many things that we tend to fix our attention on in our Christian life, for example, our efforts, our failures or our own holiness. The scriptures encourage us to look away from many things and to fix our eyes on our Lord Jesus Christ. As we mature in the Lord we need to learn to look away from many of these things and look unto Him, who is our example of obedience, our inspiration for being focused and our model for right motives. What we look upon will determine how we respond to our challenges. If we look to our own efforts, we will feel the weight of failure, when we don't see the results we expect. Every other thing we look upon, apart from Jesus, will definitely affect how far we can go in the things of God.

SCRIPTURE READING: Hebrews 12:1-4, Matthew 14:25-31, Mark 4:18-20, 1 Peter 5:8-9

PERSONAL APPLICATION: Make a conscious effort to focus less on your own ability, your past and your weaknesses. Take on a new perspective where Jesus is your focus. Exchange your weakness for His strength, your past for His future. In Jesus, your victory is guaranteed. Set time apart today to seek God's face and His guidance for your undertakings regardless of whether in your eyes they are trivial or great.

LEARNING TO SAY 'NO'!

"Women received back their dead, raised to life again. There were others who were tortured, refusing to be released so that they might gain an even better resurrection."
Hebrews 11:35 NIV

Sometimes to get the best, you must be willing to deny yourself certain things that you might even consider to be good. Good is often the enemy of best! Jesus said that anyone who wants to be His disciple must first deny himself; because whoever desires to save his life will lose it, but whoever loses his life for his sake will find it (Matthew 16:24-25). To gain certain things, you must be ready to lose some. Apostle Paul said he counted as loss those things that were gain to him that he might gain Christ (Philippians 3:7-9). He said, "All things are lawful for me, but all things are not helpful. All things are lawful for me, but I will not be brought under the power of any" (1 Corinthians 6:12). Daniel lived a life of self denial; he purposed in his heart that he would not defile himself with the king's delicacies and wine; he therefore ate vegetables and drank water instead (Daniel 1:8). At the end of the period, when they were tested by the king, Daniel and his friends were ten times better than their peers! Maturity is the ability to delay gratification; you must exercise control over your desires and appetites. What you can't say 'No' to has power over you.

SCRIPTURE READING: Matthew 16:24-26
PERSONAL APPLICATION: If self denial is an area you struggle with, ask yourself this simple question: "Why do I find it hard to say no?". Finding the answer to that question may require you to dig deep. Be sincere with yourself, look into God's Word, pray and receive the grace and strength you need. Rev. Kola often says that there is a price to pay and a position to take for the privileges of God to be enjoyed. Sometimes the price one pays is to simply say 'No!' to the flesh.

GIVE MORE OF YOURSELF

"Give, and it will be given to you: good measure, pressed down, shaken together, and running over will be put into your bosom. For with the same measure that you use, it will be measured back to you."
Luke 6:38

Giving is a major key to the operation of grace in our lives. The attitude and stance of being a giver activates grace in the life of a believer. I am talking about the giving that is motivated by the love of God—AGAPE. It is our privilege to give; it delivers us from selfishness. It increases our capacity to receive and develops our confidence in God's ability to sustain us. The condition for this is if we give as unto the Lord. To glorify God in our giving, he must be our focus. The role God plays in our lives should be central in all we do. We are instructed in the Word to do all things as unto the Lord. Whatever good anyone does, he will receive the same from the Lord. Our reward is from the Lord not from the ones who we give to. Giving is a manifestation of grace and it leads to more grace. If you want more of God in your life, give more of yourself to Him.

SCRIPTURE READING: John 3:16, Luke 6:38 *AMP*
PERSONAL APPLICATION: God gave His best for us! Can you recognise areas in your life where you need to be more generous towards God and others? Remember, if you want more of God in your life, give more of yourself to Him.

IMPROVE YOUR SELF TALK

"I have strength for all things in Christ Who empowers me [I am ready for anything and equal to anything through Him Who infuses inner strength into me; I am sufficient in Christ's sufficiency]."
Philippians 4:13 AMPC

What do you believe about yourself? How do you see yourself? Do you see yourself as a highflier or as a 'low-flier' supported by occasional gusts of wind? Do you have enough 'yeast' in you to rise above the hostilities and challenges in your life? How you see yourself really matters; so also is what you believe about yourself. When Gideon was told he was the one to save Israel from the oppression of the Midianites, his response was, "how can I rescue Israel? My clan is the weakest in the whole tribe of Manasseh, and I am the least in my entire family!" (Judges 6:15 *NLT*). What is your self-talk like? Whenever you say you can't, doubt and fear will rise up in you like a giant! When the spies were sent out to spy on the land God said He was giving the Israelites, ten of the twelve came back with an 'evil report'. They said, "We can't go up against them! They are stronger than we are!" (Numbers 13:31 *NLT*). They said, compared to the giants in the land, they were like grasshoppers! The way you see yourself will determine how you see your challenges. You can begin to see yourself the way God sees you; based on the potential He's put within you. The angel called Gideon a mighty man of valour! He called him a 'mighty hero'. Instead of you saying you are not able, say, 'I am well able!'. Caleb said to the people, "Let us go up at once and take possession, for we are well able to overcome it" (Numbers 13:30). Instead of saying you can't, say 'I can!'. We are in Christ and Christ is in us; and that is what matters.

SCRIPTURE READING: Judges 6:11-16
PERSONAL APPLICATION: Rise up today and begin to make this confession: "I can do all things [which He has called me to do] through Him who strengthens and empowers me [to fulfil His purpose—I am self-sufficient in Christ's sufficiency; I am ready for anything and equal to anything through Him who infuses me with inner strength and confident peace]" (Philippians 4:13 *AMP*).

DON'T UNDERESTIMATE YOUR MIND

"Don't copy the behaviour and customs of this world, but let God transform you into a new person by changing the way you think. Then you will learn to know God's will for you, which is good and pleasing and perfect."
Romans 12:2 NLT

When God told the children of Israel to take the land, their response was that they were like grasshoppers. It is possible for God to say something, mean something, and plan something; it is also very possible for us because of the state of our mind to stop that thing from coming to pass in our lives.

By the time we turn twelve, most of our minds have already been formed. For example, when we pour a glass of water, the water takes the shape of the glass. Why? Because the glass already has a form, so anything we pour into it will be defined by its form. The same is true of our minds. The children of Israel had the Hittites and the Jebusites to overcome in the promised land. The Hittites and the Jebusties represent the things in our minds that we have to overcome. The promised land is not a type of heaven because there are no Hittites we need to overcome in heaven. The promised land is the will of God being done in our lives, and there are obstacles, oppositions and resistances to the will of God being done in our lives. These obstacles are not necessarily physical obstacles or circumstances, they are things that have been formed in our minds that we need to overcome.

SCRIPTURE READING: Romans 11:33-12:2

PERSONAL APPLICATION: Changing your way of thinking is not automatic. You have to refuse and recognise what your obstacles, experiences and cultural expectations are (i.e. your individual strongholds); then be open to receive God's Word in order to change your perspective and thoughts.

DON'T SETTLE FOR LESS

"Giving thanks to the Father who has qualified us to be partakers of the inheritance of the saints in the light."
Colossians 1:12

Good is the enemy of best! Don't aim for average in life; aim for the highest, the exceptional, the extraordinary and the best! You deserve the best because of the value God has placed on you. God has placed so much value on humanity by creating us in His own image and after His likeness, and by giving us dominion over all His other creation. Even when man fell into sin and came short of God's glory, God sent Jesus, who took our sin upon Himself to redeem and restore mankind. God bought us back with the precious blood of His only begotten Son. The price you are willing to pay for something shows the value you placed on it. God could have left humanity to rot in their own sin, but He cared too much to do that. Jesus said that you are of more value than the birds of the air and the grass of the field. And if God feeds the birds, who neither sow nor reap; and clothes the grass, which does not toil or spin; then he will do much more for us, because we are of more value than them. God does things for us that are much more and not much less!

SCRIPTURE READING: Psalm 139:13-18, Matthew 6:25-34,
PERSONAL APPLICATION: God demonstrated how much He values us by sending Jesus to die on the cross for us. The problem is that we do not place as high a value on ourselves, and therefore shortchange ourselves out of a lot of things. Search out scriptures that talk about how much God loves you, how much He thinks about you and what His thoughts are about you. Allow that reality to soak in on you and begin to change the way you see and value yourself.

THE THINGS THAT MOULD US

"For as he thinketh in his heart, so is he: Eat and drink, saith he to thee; but his heart is not with thee."
Proverbs 23:7 KJV

Every depression and every mental situation that people face today is an abuse of the laws of the mind. As we were growing up, the enemy built blocks of rejection, hatred, jealousy, envy and selfishness into our minds. Whatever we expose our minds to determines what we expose our lives to, which in turn determines what we experience. The world has squeezed us into its mould. We are already squeezed and formed, even as we read this.

In an environment where God is believed in and He is real, people do not have a problem believing God for things because they know that God is as tangible as anything else they can imagine. In other environments, the mould is so set in its ways that God is out of the equation, because He is a foreigner and a stranger. The mould says, 'I can do what I want to do', 'I serve God when I want!'. These attitudes are a function of a mould that has been programmed by the world. If we are going to be serious believers in an environment like this, we cannot afford to live like everybody else. We cannot afford to live by the way we feel about certain things, because our feelings have been informed by the world which has moulded us.

SCRIPTURE READING: 2 Corinthians 3:7-18

PERSONAL APPLICATION: What are the things you have exposed your mind to that have informed your belief systems and reality? It is not too late to change the way you think. 1 Corinthians 2:16 tells us that we have the mind of Christ. Let us embrace the reality of the mind of Christ, and allow His Word rather than the world to affect what we think and the way we think.

DON'T BE INTIMIDATED

"For God has not given us a spirit of fear,
but of power and of love and of a sound mind."
2 Timothy 1:7

"This is why I remind you to fan into flames the spiritual gift God gave you when I laid my hands on you. For God has not given us a spirit of fear and timidity" (2 Timothy 1:6-7 *NLT*). Don't be intimidated by what you see outside you, remember that the One who is in you is greater than he who is in the world. The ten spies were intimidated by the giants they saw in the land; and so they said they couldn't take the land, which God had already given them. They said they were like grasshoppers in their own eyes, and in the eyes of the people too. But Joshua and Caleb said, "Let us go up at once and take possession, for we are well able to overcome it" (Numbers 13:30). They saw the people as bread for them. David ran towards Goliath; he wasn't intimidated by him at all. "For God has said, 'I will never fail you. I will never abandon you.' So we can say with confidence, 'The Lord is my helper, so I will have no fear. What can mere people do to me?'" (Hebrews 13:5-6 *NLT*). Don't let past failures discourage you from aiming higher. You might need to do some analysis and evaluation of your past attempts. Perhaps your goals were not realistic in the first place, maybe your methods were wrong. You might need to find your own niche and set the right goals for you! For instance, David refused to fight Goliath in Saul's armour; he told Saul, "'I cannot walk with these, for I have not tested them.' So David took them off" (1 Samuel 17:39). He got himself five smooth stones from the brook and his sling; and he went after Goliath.

SCRIPTURE READING: Jeremiah 1:1-19
PERSONAL APPLICATION: Don't pray for your challenges to get smaller, rather pray that you grow bigger so that you can face and rise up to them. Ask God for wisdom to handle your challenges. Turn the stumbling blocks into stepping stones and the opposition to opportunities for promotion.

PASSING THE OBEDIENCE TEST

"And there we saw the giants, the sons of Anak, which come of the giants: and we were in our own sight as grasshoppers, and so we were in their sight."
Numbers 13:33 KJV

The grasshopper complex is the mentality or mind-set that prevents full obedience to God through intimidation from other factors. We feel paralysed in the face of odds against God's will in our lives. The story from the book of Numbers shows us how God's instruction to take the land was met with opposition in the minds of those who were to receive the promise. From God's perspective, the land had been given. How to take it practically involved a fight with the inhabitants, the strategy for that was yet to be given (Read Numbers 13). God told them the land was flowing with milk and honey and they found it so. Now God did not tell them about the giants. Is that not like God? Not to tell you of the nature of your opposition if you do not ask Him? David was not told about Goliath when Samuel anointed him King. Whenever God stirs your heart to obey Him, He never tells you much about the opposition you will face in the course of your obedience. Joseph had no clue what slavery or imprisonment awaited him in his life's journey. I believe submission or obedience to God is incomplete without the opportunity to do otherwise. Adam's obedience was tested with the presence of the tree that was not to be touched. Without the opportunity to disobey, obedience cannot be fully tested. Without the opportunity to rebel, submission cannot be fully tested. There will be giants of opposition to your obedience to God's instructions. God's program for your life demands your participation. Your involvement includes your willingness, obedience and submission to His Word and ways.

SCRIPTURE READING: Numbers 13, Luke 1:26-38
PERSONAL APPLICATION: Today, ask God to tell you what He wants from you. Then receive the grace and strength to obey. The Israelites had to put on a willing and fighting attitude to enter into the promised land; you must be determined not to back down from obeying God.

FAITH OR PRESUMPTION

"Examine yourselves as to whether you are in the faith. Test yourselves. Do you not know yourselves, that Jesus Christ is in you?—unless indeed you are disqualified."
2 Corinthians 13:5

To presume is: to suppose to be true; to take for granted; to take the liberty; to be impudent, etc. *The Message Bible* puts it this way, "Test yourselves to make sure you are solid in the faith. Don't drift along taking everything for granted" (2 Corinthians 13:5). The easiest way into presumption is to stop hearing from God! Faith does not come by having heard but by hearing the Word of God. Man does not live by the Words that proceeded out of the mouth of God, but by every Word that proceeds from His mouth! Can you imagine what could have happened if Abraham stopped hearing from God after the first instruction to go offer his son Isaac as a burnt sacrifice (Genesis 22)? The child of promise would have been killed! We must learn to keep our ears glued to the mouth of God. It is not just about what God told you yesterday, it is also about what He is saying now! It is not just about God's written commandment, it is also about His voice (Deuteronomy 28:2, John 10:27). A lot of folks are presuming on God; His manifest presence, His ability and willingness, His grace, His mercy, etc., and they take a plunge into the deep, claiming to be in faith. David didn't presume on God, rather He asked, "shall I pursue these troops? Shall I overtake them?" And the Lord answered him, "pursue, for you shall surely overtake them and without fail, recover all" (1 Samuel 30:8). A lot of folks are in presumption while claiming to be doing great things for God. They start something in the flesh and expect God to come and bless it. Understand this clearly, God cannot be blackmailed. He will not pay for what He did not order!

SCRIPTURE READING: 1 Samuel 30:1-8, 17-20
PERSONAL APPLICATION: It's time to get serious with our relationship with God. Setting out time daily to read His Word, worship and hear from God builds our intimacy with Him. God wants to speak to us about our challenges and answer us, but we need to be ready to pay the price of relating with Him. Through intimacy with God, we can hear His voice more accurately. So, get your orders correctly from Him and even after you have heard from Him, stay in touch with Him.

A HEART OF OBEDIENCE

"If you are willing and obedient,
You shall eat the good of the land"
Isaiah 1:19

Obedience implies staying under and listening. This is derived from the Greek meaning of the word. Job 22:21-22 says, "Now acquaint yourself with Him, and be at peace; Thereby good will come to you. Receive, please, instruction from His mouth, And lay up His words in your heart." In Job 36:11 we read, "If they obey Him and serve Him, they shall spend their days in prosperity, and their years in pleasures." In Isaiah 1:19 we read, "If you are willing and obedient, you shall eat the good of the land". Obedience to God is the bedrock of progress in God. There are reasons why many vacillate in their obedience to God. One such reason is a lack of proper foundation in their life in Christ. To lay a right foundation is to have a heart commitment to revealed truth. Too many give only a mental assent to truth without a heart process. A heart commitment involves a process wherein the true state of your heart is made to have an encounter with the reality of God's Word.
Our heart attitude should be humble, meek and lowly. Many have hearts that are neither teachable nor submissive. It is not what is in our heads that change us or produce real power, it is what is in our hearts that we act on that makes the difference.

SCRIPTURE READING: Matthew 5:3-8 *AMP*
PERSONAL APPLICATION: Our heart attitude should be as described in Matthew 5: 3-8. What is your heart attitude after a major victory or increased knowledge? Are you full of yourself? Are you full of your own knowledge or of your own opinion? We must be meek - in total submission to God, humble and strong.

GOD FIGHTS FOR YOU

"The Lord will fight for you and you shall hold your peace"
Exodus 14:14

When Potiphar's wife lied against Joseph, and he was imprisoned as a result, there was no record that he fought back. But God fought for him in more ways than one. Not only did he enjoy such great favour and prosperity while he was in prison; the Lord promoted him to become second to Pharaoh in the land of Egypt! Psalm 37 tells us not to worry about the wicked or be envious of evil doers; but to commit everything we do to the Lord. Psalm 37:37 says a wonderful future awaits those who love peace - hallelujah! This Psalm depicts the life of Joseph. It's really not worth worrying yourself about evil doers; the Bible says it only causes and leads to harm (Psalm 37:8). "Never pay back evil with more evil. Do things in such a way that everyone can see you are honourable. Do all that you can to live in peace with everyone. Dear friends, never take revenge. Leave that to the righteous anger of God. For the Scriptures say, "I will take revenge; I will pay them back" says the Lord. Don't let evil conquer you, but conquer evil by doing good" (Romans 12:17-21 *NLT*). Whenever we take laws into our own hands, and fight back, we do more harm than good; but when we hold our peace, God fights for us. The battle becomes the Lord's when we turn it over to Him. God told Jehoshaphat and the people, "You will not need to fight in this battle" (2 Chronicles 20:17). Joseph's brothers meant evil against him, but God meant it for good (Genesis 50:20).

SCRIPTURE READING: Psalm 37, Exodus 14:10-31
PERSONAL APPLICATION: God is able to turn any situation around and make it work out for our good, if we will hold our peace, and let Him fight for us.

CLEANSING OUR SOULS

"that He might sanctify and cleanse her with the washing of water by the word"
Ephesians 5:26

As I've said many times, even though we are not of the world, we are in the world. Every day of our lives we are being exposed to the influences of the world that we are called to live in and influence. This daily exposure allows deposits to be made on our souls, which need to be cleansed and washed away regularly. What Jesus did for His disciples in John 13:1-17 is symbolic. Jesus, the living Word, washed the feet of His disciples. Likewise, we are cleansed with the washing of water by the Word. Ephesians chapter 5 describes how Christ loves the church and gave Himself up for it, "that He might sanctify and cleanse it with the washing of water by the word" (Ephesians 5:26 *KJV*).

We must note that it was the disciples who were with Jesus who had their feet washed by Him. In essence, for a cleansing to take place, we must be in His presence. It was also the living Word that washed the feet of the disciples. What I am saying is that one of the ways we come into God's presence is through prayer. It is also in the place of prayer that the atmosphere is made conducive for the Holy Spirit to breathe upon the Word and make it come alive. Prayer creates the atmosphere needed for us to receive cleansing of our souls from the daily contamination to which we are exposed. Because the exposure is daily, cleansing should be daily—meaning prayer should occur on a regular basis.

SCRIPTURE READING: John 13:1-17

PERSONAL APPLICATION: Toxic attitudes, behaviours and cultural influences that you allow into your life put your soul in danger. You can't avoid contact with such things in this world, but you don't have to be contaminated by them. You can detoxify your soul and start experiencing the pure life that God wants you to enjoy. You have to realise that everything you allow into your mind counts and you have to identify the lies that have deceived you and replace them with the truth of God's Word.

SEPARATED, DEDICATED AND HOLY

"I beseech you therefore, brethren, by the mercies of God, that you present your bodies a living sacrifice, holy, acceptable to God, which is your reasonable service."
Romans 12:1

Consecration is the quality decision made to keep oneself separated, dedicated and holy unto the Lord. Sanctification is the act of separation unto God. Consecration helps us to stay consistent in being doers of the Word. It helps our intimacy with God. It keeps us from yielding to the flesh and hence to the enemy, Satan. It calls for being hard on oneself and having the mind to suffer in the flesh. To present your body as a living sacrifice is a decision that anything that will not please God will not be allowed on or in your body. When sacrifices are offered, the object used for sacrifice is usually killed and offered entirely to the god they are worshipping. In our case, our God is the Almighty Father and we present our bodies, not dead but alive unto Him, wholly available for His service, not for sin. Only then can we truly begin the process of renewing our minds with the Word. Our minds need the discipline of choosing the thoughts we permit into our thought life. Every new insight into God's Word concerning our lifestyle demands a decision to allow that lifestyle to become ours. It is not enough to do what we like to do... we need to do what is pleasing to God. Since our recreated spirits already belong to God, it is our spirit's responsibility to present our bodies to God.

SCRIPTURE READING: Romans 12:1-3
PERSONAL APPLICATION: Paul is commanding us to totally give ourselves up to God. He does not mean to restrict the command to just our physical bodies. God asks for total, not partial devotion—body and soul, holy and acceptable to Him.

WALKING IN THE LIGHT

"Your word is a lamp to my feet
And a light to my path."
Psalm 119:105

It is strict obedience and commitment to the Word of God that delivers us from deception. God's Word has an answer to every lie of the devil. It didn't matter if the fruit would make Adam and Eve wise or not, what mattered was that God had said that they should not eat of it. It didn't matter if the king of Amalek and the best of the land would be good as sacrifice to the Lord or not, what mattered was that God had said Saul should utterly destroy Amalek and everything in Amalek. It does not matter if that unbeliever is handsome or not, or if he loves you or not, what matters is that God says you shouldn't be unequally yoked with an unbeliever. The Bible says we should abstain from all appearance of evil and that we should flee fornication. It doesn't matter if you think you can handle it or not. "He that thinks that he stands should take heed lest he falls" (1 Corinthians 10:12). I have discovered that the safest place to be is to be in the centre of the Word of God. Don't even slightly deviate either to the left or to the right. The Bible says, "And make straight paths for your feet, lest that which is lame be turned out of the way; but let it be rather healed" (Hebrews 12:13 *KJV*). There are some things which are already lame (i.e. feeble, crippled) in our lives; our emotions for example. We need to allow God's power to heal those things rather than have them completely dislocated or put out of joint. The way to have that done is by making straight paths for our feet. And the way to make straight paths for our feet is by ordering our steps in the Word of God. There is no occasion for stumbling for anyone who walks in the light.

SCRIPTURE READING: Matthew 5:14-16, John 8:12, John 1:4-5, 1 John 1:5-10

PERSONAL APPLICATION: As we learn God's Word and live accordingly, our lives will reflect the brilliance of God. The light of God's Word that we shine forth overcomes the darkness of this world.

ACTIVATING NEW SEASONS

"To every thing there is a season,
and a time to every purpose under the heaven"
Ecclesiastes 3:1 KJV

The life that stays connected to heaven to hear the next instruction is the life that will not miss out on God's will. When competition, comparisons and copying everyone else go on, specific instructions are lost and specific purposes never get achieved. The will of God unfolds in times and seasons. God's ultimate purpose is that we be conformed to the image of His Son, Jesus Christ. He will build character, faith, selfless service and total dependence on God into our souls through all that we experience in His will. Even in our disappointments, He can still work out something good if we let Him. Our focus must be on Him in His glory, our motive must be His love and our hearts should be totally yielded to the lessons he wants us to learn (not learning the wrong lessons). Our promptness in obedience is also a sterling quality if we are going to understand times and seasons. We cannot harbour sin, offence, bitterness and any such vice if we hope to 'navigate' accurately during the times and seasons that come upon us in our pursuit of God's will. Biblical characters all went through their various times and seasons and the effect of their seasons can be seen in the outcomes they had in their lives. God prepares us for what He has prepared for us. His preparation will take you through various seasons in your life. The lessons you learn and the tests you pass will determine your readiness for the next phase of His will for your life. Failed tests lead to repetition of phases and delayed progress. As we deepen our intimacy with God we will see more clearly the intentions of His heart for us. Whatever we go through, His intention is to do away with anything in us that is not in harmony with His nature. When we recognise in ourselves any such thing, we cooperate with Him by our repentance and willingness to deal with such traits in us. Let us learn to cooperate with God in all we go through in life.

SCRIPTURE READING: Ecclesiastes 3:1-15, Deuteronomy 1:34-46
PERSONAL APPLICATION: Obedience to heaven's instructions is the key to flowing with God's times and seasons. Let us keep our ears open to firstly hear and then to constantly obey God's instructions to us. This is the secret to staying in God's will.

SAYING 'NO' TO UNGODLINESS

"For the grace of God has appeared that offers salvation to all people. It teaches us to say "No" to ungodliness and worldly passions, and to live self-controlled, upright and godly lives in this present age"
Titus 2:11-12 NIV

The Bible says clearly that we should not continue to sin and expect grace to abound. Grace does not condone sin, rather it teaches us to deny sin. Grace much more abounds where sin abounds, so we can have what it takes in God to overcome sin (Romans 6:1). God's grace is always sufficient for us to handle the pressure of these present times. Jesus said to the Ephesian church, "Nevertheless I have somewhat against thee, because thou hast left thy first love. Remember therefore from whence thou art fallen and repent and do the first works" (Revelations 2:4-5 *KJV*). We can all come to realise where and what we have fallen from and get back. We need to get back to being sensitive to God and to His Spirit. God is looking for 'barefoot priests' who will be sensitive to Him. Jesus said in John 10:27, "My sheep hear my voice and I know them and they follow me." God told me that I need to hear His voice and follow Him even in the 'small' things of life. The truth is that if we don't learn to hear His voice and follow Him in those small things, we will never be able to do so in the big things. Actually, those who ignore God's leading in small, day to day things while trying to be led in the big things open up themselves to hearing strange voices. It also works negatively. If we have been condoning the so called small sins in our lives, we are only being set up by Satan for the 'big' sins. I am yet to see anyone fall into a 'big' sin who hasn't been condoning the 'small' sins at different times in the past.

SCRIPTURE READING: Titus 2:11-14
PERSONAL APPLICATION: It is not merely the law of God or even the fear of getting caught that teaches us to say no to sin. It is God's amazing grace that has the power to teach us to say no to ungodliness and to live a life that is pleasing to Him. This is the sanctifying power of the grace of God. Receive God's enabling grace today.

THE SECRET OF SUCCESS

"This Book of the Law shall not depart from your mouth, but you shall meditate in it day and night, that you may observe to do according to all that is written in it. For then you will make your way prosperous, and then you will have good success."
Joshua 1:8

Daniel was an example of a man with an excellent spirit. He had values that were consistent with godliness. He purposed in his heart not to defile himself and deepened his consecration to God. His purpose was to glorify God by doing whatever pleased God at all costs. God was the top priority in Daniel's life. This is the secret of the excellent spirit that Daniel had. His natural disciplines were not lagging behind his spiritual ones either. They could not find fault with him in any area of his life. They knew the secret of his success was found in his relationship with his God. Success from an eternal perspective is, when all is said and done, the purpose of God has been fulfilled, the potential that God gave is maximised and His Name has been glorified. Real fulfilment is found in fulfilling God's plans and purpose for our lives. God's purpose includes the revelation of the nature of Jesus Christ in our human lives. Utilising God's Word to see His will done on earth is included in His plans. Participating with God by acting in faith and obedience are all part of succeeding in God. No one else should take the credit or glory for the good things that happen in our lives other than God Almighty. In life or death let His glory be our priority.

SCRIPTURE READING: Daniel 1:1-21
PERSONAL APPLICATION: Know this, that the secret of your success is found in your relationship with God. It was true for Daniel, and it is just as true for you. Stop turning to every other thing in a bid to find fulfilment. Your fulfilment is found in God and in the discovery and execution of His plan and purpose for your life.

THE FOCUS OF OUR EXPECTATION

"Consider him who endured such opposition from sinners, so that you will not grow weary and lose heart."
Hebrews 12:3 NIV

Our focus determines our strength; if you focus on the wrong thing, you are going to become weary and then give up. Satan knows that if you don't give up, you will win- as long as you are standing on solid ground. So he, being the god of this world, manipulates things in the natural, including people, just to make you give up! Jesus said people ought to pray and not to give up (Luke 18:1). We are told not to grow weary while doing good, because we shall reap in due time if we do not lose heart (Galatians 6:9). When it comes to biblical expectation, our focus must be on God Himself and His Word because He is the source of every good and perfect gift. If God isn't your focus, you will be moved by the negative and discouraging things around you. Our focus also influences and governs our motives. If your focus is success, fame, money, etc. then you will be driven and motivated by those things. This explains why some folk's motivation doesn't last! We must rather be driven by the love of God (2 Corinthians 5:14) - and not by the love of money! The Bible says the love of money is the root of all evil. God was Abraham's focus. He also saw God as his source (Genesis 14:22-23). The Bible says, "After these things, the word of the Lord came to Abram in a vision, saying, Fear not, Abram, I am your Shield, your abundant compensation, and your reward shall be exceedingly great" (Genesis 15:1 *AMPC*). The Scriptures say, he who believes in, trusts in and relies on Jesus- the chief Cornerstone, shall never be disappointed or put to shame (1 Peter 2:6).

SCRIPTURE READING: Psalm 16:8-9, Psalm 62:5-8
PERSONAL APPLICATION: Spend some time searching yourself. On what or whom is your focus and expectation fixed? What or who is driving you? Do you see God as your source? Determine afresh today to put the whole of your belief, trust, reliance and expectation on the Lord. 1 Peter 2:6 assures you that you will not be disappointed or put to shame.

SETTING AND ACHIEVING GODLY GOALS

"And the Lord answered me: 'Write the vision; make it plain on tablets, so he may run who reads it. For still the vision awaits its appointed time; it hastens to the end—it will not lie. If it seems slow, wait for it; it will surely come; it will not delay.'"
Habakkuk 2:2-3 ESV

There are different areas of our lives where we can set goals. The Lord Jesus Christ grew in stature, in wisdom, in favour with God (spiritual) and in favour with man (social) (Luke 2:52).

So, if we set spiritual, relational, as well as our leadership and personal development goals, and we put a workable plan in place to accomplish these goals, in the light of our peculiar circumstances, we can see growth in all areas of our lives. Otherwise, we let other certain areas suffer as we neglect vital aspects of our lives in view of other desires we may have. Many have let key relationships suffer as they went about their businesses or ministry. We need physical goals for fitness, and proper dieting. We need career goals too. But we also need soul winning goals as well as spiritual growth goals.

Goals bring about discipline in our lives. Write down your goals, achieve them and enjoy doing so! Review your goals from time to time to set ones that are more demanding on you as you improve and stretch yourself. Keep growing as you allow your goals to bring discipline into your life. God set the goal to work for six days and rested on the seventh; you also should have goals for resting at least one day out of seven. Remember goals can be the blueprint for the life God wants you to have, if you set them according to His Word and after thoroughly praying through. Goals for sharing your faith, for your service to benefit others and your spiritual growth will all bring discipline to your life.

SCRIPTURE READING: Proverbs 21:31

PERSONAL APPLICATION: When someone sets a goal to read 25 books in a year, the person suddenly realises that there are many ways to read books, like audio books while driving, etc. Challenges bring about creativity, when we allow ourselves to take them on. Watch out for creative ideas as you set goals.

TRUSTING GOD

"Trust in the Lord with all your heart;
do not depend on your own understanding."
Proverbs 3:5 NLT

'Trust' means firm belief in the reliability of truth, strength, etc. of a person or thing; also, it is the state of being relied upon. Trusting God, therefore, means relying on and depending on Him. It implies putting one's entire weight on Him; abandoning oneself to Him completely and committing oneself totally to Him. It is being in a place where if God doesn't catch you, you would fall and if He doesn't help you, you would fail. "Heal me, O LORD, and I shall be healed; save me, and I shall be saved" (Jeremiah 17:14). If God doesn't help you, vain is the help of man. Believing God's Word will lead to trusting in Him; you don't rely on what someone says if you didn't believe in what they said in the first place! God is trustworthy. The Bible says "It is impossible for God to lie" (Hebrews 6:18). You can count on what He says (read Numbers 23:19-20 *NLT*). God not only has a desire to do what He says, but He also has the ability to do so. Sometimes, friends want to help but might still fail, because they don't have the ability to back their words. But when dealing with God, it is okay to put all your eggs in one basket; because He is faithful and able, we can count on Him. God wants to show Himself strong on behalf of those whose hearts are loyal, or fully committed to Him (2 Chronicles 16:9). Do you know that Jesus went to the cross fully trusting God to raise Him up from the dead? Romans 8:11 also tells us that God was the one who raised Christ from the dead. The truth is, if we can't trust God to keep His Word to us while we are here on earth, how could we say we truly trust Him with our eternal destiny?

SCRIPTURE READING: Proverbs 3:5-6, Numbers 23:19-23
PERSONAL APPLICATION: When times are tough and things are not going our way, that's when we find it difficult to trust God. We doubt, we lack faith in His promises and we worry about our future. This is the exact opposite of how God wants us to react to the difficult circumstances in our lives. He wants us to trust Him and believe in Him even when we think things are going to get worse.

UNDERSTANDING INSECURITIES

"I prayed to the Lord, and he answered me.
He freed me from all my fears."
Psalm 34:4 NLT

We all have insecurities, and these come up very much in our interpersonal relationships. The foundation of this problem is the fallen nature of man. When Adam and Eve fell from glory, the first sign of their state was fear when they heard the voice of God. Fear is the foundation of all insecurities. Fear of failure, fear of losing out, fear of the unknown, and all aspects of fear have their root in the Adamic nature. In interpersonal relationships, these fears show up as insecurities. Why are we usually insecure? We are human, we have our fears and doubts; and we are not usually sure what lies ahead of us. After getting born again, we need to reorder our priorities. We cannot allow ourselves to keep on living in the fears that are rooted in the old man (Adam's) nature. We can only stop fear when we let our faith in God define our lives. Fear and faith are reciprocals. The only reason we can live outside the boundaries of fear is because we believe that God is there in the future and in our peculiar experiences. Faith believes that God is a rewarder of those who diligently seek Him. There is diligence in seeking God, and allowing His Will and Word to influence every area of our lives. Becoming strong in faith is the answer to our insecurities.

SCRIPTURE READING: Genesis 2:25-3:10
PERSONAL APPLICATION: What do we do about our insecure thoughts and fears? Remember, fear and faith are reciprocals. Feeding one, leads to starving the other. Choose to feed your faith by the Word of God and starve your doubts and fears.

STOP THE ATTACK

"If any nation comes to fight you,
it is not because I sent them.
Whoever attacks you will go down in defeat."
Isaiah 54:15 NLT

Satan always tries to contest what God has done for us, and seeks to discredit God by trying to bring those things back on us. After Lazarus was raised from the dead, the religious leaders plotted to kill him again. Jesus calls the devil, "the thief" who has come to steal, kill and destroy (John 10:10). A thief steals what belongs to others. If those things weren't yours in the first place, Satan wouldn't be called a thief! Jesus said to the woman, while she was still bent over, "Dear woman, you are healed of your sickness", even before He laid hands on her (Luke 13:12 *NLT*)!
You are already the healed of the Lord; you are already delivered; you are already blessed. You are not about to be, you already are. God is not the one attacking you. Jesus made it clear who the thief is. God is not the one who is robbing you of your health, your family, your joy, your peace, and all the good things. Instead, He is the One who has given us all things freely to enjoy (James 1:17)! God has also promised us deliverance whenever we face any attack. "If anyone attacks you, don't for a moment suppose that I sent them, and if any should attack, nothing will come of it." (Isaiah 54:15 *MSG*). Jesus defeated the devil on the cross, destroyed his works, and gave us the authority over him. You have the authority, so exercise it; don't just watch Satan steal, kill and destroy. If the devil isn't stopped, he carries on until there is a total destruction. When Herod succeeded in killing James, he took Peter too. He would have killed Peter if the church had not stopped him. Somebody needs to stop the devil.

SCRIPTURE READING: Romans 8:28-39, 1 Samuel 30:8
PERSONAL APPLICATION: Command Satan and those wicked spirits to take their hands off what he has stolen from you; e.g. your finances, your health and so forth. Declare what God says about your finances, your health and anything else you are trusting Him for. Keep standing on God's Word, and don't back down. Remember, your victory has already been settled in Christ Jesus. The weapons of our warfare are not carnal: you have the Word of God which is alive and full of power (Heb. 4:12), the Name of Jesus which is above every other name (Phil. 2:10) and the Blood of Jesus which speaks better things for you (Eph. 1:7, Rev. 12:11).

FAITH GOES BEYOND

"When Jesus heard it, He marveled, and said to those who followed, 'Assuredly, I say to you, I have not found such great faith, not even in Israel!'"
Matthew 8:10

More often than not, we try to limit God to the natural. If something we think should be in place naturally is not there, we feel nothing can change it. We then close the door in the face of God's ability. But if we have our minds informed by the Word of God, it builds faith in our hearts. Sometimes, the Spirit of God will nudge you to exercise faith and belief in God for something that is beyond what you are and where you are. He does this to enlarge your capacity. What you need to do is to get into the Word of God and build yourself up in faith so that you begin to have a confident assurance and conviction of what God can do.

Faith is not limited to the meeting of our needs but is also essential for the furtherance and expansion of the Kingdom. When Elisha asked Elijah that he might receive the double portion of his spirit, Elijah said he had asked for a hard thing. But Elisha must have had enough faith because he opened his mouth and asked for double. Obviously, Elisha knew something—he knew God was able. Although he had asked Elijah for this double portion, he knew Elijah could not provide it; it had to be God.

Elisha not only knew a principle—he knew God. On the basis of that knowledge and his faith, Elisha asked and stayed until he received it. The longer he stayed, the greater his capacity to accommodate a double portion became, and the greater his ability to receive it.

SCRIPTURE READING: 2 Kings 2:1-14

PERSONAL APPLICATION: How many things have we limited God from doing in our lives because we couldn't see how He could do it? Faith isn't faith because we can see the solutions, faith is faith because we trust in Him who has promised. Let us put all our trust in God, how He does it is not our concern, just know beyond a shadow of any doubt that He is able!

THE POWER OF EXPECTATION

"I have not spoken in secret,
In a dark place of the earth;
I did not say to the seed of Jacob,
'Seek Me in vain';
I, the Lord, speak righteousness,
I declare things that are right."
Isaiah 45:19

To expect means, "to look forward to; to regard as likely to happen, to anticipate the occurrence or the coming of; to look for with reason or justification." The man at the Gate Beautiful gave Peter his attention, "expecting to receive something from them" (Acts 3:5). Though he was expecting to receive alms, he got more than that - he got his legs walking and leaping! A lot of people don't get anything because they expect nothing. Though God usually goes beyond our expectations (Ephesians 3:20), He still needs our expectations to work with. He said His thoughts towards us are, "of peace, and not of evil, to give you an expected end" (Jeremiah 29:11). David asked, "What shall be done for the man who kills this Philistine and takes away the reproach from Israel?" (1 Samuel 17:26). Though David fought against Goliath to remove the reproach from Israel, he looked forward to the reward also! The Bible says, "the ploughman ought to plough in hope, and the thresher ought to thresh in expectation of partaking of the harvest" (1 Corinthians 9:9-10 *AMPC*). God is a rewarder of those who diligently seek Him (Hebrews 11:6). He said, "I did not say to the seed of Jacob, 'Seek Me in vain'" (Isaiah 45:19). The *Amplified Bible, Classic Edition* is more explicit, "I did not call the descendants of Jacob [to a fruitless service], saying, Seek Me for nothing [but I promised them a just reward]." No wonder in Malachi 3:14, when the people said it was useless to serve God and was not of any profit that they had kept His ordinance, God said their words were harsh against Him! He said He was going to make a difference between the righteous and the wicked; between one who serves Him and one who doesn't. God has pleasure in the prosperity of His servant (Psalm 35:27).

SCRIPTURE READING: Mark 10:46-52
PERSONAL APPLICATION: It is time to start believing that He who has promised is able to perform it (Hebrews 10:23). Put all your hope and expectation in God! He is faithful.

A VITAL RELATIONSHIP

"Jesus said, "This is how you should pray:
'Father, may your name be kept holy. May your Kingdom come soon.
Give us each day the food we need, and forgive us our sins,
as we forgive those who sin against us.
And don't let us yield to temptation.'"
Luke 11:2-4 NLT

Prayer has become a chore or religious obligation for some Christians, because the vital element of relationship has been removed. Unfortunately, some Christians lack what I call a vital relationship with God. A vital relationship is "an ongoing relationship that involves interaction and exchange between the parties involved". It is a real relationship whereby we are conscious of the presence, needs and interests of the parties in the relationship. Some Christians are lacking this vital relationship with the Father. Some think God is a distant old man, who has rules and regulations that His children must strictly obey or they will be punished immediately. For others, God is God, but He is not really real to them. Yes, they believe He is out there, but He is not really involved. As a result, they cannot sense the consciousness of His presence and His willingness to interact. This is a mentality that makes prayer a religious duty, an obligation we just have to observe. Recognising that prayer is not a religious duty, but an expression of a vital relationship, transforms prayer into a joy and a delight. This makes prayer not just a duty, but an opportunity to interact and fellowship with a loved one. It is only at this point that prayer can become a lifestyle, which it is meant to be.

SCRIPTURE READING: Matthew 26:36-46

PERSONAL APPLICATION: For us to be successful and win in the world, we must develop a lifestyle of prayer. Begin to see prayer as an expression of relationship rather than merely as a religious duty. Spend time today developing a vital relationship with your Heavenly Father in prayer.

BREAK THE CYCLE

"Those who regard worthless idols
Forsake their own Mercy."
Jonah 2:8

No matter how far you've gone, you can return to God. God says, "return to Me and I will return to you" (Malachi 3:7). I don't think you have gone as far as the prodigal son, who had finished all his inheritance on wild living. The Bible says he went to a distant country. After he had spent everything he had, he became a tender of pigs and no one would give him the pigs' food even though he longed for it. How far can you go? And if you have gone that far or further, you are welcome to come back. The prodigal son one day decided to return, and he was shocked that his father could receive him, especially with so much celebration! What if he had allowed guilt, condemnation and fear to keep him in that distant country? He would have missed out on the mercy that was waiting for him. Satan uses this lie to keep people in bondage to sin, and to keep them deeper in sin and further away from God.
Take another example. Jesus said if a man looks at a woman to lie with her he has already committed adultery with her (Matthew 5:28). Jesus here was teaching on the reality of thoughts. Your thoughts are as real in the spirit realm as your physical acts are. And if you nurse a lustful thought in your mind long enough, you will carry it out physically. But Satan turns around to tell somebody to go ahead and commit the 'full' sin of adultery since he has already lusted in his heart. His aim is to trap that brother. What the brother should do is to repent of the sin of lust in his heart, he should cast down the imagination and take that thought captive and replace it with thoughts that are pure, honest and of good report (2 Corinthians 10:3-5, Philippians 4:8). There is a cycle of sin; it starts with lust, then the actual sin and then death (James 1:15). You can break that cycle before the sin is committed! It is easier to deal with lust than to deal with the physical sin of adultery.

SCRIPTURE READING: John 6:37, James 1:12-16
PERSONAL APPLICATION: Is there something in your life, now or previously, that is preventing you from coming to Christ? Remember, whoever comes to Him, He will never cast out. Make a decision today to return to God, and break every cycle of sin in your life.

THE POWER OF THE HOLY SPIRIT

"But you will receive power when the Holy Spirit comes upon you. And you will be my witnesses, telling people about me everywhere—in Jerusalem, throughout Judea, in Samaria, and to the ends of the earth."
Acts 1:8 NLT

Acts 1:8 makes it clear that the purpose of receiving the Holy Spirit's power is to become proof-producers. The enemy lies to us telling us we are shy or timid. Many sincere believers say this to themselves, thinking they are telling the truth. It is deception. You have *dunamis* power at work in you. You shall receive power in action, a mighty force, and a supernatural energy! That is the reason you can be an effective witness. The Greek word translated as 'witness' is *'martus'*. It is the word from which we get our English word 'martyr'. A martyr is one who can vouch for, guarantee, or prove what he has seen, heard or knows. They are so definite about it that they are willing to lay down their lives if need be. Listen to T.L. Osborn's lesson on soul winning, "You shall receive virtue, miracle ability, supernatural energy, after that the Holy Ghost is come upon you, for a specific purpose: to enable you to give absolute evidence and miraculous proof of my resurrection. It is this power working in you that will actually demonstrate and exhibit the proof of your testimony so as to verify your claims as with documented credentials. And you are to exhibit this supernatural evidence of my resurrection in your cities and country and unto the inner and hidden parts of the earth, yes, even to the remote and last frontier of civilization." When you receive the Holy Spirit, you have what it takes to back up your claim that Jesus is alive and well.

SCRIPTURE READING: 1 John 1:1-4
PERSONAL APPLICATION: Has God done anything in your life? Sharing the great news of salvation is not just for evangelists. We are all called to do it. For the person you share with today, you may be the only opportunity they have to hear the Gospel. Receive the power of the Holy Spirit to be an effective witness today!

EXALTED IN DUE TIME

"And Moses said to the people, "Do not be afraid. Stand still, and see the salvation of the Lord, which He will accomplish for you today. For the Egyptians whom you see today, you shall see again no more forever."
Exodus 14:13

When we do not take the law into our hands, but forgive, we allow God to take care of the situation. God is able to turn around for good, even what others meant for evil, if we would allow Him to do the judging. Doing what is good and right no matter what, offers us protection in itself! "And who is he who will harm you if you become followers of what is good?" (1 Peter 3:13).

God has His ways of doing things, and His ways are completely different from the ways of the world. In God's kingdom, the way up is down; anyone that would be the leader, must be the servant of all - "Therefore humble yourselves under the mighty hand of God, that He may exalt you in due time" (1 Peter 5:6). We get by giving - "Give, and it will be given to you: good measure, pressed down, shaken together, and running over will be put into your bosom. For with the same measure that you use, it will be measured back to you" (Luke 6:38). We live by dying - "Most assuredly, I say to you, unless a grain of wheat falls into the ground and dies, it remains alone; but if it dies, it produces much grain" (John 12:24). Though we live in the world, we do not fight like the world, using worldly or fleshly weapons; but our weapons are mighty and effective through God. "The world is unprincipled. It's dog–eat–dog out there! The world doesn't fight fair. But we don't live or fight our battles that way—never have and never will" (1 Corinthians 10:3 *MSG*). Remember, "And we know that God causes everything to work together for the good of those who love God and are called according to His purpose for them" (Romans 8:28 *NLT*). So, learn to win God's way!

SCRIPTURE READING: 1 Peter 2:21-23, Romans 12:19 *MSG*, Proverbs 20:22 *NLT*
PERSONAL APPLICATION: Sometimes we have to let go and 'let God'. When we live in the knowledge that the battle belongs to the Lord, then we also have to pray, stand still and see what our God will do, no matter how long it takes.

THE GOAL OF THE GOSPEL

"Then Jesus said to His disciples, "If anyone desires to come after Me, let him deny himself, and take up his cross, and follow Me."
Matthew 16:24

What was the apostolic mind-set that the first century church had towards the Gospel? The goal of the Gospel was to restore mankind to becoming the dwelling place of God. God made man in His image and likeness and designed us to function within the context of fellowship with Him. All of this was lost as a result of the fall. Thank God for Jesus our Saviour and Lord, whose sacrifice on the Cross has been sufficient to restore us to the place of sonship with the Father.

There has been a subtle, but profound perversion of the Gospel in modern times. The message has been changed from Jesus having come to save us from our sins, to Him having come to save us from our problems. This is not to imply that the Lord does not save us from our troubles, but that it is a very shallow foundation upon which someone is converted to the Lord, and could be the reason for impure motives and inconsistencies in many lives. Our desperation to come to the Lord should be because of the conviction of sin and not because of our problems. Some people may not relate the problems they encounter, to the wrong foundation in their lives. The Gospel we received the day we became born again, determines the disciple we become. Many preach and try to impart the hope and the benefits of the resurrection, without dying to our self-life on the Cross. This is a delusion of high proportions. Many are made to feel better about themselves, but their spiritual condition is still questionable. Reading through the Bible we see that Jesus demanded total commitment from His disciples. They had to be willing to leave everything to follow Him. This is true discipleship.

SCRIPTURE READING: Hebrews 12:1-2, Luke 14:25-33, Matthew 16:24-26 *AMP*
PERSONAL APPLICATION: Christ paid the price. He made the choice to give up His life for us even before we chose Him. What do you need to lay aside today in order to truly follow Him?

CULTIVATING HEALTHY RELATIONSHIPS

"And let us consider one another in order to stir up love and good works"
Hebrews 10:24

There are things you can never break through as a one-man or one-woman riot squad. In God's economy, there is no such thing as a self-made man. In the maturing process, we move from dependence to independence and then to inter-dependence! We need others as much as they need us! A healthy relationship is neither dependent nor independent, but inter-dependent.

Daniel had his own company - Shadrach, Meshach and Abednego. He was not alone in his consecration and in his prayers. After Peter and John were released from prison, they went to their own company, and reported all that happened to them; and they all raised their voice to God in one accord in prayer.

They say everything rises and falls on leadership; but in team-leadership, things don't have to fall, because they can make up for the weaknesses of one another. Jesus had twelve disciples, He also had the seventy; He never sent them out in ones, but in twos! "Two people are better off than one, for they can help each other succeed. If one person falls, the other can reach out and help. But someone who falls alone is in real trouble. A person standing alone can be attacked and defeated, but two can stand back-to-back and conquer. Three are even better, for a triple-braided cord is not easily broken" (Ecclesiastes 4:9-12 *NLT*).

SCRIPTURE READING: Proverbs 27:17, Daniel 1:8-21

PERSONAL APPLICATION: Do you have people who will stand with you in all things, who will challenge you in order to sharpen your faith and your walk with God?

GOD'S TRUTH

"My son, keep my words,
And treasure my commands within you."
Proverbs 7:1

The Bible is God's truth speaking to His people everyday. You must realise that these are not just printed words on the pages of a book. The Bible is the inspired Word of God that is able to save and deliver. The Christian life is not about just having some knowledge of the Bible, but having a reverence in your heart for God's Word. Once a healthy respect for God's Word is developed and maintained, you will be able to locate your destiny in it and the tangible deposit of God can be transmitted into your spirit. For instance, John the Baptist had been anointed from the womb of his mother to prepare the way for the Messiah. He still located himself in the Word of God. When he was asked who he was, he answered by the Word—"I am the voice of one crying in the wilderness; make straight the way of the Lord" (John 1:23). If he had treated the Word of God with an attitude of levity, he would not have found what had been written about him.
Your attitude goes a long way as far as God's Word is concerned. If you are to fulfill the destiny you have in God, you must wake up and recognise, reward and celebrate everything about Him in your life. You must locate yourself in His Word and recognise that He has deposited all the potential that you need to fulfill your destiny in Him. You must rise up and cultivate the right attitude towards everything of God around and inside you, because it will determine how far you go in fulfilling your God-given destiny. God is waiting for you to wake up and be empowered to fulfil destiny because He has made the provision for all you need, in His Word and inside of you.

SCRIPTURE READING: John 15:1-8
PERSONAL APPLICATION: For any of God's people to be effective for Him, they need to abide in His Words so His Words can abide in them. Are you spending enough time in God's Word? Set yourself a target today to spend time daily learning the scripture so that at the right time, God Himself can use those Words to reveal His purpose to you.

THE BASIS OF OUR FELLOWSHIP

"That which we have seen and heard we declare to you, that you also may have fellowship with us; and truly our fellowship is with the Father and with His Son Jesus Christ."
1 John 1:3

The Bible says, "our fellowship is with the Father and with His Son, Jesus Christ" (1 John 1:3). God is our Father, and that is the basis of our fellowship with Him! Whereas you could have a relationship without being in fellowship, you cannot have any meaningful fellowship without having a relationship in place, first and foremost. Jesus taught His disciples to pray to their Father. He said, "pray to your Father who is in the secret place; and your Father who sees in secret will reward you openly. And when you pray, do not use vain repetitions as the heathens do. For they think that they will be heard for their many words. Therefore do not be like them. For your Father knows the things you have need of before you ask Him. In this manner, therefore, pray: Our Father in heaven, Hallowed be Your name" (Matthew 6:6-9). We must therefore know God as our Father, see Him as such, and address Him in that manner; to have that fellowship with Him in prayer. God is the Father from whom the whole family in heaven and earth is named (Ephesians 3:14-15). That is the basis upon which we pray and expect Him to hear us, and upon which we ask Him for our 'daily bread' and other needs.

SCRIPTURE READING: Romans 8:12-17
PERSONAL APPLICATION: The depth of a relationship is directly linked to how well we know one another. God knows us very well, but do we know Him as well? Make a decision today to get to know Him better by studying and meditating in His Word.

GLORY HUNTER

"But now, thus says the Lord, who created you, O Jacob,
And He who formed you, O Israel:
'Fear not, for I have redeemed you;
I have called you by your name;
You are Mine.'"
Isaiah 43:1

One of the greatest battles in dealing with insecurities is the identity battle. Who are you? What do you have? Where are you going? What are you here for? We need to develop our confidence in who we are in Christ, what we have in Him and what we can do through Him. This is the basis of a life free of insecurities. We all grow from one dimension to another. Too many link their identities to their achievements and possessions. They measure their worth by their possessions and the opinions of others. The Scripture that God used to deliver me from a major insecurity problem was John 5:44. It reads thus in the Amplified Translation, Classic Edition, "How is it possible for you to believe [how can you learn to believe], you who [are content to seek and] receive praise and honour and glory from one another, and yet do not seek the praise and honour and glory which come from Him who alone is God?" Too many times we unconsciously seek these things from one another without considering God's opinion on the matter. It brought a major deliverance to me when I began to internalise the reality of this Scripture. I am still interested in people, I love them, but I no longer seek the glory that comes from them as I used to. At least, I am working towards this as a reality in my life. When such honour comes I appreciate it, receive it and give God the glory for making it possible, but I do not try to hunt for it.

SCRIPTURE READING: John 5:30-47
PERSONAL APPLICATION: The satisfaction that arises from acclaim and honour given to us from people is short-lived. It leaves us looking for more. Ask your Heavenly Father to show you how much He accepts and approves of you instead. The praise, honour and glory which comes from God is the only thing that will bring true satisfaction and worth to you.

THE PRINCIPLE OF DIVINE REVELATION

"Surely the Lord God does nothing,
Unless He reveals His secret to His servants the prophets."
Amos 3:7-8

In Genesis 41, Pharaoh had two dreams and Joseph was called upon to interpret them. There was going to be seven years of abundance that would be followed by seven years of famine. God not only gave the interpretation of the dreams through Joseph, but also the wisdom as to how to handle the years of abundance and the years of famine. In this one story, we can see: [i] the place of divine revelation, "Where there is no revelation, the people cast off restraint" (Proverbs 29:18 *NLT*); [ii] the place of using what Joseph had (i.e. the gift of interpreting dreams), "a spiritual gift is given to each of us so we can help each other" (1 Corinthians 12:7 *NLT*); [iii] the place of divine wisdom, "wisdom is profitable to direct" (Ecclesiastes 10:10). Divine revelation will always lead to divine instruction, so that we can know what to do with what has been revealed to us, and enjoy its full benefits. When they acted on Joseph's instructions they were sustained throughout the famine.
Elisha told the widow to sell the oil, pay her debts and live off the remainder! Divine revelation also demands from us a lifestyle of hard work, diligence and discipline. A man who is diligent in his work or 'prompt in his business' will stand before kings and not before unknown men (Proverbs 22:29). A lot of times we cut off from God and the vessels He uses to give us divine revelation, so we dry up soon. Elijah had to stay connected to God for his continuous provision to be guaranteed. God will often give you divine ideas to get out of the financial crisis, and put you on top of the situation. (See Genesis 30:31). Somebody said, poverty is not just about the lack of money, but the lack of ideas. God wants to open the windows of heaven above you and pour out such a blessing on you that there won't be enough room to contain it.

SCRIPTURE READING: Joel 2:28-29, Genesis 30:29-43
PERSONAL APPLICATION: God wants to pour out His Spirit on us and His heart to us. We need to dwell in His Word and to stay connected to God and His people, to be able to deal with God's revelations and instructions.

FAITH THAT PREVAILS

"And from the days of John the Baptist until now the kingdom of heaven suffers violence, and the violent take it by force."
Matthew 11:12

Prevailing faith is that which holds its own when the going gets tough. The Kingdom of God suffers violence, and the violent take it by force. There is a fighting spirit behind the faith that prevails. The ingredients of faith are as follows: believing His Word, speaking and acting on the Word of God. The ability to stay consistent in faith is called patience. Patience is the staying power of faith. The power of faith is found in the revelation of Christ in our hearts: His work on the cross and His present ministry on the right hand of God the Father. We believe, and therefore speak, because we have the spirit of faith. God says it, we lay hold of it and we possess its fulfilment by faith. The faith that refuses to give in when circumstances are contrary is the prevailing faith. The trying of our faith works patience and when patience has had its full work, we will be entire, wanting nothing. Our faith is more precious than gold. Gold is purified through the fire of testing. Prevailing faith comes forth brighter and stronger after the trials have come and gone. The faith that prevails is that which is founded on the finished work of Calvary, with a revelation of the present work of Christ in the heavens on our behalf.

SCRIPTURE READING: Hebrews 11:8-12, Romans 5:1-5
PERSONAL APPLICATION: The things we value most are often the things that cost us most. How much sweeter is answered prayer when we have gone past unbelief, fear, worry, doubt and come out victorious? Be encouraged today to pray more about the things that you have almost given up on because you can't 'see' an answer. Remember, your time is in the now, but God's timing is perfect for you.

BUILDING ON THE ROCK

"Therefore whoever hears these sayings of Mine, and does them, I will liken him to a wise man who built his house on the rock:"
Matthew 7:24

Jesus likened those who hear His words but don't do them, to the foolish builder who built his house on the sand. He built a house quite all right but not on the rock; he built on sand, representing human and fleshly opinions and standards. Jesus said, great was the fall of that house when the storms came! It will take the storms of life to reveal what we and our lives are made of and built upon.
"Except the LORD builds the house, they labour in vain who build it" (Psalm 127:1). Those people did build, but their labour was in vain; like the foolish builder Jesus spoke about. How painful it is to find out at the end of the day that one's labour had only been in vain! There is a way that seems right to man, but the end of it is destruction. It's the end of it that is destruction - not the start of it. Yet people have built marriages, families, ministries and even lives, on every other thing but the Word. This is because it is easier to build on sand than on the rock. Did you notice that the man that built on the rock had to dig deep to get to the rock? Sand is superficial and the human nature loves superficiality. Sand is commonly found around, and our nature likes what is common - the opposite of 'holy' is 'common'. You don't need much effort to build on sand, and the human nature doesn't enjoy hard work; but if you want to be happy in life, you must labour to build properly, on the Word of God. Build on Christ, the solid Rock.

SCRIPTURE READING: Matthew 7:24-29, Proverbs 14:12-13 *MSG*
PERSONAL APPLICATION: It is time to examine the areas in your life where you are building on sand. Most of the time, it will be areas where you have allowed public opinion, popular votes or your desires to determine what you do. Go to God and build on His Word.

BUILDING A SPIRITUAL HOUSE

"You also, as living stones, are being built up a spiritual house,
a holy priesthood, to offer up spiritual sacrifices
acceptable to God through Jesus Christ."
1 Peter 2:5

There must be no room for strife, jealousy or any work of the flesh if we intend to build a spiritual house. Unfortunately we allow these things, without any consideration for their impact on what we are building. Some gather stones and imagine they have a building. Stones need to be shaped into particular frames before they fit into the design of the house. We are called 'living stones' in 1 Peter 2:5, that are being built up as a spiritual house, a holy priesthood, to offer up spiritual sacrifices acceptable to God through Jesus Christ. Jesus said He will build His church and the gates of hell will not prevail against it (Matthew 16:18). His church is His people called out of darkness into His marvellous light, who will do His bidding, express His will on earth as they bring recognition to Him and glory to His name. They are trained, developed and shaped for His purpose as they yield to His Spirit, follow after His Word and get connected with His plans and purposes. These principles are not without the relational content. The currency of the Spirit is relationships. God connects people for His purpose to be fulfilled on earth. Many of the ingredients that God wants to bring into people's lives are inside other human beings. When God wants to put something into your life, He may connect you with others who already have some of it, and through the relationship build more of the substance into both parties. The rubbing off on one another in a correct way is the pattern for building a spiritual house. When the house is built accurately, the Lord Jesus will be displayed as the chief cornerstone for all to see.

SCRIPTURE READING: Ephesians 2:19-22, 1 Peter 2:4-12
PERSONAL APPLICATION: God has called us out of darkness and into His marvellous light. We have the great responsibility to show God's goodness. Jesus is coming for a spotless church—that means we must do away with the works of the flesh, and the activities of darkness. Let us build a church that radiates God's glory.

THE END DOES NOT JUSTIFY THE MEANS

"For if you live according to the flesh you will die; but if by the Spirit you put to death the deeds of the body, you will live."
Romans 8:13

King Saul was told to utterly destroy Amalek and everything he found there. God said to him specifically in 1 Samuel 15:3, "Now go and attack Amalek, and utterly destroy all that they have, and do not spare them. But kill both man and woman, infant and nursing child, ox and sheep, camel and donkey" (see 1 Samuel 15:1-3). Clear enough, isn't it? But what did Saul do? The Bible says that he spared the king, the best of the sheep and cattle, the fat calves and lambs and everything that was good. Do you know his reason for sparing them? It was to sacrifice them to the Lord. Before you go on and condemn Saul, you need to first of all remove the log in your own eyes. How many times have you brought proceeds of lust, immorality, fraud and cheating to sacrifice to God? Haven't you been paying tithes on, and giving testimonies to the 'glory of God' about what you didn't get His own way? Amalek represents the flesh, that is, the carnal desires, carnal thoughts and actions. We all have sanctified our flesh instead of utterly crucifying the flesh on the cross of Christ. A lot of singing, dancing and clapping, and even giving in the church today is done in the flesh. Listen, nothing done in the flesh can please God (Romans 8:8). The flesh stinks. Those who worship God must do so in the Spirit (i.e. a heart thing) and in truth (in reality, in integrity) (see John 4:24). God seeks such worshippers. Samuel told Saul that to obey is better than sacrifice and to heed is better than the fat of rams. The only sacrifice that pleases God is one done in obedience to Him that is, in faith not in the flesh!

SCRIPTURE READING: 1 Samuel 15:1-35
PERSONAL APPLICATION: Good intentions or good motives do not justify lack of or partial obedience to God's instructions. Do not tolerate the flesh and its wants and desires, crucify it! It is time to self reflect: have you given anything to God out of the flesh? Repent before God and make the decision to only offer to Him what is done in spirit and in truth.

THE SPIRIT AND LIFE OF GOD

"But there is a spirit in man,
And the breath of the Almighty gives him understanding."
Job 32:8

We read how the early church stayed filled with the Spirit after the day of Pentecost. Acts 4:31-37 shows us that the unity they experienced was a result of being filled with the Spirit. Jesus said He came that we may have life and have it more abundantly. The Word is the carrier of God's life, likewise the Spirit is the energy of God who works in us to bring about the intake of life and power. The more of the Word of God you get into your spirit, the more life you have access to. The life is the life of God and cannot be lived with the wits of the natural man. It takes a special learning to know how to live the life of God. It is a life form that is higher than the human life, having its demands and its required environment. Jesus was the only one who lived that life in His days on earth. That is the reason for the differences we read about in the life He lived and the lives others did. He perceived, while others used their minds to think. He knew things supernaturally, while others depended on natural sources for information. All these were functions of the life he had. He gave us His life so we can live like He did. Our recreated spirits are the reservoirs for this life. It will affect every other thing in us. When we abide in Him and His Word abides in us, we will ask whatever we need and it shall be done for us (John 15:7). His life is our guarantee for the victory we need on earth. The flesh must be crucified for this life to flow. Be filled with the Spirit and life of God.

SCRIPTURE READING: Acts 4:1-37
PERSONAL APPLICATION: One of the ways to be filled with more of the Spirit and life of God is to spend more time with Him. Determine today to spend more time in the Word of God, in prayer and in obedience to His instructions.

THINK LIKE GOD THINKS

"For as the heavens are higher than the earth,
So are My ways higher than your ways,
And My thoughts than your thoughts."
Isaiah 55:9

God's thoughts and ways are higher than yours - not lower. God doesn't think thoughts of lack, shortage or impossibilities. Jesus fed the five thousand men in a deserted place, with just five loaves of bread and two fish; and there were twelve baskets of leftovers. The disciples' thoughts were that Jesus should send the crowds away so they could go and find food to buy. But Jesus' thoughts were higher - He said to them, "You give them something to eat" (Mark 6:37). God's ways and thoughts will always challenge ours. Elisha asked a widow who was in so much debt, that her creditors threatened to come and take her sons away, "Tell me, what do you have in the house?" She said she had nothing, except a pot of oil. The question was meant to challenge her mind-set. Elisha told her to go borrow vessels from everywhere, from all her neighbours' empty vessels; not just a few - and to fill them with the oil. After she had done that, she sold the oil, paid off her debt, and she and her sons lived on the rest (2 Kings 4:1-7). God is more than enough; don't ask for less - but ask for more! "And God is able to make all grace (every favour and earthly blessing) come to you in abundance, so that you may always and under all circumstances and whatever the need be self-sufficient [possessing enough to require no aid or support and furnished in abundance for every good work and charitable donation]" (2 Corinthians 9:8 *AMPC*)

SCRIPTURE READING: Psalm 34:8-10, Psalm 50:10-11
PERSONAL APPLICATION: Make up your mind to think big today. Do not settle for less! The God we serve is able and willing.

THE PERSON, PRESENCE AND POWER OF GOD

*"One thing I ask from the Lord, this only do I seek: that I may dwell
in the house of the Lord all the days of my life
to gaze on the beauty of the Lord
and to seek him in his temple."
Psalm 27:4 NIV*

Having God's presence in our lives is a function of what we allow ourselves to dwell on, in our thoughts as well as in our attitudes and words. A worshipful heart, full of reverence for God is a sure way to attract and keep His presence with us. The foundation for this is a decision to dedicate our lives to God and do only what pleases Him. When we honour His person (this is a product of our fear of God), we will watch our life's choices. These guarantee that whenever His power is needed in our lives, we can count on Him. He is indeed a present help in time of trouble.

SCRIPTURE READING: Psalm 27:4-8 *AMP*
PERSONAL APPLICATION: We do not need to wait until problems hit us before coming into God's presence. Make up your mind today, to cultivate the habit of dwelling in His presence.

FREE FROM DECEPTION

"But be ye doers of the word, and not hearers only, deceiving your own selves."
James 1:22 KJV

I have discovered that nothing else opens up a believer to deception as much as hearing (or reading or even preaching) the Word without being a doer of it. The Bible says that Satan is a liar and when he lies, he speaks his native language. But the Word of God is the Truth, Hallelujah! Satan has no power against the truth. The Spirit of Truth is the answer to the spirit of error. What uncovers the lies of the devil is the Truth of God, which is His Word. It does not matter who is doing what, it does not matter what results they are getting, it does not matter how much of the 'power' seems to be flowing. What matters is obedience to the Word of God. What will last is what is done in obedience to God. The antichrist will deceive many by the mighty signs that he will do. The truth is that Jesus didn't design His people to follow signs, signs are supposed to follow us. The Bible says that the spirit of antichrist is now already in the world (1 John 4:3). The Bible says teachers will be judged by a more severe standard or with special strictness, so not many should be teachers (James 3:1). It is so amazing that we don't think so anymore. Rather we teachers (or leaders) think we can do anything, say anything and get away with it. No! That is deception. The Bible says to whom much is given, much is expected. We shall be beaten with many stripes if we are found wanting. We really need to get back into the unchanging Word of God. I love the Word! It doesn't care about what I think or what I feel, it only cares about what God thinks and feels. No wonder the Bible says, "Let the wicked forsake his way, and the unrighteous man his thoughts, and let him return to the Lord... for my thoughts are not your thoughts, neither are your ways my ways saith the LORD" (Isaiah 55:7-8). God's ways and thoughts are so much higher than our ways and thoughts that we can't fathom it in the natural.

SCRIPTURE READING: Galatians 6:7, Proverbs 24:12, James 1:21-27
PERSONAL APPLICATION: Most of us at one stage or the other have ignored the Holy Spirit's prompting to do something in our faith walk. Today, let us make a fresh commitment to do God's Word and follow His leadings and promptings.

THE PLACE OF FATHERS

"As for Me, behold, My covenant is with you,
and you shall be a father of many nations."
Genesis 17:4

A spiritual father is one that has been privileged in God to pour his spiritual composition to affect the composition of another, a leader whose influence has had a definite impact in shaping the spiritual destinies of others. A father nurtures, chastises, encourages and helps one into the path of destiny. A father is not necessarily one that leads you to salvation. In the natural a man can impregnate a woman, but it takes more than that to father a son. It involves an enduring process to be a father. The pain, agony, confusion and commitment spell fatherhood. It is never for selfish ends when it comes to true spiritual fathering; it is for godly purposes. Many spiritual fathers qualify by their life of obedience; like how Abraham became a father to us all by his obedience to God. A father has walked with God and has scars to show for it. He is not a starter who has knowledge, he has proven the Word of God in the trying places. He knows what he is talking about when he talks. He has been there. He gives what he has received of the deposits of God put in him through others ahead of him, and in his walk with God. A father imparts and helps you to navigate the murky waters of life. You can rest your case when you go through with the counsel of a God-connected father. When Peter said elders should be examples in 1 Peter 5:3, it implies patterns for others under them. Fathers chart a pathway in the Spirit for sons. Abraham's walk with God became a pattern for Isaac; Isaac's walk became a pattern for Jacob. Jacob rested in an area surrounding where his fathers had raised altars to God (Genesis 28); He had an open heaven without effort on his part. The labours of the fathers create a pathway for the sons in the Spirit. The impartation of a father can totally change the natural course of events for a son. Live a life of obedience to God and to His Word—you will be drawn to your spiritual father.

SCRIPTURE READING: Malachi 4:5-6
PERSONAL APPLICATION: Read Genesis chapters 21-22, then 24-26 and consider the spiritual and natural inheritance Isaac had from his father. Has God placed spiritual fathers in your journey of faith who have impacted you? How can you recognise the spiritual fathers God brings your way?

GIVING YOUR BURDENS TO THE LORD

"Therefore humble yourselves under the mighty hand of God,
that He may exalt you in due time, casting all your care upon Him,
for He cares for you."
1 Peter 5:6-7

We are to cast all of our cares, not just some of them, on God; and if we do, we no longer have them. He now has them. Which means, if we still have them, He doesn't have them! God can't do anything about our cares if we don't give them over to Him. "Give your burdens to the Lord, and He will take care of you. He will not permit the godly to slip and fall" (Psalm 55:22 *NLT*). We must believe that God truly cares about us and what we are going through; that truth must soak in on us. Deep within us, we believe nobody really cares about us - at least not as much as we care; but we must let these words change that. Then we can truly cast our cares on God, knowing He truly cares about us affectionately and watchfully.

We cast our cares on God, by presenting our requests to Him in prayer. "Be anxious for nothing, but in everything by prayer and supplication, with thanksgiving, let your requests be made known to God; and the peace of God, which surpasses all understanding, will guard your hearts and minds through Christ Jesus" (Philippians 4:6-7). Take note of the two absolutes in that verse; "Be anxious for nothing, but in everything by prayer..." Also, the peace of God only comes to keep our hearts after we have cast our cares on Him, and not before. We can expect to enter into God's rest when we cast all our cares on Him. When Jehoshaphat was told that a great multitude was coming against him, naturally, his first reaction was to be afraid. But then, he decided to turn that care and anxiety over to God; he set himself to seek the Lord, and proclaimed a fast throughout all Judah (2 Chronicles 20:3-4). God gave them the victory. Great things happen when we cast our cares on the Lord.

SCRIPTURE READING: Matthew 6:25-34, Philippians 4:6-8

PERSONAL APPLICATION: What do you need to take to God in prayer? Do so right now and leave it with Him! Whenever fear and anxiety come, use scriptures like Psalm 55:22 and Matthew 6:30 as your daily confession. Personalise them by putting your name and situation into them. Leave it in God's hands - He is able!

FULFILLING YOUR DESTINY

"As long as the earth endures, seedtime and harvest, cold and heat, summer and winter, day and night will never cease."
Genesis 8:22 NIV

God's will does not automatically happen, and everything that happens to you is not necessarily God's will for your life. That is not a scriptural way of thinking. There are other causes for situations that occur in our lives. The laws of sowing and reaping would be negated if God were the source of all you reap. He has allowed these laws to function and we need to know how to apply them rightly. "Whatsoever a man sows, that shall he also reap" (Galatians 6:7).

Your destiny has a lot to do with your character, attitude and knowledge. Our ultimate goal is to be conformed to the image of Christ Jesus. The extent to which we conform to the image of Christ is the extent to which our destiny in God is being realized and fulfilled. Our destiny is not necessarily in getting an end result but an ongoing and unveiling of His plans and purposes for our lives. Our destiny demands our diligence, excellence and striving for progressive development. It means we will engage our minds, develop the skills needed, discipline ourselves and grow up in all areas of life. Welcome to the journey that leads to fulfilment!

SCRIPTURE READING: Genesis 45:1-15

PERSONAL APPLICATION: God is more interested in our characters being developed, so that we can be ready for what lies ahead. Ask God to open your eyes to see which areas in your life need adjusting.

ENLARGE YOUR CAPACITY

"And it will be said,
'Build up, build up, prepare the way,
Remove every obstacle out of the way of My people.'"
Isaiah 57:14 NASB

"Enlarge the place of your tent, and let them stretch out the curtains of your dwellings; do not spare; lengthen your cords, and strengthen your stakes. For you shall expand to the right and to the left, and your descendants will inherit the nations, and make the desolate cities inhabited. 'Do not fear, for you will not be ashamed; neither be disgraced, for you will not be put to shame...'" (Isaiah 54:2-4).
A lot of people do not aim for more in life because they don't want to be stretched; they avoid anything that could stretch them physically, mentally, emotionally, or even spiritually; all they do is to try to maintain the *status quo*. In the parable of the talents, the servants were given talents according to each man's capacity. Have a change of perspective, attitude and approach towards your problems. See your challenges as an opportunity for growth, increase and promotion. "Arise, shine; for your light has come! And the glory of the Lord is risen upon you. For behold, the darkness shall cover the earth, And deep darkness the people; but the Lord will arise over you, and His glory will be seen upon you" (Isaiah 60:1-2). You are an eagle; and you are meant to soar above the storms.

SCRIPTURE READING: Judges 6:1-6, 11-16, Isaiah 54:1-10
PERSONAL APPLICATION: Don't pray for the challenge to get smaller, but that you grow bigger. Develop yourself. Ask God for wisdom to handle the challenges. Turn the stumbling blocks into stepping stones; and the opposition to opportunities for promotion. "When they cast you down, and you say, 'Exaltation will come!'" (Job 22:29). Also, surround yourself with the right company—those who encourage you to stretch yourself and grow in excellence.

WHY GIVE?

"Give, and it will be given to you: good measure, pressed down, shaken together, and running over will be put into your bosom. For with the same measure that you use, it will be measured back to you."
Luke 6:38

In 2 Corinthians 8, we see how the churches of Macedonia gave in response to some needs in other churches as Paul had informed them. This grace of giving was so prevalent amongst them that he said that despite the great trial of affliction, the riches of their liberality revealed the abundance of their joy and the depth of their poverty. I believe they gave joyously despite their poverty because of the grace of giving. The churches in Corinth were encouraged to abound in the grace of giving. We should too. We see the definition of grace in 2 Corinthians 8:9. Jesus, who was rich, became poor for our sakes so that we may become rich. He impoverished Himself to enrich us. Giving positions you for more grace from God, so you can do more for His Kingdom and He can do more through you. It delivers you from selfishness and breaks your dependence on the natural things you can see, touch and taste. It also enlarges your capacity to receive from the Lord through others. On top of that, through your giving, you lay up for yourself treasures in heaven for the time to come. We are instructed in the Word to do all things as unto the Lord and in the name of the Lord. Whatever good anyone does, he will receive the same from the Lord (Ephesians 6:8). Our reward is from the Lord, not from the ones who we give to.

SCRIPTURE READING: 2 Corinthians 8:1-15, Ephesians 6:7-8
PERSONAL APPLICATION: Convert everything you do in and for God's Kingdom into a seed. How much of your time and resources would you give if you were conscious of the fact that you have a heavenly account? And whatever you sow, that is what you will reap.

SALT AND LIGHT

"You are the salt of the earth; but if the salt loses its flavour, how shall it be seasoned? It is then good for nothing but to be thrown out and trampled underfoot by men."
Matthew 5:13

Jesus calls believers 'salt' and 'light' in Matthew 5:13-14 and Luke 14:34. Salt mixes and influences whatever it comes in contact with. It enhances the flavour and preserves. Jesus is the light of the world and when He comes into our lives, we become lights ourselves. Darkness represents ignorance and the Bible says darkness cannot overpower light. Light represents development and enlightenment. "Have salt in yourselves and be at peace with one another" (Mark 9:50). "Let your speech always be with grace, seasoned with salt, that you may know how you ought to answer each one" (Colossians 4:6). We have all been affected by our nature, nurture and environment. It's time to let our new-found relationship with God through our Lord Jesus Christ affect us so thoroughly that we can in turn influence others for Christ.

SCRIPTURE READING: Matthew 5:13-16
PERSONAL APPLICATION: When you pray, you can ask God for His nature to rub off on you. It is possible for our speech, our actions and our thoughts to reflect God's nature. Jesus is the light of the world—and as He is, so are we to be.

A ROCK OF OFFENCE

"He will be as a sanctuary,
But a stone of stumbling and a rock of offense
To both the houses of Israel,
As a trap and a snare to the inhabitants of Jerusalem.
And many among them shall stumble;
They shall fall and be broken,
Be snared and taken."
Isaiah 8:14-15

In the building of His church, Jesus is the chief cornerstone. In the process of development of His body on earth, His cross is an offence to many who do not get aligned with his Kingdom purposes and focus. The response to offences will determine the direction of the remaining part of one's life, if care is not taken. If our response is wrong, we will fall into Satan's trap; and if we get it right, we are on our way to a life of fulfilment in the purposes of God. The source and purpose of offences always differ and we need to recognise them for what they really are. Offences can lead to bitterness, and the root of bitterness, will defile many and open the door to other demonic activities in a person, family or church. In the course of our spiritual development, offences come to test, prove and determine what is inside our hearts. Our pride, selfishness and greed can get confronted almost without any announcement, and the manner of confrontation may be through an offence from someone else who is maybe immature, or someone in authority over us. Whichever way, it is for our good that after being angry we settle down to deal with what that offence has revealed in us. This is letting the cross work in us to bring death to the works of the flesh, the pride of life and other issues in our lives. Too many times we let the offence remain, and we get wounded and bitter instead of better.

SCRIPTURE READING: Hebrews 12:14-17
PERSONAL APPLICATION: It's time to take stock of your spiritual life. Is there any area where you have allowed offence to water down your commitment, your accountability, your quiet time? Offence is a rock that springs up and takes the form of many things. Ask God to reveal any area of offence in your heart. Receive the grace to kick out offence the next time it tries to jump at you.

THE SPIRIT OF EXCELLENCE

"And in all matters of wisdom and understanding about which the king examined them, he found them ten times better than all the magicians and astrologers who were in all his realm."
Daniel 1:20

People of excellence are people of quality! Quality reflects in the way you talk, the way you relate with and treat others, your appearance, the use of your time, the services you offer, the way you keep your home, your organisational abilities, and so forth. That is, though excellence starts from within, it is meant to be worked out! An example is the visit of the Queen of Sheba to Solomon in 1 Kings 10:4-5. Excellence attracts the right people to you. She came all the way from her country because of what she heard, which wasn't even half of what she saw when she came - imagine that! Excellence attracts means and wealth to you. She gave to Solomon one hundred and twenty talents of gold, spices and jewels, though Solomon was already a very wealthy king himself. Excellence attracts quality people and things to you, because quality attracts quality. People of excellence don't stay poor or unnoticed for long! "Do you see a man who excels in his work? He will stand before kings; he will not stand before unknown men" (Proverbs 22:29). Or, "Do you see any truly competent workers? They will serve kings rather than ordinary people" (*NLT*). Clearer still: "Observe people who are good at their work- skilled workers are always in demand and admired; they don't take a back seat to anyone" (*MSG*). However, it is the way you treat the people you meet on your way to the top, that will determine if you will ever get there, and how long you will stay there, if you do! You must learn to treat everyone right - rich or poor; that is the spirit of excellence. Don't always look for 'connections', rather look for relationships instead. Don't look for what you can get, always look for what you can contribute to add value to people and things. Don't use people, rather build and invest in people - that is the spirit of excellence.

SCRIPTURE READING: 1 Kings 10:1-10, Luke 2:42-52
PERSONAL APPLICATION: In all you do and say, remember that you represent Jesus here on earth. Luke 2:52 says that Jesus grew in wisdom, stature and favour with God and all the people. Ask God today to fill you with all of these things, so that when you encounter new opportunities or new relationships, you can radiate God's excellence.

THE CANDLE OF THE LORD

"For You will light my lamp; the Lord my God will enlighten my darkness."
Psalm 18:28

Darkness, in spiritual terms, is not an absence of natural light but an absence of understanding. Many grope in the dark today because there is no light inside them. Many judge the things of God by the natural circumstances of their lives, hence they miss God completely. The Psalmist cried out to God for his candle to be lit. Many of us need to cry out this prayer to God to light our candles again, so that in His light we shall see light. Little wonder that Paul the apostle prayed for the Ephesians that God would 'flood their hearts with light'. It is written in 1 Corinthians 4, that if our Gospel be hid, it is hid to them for whom the god of this world has blinded their minds. It seems to me that many believers' minds need to be delivered from blindness in many aspects of their walk with the Lord. Our spirits are the candle of the Lord. His light comes by the entrance of His Word, and our understanding gets flooded with light by the power of the Holy Spirit, who grants us the revelation of His Word. This light is the secret behind divine direction, understanding purpose and putting meaning into our life experiences. As we expose our hearts to the Word, the light gets brighter and brighter by the operation of the Spirit of truth at work inside us. When the Word and the Spirit operate together, light manifests. As we read in Genesis 1, "Let there be light" and there was. The Word was released and the Spirit was already brooding on the face of the deep. Light became a reality as God's Word interacted with His Spirit. The fact that the Word needs entrance suggests that it is not just hearing but receiving the Word that is necessary. What hinders the entrance of the Word? Strongholds! Strongholds are 'houses of thoughts' built over time in our minds that have the ability to hinder us from receiving truth. They form the preconceptions and proud arguments or reasoning that stand against proper acceptance and understanding of truth. It takes the weapons of warfare to pull down these strongholds and cast down imaginations. These weapons include the name of Jesus, the Word of the living God and the power of the Holy Spirit.

SCRIPTURE READING: Ephesians 1:15-20, 2 Corinthians 4:3-7
PERSONAL APPLICATION: When next you go to God for guidance or direction, ask Him to reveal the strongholds in your mind, that may stop you from accurately receiving from God. Then, pray Ephesians 1:15-20 over yourself to ask for light to shine in your heart. Expect every darkness in your life to be enlightened.

A SUPERNATURAL ENCOUNTER

"A renewal in which there is no [distinction between] Greek and Jew, circumcised and uncircumcised, [nor between nations whether] barbarian or Scythian, [nor in status whether] slave or free, but Christ is all, and in all [so believers are equal in Christ, without distinction]."
Colossians 3:11 AMP

When God created mankind, He blessed them, and commanded them to be fruitful and multiply and to have dominion. To bless means, to empower to prosper; "The blessing of the LORD makes one rich" (Proverbs 10:22). But when man sinned, they came under a curse; they came short of the glory of God. Man needed another encounter with God through Jesus Christ, the Saviour of mankind. He came to redeem man from the curse, so that they can come under the blessing again! Anyone who is in Christ has a new life and a new beginning; "old things have passed away; behold, all things have become new" (2 Corinthians 5:17). Christ gives you a new identity - a spiritual one; you are no longer being evaluated from a human point of view, i.e. by what you have or how you look. In Christ, all the walls of segregation - race, class and gender were broken down. "There is neither Jew nor Greek, there is neither slave nor free, there is neither male or female, for you are all one in Christ Jesus!" (Colossians 3:11). No more limitations: "I have strength for all things in Christ who empowers me (I am ready for anything and equal to anything though Him who infuses inner strength into me; I am sufficient in Christ's sufficiency)" (Philippians 4:13 *AMPC*).

SCRIPTURE READING: Genesis 1:26-28, Acts 9:3-9, 19-22
PERSONAL APPLICATION: What challenges are you currently facing? What opportunities are you yet to take on? Ask yourself 'what would I do differently if I knew I had all the strength and ability to do it?' Now tell yourself, 'I have all that I need for this task'. You can use Philippians 4:13 as your daily confession. God has given you all that you need to prosper, to overcome and to be successful.

OUR BLESSINGS, PROVISIONS AND BENEFITS IN CHRIST

"Bless the LORD, O my soul, And forget not all His benefits"
Psalm 103:2

Let us start with a general view of our many blessings and provisions. The book of Psalms captures many of such benefits that are available to us in God. We are the seed of Abraham so the blessings of Abraham belong to us. We have this access through our faith in the Lord Jesus Christ. We have a part to play and God plays His part as we play ours. "Bless *and* affectionately praise the LORD, O my soul, And all that is [deep] within me, *bless* His holy name. Bless *and* affectionately praise the LORD, O my soul, And do not forget any of His benefits; Who forgives all your sins, Who heals all your diseases; Who redeems your life from the pit, Who crowns you [lavishly] with lovingkindness and tender mercy; Who satisfies your years with good things, So that your youth is renewed like the [soaring] eagle" (Psalm 103:1-5 *AMPC*). Our benefits include forgiveness of sins, healing for all diseases, redemption from corruption and being crowned with loving kindness and tender mercy, amongst other things. Through our Lord Jesus and His sacrifice on the cross, we have access to these benefits. We however need to appropriate them into our lives and situations, otherwise they will not happen automatically. 'Not to forget' means 'to remember'. In the Holy Communion, we are told to eat the bread and drink the cup in remembrance of our Lord Jesus and His sacrifice for us. What are we to re-member? The benefits that are ours as a result of what He did for us. What we can remember we can re-live. As we remember these benefits we can experience them again and again.

SCRIPTURE READING: Deuteronomy 28:1-14, Matthew 26:26-28
PERSONAL APPLICATION: Do you know that participating in the Holy Communion is re-living what Jesus did for us on the cross? If you are trusting God for something, you can set aside some time everyday to partake of the bread and the cup. Use this as your point of faith to partake of every blessing you desire to experience.

QUIETING THE STORM

"He got up, rebuked the wind and said to the waves, "Quiet! Be still!" Then the wind died down and it was completely calm."
Mark 4:39 NIV

Today's study comes from Mark 4:35-41. Jesus said to His disciples, "Let us cross over to the other side". But as they were in the boat, with Jesus, a great storm arose... There are vital lessons to learn from this story:
1) Jesus had given His word to His disciples - "Let us cross over to the other side" before the storm arose. God's Word is always ahead of any situation and circumstances, that the enemy might throw against us. The fact that we have the Word will not necessarily stop storms from arising; but we must always hold fast to the Word in the midst of the storm. If He says, "let us cross over to the other side," you must hold on to that.
2) Jesus was in the boat with them, when the storm arose. Some people think life will be an easy ride because the Lord is with them; this story, as well as many others prove they couldn't be further from the truth! Jesus was at the wedding in Cana of Galilee, when they ran out of wine. In the story of the wise and foolish builders (Luke 6:46-49) Jesus didn't say, 'if' but 'when' the floods arose. It is whether your house has been built on the right foundation of the Word of God, or not, that matters. However, having Jesus in the same boat with you can make all the difference, when the storm arises.
3) Jesus rebuked the wind and spoke to the sea. He didn't speak about the sea, he spoke to it. Jesus said, "whoever says to this mountain..." (Mark 11:23). We often talk about the storm, the mountain and all the problems we are facing, but rarely talk to them. We can talk about them as much as we want, but nothing changes until we start speaking to them. The more we think and talk about our problems, the bigger they become! We must say exactly to the storm and the mountain, what we want to see happen.

SCRIPTURE READING: Isaiah 32:17-19, Mark 4:35-41
PERSONAL APPLICATION: It is often in difficult situations that we come face to face with how much we actually trust God and believe His Word. Remember, His Word says He will never leave you or forsake you... and that means under any circumstance whatsoever! What a promise!

A 'RUBBING OFF' ON US

"But we all, with unveiled face, beholding as in a mirror the glory of the Lord, are being transformed into the same image from glory to glory, just as by the Spirit of the Lord."
2 Corinthians 3:18

To rub off on, is for something to become part of someone because they've been in a place where it was present. It is usually said about a quality, skill, condition, or interest. People pick up the qualities or characteristics of others, because they have been with them and learned from them. "He who walks with wise men will be wise, but the companion of fools will be destroyed" (Proverbs 13:20). Elijah told Elisha that he could only receive the double portion of his spirit, if Elisha saw him when he was taken away (2 Kings 2:10)! Elisha knew that the secret was to stay in fellowship with Elijah, "as they both continued on and talked, that suddenly a chariot of fire appeared with horses of fire, and Elisha saw Elijah as he went up by a whirlwind into heaven..." The other sons of prophets acknowledged that the spirit of Elijah was now resting on Elisha! As we stay in fellowship with God, His qualities and characteristics will begin to rub off on us; and others around us will begin to see the difference in our lives. When Moses came down from the mountain, after spending forty days and nights in God's presence, his face shone; the Israelites saw the radiance of his face, and were afraid to come near him (Exodus 34:30). We shouldn't therefore remain the same as we stay in fellowship with God, but should expect to take on His attributes, qualities and characteristics. For example, 2 Corinthians 2:14 says, "Now thanks be to God who always leads us in triumph in Christ, and through us diffuses the fragrance of His knowledge in every place". As we spend time with God, His fragrance rubs off on us - we begin to 'smell' like God! The goal is to be used of Him to spread the knowledge of Christ everywhere, like a sweet perfume. We can spread His fragrance of love, joy, peace, confidence, forgiveness and healing wherever we go and to all the people we interact with.

SCRIPTURE READING: Exodus 34:29-35
PERSONAL APPLICATION: We should also expect other attributes and characteristics of God to rub off on us; like His holiness, His faithfulness, His integrity, and so forth (Deut. 32:3-4). There should be more of the fruit of the Spirit manifesting in our lives - love, joy, peace, longsuffering, kindness, goodness, faithfulness, gentleness, self-control (Gal. 5:22-23). Jesus said we can't bear fruit except we abide in Him, the vine; therefore, we will bear fruit if we abide in Him!

GIVING YOUR BEST

"For the Lord is the God of knowledge;
and by Him actions are weighed."
1 Samuel 2:3

When it comes to giving, our attitude must be right. It is usually said that your attitude will determine your altitude in life. David said in 2 Samuel 24:24 that he would not offer burnt offerings unto the Lord his God of that which costs him nothing. He valued God so much and measured worth to him that he would not offer anything for free - no wonder he had great favour with the Lord throughout his lifetime! In Deuteronomy 16:16 there is a command not to appear before the Lord empty-handed, which still applies to us today. We must honour the Lord with our giving and it must not be the things that are not precious in our sight. We must seek to always give our best in everything. Many times also, your giving shows the kind of person you are, because your attitude will say it all. In the case of Cain and Abel, (Genesis 4:1-14) God had respect for the offerings of Abel because his attitude was right. The Bible says in Genesis 4:4, "And Abel, he also brought of the firstlings of his flock and of the fat thereof." He gave the Lord his choicest offering. In verse 3, it says that Cain brought of the fruit of the ground an offering to the Lord. It wasn't a choice offering he gave to the Lord. The Bible says God is a God of knowledge by whom actions are weighed. He knows our hearts and sees the attitude and motive behind every giving. The Bible says God loves a cheerful giver.

SCRIPTURE READING: 2 Samuel 24:18-25, Acts 20:35
PERSONAL APPLICATION: It is important to know that all giving should be willingly and cheerfully done. Some giving is sacrificial and the Bible says that, "He who continually goes forth weeping, bearing seed for sowing, shall doubtless come again with rejoicing, bringing his sheaves with him" (Psalm 126:6). The giving of Christ was sacrificial because He was precious in God's sight. God did not give an angel, He gave His very best. This should be our attitude as well. We should always aim at giving our best.

BECOMING A BETTER PERSON

"I'm telling you to love your enemies. Let them bring out the best in you, not the worst."
Matthew 5:44 MSG

The Bible admonishes, "Don't let evil get the better of you" (Romans 12:21). Don't come 'down' to the level of your opponent; that is what happens when you get even with them, you really come down, not up! Instead of being like God, you become like them; you become the very thing you hate in them. For instance, if someone was nasty to you, you will have to be nasty too, to get back at them. Rather than allow evil get the best of you, you turn it around and get the best out of the situation. What can you learn from the evil being done to you, so you can become better and not bitter? "Dear brothers and sisters, when troubles come your way, consider it an opportunity for great joy. For you know that when your faith is tested, your endurance has a chance to grow. So let it grow, for when your endurance is fully developed, you will be perfect and complete, needing nothing" (James 1:2-4). That is, let your trials work for you. Our light and momentary afflictions are nothing, compared to the glory that will be revealed in us (2 Corinthians 4:17-18). The wrong you suffer can bring the best out of you, "if the rulers of this age had known the wisdom of God, they would not have crucified the Lord of glory" (1 Corinthians 2:7-8).

SCRIPTURE READING: Matthew 5:43-48
PERSONAL APPLICATION: Pray for those who hurt you. It is easier to love someone who has hurt you if you are willing to pray for them. When you pray, God will open your heart to see them as He sees them, rather than how you might see them. Through prayer, God is able to soften your heart, enabling you to love them no matter what they have done, no matter how they have treated you, no matter how they have insulted you. His grace is sufficient.

THE POWER OF PURPOSE

"There is a time for everything,
and a season for every activity under the heavens"
Ecclesiastes 3:1 NIV

God is revealing His purpose to us in Christ. Everything God does has a purpose. The prophetic teachings coming into the Body of Christ are for a purpose. The purpose of all these teachings is Christlikeness. The changes that Moses, Joseph and others went through, before they came to the fulfilment of purpose, can be likened to the changes that produce Christlikeness in us. How do you relate with the experiences in your life? Your attitude matters a lot. How much of Christ is reflected in you? Like Esther, can you also say, "if I perish, I perish"? (Esther 4:16). Like Ruth, can you forsake all and follow after covenant love? We need a sense of purpose. As we act on God's Word let us stand true to His Word and character. Read Mathew 5 and see the beatitudes. No matter what we are going through, if we would pray in the Spirit, speak God's Word, keep our hearts tender before God and walk in love, God will work out His purpose in our lives.

SCRIPTURE READING: Matthew 5:1-16
PERSONAL APPLICATION: Do you know what God's primary purpose for your life is? If your answer is no, spend time in prayer and in the Word of God to seek it out. "It is the glory of God to conceal a matter; but the glory of kings is to search out a matter" (Proverbs 25:2).

HANDLING FINANCIAL CRISIS

"Cast your burden on the Lord,
And He shall sustain you;
He shall never permit the righteous to be moved."
Psalm 55:22

We must settle it in our hearts that no matter what the cause of the famine or financial crisis is, God's will is for His people to be sustained in it. "Behold, the eye of the LORD is on those who fear Him, On those who hope in His mercy, To deliver their soul from death, And to keep them alive in famine" (Psalm 33:18-19). To sustain means: to maintain, nourish, provide food, to supply the means necessary for living, etc. This was the same word used by Joseph, when he promised his brothers that he would provide for them and their young ones (Genesis 50:10). God promised to make a way in the wilderness, and rivers in the desert (Isaiah 43:19). With every trial, God will always make a way of escape for His people. God doesn't want His people to suffer with the world. After Elijah declared that there was going to be a famine as a result of God's judgment, he was told to go to brook Cherith, where he was fed (1 Kings 17:2-3). And even when the brook dried up, Elijah was sent to Zarephath to be sustained by a widow. Elijah, the widow and her household were sustained throughout the famine - the bin of flour was not used up nor did the jar of oil run dry until the famine was over! In times of financial crisis or recession, we are not meant to panic like the people of the world. Jesus said men's hearts will fail them from fear and expectation of those things which are coming on the earth (Luke 21:26). God does not want us to be moved by the things happening around us. He said He will shake the heavens and the earth, indicating the removal of things that can be shaken, so that the things which cannot be shaken (i.e. the Kingdom of God) may remain (Hebrews 12:26-29). Every man-made thing, helpful as it may be while it lasts, will be shaken; only the Kingdom of God, and everything established on it will remain unshaken. Our faith should, therefore, not rest on the wisdom of men but on the power of God (1 Corinthians 2:5)!

SCRIPTURE READING: 1 Kings 17:2-15
PERSONAL APPLICATION: God is our source. It is He that gives us the power to get wealth. Look upon your income as being from the Lord; this makes it much easier to navigate through economic downturns and tough financial situations.

WAITING ON THE LORD

"Wait on the Lord; be of good courage, and He shall strengthen your heart; Wait, I say, on the Lord!"
Psalm 27:14

To wait means to look for, expect, hope, waiting hopefully. This means that you do not worship, study, pray and meditate just to carry out your Christian duty. You do these things to look, expect and hope for more of God in your life. It takes hunger to do so. That is how spiritual hunger is cultivated. The fullness of life is available in the presence of God. Remember you are a partaker of his divine nature (2 Peter 1:3 -4). To partake means, 'to take portions of'. Whenever we think of our giving to God, it has become normal to give God little things. We do this to our own fulfilment in life. When we think of our usual offerings, we give God little; is it a wonder we do not really get satisfied? It is time to be bountiful towards God. He that soweth sparingly reaps sparingly. God will give Himself to anyone who gives himself to Him. It is time to make meaningful progress with God. If God is God, let us serve Him as God fully. He deserves all our affection and attention. Why don't you tithe your 24 hours and give 2.4 hours of your sleep and leisure time to God, to wait on Him and see what remarkable progress He will bring into your life, family, and future?

SCRIPTURE READING: 2 Peter 1:3-4, Isaiah 40:31
PERSONAL APPLICATION: Are you feeling tired? Weary perhaps? God's promise to those that wait on Him is that He will renew their strength. Are you in a 'waiting season'? Be encouraged, God is always on time!

EXPOSING THE WORKS OF DARKNESS

"Be sober, be vigilant; because your adversary the devil walks about like a roaring lion, seeking whom he may devour."
1 Peter 5:8

In 1 Peter 5:8, Peter admonishes us to be sober and vigilant. Beloved, you cannot afford to be careless in any area of your life. It is like leaving your front door wide open whilst living in a rough neighbourhood! Don't give Satan room in your thought life, in your utterances, in your emotions, in your marriage and so forth. Keep him out by being sober and vigilant. Satan is the ruler of darkness, he loves secrecy, that is his domain. Expose lust, pride, rebellion, sexual immorality, sin and so on. Bring them out in the open. It is whatever he has in you that he will place a demand upon, either now or in the future! Satan won't use what is outside you to get you, he'll use what is inside of you. So expose it, or it will explode one day on your inside like a time bomb that's been ticking away unnoticed. The truth is that whenever we are actually ready to deal with issues in our lives, then we will be ready to expose them. When you are truly ready to be delivered from the sinful habit of addiction, bring it out into the light. That breaks Satan's control over you. If we are going to be free and not come under bondage to Satan and sin, we must expose the unfruitful works of darkness in our lives.

SCRIPTURE READING: 1 John 1:5-10
PERSONAL APPLICATION: Let us be quick to acknowledge any sin in our lives, to expose it before God, repenting of it, and asking Him for and receiving His forgiveness. God is faithful to forgive.

INTIMACY WITH GOD

"I will instruct you and teach you in the way you should go;
I will counsel you with my loving eye on you."
Psalm 32:8

Intimacy implies familiarity, closeness, understanding, confidence and relationship. To cultivate intimacy means acceptance for, measuring worth to, and getting to recognise fine and delicate details about the one you are getting intimate with. Intimacy is a function of quality time spent together. This requires focus and intensity. Intimacy is to be enjoyed, not endured. It can only happen when love is flowing out of a sense of deep appreciation, honour and understanding. When we direct our hearts' efforts towards God to cultivate intimacy with Him, we begin to see the deadness of religion without a personal relationship with God through the finished work of Calvary. It is not enough to have a salvation experience; it must lead us to pursue a meaningful and personal relationship with God through Christ. To have His presence, His power and see His purposes fulfilled we need to be intimate with Him. "The secret of the Lord is with those who fear Him; and He will show them His covenant" (Psalm 25:14). "I will instruct you and teach you in the way which you shall go: I will guide you with my eye" (Psalm 32:8). To be guided with the eye implies a degree of intimacy to recognise any changes in the eye. This intimacy will help us navigate the way into God's purpose for us. God Himself wants us to draw closer to Him and to know the deep things in His heart for us, for His Kingdom and for Himself (James 4:6-10). God and His Word are one (John 1:1-3). The Word becomes our access to intimate knowledge of God. Whenever the Word is approached correctly, you can count on the Holy Spirit to help and guide you into intimacy with God. To be close to God must become a passion in our hearts for it to come to pass. It will take a disciplined life that sets intimacy with God as a goal.

SCRIPTURE READING: Psalm 25:4-14
PERSONAL APPLICATION: One sure way of going deeper into intimacy with God is to make personal worship a daily priority. Express affection to your Saviour. Give admiration and love to your heavenly Father. Fall on your knees and raise your hands in praise!

AGREEING WITH GOD

"My God, I have come to do what you want.
Your law is in my heart."
Psalm 40:8 NIV

Mary submitted to God's plan for her life, even at the risk of her marriage to Joseph and even her own life - she could have been stoned to death, according to the law of Moses, for being found pregnant without being married! That level of submission she demonstrated brought her into a state of blessedness or happiness; "Blessed are you among women..." (.Luke 1:42). "Blessed (Happy, to be envied) is she who believed for there will be a fulfilment of those things which were told her from the Lord." And Mary said, "For behold, from now on all generations [of all ages] will call me blessed and declare me happy and to be envied!" (See Luke 1:45, 48 *AMPC*).

The secret to happiness in life is found in saying 'yes' to God. The Bible says He is the Potter and we are the clay, and "woe to him who strives with his maker" (Isaiah 45:9). It is woeful indeed, because it can only lead to a lifetime of misery, pain, unfulfillment and frustration. God sent Jonah to Nineveh, "But Jonah got up and went in the opposite direction to get away from the Lord" (Jonah 1:3 *NLT*). He boarded a ship leaving for Tarshish, but as they sailed, the Lord hurled a powerful wind over the sea, causing a violent storm that threatened to break the ship apart. Fearing for their lives, the desperate sailors shouted to their gods for help and threw the cargo overboard to lighten the ship. They later found out who the cause of all their woes was; so they reluctantly agreed to throw Jonah into the sea, and there was calm. Jonah ended up in the belly of a fish; and when he repented, he got out and went in the right direction. "Submit to God, and you will have peace; then things will go well for you. Listen to His instructions, and store them in your heart. If you return to the Almighty, you will be restored – so clean up your life" (Job 22:22-23 *NLT*).

SCRIPTURE READING: Jonah 1 and 2

PERSONAL APPLICATION: God will not ask anything of us that we are not capable of doing. But how will He ask us? It may be a gentle stirring of the soul, a pang of conscience, or an unexplained feeling of elation. If today you hear his voice, have the confidence to say "YES".

THE NEW CREATION

"Therefore if any man be in Christ, he is a new creature: old things are passed away; behold, all things are become new."
2 Corinthians 5:17 KJV

The born-again man has a new and old nature living in him. He needs to know how to put one to death and let one come alive in him. The cross is the instrument of death for the old nature and faith in Christ is the key to life for the new nature. Christ is to be formed in us through the process of the cross and the application of in-Christ truths in our lives. We must realise the power of the new creation and death that exists in the old creation. Sin has wrecked the old through selfishness and disobedience, but righteousness has been wrought through selflessness and obedience of Christ. We must begin to reckon ourselves dead to sin and alive unto God. As we reckon ourselves dead, the Holy Spirit will make it a reality in our lives. We need to understand the new creation. It is by faith in Christ and it involves the suffering of the flesh, denying it and subjecting it to the reality of the Word. Whatever the old creation lost, the new regained it better than what was lost (see Romans 4-6). Righteousness is more powerful than sin; faith more than fear; love more than hate, etc. Jesus Christ is the example of the new. He was totally subject to God, lived above sin, above Satan and the world. He is the perfect example of the new creation. If you are born again He is your pattern to follow.

SCRIPTURE READING: Romans 6:1-14
PERSONAL APPLICATION: As a new creation you are no longer a slave to sin, as you formerly were. You have the choice to either "let sin reign" or to count yourself "dead to sin". You have been given the power to choose the latter!

CULTIVATING THE RIGHT HABITS

"when I call to remembrance the genuine faith that is in you, which dwelt first in your grandmother Lois and your mother Eunice, and I am persuaded is in you also."
2 Timothy 1:5

"Even a child is known by his doings..." (Proverbs 20:11). "Train up a child in the way he should go, and when he is old, he will not depart from it" (Proverbs 22:6). Start cultivating the right habits now - by thinking the right thoughts, speaking the right words and doing the right things; and like it's been said, your habits will take you into your future. Determine the kind of future you want now, and start working your way towards it. Don't wait till you are older, or richer, or bigger, or better; start now! You can determine and generate your own climate. Even in the wilderness, the Israelites carried their own climate; they had a pillar of cloud by day - to protect them from the scorching desert sun, and the pillar of fire by night - to keep them warm. You can be an oasis in the desert. You are in the world but not of the world. You can be bigger on your inside than your outside. Don't let your environment or circumstances condition you or shape you, or determine what you do. Give your best all the time. If you develop yourself, and grow bigger on your inside, it is either your environment changes or you are taken out to a more progressive place. "You can't keep a man from rising, who has enough yeast in him to rise."

SCRIPTURE READING: Philippians 4:8-9, Proverbs 22:29
PERSONAL APPLICATION: Our thoughts form the basis for, and are largely revealed in our words and actions. Learn to bring your thought life into submission to God's Word by training yourself to think biblically about every aspect of your life.

THE REVELATION OF PURPOSE

"Where there is no revelation, people cast off restraint; but blessed is the one who heeds wisdom's instruction."
Proverbs 29:18 NIV

God is a God of purpose. He does nothing without purpose in mind. Purpose is the reason for being; it is the original intent in the heart of the manufacturer, in this case in the heart of the Creator. Our time on earth has been given to us to fulfil the Creator's purpose. Vision is the revelation of purpose. When vision is revealed it gives direction and challenges purposeful living. The prophetic revelation of God's purpose is one of the greatest stabilizers in a human life. No more strife or competition to out-smart another person, because you are as unique as God's vision for you. Nobody has your peculiar flavour; the combination of your experience, exposure and gifting cannot be matched anywhere else. Vision helps you to take your place in God. Your pursuit of vision is your pursuit of meaning in life. Your vision from God is to be accomplished in the time frame God has allocated. God's vision for your life will preserve you. One cannot kill a visionary who is on course with God's vision for their life. You are protected within God's vision that you are pursuing. The vision will keep you through all the stages of development. As you go through process the vision matures in you. Do not allow God's vision for your life to become polluted with rivalry, competitive jealousy or carnal desires of the flesh. The vision will cause you to grow as it grows in you. You will be bigger than unforgiveness and bitterness. It will also deliver you from insecurity and the things that plague people with small minds. The vision will give you what it takes to help the vision of others. It will deliver to you authority in life after you have passed the tests and wilderness experience.

SCRIPTURE READING: Jeremiah 29:11-13
PERSONAL APPLICATION: The easiest way to discover the purpose of an invention is to ask the creator of it. The same is true for discovering your life's purpose; ask God!

BELIEVING GOD'S WORD

"Jesus said to him, 'If you can believe, all things are possible to him who believes.' Immediately the father of the child cried out and said with tears, 'Lord, I believe; help my unbelief!'
Mark 9:23-24

Ordinarily, to believe simply means 'to accept as true or conveying truth'. God told Abraham that his descendants would be innumerable, when as yet he had no child; and he believed God. To believe God means to accept as true whatever He says to you or about you, and to be persuaded that God's Word is true. It also means to agree with God and His Word. When Mary was told by angel Gabriel that she was going to be the mother of the Lord, she answered the angel, "Behold the maidservant of the Lord! Let it be to me according to your word" (Luke 1:38). "Stop quarrelling with God! If you agree with Him, you will have peace at last and all will go well for you" (Job 22:21 *NLT*). When you believe what God says, His power will be released to produce results in your life; "Blessed is she who believed, for there will be a fulfilment of those things which were told her" (Luke 1:45). Jesus would ask someone in need of a miracle, "Do you believe I am able to do this?" (Matthew 9:28). Jairus came to ask Jesus to come heal his sick daughter, but he got a report that his daughter was already dead. Jesus turned around and said to him, "Don't be afraid, only believe" (Mark 5:36). Jesus told the father of the epileptic, "If you can believe, all things are possible to him who believes" (Mark 9:23). The same power that raised Christ from the dead and sat Him at God's right hand, is also at work towards those who believe (Ephesians 1:19-20).

SCRIPTURE READING: Galatians 3:5-9
PERSONAL APPLICATION: Can you be persuaded that God's Word is true, even when life's circumstances are telling you the complete opposite? Keep standing on the Word of God, keep believing Him no matter what. Do not withdraw your faith. There will be a fulfilment of all He has promised.

UNDERSTANDING THE WILL OF GOD

"'My food,' said Jesus, 'is to do the will of Him who sent Me and to finish His work.'"
John 4:34 NIV

God's will has to do with His plans and purpose on earth. It is dynamic in character, based on principles, and gives God the liberty to do what He wants to do in our lives. The will of God is not passive or static. It demands our engagement, as we participate with God. Many are waiting passively for God's will to happen. As a result, the wait is usually endless. All His plans have processes involved. The individual will be processed to come into harmony with God's perspectives before the expression of the will can commence. Our lack of understanding of the process is what leads to frustration. When we are going through the process, we are participating in His will.

The principles involved in process are as follows: we come to a place where it is all about Him in us. The cross takes its role in us as we put the flesh under, pride is confronted and dealt with and any other thing that may seek to take credit for what He is doing in us will go. Secondly, the gifts in us come from Him and He takes the credit as we give Him the liberty to do as He wills in and through us. To understand this we need to renew our minds (Romans 12:2) and we also need to prove His will in our lives. As we internalize truth, we confront our inner attitudes and yield to truth so our bodies indeed become the temple of our God just like the body of Jesus. Our will comes into alignment with His. Our will is to do His will. When God is at liberty to express Himself in us, we will be at liberty to be all He wants us to be. In Matthew 11:28-30, we see that God's yoke looks like bondage but gives great freedom. Satan's yoke looks like freedom but brings great bondage.

SCRIPTURE READING: Ephesians 5:15-17, Colossians 4:5

PERSONAL APPLICATION: Case Study: Read the story of Joseph (Genesis chapters 37-45:8) to see the process he had to go through in order to fulfil the will of God. Oftentimes, the path and process God would have us take don't line up with our expectations and can cause confusion and uncertainty. It is in those times we need to seek Him and gain assurance from Him that we are still in the centre of His will.

TWO ARE BETTER THAN ONE

"Two are better than one, because they have a good reward for their labour..."
Ecclesiastes 4:9

People who make a difference are never an island to themselves. They always recognise the role and the place of others. They work with others to achieve a common goal. Somebody said, a lot more will be done if nobody cares who gets the credit! Esther knew she couldn't act alone, so she asked Mordecai and all the Jews in Shushan to pray and fast for her; and she and her maids also fasted, before she went in to see the king (Esther 4:16). Daniel did not act alone, he acted with his three friends in his decision not to defile himself with the king's meat (Daniel 1:11-15). Also when he needed to know the interpretation of the king's dream he went to his friends and they all prayed together. God answered their prayer by revealing the dream and its interpretation to Daniel. When the king promoted Daniel he also petitioned the king to promote his friends (Daniel 2:17-19). The women who struggled for women's suffrages in Great Britain and the United States worked in consonance. Sylvia Parkhurst (1911) said, "All over America, the suffragists declare that they gained hope and inspiration from our own Great British Movement. In the early day of our long struggle, it was we who drew our inspiration from them. Our movements act and react on each other." In Great Britain, the women won the right to vote in 1918, and their counterpart in the U.S. won theirs in 1920. Those who make a difference always desire and aim for things that are bigger than them and so could never be accomplished in their strength alone. They always recognise and acknowledge their need for others. "Two are better than one, Because they have a good reward for their labour. For if they fall, one will lift up his companion. But woe to him who is alone when he falls, For he has no one to help him up." (Ecclesiastes 4:9-10).

SCRIPTURE READING: Ecclesiastes 4:9-12, Acts 2:42-47
PERSONAL APPLICATION: Go to God in prayer and ask Him to reveal the relationships and people He has placed around you. God can reveal the purpose and role that you play—and others play in this season of life. As we make ourselves available to God, He can use us and those around us to fulfil His plans.

FRUITFULNESS: A HEAVENLY PERSPECTIVE

"But while men slept, his enemy came and sowed tares among the wheat and went his way."
Matthew 13:25

The parable of the sower in Matthew 13 shows how the seed is the Word. The explanation makes it plain that God intends for His seed to be sown in our hearts and the different conditions of the heart also help us recognize the reason for a lack of harvest in our lives. We want the harvest but are we planting the seeds? Are we treating our hearts with the right ingredients to give proper conditions for the seed to grow? The cares, lusts for other things and the deceitfulness of riches, enter to choke the reproductive systems of our hearts and we bear no fruit at all. Further on in Matthew 13 is another parable that sheds more light on Kingdom fruitfulness. From verses 24-43, we read about the wheat and the tares and the enemy planting tares while men slept. The explanation here says the good seeds are the sons of the Kingdom. How can this be? The sons of the Kingdom are the ones in whom the seed (the Word) has become flesh, as in Jesus, and they can carry out the work of the Kingdom in the face of opposition and contradictions of men. It boils down to how much we let Christ be formed in us: this is the surest way to see 100-fold fruitfulness in our lives. It is time to set our hearts on much fruit to glorify the Father and reflect the Son on earth.

SCRIPTURE READING: 2 Peter 1:1-10, Matthew 13:1-43
PERSONAL APPLICATION: Choose to be fruitful in every area of your life. Declare war on barrenness. See 2 Peter 1:2-8 and learn what to do practically to avoid unfruitfulness. It is our responsibility, as we yield to and are built up in Christ, to ensure fruitfulness in our lives.

UNFAILING, UNCONDITIONAL LOVE

*"And this hope will not lead to disappointment.
For we know how dearly God loves us, because he has given us
the Holy Spirit to fill our hearts with his love."
Romans 5:5 NLT*

Now hope does not disappoint, because the love of God has been poured out in our hearts by the Holy Spirit who was given to us (Romans 5:5). God's love is unfailing; it never ends. God's love is unconditional; it's not based on our own goodness, but on His! We can always count on His goodness; the psalmist said, "Surely goodness and mercy shall follow me all the days of my life" (Psalm 23:6). Another word for love is mercy or compassion. Blind Bartimaeus cried out, asking Jesus to have mercy on him and Jesus healed him of his blindness (Mark 10:46-47). People often come to God based on their own goodness or some come asking for 'justice' or their 'rights', when they should be asking for mercy! If God would mark iniquity, the Bible says nobody will stand; but thank God mercy triumphs over judgment. God gave Jesus to the world- not because we deserve Him but because He loved the world (John 3:16). We are more than conquerors, through Him who loved us (Romans 8:37). It is through His mercies we are not consumed, because His compassions don't fail (Lamentations 3:22). The multitudes who had come against Judah were all defeated as the singers began to sing and to praise saying: "Praise the Lord, For His mercy endures forever" (2 Chronicles 20:21-22). Judah spent three days gathering the spoil because there was so much; there was an abundance of valuables and precious jewellery, more than they could carry away! We are told to come boldly to the throne of grace, expecting to obtain mercy and find grace to help in time of need (Hebrews 4:16).

SCRIPTURE READING: Ephesians 3:14-21
PERSONAL APPLICATION: How wonderful to know that God's love for us is not based on our own goodness! Don't let anything keep or separate you from God. Don't let any lie from hell, any fear, condemnation or shame keep you from God. Come boldly to the wonderful throne of grace today and obtain grace and mercy to help in times of need.

EXPOSE THE MOTIVE

"The heart is deceitful above all things,
And desperately wicked; Who can know it?
I, the Lord, search the heart, I test the mind,
Even to give every man according to his ways,
According to the fruit of his doings."
Jeremiah 17:9-10

Our motives and focus will either undermine or undergird our activities of faith and our experience of the divine results we expect. Our experience and activities as Christians are usually as real or as meaningless spiritually as much as our motive and focus permit them to be. Some things are not acceptable to God simply because the motive of the doer is not the right one. Ananias and Sapphira felt they were doing what was expected of them, or rather what would please God. Their motive was not right. Wrong motives usually lead to wrong actions and wrong results follow. Now giving was right but the wrong motive undermined their giving and it led to their death. Read Acts 5. An activity in itself may be right but your motive will make it wrong before God. He sees the motive of your heart and rewards accordingly. What is the right motive for everything you do in God?

SCRIPTURE READING: Acts 5:1-11, Jeremiah 17:5-10
PERSONAL APPLICATION: Spend some time examining your heart. What are the motives behind your actions? We've learnt today that an action may be 'right', but the motive behind the action makes it wrong. Ask God to purify your heart and motives (even the hidden motives of the heart) so that everything you do will be an acceptable offering, pleasing before the Lord.

THE SECRET OF INCREASE

"We are confident that you are meant for better things, things that come with salvation."
Hebrews 6:9 NLT

Don't despise what you have, it may look small, but it has great potential. Esau despised his birthright and traded it for some bread and lentil stew (Genesis 25:32). The disciples didn't think the five loaves of bread and two fish were anything to be reckoned with, when talking about feeding five thousand men; but Jesus thought differently, because He understood the seed principle. The Lord asked Moses, "What is that in your hand?" (Exodus 4:2). God will use what you have to get what you need. Elisha asked the widow, "What shall I do for you? Tell me, what do you have in the house?" (2 Kings 4:2). So whenever there is a need in your life, don't look outside, but look inwards. Don't worry about what you don't have, but look closely at what you have - that is where the answer is. Look at the qualification you've got; the skills you've acquired - formally and informally; your past experiences - the good and the bad; your natural talents and abilities, and even your disabilities, etc. The key to your breakthrough is hidden somewhere between those things. Contentment looks inwards, it says, "I've got something". But covetousness always looks outward, it says, "If only I had or could have". Be thankful for what you have - it is a major key to increase.

SCRIPTURE READING: 2 Kings 4:1-17
PERSONAL APPLICATION: Your attitude determines your altitude in life; embrace an attitude of gratitude towards what you've got. Acknowledge the good things in you - "the sharing of your faith may become effective by the acknowledgment of every good thing which is in you in Christ Jesus" (Philemon 1:6). You've got good things going on for you in Christ Jesus.

REVEALING OUR PROGRAMMING

"Do not conform to the pattern of this world, but be transformed by the renewing of your mind. Then you will be able to test and approve what God's will is—his good, pleasing and perfect will."
Romans 12:2 NIV

Our lives are greatly determined by our decisions and our decisions are based on the accuracy of knowledge we have. No wonder the same Apostle had earlier said, "I wish above all things that you prosper and be in health even as your soul prospers" (3 John 2). Soul prosperity leads to material prosperity and health. The soul of a human being comprises the mind, will and emotions. All these are affected by the programming we have all received through our nature, nurture and culture. For many, the process begins when we can have the courage to ask why we think, say and do the things we do, the way we think, say and do them. The answers to these questions will reveal the internal programming at work in us. When God's reality (truth) is not in us then lies have found their way into us. Satan's greatest access into the human race is by injecting thoughts into the mind. The grafting of truth into us as we humbly receive the truth is what will save our souls from all the junk we have imbibed into our minds, emotions and wills. "So get rid of all uncleanness and the rampant outgrowth of wickedness, and in a humble (gentle, modest) spirit receive and welcome the Word which implanted and rooted [in your hearts] contains the power to save your souls" (James 1:21 *AMPC*).

SCRIPTURE READING: Matthew 15:1-20
PERSONAL APPLICATION: Take time to pause and reflect on your motives, focus and intentions. They fuel what you say and do. In order for you not to be defiled, as Matthew 15:1-20 highlights, you must deal with the things inside you so that they don't come out and defile you.

WASTE NOT, WANT NOT

"And if one member suffers, all the members suffer with it;
or if one member is honoured, all the members rejoice with it."
1 Corinthians 12:26

In Acts 4:34-35, no one lacked in the church because those who had possessions sold them and the proceeds were distributed by the apostles to each one as anyone had need. When famine hit the world, and there was food in Egypt as a result of Joseph's influence, Joseph sent for his father and his brothers and their families. He said to his brothers, "God sent me before you to preserve a posterity for you in the earth, and to save your lives by a great deliverance" (Genesis 45:7). God arranged the Body of Christ in a way that there should be no lack in the Body! If we would follow that plan of wealth distribution, there would not be any lack anywhere! If we understood this principle, we wouldn't indulge in wastage; but those who had excess would instead send it to where there was need. After the miracle of feeding five thousand men, Jesus commanded His disciples to gather up the remaining food, "so that nothing is lost" (John 6:12). As good stewards, we must learn to manage properly the resources God has committed to us; the Bible says, it is required of a steward to be faithful. Wastage is a revelation of poor management and a mark of unfaithfulness; which always eventually leads to poverty.

SCRIPTURE READING: John 6:1-14
PERSONAL APPLICATION: Ask God today to help you place value on what He has already given you. We take care of the things we value and are in a better place to give to those in need. God rewards faithfulness, so when you are faithful in little, He will multiply your resources.

LOVE, LOVE, LOVE

"Though I speak with the tongues of men and of angels, but have not love, I have become sounding brass or a clanging cymbal."
1 Corinthians 13:1

The first and second commandments of God are to love the Lord our God with all our heart and to love others too! Jesus says, "If you love me, keep My commandments." He also says in John 15:10, "If you keep my commands, you will abide in My love as I have kept my Father's commands and abide in His love." If you love Him, you will keep His commands and if you do, you will abide in His love. Any attempt at loving others without first loving God will amount to selfish love (1 Corinthians 13) The love for God should be your true motive to love others. Without love everything loses its benefit and validity before God and His Kingdom. Others may seem to benefit from it but God's Word declares it is nothing. No impact spiritually, no rewards from heaven, will rest on such activities even if others celebrate you for doing them. It is lacking in the essential ingredient of love for God.

SCRIPTURE READING: 1 Corinthians 13:1-13
PERSONAL APPLICATION: You cannot give what you do not have. The more time you spend with God and His Word, the more of His love you have to give to others. Ask God to purify your motives today so that everything you do is born out of love. Read 1 Corinthians 13 in *The Message Bible*, and use it to make daily confessions.

DO SOMETHING POSITIVE

"And let us not grow weary while doing good, for in due season we shall reap if we do not lose heart."
Galatians 6:9

A lot of people blame others for the negative outcome of their lives, whereas, they themselves are to be blamed! You are ultimately responsible for your own actions. Jesus said that a good man out of the good treasure of his heart brings forth good things; so stop allowing what people have done to you to determine the outcome of your life. Joseph was a great example, he was hated by his brothers; he went from the pit to Potiphar's house (as a slave), and to the prison (for saying no to Potiphar's wife). Yet, we never heard him once blame his brothers or Potiphar's wife; instead, he maintained fellowship with God and used every circumstance he found himself in as an opportunity to make his own contribution to the lives of others. Joseph also obviously used every opportunity to develop himself in his skills and gifts, so that when Pharaoh sent for him, he was ready for the palace. None of the evil done to him was strong enough to stop him; Joseph conquered evil with good! It is therefore not enough not to sow bad seeds in retaliation, you must also make sure you are sowing the right seeds, so you can have a harvest to look forward to. Don't be passive, but be active; don't be too preoccupied with trying to defend or protect yourself or your position; you must step out to make some positive deposits. Do the exact opposite of what your flesh wants to do to the one who has wronged you. We must always conquer evil by doing good, rather than allow evil to get the best of us.

SCRIPTURE READING: Galatians 6:8-10, Matthew 12:35
PERSONAL APPLICATION: Today, take stock of your current actions; are they good seeds? Are they motivated by love? No matter what comes your way, you are responsible for how you respond. Spend time asking God to give you the strength and willingness to sow the right seeds.

MOTIVES AND FOCUS

"looking unto Jesus, the author and finisher of our faith, who for the joy that was set before Him endured the cross, despising the shame, and has sat down at the right hand of the throne of God."
Hebrews 12:2

In looking to Jesus, we receive strength as we take on His attributes, motives and focus. It was His love for the Father that kept Him on the cross and His focus was pleasing the Father and not Himself. Go and do likewise. May the Lord grant us all understanding. He esteemed His love for God above the shame He faced and His desire to please God above the pain He went through. What do we esteem today as valuable? Our motive and focus will determine our values today. If you are selfish your values will reflect it. The reason why many suffer failure is attributable to wrong or selfish motives and wrong focus in their Christian service. Let your motive be love for God and then for His people. Let your focus be Christ and His pattern of the Cross. You will not fail but be fulfilled in life. In Jesus' Name!

SCRIPTURE READING: Hebrews 12:1-3
PERSONAL APPLICATION: Recognise the things that may distract or cause you to turn your focus away from Jesus. Spend time bringing these things to God in prayer, and allow Him to deal with your motives. Ask God to refine your values, focus and motives so that no matter what comes your way, He remains your focus.

TURN TO GOD

"When hard pressed, I cried to the LORD;
He brought me into a spacious place."
Psalm 118:5 NIV

"And let the peace (soul harmony which comes) from Christ rule (act as umpire continually) in your hearts [deciding and settling with finality all questions that arise in your minds, in that peaceful state] to which as [members of Christ's] one body you were also called [to live]. And be thankful (appreciative), [giving praise to God always]" (Colossians 3:15 *AMPC*). You're not in a good position to make the right decisions when you are full of worries, fears and anxieties. The best time to hear from God is surely not when you are in such a state; you would most likely hear from your pain and distress. After Elijah's victory on mount Carmel, he soon slumped into a state of discouragement and despair because Jezebel was now after his life. He went out to hear from God, and God was not in the strong wind that passed, nor was He in the earthquake and the fire; but He was in a still small voice (1 Kings 19:11-12). The Lord, as our shepherd, leads us beside the still and restful waters (see Psalm 23:2). After the Amalekites had raided David and his men, taking their families and possessions; David was greatly distressed, because the people were so grieved that they spoke of stoning him. David desperately needed to hear from God, to know the way forward. But he couldn't accurately hear from God in his distress, so he first encouraged himself in the Lord, and then inquired of the Lord. Encouraging himself in the Lord, took David out of the place of distress and brought him into a place of peace - where he could hear from God! "Therefore with joy you will draw water from the wells of salvation" (Isaiah 12:3).

SCRIPTURE READING: 1 Kings 19:11-12
PERSONAL APPLICATION: Like David, you can encourage yourself in God. No matter what you are going through, there are enough of God's written promises to encourage you and silence your fears. God is in the still, small voice; as you turn to Him today, let go of all anxieties, fears and doubts, and get ready to hear from Him.

A LIFE OF OBEDIENCE

"His mother said to the servants, 'Do whatever he tells you.'"
John 2:5 NIV

Obedience to God is the bedrock of progress in God. There are reasons why many vacillate in their obedience to God. One such reason is the lack of a proper foundation in their life in Christ. To lay a right foundation is to have a heart commitment to revealed truth. Too many give only a mental assent to truth without a heart process. A heart commitment involves a process wherein the true state of your heart is made to have an encounter with the reality of God's Word. If you harbour strife, pride, fears and unbelief in your heart, it will hinder the process that God's Word will minister in your heart. You cannot deal with whatever you do not confront in your heart. What you do not deal with will hinder the proper placement of the seed of God's Word in your heart and any matter not dealt with will deal with you. The power of the Kingdom of God is available to those who allow His Kingdom to be formed in their heart. Real spiritual work is a heart work. Our heart attitude should be humble, meek and lowly. It is not what is in our heads that changes us or produces real power, it is what is in our hearts that we act on that makes the difference. What is your heart attitude after a major victory or increased knowledge? Are you full of yourself? Full of your knowledge or of your opinion? We must be meek, humble and strong. With this in place, entering a life of obeying the proceeding Word of God will not be a problem. A sensitive, prayerful heart will pick up the proceeding Word from God.

SCRIPTURE READING: 1 Samuel 15:22-23

PERSONAL APPLICATION: 1 Samuel 15:22-23 tells us that to obey is better than sacrifice. However, why is it sometimes hard to obey? How can we come to that place where we can just do whatever God asks us to do?

SELFLESS FAITH

"Go, gather all the Jews who are present in Shushan, and fast for me; neither eat nor drink for three days, night or day. My maids and I will fast likewise. And so I will go to the king, which is against the law; and if I perish, I perish!"
Esther 4:16

God's will for each and every one of us is to make a difference on earth. Whoever you are, wherever you are and whatever you do, you can make a difference. If Esther had only thought about herself, she would have remained silent in the palace; after all, nobody knew her true identity. Esther put her life on the line for her people. "And they overcame him by the blood of the Lamb and by the word of their testimony, and they did not love their lives to the death" (Revelation 12:11). The Apostle Paul said he didn't count his life dear to himself, so that he might finish his race with joy and the ministry he had received from the Lord Jesus Christ (Acts 20:24). We are to run the race set before us with endurance, that is, with perseverance (Hebrews 12:1). If you will make a difference, you have to stop thinking only about yourself – your needs, your desires, your reputation, your comfort, etc. Ruth refused to return to her people and to her gods; she clung to Naomi. She didn't make a selfish decision. She committed herself to Naomi, to Naomi's people and to her God; she committed herself to a lifelong relationship. Boaz said to her, "It has been fully reported to me, all that you have done for your mother-in-law since the death of your husband, and how you have left your father and your mother and the land of your birth, and have come to a people whom you did not know before" (Ruth 2:11). People who make a difference don't think only about themselves, they are sacrificial. The women who fought women's suffrages in Great Britain campaigned relentlessly for about fifty two years; some of them faced trials and were jailed, and even went on hunger and thirst strikes! To make a difference, we must move from success (personal) to significance. It is not just for us or our immediate family; it is for generations to come.

SCRIPTURE READING: Esther 4:1-16
PERSONAL APPLICATION: People who make a difference don't think only about themselves, they are sacrificial. If you were in Esther's situation, what would you have done? Are you willing to make the transition from personal success to significance? Are you ready to pay the price?

UNDERSTANDING GRACE

"Let us then with confidence draw near to the throne of grace, that we may receive mercy and find grace to help in time of need."
Hebrews 4:16 RSV

Grace in the first dimension brings us to salvation or brings salvation to us. The same grace now teaches us how to live holy in the sight of God and in the face of all the ungodliness due to the fallen nature and corruption all around us. This is grace in the second dimension. It is the same grace, but has progressive effects in our lives. In order for this dimension of grace to be effective, we need to understand that ungodliness reduces the effect of grace in our lives. Grace is God's energy in us to accomplish God's purposes. Anything that reduces the effect of grace in our lives will eventually reduce the workings of God and frustrate the purpose of God in our lives. That inner working of grace is the key to almost everything God wants to get done in our lives. Watch out for the things or relationships that hinder the operation of grace in your life.

SCRIPTURE READING: Titus 2:11-14, Romans 11:4-6, Ephesians 3:2-7
PERSONAL APPLICATION: The grace of God enables us to do all that He calls us to do effectively and efficiently. We must seek His grace. If we attempt to do things in our own strength, we will lack commitment, consistency and the ability. Receive God's grace today.

VICTORY OVER THE DEVIL AND NEGATIVE CIRCUMSTANCES

"For we walk by faith, not by sight."
2 Corinthians 5:7

God is all-knowing; therefore nothing catches Him unawares. We are not all-knowing, but as we fellowship with God in prayer, He reveals to us things that we need to know to keep ahead of the devil and circumstances so we can be victorious in life! The revelatory gifts of the Holy Spirit, i.e. the word of knowledge, the word of wisdom, and the discerning of spirits, are also very pivotal to this. When the king of Assyria was at war with Israel, Elisha was able to supernaturally know his plans of war and leak them to the king of Israel. When the king demanded to know who among them was the traitor, one of the officers replied, "Elisha, the prophet in Israel, tells the king of Israel even the words you speak in the privacy of your bedroom!" (2 Kings 6:12 *NLT*). After Elijah announced to King Ahab that there was going to be a famine in Israel for several years, the Lord told Elijah to go to the brook Cherith, where He had commanded the ravens to feed him. When the brook dried up, God told Elijah to go to Zarephath where He had commanded a widow to sustain him (1 Kings 17:1-9). We have God's promises for sustenance, even in famine and evil times. The Bible says, "They will not be disgraced in hard times; even in famine they will have more than enough" (Psalm 37:19 *NLT*). We see this also in Job 5:19-22 *NLT,* "From six disasters He will rescue you; even in the seventh, He will keep you from evil. He will save you from death in time of famine, from the power of the sword in time of war. You will be safe from slander and have no fear when destruction comes. You will laugh at destruction and famine; wild animals will not terrify you."

SCRIPTURE READING: Acts 27:9-12
PERSONAL APPLICATION: To enjoy victory over the devil and negative circumstances, we must learn to stay in close fellowship with God to get directions from Him. Jesus said, "Man shall not live by bread alone, but by every word that proceeds out of the mouth of God" (Matthew 4:4).

BUILDING AN ALTAR UNTO THE LORD

"The Lord appeared to Abram and said, 'To your offspring I will give this land.' So he built an altar there to the Lord, who had appeared to him."
Genesis 12:7 NIVUK

An altar was a place of offering sacrifice to God; a place of offering to God that which was due Him. The men of old never conceived of God as One with whom they related without the concept of offering. The very thought of God elicited in them offering something to Him. You should not think of God without the reverential awe that makes you ponder, "What can I offer to my God?" Today our altars are not physical buildings but places of communion with God. Our hearts' reverence for God is our altar of sacrifice to God. The men of old put God first, His Kingdom first, His will first. He was their number one. They allowed the authority of God to hold a prominent place in the scheme of things in their lives. Isaac built an altar, a memorial unto God. God wants to take us into heights of His will and pleasure but our value-system has not put such importance on God or His will and Word in our lives. At the altar, we meet with God. We get direction, wisdom and a whole lot of godly input from this meeting point. Every endeavour in life can be enriched at this place. The value we place on God and the things of God will determine how we move on with God. When Paul, the apostle said He was not ashamed of the heavenly vision; he allowed God's Word to be the basis for a turning point in his life. The place you give God's Word is the place you give God in your life. Build an altar today in your heart made up of God's Word and worship God in Spirit and truth.

SCRIPTURE READING: Genesis 12:1-9, Mark 12:28-33
PERSONAL APPLICATION: Who is Number 1 in your heart? Your job, your family, your reputation, your friends, your needs? The list can go on... or is it God? Repent before God and ask Him to remove any and every foreign god from your heart. Rededicate yourself wholly and unreservedly to Him only!

BE A GOOD EXAMPLE

"Be ye followers of me, even as I also am of Christ."
1 Corinthians 11:1 KJV

You must be a good example. People like to follow a leader who leads, not just by their words, but also by their corresponding actions. "Don't lord it over the people assigned to your care, but lead them by your own good example" (1 Peter 5:3). The Pharisees lost credibility as leaders because, though they were meant to be the custodian of the law, their lifestyle was contrary to what they taught; Jesus said the people shouldn't follow their ways. People will choose a leader whose lifestyle matches their teachings. "Remember your leaders who taught you the word of God. Think of all the good that has come from their lives, and follow the example of their faith." (Hebrews 13:7). People would first of all buy into a leader before buying into what he or she says. It's easier to motivate people by being an example to them. You can motivate people to pray, by you being a praying person yourself; you can motivate people to serve by you being a servant-leader yourself, and you can motivate people to give by being a giver. Like leader, like followers; like shepherd, like flock!

People will follow a leader who is not an end in themselves. The centurion said to Jesus, "For I also am a man under authority, having soldiers under me. And I say to this one, 'Go,' and he goes; and to another, 'Come,' and he comes; and to my servant, 'Do this,' and he does it." (Matthew 8:9). It looks like we can't exercise more authority in our lives, than we ourselves are under. Jesus Himself was under the authority of God; He said, "I do nothing of Myself; but as My Father taught Me, I speak these things" (John 5:30)

SCRIPTURE READING: 1 Peter 5:2-7, 1 Timothy 4:12

PERSONAL APPLICATION: If you are not a good student, you won't be a good teacher; and if you are not a good servant yourself, you won't be a good leader. Samuel served God under Eli. Who do you serve under? Who do you study after? Who is your teacher or mentor? Who speaks into your life? Who do you check things up with?

A WILD HORSE

"And whoever falls on this stone will be broken;
but on whomever it falls, it will grind him to powder."
Matthew 21:44

As I interact with believers from different walks of life, I constantly come across those who seem to have it all together in terms of being in the Lord but still lack one quality. The word that keeps ringing in my heart is 'brokenness'. Matthew 21:44 says, "And whoever falls on this stone will be broken; but on whomever it falls, it will grind him to powder". The former is a choice we make to yield to God and His ways, and the latter is the judgement of God upon the obstinate. A wild horse is no good for winning races. It has the strength but not the discipline. The potential is there, but not the skill to win. Many come to the Lord in much the same way, wild, unbroken and unusable by God or man. Wild and rebellious is the description of the carnal man where God is concerned. Talking about horses, remember the colt Jesus rode into Jerusalem when they threw palm leaves on the ground to receive Him? Imagine the animal thinking that all of the attention was for it and not its rider. Without its rider, the animal was like any other. In a sense those who are being used of God are like that; the Master rides us to fulfil His plans and purposes. What is done to 'break in' a horse? The horse is made to realise that it won't be hurt, it is loved, then it undergoes a process of training with a bit in its mouth and eventually the control of its movement is regulated by the bit in its mouth. God lets us know He loves us so we can submit to His corrections. Rebuke and chastening cause pain no matter how nice we try to be about it. Our mouth plays a major role in the process as well as our heart and the contents therein. God's training includes receiving correction, instruction and rebukes and getting on, with the joy of the Lord as our strength. The virtues that go along with brokenness are: being teachable, willingness to obey and the ability to receive correction without offence or pride. Wholeness, through yieldedness, is when in our dependence on God, we take our rightful position and with joy, do His will. God usually directs those who fear Him and are contrite in heart. The fear of God, meekness and brokenness all enhance our walk with God towards our destiny. Stay yielded and teachable in God.

SCRIPTURE READING: Matthew 11:29-30, Hebrews 12:4-12
PERSONAL APPLICATION: The next time you face an opportunity to be 'broken', instead of complaining and grumbling, go to God in prayer. Ask Him to give you His perspective and receive humility to undergo His process for your life.

THE TRUE VINE

"I am the vine, you are the branches. He who abides in Me, and I in him, bears much fruit; for without Me you can do nothing."
John 15:5

We take our text today from John 15:1-16. The discussion our Lord was having here is very eye opening into the mind and ways of God. For there to be a true vine, it implies that there is a possibility of a false one. What can be called a false vine if a vine is a life-source? It will be something that looks like it, but lacks the life producing capacity of the vine. Religion will fit the picture. Many treat religion as a vine when one considers the hold it has on many people around the world. Religion is a false vine. It may have similarities with the real thing but it lacks the ability to give life. The vine gives life to all who are connected with it. Jesus is the true vine, the true life source, and the correct one to be connected to. The Father is likened to the vinedresser, the one who is taking care of the growth of the vine. What a picture of similar purposes but distinction of labours. Every branch in Christ that does not bear fruit is taken away and the ones who bear fruit are pruned to enable them to bear more fruit. Is it possible to be connected and not be fruitful? Yes. This means that though the connection is in tact, there could be other factors that may hinder fruitfulness. To understand this we may need to get the picture of us humans being like branches. The picture is found in Romans 11:12-24; here Paul was discussing the wild olive branches (Gentiles) connected to the cultivated olive tree (the tree of Christ that the Jews are natural branches to). The picture becomes clear, in that in our pre-Christian days, we were like wild olive trees having a nature not subject to God or His laws. Our old nature can hinder our fruitfulness even if we get connected to Christ as the Vine. There is a need to do an internal re-configuration in our make up to make us fruitful. Abiding in Christ is the key to much fruit. When God prunes, He takes away that which hinders the flow of His life in us. Fruitfulness is as a result of the over flow of life. When we bear much fruit, the Father is glorified.

SCRIPTURE READING: John 15:1-16, Romans 11:11-24, Matthew 7:17-20
PERSONAL APPLICATION: Jesus is ready to prune any branch that does not bear fruit. Pruning is not a comfortable process. Ask God to help you embrace process to internally reconfigure your makeup, and give you the willingness to bear the right fruit.

UNDERSTANDING GOD'S CHARACTER

"For God is not unjust to forget your work and labour of love which you have shown toward His name, in that you have ministered to the saints, and do minister."
Hebrews 6:10

God is just. It would amount to injustice on God's part to forget our labour in Him! The Bible says it shall be well with the righteous, and they shall eat the fruit of their doing (Isaiah 3:10); they will also be rewarded on earth; not only the hereafter (Proverbs 11:31)! "But the godly will flourish like palm trees and grow strong like the cedars of Lebanon. For they are transplanted to the Lord's own house. They flourish in the courts of our God. Even in old age they will still produce fruit; they will remain vital and green. They will declare, "The Lord is just! He is my rock! There is no evil in Him!" (Psalm 92:12-15 *NLT*). It is God's justice that ensures people reap what they sow; either good or bad! "Don't be misled–you cannot mock the justice of God. You will always harvest what you plant" (Galatians 6:7 *NLT*). God is also faithful, so we expect Him to do just what He says! "Let us hold fast the confession of our hope without wavering, for He who promised is faithful" (Hebrews 10:23). The *New Living Translation* says, "for God can be trusted to keep His promise." If we confess our sins, we expect God to forgive us our sins and cleanse us from all unrighteousness, because He is faithful and just (1 John 1:9). We can always count on God's faithfulness at any time to do what He says; knowing that, "He who calls you is faithful, who also will do it" (1 Thessalonians 5:24).

SCRIPTURE READING: Deuteronomy 32:1-4 *AMPC*, Psalm 92:12-15, Psalm 103:1-22
PERSONAL APPLICATION: As a believer, it is important to know God and His character. Spend time studying and meditating on the passages in todays devotional over and over again—until God's character becomes so real to you.

BUILDING THE CHURCH OF CHRIST

"And I also say to you that you are Peter, and on this rock I will build My church, and the gates of Hades shall not prevail against it."
Matthew 16:18

"I have been crucified with Christ; it is no longer I who live, but Christ lives in me; and the *life* which I now live in the flesh I live by faith in the Son of God, who loved me and gave Himself for me" Galatians 2:20. When Christ is allowed to be in His church, offences will show up that will reveal the hearts of people there. As Christ builds His church, He builds His Word into the hearts of His people by dealing with the mind-sets and desires that are contrary to His will in them. Many things need to be rooted out, pulled down and destroyed before real building and planting can be done in our lives. When the contents of the heart of people are ignored, it is not the church of Christ that is being built, but a place where Satan has access to strike. He uses offence to carry out his operations. Offence in the heart of an unbroken person will trigger a lot of bitterness. That becomes the workshop for the enemy to carry out his masterly destructive schemes. Whatever needs to die to let Christ live in us should be allowed to die. This should bring a change of disposition in us as we seek to let Christ be formed in us. What the enemy planned for destruction can now become a stepping-stone to greater heights in God.

SCRIPTURE READING: Jeremiah 1:9-10, Nehemiah 2:17-20, Hebrews 12:14-15
PERSONAL APPLICATION: Offences are always bound to arise. How we deal with them will build our character and reflect God's glory. Submit yourself to God. As He builds you, ask Him to reveal areas in your life that need to be rebuilt to reflect Him.

THE SACRIFICE OF CHRIST FOR US

"Christ redeemed us from the curse of the law by becoming a curse for us..."
Galatians 3:13

"Surely He has borne our griefs (sicknesses, weaknesses, and distresses) and carried our sorrows and pains [of punishment], yet we [ignorantly] considered Him stricken, smitten, and afflicted by God [as if with leprosy]. But He was wounded for our transgressions, He was bruised for our guilt and iniquities; the chastisement [needful to obtain] peace and well-being for us was upon Him, and with the stripes [that wounded] Him we are healed and made whole" (Isaiah 53:4-5 *AMPC*). Jesus took our place on the cross; He became as we were, so we can become as He is! He became sick, that we might be well (1 Peter 2:24). He was broken, that we might be made whole. He became sin, that we might be made righteous (2 Corinthians 5:21). He bore our shame, that we may share His glory (Colossians 1:27). He was rejected, that we might be accepted in the beloved (Ephesians 1:6). He became poor, that we, through His poverty, might be made rich (2 Corinthians 8:9). He became a curse that we might be blessed (Galatians 3:13:14). The curse of the law is threefold; spiritual death, sicknesses/diseases, and poverty. Jesus bore them all for us on His cross. If we would base our expectations on the sacrifice of Jesus for us, instead of on our own power or holiness, then we could be sure of always being victorious. We can always overcome the devil and his cohorts by the blood of the Lamb, Jesus Christ (Revelation 12:11)!

SCRIPTURE READING: Galatians 3:1-14, Philippians 2:5-11
PERSONAL APPLICATION: Scripture teaches us how we should live our lives, based on the example of Christ Himself and His sacrifice on the cross. Is there anything in how you live your life that needs to be realigned with the example Christ sets?

CULTIVATING THE RIGHT ATTITUDE

"These were more fair-minded than those in Thessalonica, in that they received the word with all readiness, and searched the Scriptures daily to find out whether these things were so."
Acts 17:11

There are attitudes we must embrace to enhance the fulfillment of our destiny. It is very necessary that we cultivate these attitudes, particularly as it is often said that your attitude will determine your altitude in life. Having the right attitude is very important because it either makes you or mars you. If you want your destiny to be what God has planned it to be, you must have an attitude towards the things of God that shows respect, reverence and gravity.

Attitude can be likened to your response to a person or a thing as reflected in your thoughts and actions towards that thing or person. The way you respond to what God tells you really matters, and how you act on it goes a long way in enhancing your destiny. Many times, God may speak to your heart or even through His people. What you do with what is said will determine the results you get. "My son, keep my words, and treasure my commands within you" (Proverbs 7:1).

Your attitude must be right for you to reach great heights in Christ. Even when God is telling you what you ordinarily cannot comprehend, still respect what He is saying. The fact that a particular Word of God works for someone else does not mean it will automatically work for you. Your attitude towards it will determine whether it will work for you or not. It is not because God does not want it to work for you, but if you have no respect for it, then it will not work for you. Even that respect has to be firmly established before the Word begins to produce in your life.

SCRIPTURE READING: Mark 4:23-25 *AMPC*

PERSONAL APPLICATION: How do you know when you are hearing from God? God has given you the tools to know His voice and to hear instructions, but you need to have a heart that enables you to hear and to understand.

MAKE YOUR TRIALS WORK FOR YOU

"not returning evil for evil or reviling for reviling, but on the contrary blessing, knowing that you were called to this, that you may inherit a blessing."
1 Peter 3:9

You can develop a strong prayer life, intimacy with, and dependence on God through your tests and trials. The Bible says of Jesus, "Who, in the days of His flesh, when He had offered up prayers and supplications, with vehement cries and tears to Him who was able to save Him from death and was heard because of His godly fear, though He was a Son, yet He learned obedience by the things which He suffered" (Hebrews 5:8). The Apostle Paul said he has learned in every circumstance, how to abound and how to be abased; the secret of facing every situation, whether well-fed or going hungry. He said, "I have strength for all things in Christ Who empowers me [I am ready for anything and equal to anything through Him Who infuses inner strength into me; I am self sufficient in Christ's sufficiency]" (Philippians 4:13 *AMPC*). Also in 2 Corinthians 12:9-10, "Each time He said, 'My grace is all you need. My power works best in weakness.' So now I am glad to boast about my weaknesses, so that the power of Christ can work through me. That's why I take pleasure in my weaknesses, and in the insults, hardships, persecutions, and troubles that I suffer for Christ. For when I am weak, then I am strong".

Joseph was somebody who refused to get bitter, but got better and bigger through his trials. Joseph didn't repay his brothers or Potiphar's wife with evil, even when it was in his power to do so; instead he chose to forgive (Genesis 50:15-21). I believe that the strength to forgive his brothers came from Joseph's intimacy with God. It was in that place of intimacy that Joseph got God's perspective to all he had gone through; and that was a major secret of his strength. The Bible says those who wait on the Lord shall renew their strength.

SCRIPTURE READING: Isaiah 40:28-31

PERSONAL APPLICATION: Waiting on God and dwelling on His Word changes our perspective on the things we experience and enables us to rise above the ordinary to achieve the extraordinary. What is God calling you to seek Him and wait on Him for?

UNDERSTAND YOUR NEED TO ALIGN WITH HIS WAYS

"Commit your works to the LORD,
And your thoughts will be established."
Proverbs 16:3

Our motives, focus and priorities play a major part in our receiving consistently from God. Our needs become our avenue to come into harmony with God. Our priority should be His Kingdom. "But seek ye first the kingdom of God, and his righteousness; and all these things shall be added unto you" (Matthew 6:33 *KJV*). Put God first, place a higher value on the spiritual side of life. Our motive should be our love for God and His people. Faith works by love. Love is unconditional acceptance and divine confrontation. Love is a commandment not a suggestion or advice. Check your motives! Are you walking in strife, unforgiveness or bitterness? Release yourself from these by repenting and forgiving others. Your focus should be Jesus Christ.

"Looking unto Jesus the author and finisher of our faith, who for the joy that was set before him endured the cross, despising the shame, and has sat down at the right hand of the throne of God" (Hebrews 12:2). Our goal is to reflect His nature and power. The more you see Him, the more you are transformed to be like Him. God's kingdom is a spiritual kingdom. This kingdom is to be built in our hearts as we align ourselves with kingdom principles. We check our inner attitudes, motives and focus. Are we God-focused, kingdom-minded or earth-bound in our quest for things in this life? Are we compromising God's values, standards and methods for our needs? Many pursue things and miss God. God should be our main pursuit. His presence is the greatest solution to all our needs. Therefore His presence is our greatest need. Let the peace of God act as an umpire in your heart. Do not walk in things that your heart condemns you in! Why you do what you do is more important than what you do. Ask yourself, "Are my motives in line with God's method and ways?" Alignment with God calls for real sincerity before Him.

SCRIPTURE READING: 1 John 3:2-3

PERSONAL APPLICATION: Spend time in prayer. Examine your motives for what you say, think and do. What is God saying to you today? Are you at peace and in alignment with His Word?

A PARADIGM SHIFT

"Behold, children are a heritage from the Lord,
the fruit of the womb is a reward."
Psalm 127:3

See your children as gifts from God; and yourself as a steward over those gifts, who is also accountable to God. We must have a stewardship mentality where our children are concerned. This mind-set puts on us a great sense of responsibility and will change a lot of things in our parenting methods. For instance, in Paul's farewell speech to the Ephesian elders, he told them he was innocent of the blood of all men, because he had not shunned to declare to them the whole counsel of God (Acts 20: 26-27). Samuel told Saul that he would not sin against the LORD by stopping to pray for Saul, and he would continue to teach him the good and the right way (1 Samuel 12:23). We must not shrink from telling our kids all that God wants them to know, and from praying for them; or else we will be failing God and our children also. When you make this shift in your mentality, you will see your kids differently, and your role in their lives differently.

SCRIPTURE READING: John 17:6-19
PERSONAL APPLICATION: What example does God set for what your attitude towards your children should be? What do you need to change to align yourself with God's view of you and your children?

GOD'S VISION FOR YOU

"'For I know the plans I have for you,' declares the Lord, 'plans to prosper you and not to harm you, plans to give you hope and a future.'"
Jeremiah 29:11 NIV

God's vision is so great that no human being can fully handle it all. We all take portions of it. God's vision to bring the children of Israel out of bondage was spearheaded by Moses but could not be contained by him alone. He needed Joshua to fight the battles while he prayed; Aaron and Hur to hold up his hands, while Bezalel and others built the tabernacle of Moses. We have equated the vision that one person receives, as the totality of God's plans and purposes. We should always learn to respect and receive the portion others receive of God's overall purpose so that we can be built up. The reason for jealousy in the Body today is a lack of understanding of how God's vision works out on the earth. Every vision will go through a process as we are all being prepared for what God has prepared for us. In every given house there can be only one vision. Two visions will lead to di-vision. Moses had a vision and every one drank into the vision of Moses. As the vision matured in the people like Joshua, they began to discover their God-given portion within the same vision. Joshua had to get involved with the grace upon Moses to carry out his portion of the vision. This principle should prevail in every house that God builds. Everything in the Kingdom of God must pass through God's process to be proved, tested and established. Now the enemy means it for destruction but God will work out his will if you stay true to Him and allow uprightness of heart to prevail in you.

SCRIPTURE READING: Exodus 31:1-11
PERSONAL APPLICATION: Do you know what God has called you to do? How does this align with God's will for where you are?

DEVELOPING EXCELLENCE

"Give instruction to a wise man, and he will be still wiser;
Teach a just man, and he will increase in learning."
Proverbs 9:9

How open you are to learn, will determine how much you can observe and take in; and how teachable you are will determine the change that will take place in your life. This explains why some people spend time in some places, but come back exactly the same way they left! Decide to be open and teachable; even if it doesn't come naturally with you. God resists the proud, but gives grace to the humble (James 4:6). Don't think of yourself more highly than you ought to (Romans 12:3). Somebody said if you stop growing, you start dying. There is a price to pay for growth and development; be willing to pay the price. It will cost you money, your pride, your comfort and even what you thought you knew! Growing, however, is very rewarding. A growing leader will have a growing people or organisation; because growth challenges growth in others. People respect and commit to a growing leader, not a 'perfect' leader. Don't rest on your laurels. There is always room for improvement; improve on the last thing you did.

SCRIPTURE READING: 1 Peter 5:1-11
PERSONAL APPLICATION: Have a sober and realistic evaluation of yourself; know that no matter how much you know, there is still a lot more that you don't know. Stay open to and be willing to learn all the time.

TRUE DISCIPLESHIP

"Whoever wants to be my disciple must deny themselves and take up their cross and follow me."
Matthew 16:24 NIV

Three requirements stand out in the demands of Christ. If any will follow, he must deny himself, take up his cross and follow Jesus (Matthew 16:24). In many parts of Scripture, Jesus made it clear that following Him demands total commitment to Him, His ways and His Kingdom (Luke 14:26-33). We do not see Jesus beg His followers to follow Him or entice them with many blessings to obey Him, the way many present-day preachers do. Preaching the cross has always been offensive and preparing disciples for hardness is not popular. Strong disciples are raised when they are told the truth about entering the Kingdom through much tribulation. The persecution and perseverance of the saints of old needs to be brought back to our thoughts so that we will be prepared for any unfavourable conditions that may come our way. It is interesting to note that the heroes in the Bible, like Moses, Daniel and Joseph, all went through trying times to fulfil their destinies. If the present-day disciples are not properly equipped, their destinies remain as dreams that will never be fulfilled. The apostle Peter advised us to arm ourselves with the mind to suffer, just as Jesus gave us an example in His suffering (1 Peter 4:1). The secret of dealing a death blow to the sins of the flesh, is to die to the flesh, which spells out 'suffering in the flesh'.

SCRIPTURE READING: 1 Peter 4:12-19, Luke 14:26-33
PERSONAL APPLICATION: Do you suffer persecution in your walk with Christ? Examine what your response is and what God's Word says it should be.

SEEK HIM HUMBLY

"'For all those things My hand has made,
And all those things exist,'
Says the Lord.
'But on this one will I look:
On him who is poor and of a contrite spirit,
And who trembles at My word.'"
Isaiah 66:2

"God blesses those who are poor and realize their need for him, for the Kingdom of Heaven is theirs" (Matthew 5:3 *NLT*). It's interesting to note that this is the first, in the blessedness series! God resists the proud, but gives grace to (i.e. favours) the humble (James 4:6-7). When the king and the people of Nineveh repented, at the preaching of Jonah, God relented from the disaster that He had said He would bring upon them (Jonah 3:10). God said when He shut up the heavens and there was no rain, if His people would humble themselves, and pray and seek His face, and turn from their wicked ways; then would He hear from heaven, and would forgive their sin and heal their land (2 Chronicles 7:13-14). The psalmist said, "The sacrifices of God are a broken spirit, A broken and a contrite heart— These, O God, You will not despise" (Psalm 51:17). The Bible, however, talks about two kinds of sorrow; namely, godly sorrow - which leads to repentance and salvation; and worldly sorrow- which leads to death (2 Corinthians 7:10-11). Peter typified godly sorrow, as he remembered the words of Jesus when the cock crowed - because he had denied the Lord three times. Peter repented, and was converted indeed. Judas, on the other hand was filled with worldly sorrow, when it dawned on him that he had betrayed innocent blood; but he went on to hang himself (Matthew 27:3-5). God never gives up on us, even when we miss it; He promised never to leave us nor forsake us (Joel 2:12-13). So, we must not give up on ourselves; we can get up and get going again. Don't forget that a failure is not the one who failed, but the one who quit!

SCRIPTURE READING: Luke 18:9-14, 2 Chronicles 7:12-22
PERSONAL APPLICATION: We must never allow our past blunders to hinder our future destiny; there is still a lot more we can achieve in God, in spite of our failures. When you mess up, come before God with humility and with godly sorrow. Repent before Him, then receive forgiveness and the grace and wisdom you need to keep going. As we learnt today, God never gives up on us, so don't give up on yourself.

THE CENTRALITY OF THE WORD OF GOD

"And the Word became flesh and dwelt among us, and we beheld His glory, the glory as of the only begotten of the Father, full of grace and truth."
John 1:14

Every Word of God carries a dimension of God that can impart something of Himself into your life and future. You cannot relate with God based only on your experiences or opinions. There is more to God than what you presently know. Whatever you can discover in His Word will lead you to recovering that thing from Satan. The devil's assignment is to steal, kill and destroy (John 10:10). We are meant to cast down anything that raises itself against the knowledge of Christ (2 Corinthians 10:3-5). What if we do not have the knowledge of Christ? We will not even recognise any high thing that exhorts itself against the knowledge. The Word must be central — not feelings. You have been stolen from. Recover what is yours after you have discovered it in the Word. In this day and age we have our minds bombarded with all sorts and we need the stability that the Word of God gives. It is an anchor for our souls in this world of ours. The respect we have for God must be reflected in the respect we have for His Word. He and His Word are one (John 1:1-4)! The Word also has life and the light in the life is released as we receive the Word into our hearts. The Word of God contains the grace, power, love and anointing of God. As we respect and receive the Word, the grace and love in the Word will flow into us and equip, strengthen and prepare us to do His will. Keep the Word central.

SCRIPTURE READING: Psalm 119:33-38, John 1:1-5
PERSONAL APPLICATION: Here are some questions to think about: what is the key to walking in the reality and experiencing the power of the Word of God? What things in your life need to be adjusted? Why should you not limit the Word of God to your experience of it?

A TREE OF LIFE

"Hope deferred makes the heart sick,
but a longing fulfilled is a tree of life."
Proverbs 13:12 NIV

Truly delay is not denial; but after a long time of waiting and unrelenting disappointment, we all need that good break that can turn our lives around! What then do we need to do or how do we position ourselves, to make our expectations become realities?

1) Affirm the certainty of your expectations: the Bible says those who plant in tears will harvest with shouts of joy (Psalm 126:5, Proverbs 23:17-18 *AMPC*).

2) Stay in Faith: "Now faith is the substance of things hoped for, the evidence of things not seen" (Hebrews 11:1). The *NLT* says, it is the confidence that what we hope for will actually happen! We don't hope for what is seen, but for what is unseen; and hope that is seen isn't hope (Romans 8:24). To actualise what we hope for, we must stay believing.

3) Maintain the right focus: we must keep looking at the unseen and we must not give up. Moses endured because he saw Him who is invisible! Christ, for the joy that was set before Him endured the cross, despising the shame (Hebrews 12:2). We must, therefore, focus on God's Word—rather than the contrary evidence around us, if our hope is to be a reality.

4) Learn to maintain your joy: Understand the powerful connection between hope and joy. The secret of not quitting is to maintain your joy. As long as we maintain our joy, no matter what trials we may face, we will abound in hope, instead of giving up (Romans 15:13)! Joy keeps our hope alive and as long as our hope is alive, we will not be disappointed. Rather, we will become mature and complete, lacking nothing (James 1:2-4). Amen.

SCRIPTURE READING: Hebrews 11:1—12:2
PERSONAL APPLICATION: God's Word teaches us not to lose heart when we believe, but to have faith for the things not seen. The essence of this is to believe God that no matter what does or does not seem to happen, He is able to do what He has promised (see Romans 4:21).

WALKING IN VICTORY

"Then David spoke to the men who stood by him, saying, "What shall be done for the man who kills this Philistine and takes away the reproach from Israel? For who is this uncircumcised Philistine, that he should defy the armies of the living God?"
1 Samuel 17:26

In our destiny walk there are two dimensions to the overall picture: the God part and our part. In the story of David and Goliath you can see where our part comes into play. David took the battle to the gates of the enemy. He did something: engaging his gifts, calling and skill to see God's will fulfilled. 1 Samuel chapter 16 is an eye-opening read to see how David had confidence in the God he had spent time cultivating a relationship with. God was so big inside David that the 9-foot giant looked small to him. Others saw the giant as too big to handle, David saw him as too big to miss. David believed in and engaged his God-given talents, skills and covenant privileges. David recognized his covenant position and the giant's lack in that area. He celebrated his victories over the lion and the bear, giving God glory for them. (Many would take the credit for the uncelebrated victories in their lives, eating some ego-food). David must have felt alone but with a great awareness of God with him. He used what he had. Many do not value what they have enough to use it to face their challenges. They always feel they do not have what it takes to win. Finally, David demonstrated greater confidence in his proven armour than Saul's offer. God will not use the rod of Moses to kill David's giant. What you have, when given to God will be used to kill your giant. Your victory will release others to victory. Go ahead and walk in victory in Jesus' name!

SCRIPTURE READING: 1 Samuel 17
PERSONAL APPLICATION: How can we use what God has done in our lives to address the giants that come against us? When we give God the glory for His victories in our lives, He removes fear and enables us to face and defeat greater foes, so we can testify to others of the greatness of the Father and His Son Jesus.

UPROOTING THE FLESH

"Then His disciples came and said to Him, 'Do You know that the Pharisees were offended when they heard this saying?'
But He answered and said, 'Every plant which My heavenly Father has not planted will be uprooted'"
Matthew 15:12-13

When Baby Jesus was brought into the temple, Simeon blessed Him and said to Mary, "Behold, this child is destined for the fall and rising of many in Israel and for a sign which will be spoken against" (Luke 2:34). Do you know how many are offended in Jesus today? Many are disappointed in Him and a lot of things that seem inexplicable are blamed on Him. And we are not only talking about unbelievers, but sad to say, believers too! Jesus said to John the Baptist in the prison, "And blessed is he who is not offended because of Me" (Matthew 11:6). I want to highlight that though Jesus is called the rock of offence, the purpose for which He causes offence is not for us to stumble. Satan is the one who wants us to stumble and fall; he wants to hinder us from the purposes of God. Jesus and Satan are not on the same platform, neither are they next of kin. When they told Jesus that the Pharisees were offended at His teaching, he replied, "Every plant which My heavenly Father has not planted will be uprooted" (Matthew 15:13). God showed me from this that offences can act as that which can root out of our lives the things which are not planted by God. Things like; pride, selfishness, poor self-esteem, jealousy, rivalry, and so forth. These things are not the plantings of the Lord and they deserve to go, so they don't destroy us! Think about it, when you are offended, what is stirred up in you? Your pride of course! That is the very thing God, in His wisdom, meant for that offence to root out, if we cooperate with Him. Fire reveals the 'serpent' nature, so it can be dealt with. Over the years, I have seen that God Himself orchestrates offence for this purpose. On the other hand, if we don't allow the offence to root out what God has not planted in us, but rather we get offended, then we are the ones that will be rooted out! Simply put: God wants to use offences to root out of our lives what He hasn't planted, whereas, Satan wants to use them to root us out of where God has planted us!

SCRIPTURE READING: Luke 2:25-35
PERSONAL APPLICATION: When you feel offended and hurt, what are the thoughts that fill your heart? What is God trying to reveal in you through this offence? What needs to be uprooted?

SENSITIVITY TO GOD

"Talk no more so very proudly; let no arrogance come from your mouth, For the Lord is the God of knowledge and by Him actions are weighed."
1 Samuel 2:3

Your lifestyle carries within it what your future will be. Your words, thoughts and actions need to be disciplined in sensitivity. We err too soon with our words (James 3) and our actions (1 Samuel 2:3). Our thoughts are the battleground for evil and good. We have not been aware that these things affect the quality of our fellowship with God and hence the quality of our lives individually. Let your thoughts, words and actions line up with God's Word. You will have to exercise your faith to walk in obedience in these areas. Unbelief, doubt, fears and filth all spew out of our mouths because of the abundance of these things in our hearts. God's commandments are not grievous, they are for our good. Stay in love in your heart. Stay full of God's Word and generate hope with your words. Be sensitive to anytime the Holy Spirit in you stirs your heart towards obedience to the perfect law of liberty, as James 1 calls God's laws of the heart. The New Testament laws are primarily laws that govern our hearts. They are to get our hearts in love toward God as we reverence Him and walk in the fear of the Lord. They also help us to stay sensitive in our hearts as the Holy Spirit nudges us inside to read the Word, walk in love, stay humble, stay sincere and speak in accordance with His Word. The reason we feel low sometimes is because we have disobeyed the law of liberty — the law of the heart.

SCRIPTURE READING: Psalm 15:1-5
PERSONAL APPLICATION: How do God's people think, speak and act in accordance with God's will? What is your responsibility in becoming what God wants you to be? Read 1 Samuel 2, Psalm 15 and James 1. Pray that God enables you to discipline your thoughts and words so you can walk blameless before Him, out of love and reverence for God.

BREAK UP YOUR FALLOW GROUND

"I said, 'Plant the good seeds of righteousness,
and you will harvest a crop of love.
Plow up the hard ground of your hearts,
for now is the time to seek the Lord,
that he may come
and shower righteousness upon you.'"
Hosea 10:12 NLT

Fallow ground is ground that has been ploughed but nothing sown or planted on it. It is an empty land. God says that He wants to rain His righteousness on us but the fallow ground must be broken up. We need to plant God's Word in our hearts. Be committed to doing what God says in His Word, or else you will soon forget who the Word says you are. The mirror (i.e. God's Word) says you are the righteousness of God in Christ Jesus and a new creature in Him (1 Corinthians 5:21). It says you have been chosen before the foundation of the world by God to be holy and blameless before Him (Ephesians 1:4); it says the love of God has been shed abroad in your heart by the Holy Ghost who is in you (Romans 5:5); but you will soon forget all these if you are not a doer of the Word. This is the implication of James 1:23-24 *KJV*, "For if any be a hearer of the word, and not a doer, he is like unto a man beholding his natural face in a glass: For he beholdeth himself, and goeth his way, and straightway forgetteth what manner of man he was."

SCRIPTURE READING: Jeremiah 4:1-4
PERSONAL APPLICATION: We need to be proactive if we wish to have righteousness showered upon us. What does God expect of us when we are instructed to 'break up the fallow ground'? What role does God's Word play in the harvest of His righteousness in your life?

SECRETS TO A POWERFUL LIFESTYLE

"In your seed all the nations of the earth shall be blessed, because you have obeyed My voice."
Genesis 22:18

The quality of our lifestyle plays a major role in the way and manner in which we can minister the power of God. There is a connection between our lifestyle choice and the steady flow of God's power in our lives. When we read about how many men and women of old walked in the power of God, we seldom see the quality of their obedience and the price they paid to experience the power flowing in their lives. Yes, they do have a calling and yes, God was willing to use them to fulfil His purpose, but they paid the price none the less. Our present lifestyle makes it almost impossible to pay any meaningful price. We are so absorbed in many 'legitimate' things that it seems ridiculous to think of adding any 'price' to what we are already paying just to make ends meet or keep up with work. That is what makes this subject all the more important; we will always pay a price somewhere and some how. When we fail to pay it spiritually, it takes its toll on us in many other areas and some price will still have to be paid. Knowing that there is a price to pay and a position to take, for the will of God to be done on earth, let us labour to know and to pay the right price for the right things to be done on earth. The Bible says that if we be willing and obedient, we shall eat the good of the land. God is at work in us both to will and to do of His good pleasure. May God make us willing to be willing.

SCRIPTURE READING: 1 Corinthians 9:24-27
PERSONAL APPLICATION: Spend some time thinking about this question: what price are you willing to pay in order to grow your faith in Christ Jesus who paid the ultimate price for your salvation? May you be willing to fight to stay in the place of obedience to God, no matter the opposition.

HUMBLE YOURSELF

"I lift up my eyes to the mountains—where does my help come from? My help comes from the LORD, the Maker of heaven and earth."
Psalm 121:1-2 NIV

"God resists the proud, but gives grace to the humble" (James 4:6). That is, God sets Himself against or opposes the proud. Some of the resistance or opposition we face in life, could be because of our pride. Pride is the unduly high opinion of one's own importance or merits; the Bible says we shouldn't think of ourselves more highly than we ought to. Pride affects the way we think, the way we see things; it affects our lifestyle, our relationships and our response to things. God gives grace to the humble; humble people are teachable and they also ask for help when they need it. Prayer is asking God for help; so learn to ask for God's help in the areas where you need breakthroughs. When some nations came against Jehoshaphat, he set himself to seek the Lord, and to ask Him for help (2 Chronicles 20:3). When Paul and Silas were in prison, the Bible says they prayed and sang praises (Acts 16:23-26). When Peter was kept in prison by Herod, the church prayed to God constantly for Peter to be released (Acts 12:5). When King Nebuchadnezzar wanted to destroy all the wise men including Daniel, Daniel and his three friends sought mercies from God. And God revealed Nebuchadnezzar's dream to Daniel (Daniel 2). "God is our refuge and strength, always ready to help in times of trouble" (Psalm 46:1 *NLT*).

SCRIPTURE READING: 2 Chronicles 20:3-22
PERSONAL APPLICATION: Are there areas in your life that you need to give over to God? God is faithful to deliver you if you humble yourself and seek Him with your whole heart.

THE OBEDIENCE OF CHRIST

"During the days of Jesus' life on earth, he offered up prayers and petitions with fervent cries and tears to the one who could save him from death, and he was heard because of his reverent submission."
Hebrews 5:7 NIV

Hebrews 5:7-9 says that Jesus learned obedience through the things He suffered. Obedience is to be learned. It does not come on us naturally. He went through this as a pattern for us. We will learn obedience through what we suffer. Many suffer but never learn obedience. That is because of strongholds. Rather than learn what lessons we can derive from our experiences; many either learn the wrong lessons or learn nothing at all. He learned obedience through what He suffered in His walk with God's purposes for Him. He suffered the limitations of humanity; the contradiction of the fallen race; he suffered being subjected to human limitations of people all around Him. (They could not see what He was about and hence made wrong judgements about Him). He suffered subjecting His flesh to God's ways of doing things; things like prayer and deep supplications. He also suffered the cross experience. His obedience brought about restoration and recovery of all that Adam lost in the Garden of Eden. Through one man's obedience, righteousness has now been made available to human beings through faith in Him. Our true sacrifice in life is to walk in obedience to God. We need to develop the mind of Christ; the state of His mind is the reason why He walked in such obedience. His humility is also seen in how His mind worked. Paul says, "Let this mind be in you which was also in Christ Jesus" (Philippians 2:5). "Not my will but yours be done" (Luke 22:42). "I can do nothing of my own" (John 5:30). Let this mind be in you and you can also walk in the obedience He walked in.

SCRIPTURE READING: Hebrews 5:1-10
PERSONAL APPLICATION: Read Hebrews 5:7-9 again. How is Jesus an example of 'learning' obedience? How do you deal with suffering in your life? How can you turn it into an opportunity to learn obedience?

YOU DESERVE THE BEST

"For every beast of the forest is Mine,
And the cattle on a thousand hills."
Psalm 50:10

You deserve the best because God is your Heavenly Father! The God who made and owns everything is your own Heavenly Father! If you are a believer in Christ then God is your Heavenly Father; you are part of God's family. "God decided in advance to adopt us into His own family by bringing us to Himself through Jesus Christ. This is what He wanted to do, and it gave Him great pleasure" (Ephesians 1:5 *NLT*).
The birds do not sow or reap or gather into barns, yet God feeds them; also the grass doesn't toil or spin, yet God clothes it. If we are indeed of more value than them (and we are); then we should expect God to feed and clothe us, not primarily because of what we do, but because He is our Heavenly Father! Jesus said, you shouldn't worry about your basic needs, "For your heavenly Father knows that you need all these things" (Matthew 6:32). And for the same reason we are not to use vain repetition, as the heathens do, when praying. You deserve the best, because God Himself qualified you for it; He made you worthy and deserving in Christ! "...giving thanks to the Father who has qualified us to be partakers of the inheritance of the saints in the light" (Colossians 1:12). It also goes on to say, we have redemption through the blood of Jesus, and the forgiveness of sins. In Christ we have not only been forgiven, we've also been accepted in the Beloved- we have been made the righteousness of God in Christ (2 Corinthians 5:21)! There is actually no reason or need for you to feel unworthy anymore.

SCRIPTURE READING: Ephesians 1:3-14
PERSONAL APPLICATION: God has chosen us in Christ Jesus to be His. Christ has called us His friend. Our adoption into God's Kingdom makes us brothers and sisters of Christ Himself. Give God thanks today that of all His creation, He has chosen you. Drown every thought of unworthiness by meditating on the scriptures about God as our Heavenly Father.

WHAT WOULD GOD HAVE YOU DO

"Many sternly rebuked him, telling him to keep still and be quiet; but he kept on shouting out all the more,
"Son of David (Messiah), have mercy on me!"
Mark 10:48 AMP

For things to happen on earth, man usually plays a role. Many want to play no part and want to see things happen to them. By his Spirit, God inspires us into actions that will lead to our needed miracles. Whenever you are praying for God to do things in your life, ask to know what your role is in what He wants to do, in response to your faith. I wonder who told blind Bartimaeus to shout louder to get Jesus' attention before the miracle of sight to blind eyes happened for him. Who informed the woman with the issue of blood that she could draw on the power of God through the helm of Jesus' garment? Mary, the mother of Jesus was specifically told her role. Remember that faith will always be involved in the role you are to play, but let God help you to know it and do not let any stronghold keep you from walking in the knowledge of God.

The way to identify existing strongholds in our minds is to recognise the reactions that pop up in our minds whenever the knowledge of God comes to us. Usually what God tells us to do may look ridiculous, but the ridiculous sometimes precedes the miraculous. Your future lies in your knowledge of God. Go for all God has for you! Amen!

SCRIPTURE READING: 2 Kings 5:1-14

PERSONAL APPLICATION: What is God asking you to do today? What is it that is preventing you from obeying? Do not allow any fear or stronghold to stop you!

WORTHY OF YOUR WAGES

"Remember me, my God, for good, according to all that I have done for this people."
Nehemiah 5:19

A lot of folks don't believe they deserve any reward in life; so they don't expect any. Jesus said, a labourer is worthy of his wages; "those who work deserve their pay" (Luke 10:7 *NLT*). The truth is, you aren't being done a favour, when you are paid for doing some work! Do you work without expecting a reward? That wouldn't be humility, but false humility as a result of ignorance; because there is no basis in the Bible for that. The brother of the prodigal son was angry because his father decided to throw a party at the return of his brother. He had slaved for so many years without taking a break to enjoy any reward; whereas, all his father had was his - at his disposal! Compare and contrast him with David. David asked, "What will a man get for killing this Philistine and ending his defiance of Israel?" (1 Samuel 17:26 *NLT*). Of course they told him that the king had offered a huge reward to anyone who kills him. He would give that man one of his daughters for a wife, and the man's entire family would be exempted from paying taxes! Wow, what a reward; enough to fire anyone up for action! Is it possible that it's the lack of expectation of rewards that has produced in many cases the lack of drive and motivation to take on some tasks? God Himself has a reward system; "Anyone who wants to come to Him must believe that God exists and that He rewards those who sincerely seek Him" (Hebrews 11:6 *NLT*). God said He didn't ask folks to seek Him in vain (Isaiah 45:19)! God doesn't reward people with evil or bad things; He takes pleasure in the prosperity of those who serve Him (Psalm 35:27).

SCRIPTURE READING: Hebrews 6:9-20
PERSONAL APPLICATION: As you serve God in His Kingdom, trust that He will and is rewarding your labour of love. Whatever you are believing God for, know that He is willing to grant you your heart's desires! God is a rewarder.

DIVINE PATTERN OF SONSHIP

"I have been crucified with Christ and I no longer live, but Christ lives in me. The life I now live in the flesh, I live by faith in the Son of God, who loved me and gave himself for me."
Galatians 2:20

"For whom He foreknew, He also predestined to be conformed to the image of His son, that He might be the firstborn among many brethren" (Romans 8:29). Jesus died to set us free, however His life, death, burial and resurrection also shows us a pattern for us in living according to His will. This has to do with character formation, where inner attitudes and attributes like humility, intimacy and faithfulness are cultivated. The main issues here are that tests of character precede kingdom promotions. Jesus died and we are supposed to die to ourselves. Our flesh needs putting under. He carried His cross and we are supposed to be ready to carry ours. A body was prepared for Him as He was to lay His body in death, and we are to present our bodies as a living sacrifice. Our motives and focus come to bear on our servant heart for God's kingdom purposes. The death process of the grain of wheat comes into focus here. We undergo the process of denying self, taking up our cross and following Him (see John 12:24-26). In our death process, all the trappings of the old nature and its effects on our souls undergo death. Paul says, "I have been crucified with Christ; it is no longer I who live, but Christ lives in me; and the *life* which I now live in the flesh I live by faith in the Son of God, who loved me and gave Himself for me" (Galatians 2:20). This aspect is not popularly preached because dying to self is not always palatable neither is it found when happiness is our ultimate goal in our Christian faith. Our motive in life should be our love for God and our focus should be Christ and His Kingdom.

SCRIPTURE READING: John 12:24-26
PERSONAL APPLICATION: It's time to do some self reflection. What characteristics and attitudes can you see in yourself that need to go through the death process? We are called to conform to the image of Christ which means our character must go through transformation. Ask God to help you as you go through the process of denying self.

ENJOYING GREAT PEACE

"Great peace have those who love your law,
and nothing can make them stumble."
Psalm 119:165

Jesus told His disciples that it is impossible that no offences should come; He said, "Things that cause people to stumble are bound to come," (Luke 17:1 *NIV*). But, nothing shall offend or make to stumble, those who love God's law. *The Message Bible* puts it so clearly, "For those who love what you reveal, everything fits—no stumbling around in the dark for them" (Psalm 119:165). What then is God's law? A lawyer asked Jesus, which is the great commandment in the law? "Jesus said to him, "'You shall love the Lord your God with all your heart, with all your soul, and with all your mind.' This is the first and great commandment. And the second is like it: 'You shall love your neighbour as yourself.' On these two commandments hang all the Law and the Prophets"" (Matthew 22:37-40). Jesus gave a new commandment to His disciples, that they love one another as He had loved them- not just as they loved themselves! The focus and standard need to shift from you, to Christ; and that can only be accomplished by His help - His grace. Offences will always come, but to be or not to be offended is a choice you make; and if you choose not to be offended, you will enjoy great peace. It also works that if you have chosen to have peace in spite of everything around you, you will choose not to be offended by anything. Some people around you have chosen to be rude, selfish, unfair and unkind, but you must choose not to be negatively affected by their wrong choices. Live proactively, rather than reacting negatively to circumstances.

SCRIPTURE READING: 1 John 2:7-11
PERSONAL APPLICATION: Make a decision today that whenever offences come your way, you will steward your responses towards love. Instead of reacting in anger or doing evil, forgive, pray and bless those who hurt you. It draws you closer to God and He can take away any hurt and pain so that you don't have to bear it.

NO FOREIGN GODS

"Blessed are the pure in heart, for they shall see God."
Matthew 5:8

Don't seek God with idols in your heart - i.e. with your mind already made up, or a hidden agenda, or a wrong motive, or a preconception, or else He will answer you accordingly (Ezekiel 14:1-4)! Do you know we hear God according to the contents and disposition of our hearts? We are told to seek the Lord while He may be found, and to call upon Him while He is near; and because His thoughts and ways are higher than ours, we must forsake our own ways and thoughts, and take on His (Isaiah 55:6-9). God says two people can't walk together, except they are going in the same direction or are in agreement (Amos 3:3); and it only makes sense to know that we are the ones to align our ways with His, not the other way round! King Asa did what was good and right in the eyes of the Lord his God, because he removed the altars of the foreign gods and the high places, and broke down the sacred pillars and cut down the wooden images; and then commanded Judah to seek the Lord God of their fathers, and to observe the law and the commandment (2 Chronicles 14:1-4). So, it's time to pull down the stronghold of preconceptions, contrary mind-sets, belief systems and the high things in our lives, so we can see and hear God clearly.

SCRIPTURE READING: Psalm 24:1-6
PERSONAL APPLICATION: How can you identify if you have any idols in your heart? Sometimes you don't even know what is in your own heart. Pray according to Psalm 24:4. You can ask God to search you and reveal the inner disposition of your heart. As God reveals things to you, don't feel condemned, ask God who is merciful to cleanse and purify your heart.

RISING INCENSE

"Your prayers and your alms have come up
for a memorial before God."
Acts 10:4

Jesus said when we give, fast and pray, our Father who sees in secret will reward us openly (Matthew 6:1-4, 6, 17-18). Truly, God didn't ask us to seek Him in vain! Cornelius was a devout and God-fearing man who gave alms generously and prayed to God always. He was told by an angel in a vision that his prayers and alms had gone up for a memorial before God (Acts 10:1-4). The prayers of the saints are offered as incense before His throne (Revelation 5:8, 8:3-4), so they cannot be forgotten. The Bible says, "The earnest prayer of a righteous person has great power and produces wonderful results" (James 5:16 *NIV*). Hannah prayed and made a vow asking for a male child from the Lord, "and the Lord remembered her". In the process of time she conceived and bore a son whom she named Samuel, saying, "Because I have asked for him from the Lord" (1 Samuel 1:19-20). Zacharias was told by the angel that his prayer was heard and his wife Elizabeth was going to have a son that will be named John (Luke 1:13-14). God never forgets our prayers and our gifts, or anything we do in service to Him, even when we or others have long forgotten; because they are before Him for a memorial! The Bible says, by faith Abel offered to God a more excellent sacrifice than Cain, and through it, he being dead still speaks (Hebrews 11:4). Paul said the gift the Philippians sent to him was a sweet smelling aroma, an acceptable sacrifice, well pleasing to God. "And my God shall supply all your need according to His riches in glory by Christ Jesus" (Philippians 4:19-20).

SCRIPTURE READING: Matthew 6:1-18, Galatians 6:9
PERSONAL APPLICATION: Study the stories of Hannah, Zacharias and Cornelius. What attributes do you find in their prayer and communion with God? Commit to a life of prayer and devotion to God and ask Him to show you areas where you can offer your time, talent and treasure as an acceptable sacrifice before Him.

UNDERSTANDING BOUNDARIES

"On the same day the Lord made a covenant with Abram, saying: 'To your descendants I have given this land, from the river of Egypt to the great river, the River Euphrates'"
Genesis 15:18

Error can be defined as truth taken beyond godly boundaries. The enemy of our souls wants to keep us bound up in habits and destructive tendencies and he succeeds at this through deception and delusions. He uses thought-patterns that foster his deceptive strategies. It is the reality of godly boundaries that he blinds people to and so when they think they are free of his bondage, they now roam free to do just anything, hence they come into another dimension of bondage. A functional part of the legitimacy of anything is when its correct boundaries are known. Outside godly boundaries, a good thing becomes a curse! Within the right boundaries there lies a vast potential of the depth and width of the same thing.

The example that comes to mind is the emotional make-up of human beings. Within godly boundaries of marriage, there is such a depth of intimacy and fulfilment that is potentially available, outside marriage this emotional make-up can be the beginning of unhealthy and binding soul-ties. In life, ministry and relationships, it helps to know the boundaries God has set for us not Satan. When Adam and Eve were told not to eat the fruit of the knowledge of good and evil, it was to shield them from knowing things that they had no power to change. It also served as a godly boundary of obedience to stay in the place of blessings. Through the lust of the eyes, the lust of the flesh and pride of life, they were lured out of their boundaries and came under a curse from the same one who had blessed them. This reveals that Satan's chief operation is to bring us to a place where we are against God's way of doing things. He is empowered when we are out of God's order of things. Real freedom is when we are free to obey God, not free to do what we want to do. Many times what we want to do is linked up to what the flesh can use to hinder us from full obedience to God. Our will needs to become aligned with His in every area of our lives.

SCRIPTURE READING: Genesis 2:8-17, 3:1-19

PERSONAL APPLICATION: God gives us boundaries for our own good and protection. Are there any godly boundaries you are trying to 'free' yourself of or rebel against? Don't do it. You'll only be opening the door for Satan to come in and mess you up. Live within godly boundaries—it's the place of safety, protection and freedom.

MORE THAN ENOUGH

"Now to Him who is able to do exceedingly abundantly above all that we ask or think, according to the power that works in us"
Ephesians 3:20

A lot of folks have a mentality of poverty and shortage, instead of an abundance mentality. They always think in terms of 'not enough' rather than 'more than enough'! They always see the glass 'half-empty,' rather than 'half-full!' Jesus said, "Now if God so clothes the grass of the field, which today is, and tomorrow is thrown into the oven, will He not much more clothe you, O you of little faith?" (Matthew 6:30). God still lavishly clothes the grass, even though it might not be there for long, and doesn't think it's being wasteful! God always does things 'much more,' and not 'much less!' He is El-Shaddai; more than enough. Jesus came that we might have life more abundantly; He said, "I came that they may have and enjoy life, and have it in abundance (to the full, till it overflows)" (John 10:10 *AMPC*). Do you value yourself enough to believe you deserve the best in life, and not always look for the poorest, cheapest and lowest of things?

SCRIPTURE READING: 1 Kings 17:8-16
PERSONAL APPLICATION: Today, take the limits off God! Present your desires and dreams before God and trust that He will do exceedingly and abundantly above all you could ask or think.

PREPARING FOR GOD'S NEW THING

"See, I am doing a new thing! Now it springs up; do you not perceive it? I am making a way in the wilderness and streams in the wasteland."
Isaiah 43:19 NIV

Many things are involved in knowing and cooperating with God for the new thing to come to pass. We read for instance that when the day of Pentecost was fully come, the Holy Spirit suddenly came into the upper room (Acts 2). We generally think He does things like that without anything happening to bring it about. The truth is He inspires us to cooperate with Him while we can or He causes things to be in agreement with His will so the new thing can come to pass. He has His processes to sharpen us for His purposes. Our willingness to yield to the Spirit of God and our faith to appropriate His provision are two keys to God's new things in our lives. The yielded heart says, 'Lord, what would you have me do?'; the heart full of faith says, 'I can do all things through Christ who strengthens me!'. We yield for Him to have His way, and we take by faith what is ours in His provision. Whatever has been provided in the Word is for taking by faith. When we get loaded with the Word there is a heart full of faith and acting on the Word will produce new things and helps us to give all the cooperation to God. Our expectation plays a major role in determining the lifestyle that will get us to experience the new things that God will be doing. Our lifestyle is what determines whether we will experience the new things or if we shall just hear of it when it happens to others. When we yield to the Holy Spirit, exercise faith in His Word and build our expectation on Him, we will cultivate a lifestyle that will be conducive for God's new thing.

SCRIPTURE READING: Isaiah 43:16-19
PERSONAL APPLICATION: Make this confession: *"Heavenly Father, I am ready for something new. I am willing to participate with you to bring about the miraculous and supernatural. Lord, help me not to let fear and doubt stop the flow of greatness. Amen".*

OVERCOMING FEAR

"There is no fear in love; but perfect love casts out fear, because fear involves torment. But he who fears has not been made perfect in love."
1 John 4:18

There isn't much you can reach out for or aspire to accomplish if you entertain the fear of some evil befalling you, or the fear of death or failure or defeat or any other fears. God said, "Enlarge your house; build an addition. Spread out your home, and spare no expense! For you will soon be bursting at the seams" (Isaiah 54:2-3 *NLT*). But the key to achieving that is in the following instructions, "Do not fear, for you will not be ashamed; Neither be disgraced, for you will not be put to shame" (Isaiah 54:4). Do you know that you could even be afraid of succeeding? A lot of folks are happy to have average finances - being neither poor nor rich; so as to stay 'safe'; "give me neither poverty nor riches! Give me just enough to satisfy my needs. For if I grow rich, I may deny You and say, 'Who is the Lord?' And if I am too poor, I may steal and thus insult God's holy name" (Proverbs 30:8-9 *NLT*). But God wants you to prosper in all things (3 John 2); He wants us to make our way prosperous and have good success (Joshua 1:8). Instead of being afraid of succeeding, let's develop ourselves to handle success.

SCRIPTURE READING: Exodus 3:1-18
PERSONAL APPLICATION: Identify any fear holding you back and confront it with the Word of God. Trust that God has placed mighty potential in you, which needs to be developed in order to handle success.

LET YOUR LIGHT SHINE

"Let your light so shine before men, that they may see your good works and glorify your Father in heaven."
Matthew 5:16

We are the salt of the earth and the light of the world. We are to generate the influence that will preserve the earth and show the world the way to God and how to live a fulfilled life in Christ. God did not intend to hide the church in a place of irrelevance and obscurity. He intends that the earth be preserved by the presence of the church and the light that we carry should shine throughout the world so that people will know who God is and He will be given His rightful place in their lives. The world is ignorant of God, largely because God's agents of influence (His people) have not allowed the light to shine. We should no longer seek our own but embrace His ways and Kingdom. The outcome is a more fulfilled life that glorifies God. We seek His Kingdom and every other thing is added to us because as we get involved with His kingdom, we know how He operates and all the supplies we need are added to us. God bless you as you labour for and in the Kingdom of God.

SCRIPTURE READING: Matthew 5:13-16, Isaiah 60:1, Colossians 3:1-17
PERSONAL APPLICATION: As a believer, the Bible calls you the salt of the earth and the light of the world. God has blessed you with every spiritual blessing (Ephesians 1:3). Jesus is your perfect example on how to live your life on earth. And the Holy Spirit is your great Helper. Today, tap into God's grace to be a doer of His Word and to be a blessing to your loved ones and neighbours.

LAYING HOLD OF HOPE

"Now hope does not disappoint, because the love of God has been poured out in our hearts by the Holy Spirit who was given to us."
Romans 5:5

Hope (expectation) is the cornerstone of Christianity. The Bible has a lot to say about our spiritual hope which, unfortunately, many have lost sight of! (1 Corinthians 15:19). First and foremost is the hope of spending eternity with the Lord! (1 Thessalonians 4:17). We were saved in the hope of the redemption of our body (Romans 8:23-24). The Bible says we shall be changed in the twinkling of an eye, at the last trumpet (1 Corinthians 15:51-52). As children of God, we have the hope that we shall be like Him when He is revealed, for we shall see Him as He is. This hope has the power to purify us, if we would retain it in us (1 John 1:2-3). We were born "again to a living hope through the resurrection of Jesus Christ from the dead, to an inheritance incorruptible and undefiled and that does not fade away, reserved in heaven" for us (1 Peter 1:3-4). Apostle Paul prayed for the Ephesians; that the eyes of their understanding being enlightened, may know what is the hope of God's calling (Ephesians 1:17-18). The Bible says when we were without Christ, we were also without hope and without God in the world, but, praise God, we now have Christ (Ephesians 2:11-13). This implies we now have hope and are with God in this world! Hope in Christ isn't therefore only in the life to come, that is, in the sweet by and by; but also in this present life. The Bible says, "...training for godliness is much better, promising benefits in this life and in the life to come" (1 Timothy 4:8 *NLT*). The righteous shall also be rewarded on earth (Proverbs 11:31). "The blessing of the Lord makes a person rich, and He adds no sorrow with it" (Proverbs 10:22 *NLT*). The man who fears the Lord and walks in His ways is blessed; and those blessings are also here in this life (Psalms 112 and 128)!

SCRIPTURE READING: 1 Thessalonians 4:17, Romans 8: 23-24, 1 Peter 1:3-4
PERSONAL APPLICATION: Hope can be defined as: to trust in, wait for, look for, or desire something or someone; or to expect something beneficial in the future. We all put our trust in something, but ultimately, we are created to trust in God and depend on Him and His promises. Abraham hoped in God, he and his wife Sarah had their own son when Sarah had already passed her child bearing age; Daniel trusted in God, and he was saved from the lion's den. God is our covenant God, He does not ask us to seek Him in vain. Therefore, let us be encouraged and fix our eyes on the faithful promises of God.

BELIEVE AND RECEIVE

"For by grace are ye saved through faith; and that not of yourselves: it is the gift of God"
Ephesians 2:8 KJV

Through believing in Jesus Christ and His work at Calvary, we have come into a relationship with God. We can call Him our Father. We have received Jesus Christ as our Saviour, we have the right to become children of God (John 1:12). To become a child of God is not automatic, it is to be received by faith. We must get rid of unbelief, disbelief and rebellion to accept what has been given to us. Our relationship with God is based on the finished work of calvary! Not on our efforts! Our part is to believe and receive. It is our fellowship that is based on our decisions, choices and efforts! Our relationship, when we believe, has been sealed by the blood, and the Spirit of God acts as a down payment for the full purchase of our redemption.
Ephesians 1:11-14 (*KJV*) says, "In whom also we have obtained an inheritance, being predestinated according to the purpose of him who worketh all things after the counsel of his own will: That we should be to the praise of his glory, who first trusted in Christ. In whom ye also trusted, after that ye heard the word of truth, the gospel of your salvation: in whom also after that ye believed, ye were sealed with that holy Spirit of promise, Which is the earnest of our inheritance until the redemption of the purchased possession, unto the praise of his glory."
The potential that is available to us because of our relationship with the Father, through Jesus Christ, has put us in a totally different standing with God. We have access to things that were impossible before now. We can do all things through Him who infuses inner strength in us (Philippians 4:13).
Romans 8:16-17, "The Spirit itself beareth witness with our spirit, that we are the children of God. And if children, then heirs; heirs of God, and joint-heirs with Christ; if so be that we suffer with him, that we may be also glorified together."

SCRIPTURE READING: 2 Corinthians 5:14-21
PERSONAL APPLICATION: Believing in Jesus Christ and His work at calvary is through faith; and that grace which saved us is the gift of God. Receiving it is the best decision we can ever make.

ONLY BELIEVE

"Peace I leave with you; my peace I give you. I do not give to you as the world gives. Do not let your hearts be troubled and do not be afraid."
John 14:27 NIV

"Do not be afraid; only believe" (Mark 5:36). Those were Jesus' words to Jairus, when he was told his daughter was now dead, and there was no need to trouble the Master any further. Jairus had already cast his care on the Lord, by presenting his request to Him; and the news he got was an opportunity to take it back! Jairus was very specific in his requests; he said, "My little daughter lies at the point of death. Come and lay Your hands on her, that she may be healed, and she will live" (Mark 5:22-23). That was Jairus' faith speaking; he believed his daughter would live if Jesus laid hands on her. Many times, after we've turned things over to the Lord, contrary circumstances develop to make us take them back. Rather than yield to them, we must still maintain our stance of faith. Fear and faith are reciprocals. Fear will rob you of your faith; hence Jesus' words to Jairus, "Do not be afraid, only believe" (Mark 5:36). Faith will drive out fear. Fear is a spirit, and it's not from God; so exercise authority over it and cast it away from you (2 Timothy 1:7). Fear came as a result of the fall of man; it is foreign to your recreated spirit (Romans 8:15). To be afraid is a choice; you can choose not to fear, no matter the circumstances around you (Psalm 23:4). You can choose not to respond in fear to the things around you; but to respond in faith. Not to be afraid is a commandment from God. There are enough 'fear nots' in the Bible to take you through every day of the year.

SCRIPTURE READING: Psalm 23:1-6, Psalm 91:1-16
PERSONAL APPLICATION: Do you know that we have the power of choice to choose either to be in fear or in faith? Do you know that our response is our responsibility? Let's put a stop sign in our mind, when Satan tries to throw fear on us. Let's fight the good fight of faith, because our God is faithful. Psalm 91:5-7 says, "You shall not be afraid of the terror by night, Nor of the arrow that flies by day, Nor of the pestilence that walks in darkness, Nor of the destruction that lays waste at noonday. A thousand may fall at your side, and ten thousand at your right hand; But it shall not come near you."

YOU CAN TURN IT AROUND

"Behold, I am the Lord, the God of all flesh.
Is there anything too hard for Me?"
Jeremiah 32:27

No matter the problem or situation, the Word of God has the solution. If you seek God, He will show you the way out and the way forward. In Romans 4, from verse 16, we read about Abraham, the father of multitudes, who had no child to start with. God calls things that be not as though they were, because He lives in the timeless zone called eternity. He sees the end from the beginning. His Word paints a picture inside your heart. That picture is your future, a product of His promises. That is what hope is, an inner image in the heart. When the natural hope failed, Abraham allowed God's Word to give him a new hope. That hope was so powerful it changed him from the inside out. Meditation lets you get that Word established in your heart. When you can see it, you will act on it and speak it and get the results. That is how we were designed to function. What is on your heart? If its your past failures then you are planning to re-live them again. Replace your failures and fears with God's Word through meditation and confession. That is where the work is. Getting the inner image to be in harmony with the covenant Word of God is hard work. Too many fear-borne prayers go unanswered and God gets the blame for it. In addition to this process, waiting on God for His wisdom to know the accurate timing and needed skill necessary to carry out the things involved becomes necessary. Is it any surprise that faith is the assurance of things hoped for? The steps described so far are the steps of faith. It is time to speak to mountains after we are established in our hearts that we are mountain movers. In fact, the continuous process of speaking and feeding on the Word of God is part of the process of getting established in the Word. It is time to change all the things that can be changed by the power of the Word of God.

SCRIPTURE READING: Philippians 4:13, Mark 11:24, John 15:7
PERSONAL APPLICATION: No matter the problem or situation, the Word of God has the solution. Do you believe it? Today, challenge yourself to find the promises in God's Word that concern your situation; start to meditate on them, confess it and declare it. When you receive your answer, please remember to share your testimony with us.

DO YOU WANT TO BE WELL?

"When Jesus saw him and knew he had been ill for a long time, he asked him, 'Would you like to get well?'"
John 5:6 NLT

In John 5:6 Jesus asked a man who had an infirmity, "Do you want to be well?" It seems Jesus was challenging in that man, the mind-set that had kept him in that state for thirty eight years! The man thought he needed someone to put him into the pool before he could be healed; but Jesus simply said to him, "Rise, take up your bed and walk" (John 5:8). Jesus was challenging in him, an unhealthy dependence on people and systems. Think of so many people who are stuck today in their predicament because they are waiting for someone to get them out, instead of taking responsibility for their own breakthrough. Jesus gave the man a threefold instruction; "Rise, take up your bed and walk". The man had to rise first of all - he had to rise up in his thinking; he had to rise up on the inside, above his immediate situation and environment. He needed to rise above everything around him so he could begin to see new possibilities. He needed to rise up to break through his infirmity. Do you know that where you are, determines what you can see? "Arise, shine; for your light has come!" (Isaiah 60:1). It seems you can't shine unless you first of all arise.

SCRIPTURE READING: John 5:1-15
PERSONAL APPLICATION: Whatever it is that is keeping you down, allow the Word of God to challenge the mind-set and thinking that is keeping you there. Receive empowerment today to get up, to pick up your 'mat' and to walk!

ACCORDING TO YOUR FAITH

"He said to her, 'Daughter, your faith has healed you.'"
Mark 5:34 NIV

God has chosen to do things in response to our faith in Him. Mark 5:22-43 talks about Jairus, one of the rulers of the synagogue. His daughter was sick and he called upon Jesus for healing. That is prayer in its simplest form. Jesus responded to his call and started to go to his house. On the way, news came that the daughter had died. Jesus told Jairus, "fear not, only believe". That means prayer had set things into motion to see to the healing of the girl, a negative report should not negate the faith of this man in Jesus. Fear will steal your faith, don't let it happen. Another miracle took place that had no form of request from the needy one. The woman with the issue of blood forced herself through the crowd and touched the edge of the garment of Jesus and her ailment was healed. Jesus felt power leave Him and after recognising who touched Him, He said, "Daughter, your faith has made you whole". God wants to do things in response to our prayers and faith. Get on your knees and pray according to His Word; believe (fear not) and receive answers to your prayers.

SCRIPTURE READING: Mark 5:22-43, Mark 10:46-52, 11:22-24
PERSONAL APPLICATION: Jairus, the woman with the issue of blood and blind Bartimaeus all had faith and believed in Jesus. As a believer, if Jesus came and asked you today, "What do you want me to do for you?", what would you ask Him? Do you have the faith to receive your answer?

MODEL IT, SHOW IT, LIVE IT

"Follow my example, as I follow the example of Christ."
1 Corinthians 11:1 NIV

Children need role models. They learn from them; they copy their ways. Children literally adore and admire their role models; they want to be just like them in every way! You can model fatherhood, motherhood, success, etc. to your kids. It isn't enough to teach them; model it, show it and live it! What people see makes a greater and more lasting impact on them, much more than what they hear. Jethro said to Moses about the children of Israel, "And you shall teach them the statutes and the laws, and show them the way in which they must walk and the work they must do" (Exodus 18:20). Peter charged his fellow elders to be examples to the flock entrusted to them (1 Peter 5:3). Paul told Timothy, his son, to keep putting into practice all he had learned and heard from him, and saw him doing (Philippians 4:9) and that Timothy himself should be an example to all believers in what he taught, in the way he lived, in love, faith and purity (1 Timothy 4:12). Note that children don't do just what you say, but what you do.

SCRIPTURE READING: Proverbs 22:6, 2 Timothy 1:3-7
PERSONAL APPLICATION: It takes strength of character and a strong conviction to live a life of integrity and to be someone our kids want to follow after, especially when under pressure. May God grant you the strength and clarity of mind you need to be a role model to your children; not just to 'talk the talk' but to model it, show it and live it everyday, in Jesus' Name!

TAKE HEED WHAT YOU HEAR

"Your statutes are my delight;
they are my counsellors."
Psalm 119:24 NIVUK

Mark 4:24 says, "Take heed what you hear. With the same measure you use, it will be measured to you; and to you who hear, more will be given." The measure of thought and study we measure to the truth we hear will determine the measure of virtue and understanding that will be measured back to us. God deals with us according to the measure of respect we have for Him and His Word. Satan's greatest fear is when believers come into truth. He will do everything and anything to stop it, as we have seen. The entrance of the Word gives light. In the Word is life and the life is the light of men (John 1:4). Satan is the prince of darkness so he hates it when light comes on. We are the light of the world. When we get saved we receive the life of God and that life is the light. The Word also has life and the light in the life is released as we receive the Word into our hearts. The Word of God contains the grace, power, love and anointing of God. As we respect and receive the Word, the grace and love in the Word will flow into us and equip, strengthen and prepare us to do His will. Keep the Word central.

SCRIPTURE READING: Psalm 119:9-16
PERSONAL APPLICATION: Let us make a fresh commitment today to press into God and into His Word with a greater zeal and hunger than before. The more of His Word is in us, the more of His light will come to us.

SIN LIES AT THE DOOR

"If you do well, will you not be accepted? And if you do not do well, sin lies at the door. And its desire is for you, but you should rule over it."
Genesis 4:7

Adam and Eve lost the garden of Eden because of sin. People who hold on to their sin will have their portion in the lake of fire (Revelation 21:8). It is the cheapest thing to commit fornication and adultery these days. Lie telling is no more a sin in some quarters. The Bible says anyone that hates his brother is a murderer, like Cain. In the New Testament, hatred is murder. The truth is that if you hate anyone, you can actually physically kill the person or take his wife or do anything to harm him. The Bible says, "Love works no ill to his neighbour, therefore love is the fulfilling of the law" (Romans 13:10 *KJV*). Satan only needed a Judas who was already envious of Jesus to betray him. Judas was filled with envy, jealousy and anger when the woman with the box of alabaster oil broke it and poured it all on Jesus. Judas suddenly remembered the poor, that the oil could have been sold and the proceeds given to the poor. The Bible tells us that he didn't care about the poor and he was a thief. What does that mean? He wanted it for himself. How do you feel when another person is being honoured? Do you feel that honour should have been given to you? Please get rid of that feeling quickly because it will get rid of you if you don't. Cain was jealous and angry because he felt it was his own offering God should have accepted and not Abel's. Before he actually reached out to kill his brother God warned him, "sin lies at the door" (Genesis 4:7). Whenever you are jealous, angry or envious, remember, sin lies at the door; don't give in to it! If because of our sins, God didn't spare His only begotten Son, Jesus Christ but delivered Him up for us all, I wonder how and why He would spare anyone who refuses to accept Christ's sacrifice and let go of a life of sin.

SCRIPTURE READING: Galatians 5:16-24, Ephesians 4:17-5:20
PERSONAL APPLICATION: God has empowered us through the Holy Spirit to live above the desires and dictates of our sinful nature. If you recognise areas in your life where you give in to your 'flesh', repent and cry out to God. He is faithful and just to forgive us (1 John 1:9). Then receive the strength and grace from God to live by and produce the fruit of the Spirit (Galatians 5:22-23).

WALKING IN GOD'S PROMISES

"But the scripture hath concluded all under sin, that the promise by faith of Jesus Christ might be given to them that believe."
Galatians 3:22 KJV

Just like we believed to become God's children, we need to believe to receive from God. Romans 10:9-10 *KJV* says, "That if thou shalt confess with thy mouth the Lord Jesus, and shalt believe in thine heart that God hath raised him from the dead, thou shalt be saved. For with the heart man believeth unto righteousness; and with the mouth confession is made unto salvation." With the heart we believe unto a new nature and with the mouth we confess unto all our salvation offers. All God has done for others in the Bible can and should become our basis for expecting Him to do similar things for us. His Word is His bond. Whatever He said or did can become our solid ground for believing and receiving. Our responsibility involves connecting our need with His provisions. His provisions are conveyed to us through His promises. We take portions of His nature and ability through these promises.

SCRIPTURE READING: Hebrews 6:13-19
PERSONAL APPLICATION: Don't wait for problems to arise before standing on God's Word. The secret is to build your faith in God before any problem arises so that if and when it does, you have within you the strength to stand.

Promises for Healing: Isaiah 53:3-5, 1 Peter 2:24
Promises for Protection: Psalm 91, Psalm 27:5
Promises for Provision: Psalm 23:1, Psalm 34:9-10
Promises for Direction: Psalm 25:4-5, Psalm 27:11, Psalm 23:3, Psalm 3:6
Promises for Strength: Psalm 27:1, Psalm 18:39, Psalm 29:11, Isaiah 40:29, Philippians 4:13
Promises for Courage: Psalm 27:13, Psalm 23:6, Deuteronomy 31:6, Joshua 1:9
Promises for Success in God's will: Joshua 1:8

DO NOT BE AFRAID

"But when he saw the wind, he was afraid and, beginning to sink, cried out, "Lord, save me!""
Matthew 14:30 NIV

I have found that any time I take my eyes off Jesus, I come into tribulation and other things in the world. When I bring my focus back on Him, I have peace. Have you noticed that in your life? When Jesus was walking on water, the disciples were afraid because they thought he was a ghost. He said, "Be of good cheer! It is I; do not be afraid" (Matthew 14:27). God always comes with a message of cheer, a message of 'don't be afraid'. I have never seen God telling anyone to be afraid in the Bible. See examples of Angel Gabriel when he appeared to Mary, and Jehoshaphat when the army came up against him. God always comes with the message, 'Fear not!'.

When you look at things in the natural, you will be afraid. What you should do when you are afraid is call a prayer meeting! In 2 Chronicles 20, they lifted up their voices and prayed. For some of us, the last thing we do is pray, if we even remember to at all! But Jehoshaphat called a prayer meeting, and when the Spirit of the Lord came upon Jehaziel, the Lord said, 'Do not be dismayed.' Fear rises when we take our focus away from God.

SCRIPTURE READING: Matthew 14:22-32

PERSONAL APPLICATION: As long as Peter's eyes were kept on Jesus, he was walking on water. But when he took his eyes off Jesus and put them on the storm, and looked at the boisterous waves, he began to sink. That happens to us. Determine today to keep your eyes on Jesus. No matter the storm, do not be afraid. Be still and know that He is God.

THE POWER OF VISION

"Where there is no vision [no redemptive revelation of God], the people perish; but he who keeps the law [of God, which includes that of man]—blessed (happy, fortunate, and enviable) is he."
Proverbs 29:18 AMPC

No one can kill a visionary who is on course with God's vision for their life. You are protected within God's vision that you are pursuing. The vision will keep you through all the stages of development. As you go through process the vision matures in you. The vision will keep you from sin like it did Joseph. If you are focused on the Lord and you keep the vision pure before you, the vision will keep you from sin and contamination. Do not allow God's vision for your life to be polluted with rivalry, competitive jealousy and carnal desires of the flesh. That vision will keep you pure. Sin is a destroyer of destiny and Satan will hold you in condemnation if you allow him. Keep yourself pure; remember we have an advocate with the Father, Jesus Christ. Repent and go on if you fall. The vision will cause you to grow as it grows in you. You will be bigger than unforgiveness and bitterness. It will also deliver you from insecurity and the things that plague people with small minds. The vision will give you what it takes to help the vision of others. It will deliver to you authority in life after you have passed the tests and wilderness experience. God bless you as you let the vision speak for it will not tarry.

SCRIPTURE READING: Genesis 39:1-10, 19-23, Colossians 3:1-17
PERSONAL APPLICATION: God has called you for a specific plan and purpose (Jeremiah 29:11). Ask God to reveal to you His vision for your life. A vision will keep you on course and on track. May you run with endurance the race that is set before you (Hebrews 12:1-2).

UNDERSTANDING PURPOSE IN RELATIONSHIPS

"Can two walk together, unless they are agreed?"
Amos 3:3

We all need to understand the different goals and purposes in relationships. How far do people want to go in the relationship with you? You can't take them further than they want to go! Don't assume people want to go into the highs and the lows, or through thick and thin with you, just because they are friends with you. Jonathan loved David as his own soul, he cut a covenant with David and even helped him escape from Saul; but all that didn't mean he was going to be running around with him as a fugitive. We must know how to get the best out of people, without placing on them demands bigger than what they are willing to commit to. Because a guy is nice to a lady and buys her lunch, doesn't mean he plans to marry her. His goal might just be friendship, and not marriage; marriage is a life changing, lifetime commitment. The goals must also be mutually understood, so we don't hurt ourselves or others or, even the relationship itself! We are able to get the best out of relationships when they are clearly defined. Defining the purpose of a relationship also helps to define the boundaries for individuals and helps to prevent abuses in the relationship.

SCRIPTURE READING: John 15:14-15
PERSONAL APPLICATION: Relationships can evolve; they have the potential to develop from one level to another. What started as a business relationship can later become a personal relationship; a friendship relationship can become a mentoring relationship, etc. Unfortunately, relationships can also degenerate, if not well handled. This is why we must learn how to define and manage relationships well.

THE OLD VERSUS THE NEW

"Behold, I will do a new thing, now it shall spring forth; shall you not know it? I will even make a road in the wilderness and rivers in the desert."
Isaiah 43:19

Our text for consideration is 1 Kings 13. The story here has to do mainly with a young prophet with a dynamic message from God that was confirmed with signs following, and an older prophet who claimed to have heard from God and got this young man killed. Well, the young man was simply called a man of God. I like that, a man who lives and walks for God. The story when heard in isolation can be used to confirm many lies about God and His operations on the earth. Nothing excites satan more than a distortion of the image of God in the minds of people. To get a fuller picture of the story we need to read from chapter 11 of the book and see how compromise in the heart of people in authority releases a spirit of compromise into the community and every one can be involved and affected. There are lessons to learn from each character in this chapter we are considering. The King Jeroboam had been responding to his insecurities rather than to God's Word that made him king. Compromising the standards of God even to fulfil God's will becomes a risky business as this will lead to all kinds of things if not repented of. Thank God for His mercy. The young man of God helps us to see that there are tests of all sorts in the spirit. Only a strong intimacy with God will help us in our tests. Many have obeyed God's prophets in the Bible and experienced God's blessings. This tells us that blessings are guaranteed only as the prophet speaks the Word of God as from God. Titles bearing past obedience will not suffice. We must be current with the now Word from heaven. From the old prophet we must get it right that God is not in the business of using and dumping us. That is a lie from hell. We get too familiar with Him and tend to become presumptuous using stale methods to carry out fresh instructions. We end up not being able to carry command in the spirit. The man of God knew better than to yield to his flesh in purported obedience to the old prophet. The old prophet had lost it where God is concerned; why he was listened to surprises me. A man's clout in the society cannot be used to determine God's will in these last days.

SCRIPTURE READING: Luke 5:33-39, 1 Kings 13
PERSONAL APPLICATION: Whenever God is going to do a new thing, expect opposition from the old order and be sensitive so you don't lose your guard in your heart to know where to draw the line, as you stay in obedience to God.

PRESS TOWARDS YOUR GOAL

"The horse is made ready for the day of battle,
but the victory belongs to the Lord."
Proverbs 21:31 ESV

Nothing good just happens; you must be willing to pay the price for success. If wishes were horses, beggars would ride. You must make things happen, don't just wait for things to happen; because they may never happen. You must take the Kingdom by force! When the Amalekites raided David and his men, and took away their families and properties, David inquired from God if he should go after them. And God said to David, "Pursue, for you shall surely overtake them and without fail recover all" (1 Samuel 30:8). Work towards your goals; it will take a lot of diligence, hard work and determination, but do it! Don't forget, success opportunities often present themselves as hard work. Go the extra mile; turn the other cheek; put your hand to the plough, and do not look back. "Do you see a man who excels in his work? He will stand before kings; he will not stand before unknown men" (Proverbs 22:29). To achieve your goals, you must cut out all excesses, irrelevances and distractions; "let us lay aside every weight, and the sin which so easily ensnares us, and let us run with endurance the race that is set before us" (Hebrews 12:1). You must also learn time management.

SCRIPTURE READING: 1 Samuel 30:1-20
PERSONAL APPLICATION: No great achievement was ever produced without it first being set as a goal. Goal-setting can become a tool to help time management as well as inspire productivity and help accomplish great things in life. When written down, goals can become a blueprint for the process we choose to go through to accomplish great projects. Why don't you set some time aside right now and start writing down some goals? Then go out and start working towards them.

THE APOSTOLIC OFFICE

"Now, therefore, you are no longer strangers and foreigners, but fellow citizens with the saints and members of the household of God, having been built on the foundation of the apostles and prophets, Jesus Christ Himself being the chief cornerstone"
Ephesians 2:19-20

The apostolic office is the office that governs and operates in godly wisdom to see God's plans, purposes and processes done on earth. It can be likened to the architect in the building industry. The industry has civil engineers, quantity surveyors, estate planners, etc. Whenever anything is to be done according to specifications, all need to put their heads together. The architect is mainly in charge of the design and oversight of construction of the building project. The apostle is pretty much like that in the building of God's house. The wisdom to build, the understanding of process and the grace to break into new grounds and territories are seen in the office of the apostle (see Acts 13-14). Wisdom is the signature of the apostolic office. Apostles have grace to nurture others into their destinies. Paul fathered Timothy and Titus and helped others to be all God had ordained for them.

The first twelve who saw Jesus' ministry on earth and were eyewitnesses of His compassion stand in a unique apostolic grace and office. The book of Acts is a showcase for the apostolic office. Healings, raising the dead, breaking new grounds were common things seen in the book of Acts. Unusual miracles were done through the lives of the apostles. The Bible says that the apostles and prophets were the foundation of the church and Jesus Christ is the chief cornerstone (Ephesians 2:20). This means their lives, revelations and teachings should be the foundation upon which the church is built and the Lord Jesus stands as that which is showed off as the chief cornerstone. When the offices are functional, the gifts of the Spirit will no longer be a strange phenomenon and we can all take our places in the body as we yield to the Spirit of God within His understood boundaries for our operations and functions. God will be glorified as souls are saved, healed and established in the truth. The body will be built as we all supply our parts in the building.

SCRIPTURE READING: Ephesians 4:11-16

PERSONAL APPLICATION: Are you allowing yourself to be built up so you can take your rightful place in the Body of Christ? The early church continued in the Apostles' doctrine and were built up. The Word of God's grace will build you up and give you an inheritance amongst the saints.

PROTECTING YOUR HEART AND MIND

"Above all else, guard your heart, for everything you do flows from it."
Proverbs 4:23 NIV

"Be anxious for nothing, but in everything by prayer and supplication, with thanksgiving, let your requests be made known to God; and the peace of God, which surpasses all understanding, will guard your hearts and minds through Christ Jesus" (Philippians 4:6-7). The *Amplified Bible, Classic Edition* says, it "shall garrison and mount guard over your hearts and minds in Christ Jesus". The picture here is like that of troops sent in to protect a place. The Bible says we should keep our heart with all diligence, because out of it flow the issues of life (Proverbs 4:23); and, one way to keep our heart is by the peace of God. Jesus tells us not to worry about everyday life- "saying, 'What will we eat? What will we drink? What will we wear?' These things dominate the thoughts of unbelievers, but your heavenly Father already knows all your needs" (Matthew 6:31-32 *NLT*). 'Worry' is from the root word that means to divide into parts. It suggests a distraction, a preoccupation with things causing anxiety, stress and pressure. Jesus said in the end times, people will be terrified at what they see coming upon the earth, because the powers in the heavens will be shaken (Luke 21:26 *NLT*). But we as believers, have received a Kingdom that cannot be shaken- the Kingdom of God (Hebrews 13:27-28)! Peace is one of the components of God's Kingdom; so we can receive His peace in spite of the turbulence and turmoil around us. Most of the common diseases on earth today are stress-related; so you imagine the health benefits of having God's peace! That peace can protect our hearts and minds from all stress, panic and anxieties, if we would let it rule in our hearts.

SCRIPTURE READING: Philippians 4:4-9 *AMPC*
PERSONAL APPLICATION: When your mind becomes like 'troubled waters', full of anxieties and worries, remember that, "He leads me besides the still waters" (Psalm 23:2). Walking in God's peace takes a deliberate and conscious effort. Deliberately cast your cares on the Lord today... then leave them there!

HOW DO YOU SEE YOURSELF?

"You are of God, little children, and have overcome them, because He who is in you is greater than he who is in the world."
1 John 4:4

The Word of God is able to build you up and give you an inheritance, according to Acts 20:32. God's Word has the ability to build you up into becoming the army that will kill your giants. No Word from God shall be devoid of power. The Word of God contains His ability, nature and wisdom. These are imparted when we receive and walk in obedience to His Word. Joshua and Caleb chose the Word and measured value to it; they agreed with God and followed God fully with a different spirit. They entered the Promised Land. The way you see yourself is the way others will see you. The way you see yourself determines how hard you work, and the attitude and expectations you have. However, the key to victory is to see yourself depending on the unfailing God. Self-focus does not get the job done. It is being God-focussed that gets the job done. Christ in us the hope of glory. Greater is He who is in us than he who is in the world. He will put us over. We are able to do all things through Him who infuses inner strength in us. Our eyes should be on Him not on ourselves. Let the Lord be your strength and help you to see and be all that He wants you to be.

SCRIPTURE READING: Philippians 4:13 *AMPC*, Judges 6:11-16, Jeremiah 1:4-19
PERSONAL APPLICATION: Spend time meditating in the Word of God. Build yourself up in who God has made you to be.

A LEADER ONE WOULD CHOOSE

"Imitate me, just as I also imitate Christ."
1 Corinthians 11:1

Whenever you fly with an airline, you are most likely to hear them say something like - "Thanks for choosing to fly with us, we know you had a choice...". They recognise that you had a choice of flying with another airline, but you chose them. For them, it wasn't a right to have you fly with them, but a privilege. If people had a choice, would they choose you as their leader?

You must have a genuine love for, and interest in the people. People would choose a leader who isn't manipulating them for their own selfish gains, but motivating them for their own good and the good of all. When Israel asked for a king, so they could be like other nations, God asked Samuel to warn them what their king would do to them, how he will exploit them and use them to build himself up. Samuel was a leader who loved the people and didn't take advantage of them. In Paul's farewell speech to the elders of Ephesus, he talked about how he kept nothing back from the people that was helpful to them, his constant watch and care over them in the three years of being with them, and that he didn't exploit them by coveting their gold and silver. People don't care about what you know, until they know you care. "Care for the flock that God has entrusted to you. Watch over it willingly, not grudgingly–not for what you will get out of it, but because you are eager to serve God" (1 Peter 5:2 *NLT*).

SCRIPTURE READING: Matthew 5:13-16, Deuteronomy 28:13

PERSONAL APPLICATION: The Bible says that we are the light of the world and the salt of the earth. We are all called with a unique calling and purpose. Jesus is the ultimate example for us to follow. We choose to follow Jesus, because we know He loves and cares for us. If people had a choice, would they choose you as their leader?

ABOUNDING IN GRACE

"And with great power the apostles gave witness to the resurrection of the Lord Jesus. And great grace was upon them all."
Acts 4:33

Giving is a manifestation of grace and it leads to more grace. If you want more of God in your life, give more of yourself to Him. Remember to always give yourself first to God then to His servants in your life. Someone said that generosity is when you give what you need. There are benefits to giving as unto the Lord, with a right motive. Amongst other things, it delivers you from selfishness; it breaks your dependence on the natural things you can see, touch and taste; it stirs up the joy of giving as you see others enriched; it enlarges your capacity to receive from the Lord through others; you lay up treasures in heaven for the time to come; your giving today enriches your future. Giving also positions you for more grace from God so that you can do more for His Kingdom and He can do more through you. It is time to let your faith grow as you release it through your words; to do more for the Kingdom of God, as you give more to Him in your time, talent and treasure. If God so loved that He gave and His giving released grace to us, our giving will release more grace too. After all we were made in His image. Allowing the nature of Christ to be formed in us is a wonderful opportunity to enrich our lives and the lives of people around us. He still wants to see His image and likeness walking around the earth that He made. The ball is in our court to start the flow of grace, by giving and receiving to give more until all the earth will be filled with His glory. May His grace abound toward you that you, having all sufficiency in all things will abound to every good work. Go ahead and be a carrier of His grace and love. May the good Lord bless and keep you. Amen.

SCRIPTURE READING: 2 Corinthians 9:6-15
PERSONAL APPLICATION: The act of giving is a manifestation of God's grace, which we can experience in every area of our lives; first to Him, then to others. When we give, it must be whole hearted—no strings attached. We most certainly need the grace of God!

HAVE A GOAL IN LIFE

"I press on toward the goal to win the prize for which God has called me heavenward in Christ Jesus."
Philippians 3:14 NIV

"Where there is no vision, the people perish" (Proverbs 29:18 *KJV*). Vision has to do with seeing possibilities. God told Abraham, "Look as far as you can see in every direction–north and south, east and west. I am giving all this land, as far as you can see, to you and your descendants as a permanent possession" (Genesis 13:14-15 *NLT*). If you can see it, you can have it. What do you see yourself doing? What do you see yourself having? What do you see yourself becoming? Where do you see yourself in the next one year or five years or ten years? You must set goals to achieve your objectives; have short-term and long-term goals. Have a plan and a schedule, or else your objectives will only be a pipe dream. Plan your work, and work your plan. How often do you hear yourself at the end of a day say, 'it's amazing how time flies?' Time and tide wait for no man; even if you do nothing! Set goals to cover every aspect of your life; your spirit, soul, and body (1 Thessalonians 5:23). Make sure you keep an eye on your goal; be focused, don't be distracted. Have a good and lasting reason for your goals; for example, why do you want to get a degree? Why do you want to increase your income? Why do you want to lose weight?

SCRIPTURE READING: Romans 12:3-8
PERSONAL APPLICATION: A lot of folks are defeated in life either because they aim at nothing or they aim too low! Don't be too modest or fearful to aim high because God has not given you the spirit of fear. No matter your past experiences, you can say, "forgetting those things which are behind and reaching forwards to those things which are ahead, I press towards the goal" (Philippians 3:13-14).

THE COVENANT OF HEALING

"how God anointed Jesus of Nazareth with the Holy Spirit and with power, who went about doing good and healing all who were oppressed by the devil, for God was with Him."
Acts 10:38

We know God has been involved with healing from the days of old. Many have argued whether He still heals today. The question we need to settle is not whether God can or wants to heal, but do we really have a covenant that guarantees healing? Exodus 15:26 and 23:25-26 clearly states God's stance on healing for His covenant children. The book of Hebrews calls ours a better covenant, so if the old has healing of the physical body, the better covenant should have more than physical healing. And it does. Until we settle it in our hearts that it is God's will to heal, we shall harbour doubts in our hearts. The unchanging God is Jehovah-Rapha - the Lord that healeth thee (Exodus 15:26). Jesus came to fulfil the law and demonstrate the fullness of the old covenant blessings. When He healed the bent lady in the synagogue (Luke 13:10-13), He called her the daughter of Abraham, tying her healing to the covenant relationship established with Abraham and God. He said, "woman, thou art loosed". She immediately came up straight, healed! God is the same yesterday, today and forever. It is His will to heal and He made the provision for it. Proverbs 4 says the Word is healing to our flesh, if we find it. Jesus says these signs will follow them that believe, among other things, they will lay hands on the sick and they will recover (Mark 16:15-18). Looking at Proverbs 4 we see a method we can use to receive the promise of healing. When trusting God for healing, plant the seed of God's Word in your heart. He bore our sickness, our grief and sorrows as stated in Isaiah 53:3-5. The prayer of faith that heals is to follow the planting of the Word. Proverbs 4:20 gives us a method we can use to receive the promise of healing. Jesus must be our focus. When your eyes are upon your symptoms and your mind is occupied with them more than with God's Word, you have in the ground the wrong kind of seed for the harvest that you desire. You have in the ground the seeds of doubt. Your symptoms may point to death, but always remember God's Word points you to life! God is still healing today like He did yesterday. Receive your healing in the Name of Jesus!

SCRIPTURE READING: Exodus 12:13, Deuteronomy 7:15, Acts 10:38, Romans 8:11
PERSONAL APPLICATION: Spend time meditating on and building your faith up in God's promises of healing. He is the same God. Receive your healing!

BRIDGING THE GENERATION GAP

"I have singled him out so that he will direct his sons and their families to keep the way of the Lord by doing what is right and just."
Genesis 18:19 NLT

There is a huge generation gap, yet God is a God of generations; He thinks generationally! He is the God of Abraham, Isaac and Jacob! God wants values and virtues to be passed on generationally (Deuteronomy 6:4-9). The future of parents lies in their children e.g. what God said to Abraham and David depended on their children walking in God's ways (Genesis 18:19, 1 Kings 2:2-4). The future of every nation lies in the youths of that nation. Children don't trust their parents. Children think that they are wiser and better than their parents. Parenting is becoming an obsolete thing. Proverbs 30:11-14 describes a generation that dishonours their parents, that is pure in its own eyes, that is proud and knows it all. God ordained the family and His plan is still that children be raised in the family structure. Even Jesus was raised in a family. He had earthly parents and siblings; the Bible says that He submitted himself to Joseph and Mary (Luke 2:51). Somebody said, 'Raising children is more difficult than raising the dead'; but thank God with Him all things are possible. We can still raise godly children in an ungodly world. "And the light shines in the darkness, and the darkness did not comprehend it" (John 1:5).

SCRIPTURE READING: 1 Samuel 2:22-35, 3:19-20, Isaiah 65:23, Proverbs 22:6
PERSONAL APPLICATION: Whether you are a parent or desire to be one in future, start praying over your children. Use Isaiah 65:23 and personalise it over your children. Also, ask God to shine through where there is darkness, confusion and frustration.

OUR NEW IDENTITY IN CHRIST

"Therefore, if anyone is in Christ, he is a new creation; old things have passed away; behold, all things have become new."
2 Corinthians 5:17

The new birth starts with the injection of God's life (*'Zoe'* in Greek) into our spirits. When we receive Jesus as our Lord and Saviour having repented of our sins, we have our human spirits recreated by the Holy Spirit infusing God's life into us. We now have a new identity in Christ. We become a part of the new creation, with Jesus Christ as the head of this new creation, replacing Adam as the failed head of the old creation. This life is in our spirits but the inherited nature we had is still lodged in our souls (our minds, will and emotions). James 1:21 tells us to lay aside naughtiness, amongst other things in our souls, and receive, with meekness the engrafted Word, which is able to save our souls. Work needs to be done in our souls so we can come into alignment with the way God ordained for things to function in our lives on the earth. Our souls (the seat of our personality) have been affected by the sinfulness in our world, nature and experiences before we met Christ. Without the development of our spirits in the life of God, we can still live as people who are governed by the dictates of the human flesh and not yield to the Spirit of God who lives within us. The Corinthian church, in the days of Apostle Paul, were full of the manifestations of the Spirit in gifts yet they were ruled by their flesh according to 1 Corinthians 3. God's Word is designed to train us to walk in the victory that has been granted us through the death, burial and resurrection of our Lord Jesus Christ. Many Christians are not taking full advantage of their privileges in Christ. God raised Paul to help bring us all into the fullness of what we have become in Christ.

SCRIPTURE READING: Galatians 2:20, James 1:18-25, Romans 12:2

PERSONAL APPLICATION: It's time for a spiritual detox! Make a decision not to clog up your spirit and soul with junk. The more we expose our hearts to God's Word, the more sensitive we become to His voice and His leadings. Also, as you read His Word, ask God to reveal the meaning of His death, burial and resurrection and their roles in our identity in Christ.

YOU HAVE POTENTIAL

"For we are His workmanship, created in Christ Jesus for good works, which God prepared beforehand that we should walk in them."
Ephesians 2:10

When God created mankind in His own image and likeness, He also blessed them and told them to, "be fruitful and multiply; fill the earth and subdue it; have dominion" (Genesis 1:28). "God created human beings; he created them godlike, reflecting God's nature. He created them male and female. God blessed them: "Prosper! Reproduce! Fill Earth! Take charge!" (*MSG*). To bless, means to empower. "Remember the Lord your God. He is the One who gives you power to be successful" (Deuteronomy 8:18 *NLT*). Power also means, capacity or ability. Your potential is what you are capable of being or doing. God is the omnipotent God; He is the God of all potential. The Bible says all things are possible with God. And because you were made in His image and likeness, you are also full of potential; more so, if you are in Christ. "For we are God's masterpiece. He has created us anew in Christ Jesus, so we can do the good things He planned for us long ago" (Ephesians 2:10 *NLT*). "For God wanted them to know that the riches and glory of Christ are for you Gentiles, too. And this is the secret: Christ lives in you. This gives you assurance of sharing His glory" (Colossians 1:27). Christ has been made unto us wisdom from God (1 Corinthians 1:30). You have the mind of Christ (1 Corinthians 2:16). Everyone has something of God and from God in them (Romans 12:3-8). There is room for everyone's gifts, grace and calling.

SCRIPTURE READING: Genesis 1:26-31
PERSONAL APPLICATION: We need to pay the price in prayer and obedience to see God's power at work in our lives. Jesus retreated to the wilderness to pray and fast before He began His public ministry. Whether you want to receive power to heal the sick, share the gospel with a loved one—remember that God has given you the power and ability.

THE ATTITUDE OF A WINNER

"Do you not know that those who run in a race all run, but one receives the prize? Run in such a way that you may obtain it."
1 Corinthians 9:24

Your attitude is a function of your knowledge, thoughts and expectations in life. Paul said he had learned to abase and abound and could do all things through Christ who strengthened him. His attitude was, 'no matter my financial state, I will not let the natural control me. I am regulated internally by the presence of the Greater One in me'. A winning attitude seeks to develop, improve and be the best one can be in life. Practice daily times of worship, meditation and confession of God's Word. We are to challenge contrary thoughts and speak to mountains of doubt, unbelief, un-forgiveness, strife and bitterness or offences. Get rooted in your identity in Christ, by speaking what God says about you and acting like it is true as you form new habits. Build your expectations on the Word of God. Cast all cares on the Lord and regulate your thoughts throughout the day (read Philippians 4:6-8). Set goals for your spiritual, financial, emotional and physical health. Make plans for these to come to pass based on God's Word and strategy. Set goals that can help deepen your walk with God - faith goals as well as natural goals. Cultivate healthy relationships with people who add value to your life and who can help you become all that God planned for you to be.

SCRIPTURE READING: Proverbs 4:20-27, Ephesians 3:16-17
PERSONAL APPLICATION: What goals/expectations do you have? There is no time like the present to form the right habits to bring the right results! Practice daily: worshipping God, meditating and confessing God's Word and getting rid of un-forgiveness, strife and offence. Ask the Holy Spirit for wisdom in setting the right goals for your spiritual, financial, emotional and physical health.

CASTING YOUR CARES

"And the God of peace will crush Satan under your feet shortly."
Romans 16:20

In 1 Peter 5:8, we are told to be, "sober and vigilant; because your adversary the devil walks about like a roaring lion, seeking whom he may devour". 1 Peter 5:7 gives us a key to achieving that state of being sober and watchful - it is by casting all our cares on Him. Jesus said the thief only comes to steal, kill and destroy; one major way he accomplishes his goals is through fear, worries, and anxieties. Job said that what he always feared and dreaded had happened to him. He said, "I have no peace, no quietness. I have no rest; only trouble comes" (Job 3:26 *NLT*). Fear licences and empowers Satan and demonic forces against us; but faith paralyses their operation in our lives. What the devil can't bring you to fear, he can't bring about or bring upon you; "and be not in any way terrified by your adversaries, which is to them a proof of perdition, but to you of salvation, and that from God" (Philippians 1:28). Jehoshaphat and all Judah were prophetically instructed not to be afraid or dismayed because of the multitudes that had come against them. They were told to stand still and see the salvation of the Lord (2 Chronicles 20:17). The salvation, i.e. the deliverance of the Lord, doesn't come in the place of fear and anxiety; but in the place of peace. And Judah did see God's salvation - which also meant the defeat and destruction of their enemies; they were three days gathering the spoil because there was so much!

SCRIPTURE READING: Psalm 18:16-17, Isaiah 41:10
PERSONAL APPLCATION: We should cast our cares on God because He cares for us. Refuse to fear and settle it in your heart that the devil has forever been defeated on the Cross. Resist him and he will flee (James 4:7)!

COMMITMENT

"But be sure to fear the Lord and serve him faithfully with all your heart; consider what great things he has done for you."
1 Samuel 12:24 NIV

We all know that progress in any field is impossible without commitment to some things that make for progress. If we can conceive of a life without commitments then we see someone who is going nowhere fast with his entire life. He will flow wherever the wind blows him. Here today, gone tomorrow! As Christians, our commitment is first to God, to His principles, to His people and to His purposes on earth. Loving God includes commitment to Him. This may be the bedrock of character development and character may well be the bedrock for personal development. Our commitment to God is what produces honour for God in our hearts; this is what the Old Testament calls the fear of God. It is this that helps us love and value what God loves and values. We desire to do the things that are pleasing to God because we love Him and are committed to him. It's a choice we make. Our commitment to God is the basis of our faithfulness to Him. We are committed to Him, His Word (principles for living) and His people and purposes, no matter how life comes across to us. When our commitment goes beyond convenience, we are called faithful, and when faithfulness is beyond comfort, we are called loyal. Our commitment is also the basis for our integrity. Integrity has to do with being wholesome, saying and meaning what we say, saying and doing what we say!

SCRIPTURE READING: Proverbs 16:3, Jeremiah 38:20
PERSONAL APPLICATION: We should not have a casual/convenient relationship with God. Commit your life (your whole life—nothing hidden) afresh to Him today.

SUBMISSION ONE TO ANOTHER

"Giving thanks always for all things to God the Father in the name of our Lord Jesus Christ, submitting to one another in the fear of God." Ephesians 5:20-21

God's way is the way of love, "And yet I will show you a still more excellent way [one that is better by far and the highest of them all--love]" (1 Corinthians 12:31 *AMPC*). The love of God has already been shed in our hearts, by the Holy Sprit; the first fruit of our recreated spirit is love (Galatians 5:22). The characteristics of God's love are listed in 1 Corinthians 13:4-8; and in verse 5, "Love (God's love in us) does not insist on its own rights or its own way, for it is not self-seeking..." (*AMPC)*. We are told to "Work at living in peace with everyone," (Hebrews 12:14 *NLT*); that seems a tall order, but it isn't an impossible one! One way to achieve that is by learning to yield to others. The Bible says, "But the wisdom from above is first of all pure (undefiled); then it is peace-loving, courteous (considerate, gentle). [It is willing to] yield to reason, full of compassion and good fruits" (James 3:17 *AMPC*). Love meets all the requirements of the law, because it does no harm or wrong to a neighbour! Knowledge puffs us up, but love builds up others. The Bible says, "So let us then definitely aim for and eagerly pursue what makes for harmony and for mutual up-building (edification and development) of one another" (Romans 14:19 *AMPC*). We will experience great peace when we focus on what builds others up, rather than on what destroys; and on the things that unite us, rather than the things that divide us.

SCRIPTURE READING: Ephesians 5:21, Galatians 5:22, 1 Corinthians 13:4-8
PERSONAL APPLICATION: God's Word exhorts us to submit one to another in the fear of the Lord. Why then is it so hard to submit to one another? Parents and children, husbands and wives, friends, colleagues, and so on. Spend time thinking about this question and identify things at work within you that makes this simple command so difficult. Receive grace to first submit to the Word of God, then receive the help of the Holy spirit to do what the Word of God says.

UNDERSTANDING OUR BENEFITS IN CHRIST

"Bless the Lord, O my soul, and forget not all His benefits"
Psalm 103:2

There are many benefits (provisions and blessings based on the finished work of Calvary) available to us as believers as a result of our relationship with God through our Lord and Saviour Jesus Christ. The blessings of Abraham are ours in Christ as Jesus bore the curse of the law. A lack of knowledge of these blessings and benefits has hindered many from enjoying what rightfully belongs to them. The enemy of our souls (Satan) has lied to many about how God operates and has taken advantage of their ignorance to steal from them many of the benefits they should be enjoying. Many are not enjoying these benefits and they attribute what they are experiencing to God preventing or denying them of these benefits. The quality of knowledge we have determines the quality of decisions we make. Our decisions affect our actions, attitudes and eventually the outcomes of our lives. The choices we make affect the outcomes of our lives. We need not only to know what is available to us, but also know what we need to do to experience these benefits. There is a thief out there who is willing to steal, kill and destroy anything in sight. He is our enemy called Satan and he utilises things like our wrong thought processes, circumstances or evil influences around us to achieve his aim. We, on the other hand, have the God-given authority to stop, bind and resist him. God's power will be released on our behalf to see that he is stopped in his tracks when we put up resistance in the Name of the Lord Jesus Christ.

SCRIPTURE READING: Psalm 103:1-8, Ephesians 1:3-9
PERSONAL APPLICATION: We need to understand our benefits in Christ, and what Jesus Christ has made available for us. It will help us to recognise Satan's evil schemes and live a victorious life. Let's pray and ask God to open the eyes of our hearts to see the provisions and blessings that he has made available for us.

BE A WINNER

"Do not judge others, and you will not be judged. For you will be treated as you treat others. The standard you use in judging is the standard by which you will be judged."
Matthew 7:1-2 NLT

When we get even with people, we disobey the biblical injunction that says: "Beloved, do not avenge yourselves, but rather give place to wrath; for it is written, 'Vengeance is Mine, I will repay, says the Lord'" (Romans 12:19). Also, in repaying evil for evil, we also become guilty of doing evil! For instance, if someone, in retaliation, commits murder or steals, he will be held guilty notwithstanding. Like they say, "Two wrongs don't make a right." We usually take the law into our own hands when we retaliate, and thereby become guilty ourselves. "You must all be quick to listen, slow to speak, and slow to get angry. Human anger does not produce the righteousness God desires" (James 1:19-20 *NLT*). (Read also Romans 2:1-3 and Matthew 7:1-2).

Whenever we repay evil for evil, we also sow the wrong seeds into our own lives. "Do not be deceived, God is not mocked; for whatever a man sows, that he will also reap. For he who sows to the flesh will of the flesh reap corruption" (Galatians 6:7-8). Our thoughts, words and actions (and even inactions) are seeds; and no matter what anyone does to us, we must make sure we don't sow the wrong seeds in return. Saul was all out to kill David, but David kept running away from him and for his own dear life. Even when David had the opportunity to kill Saul, he didn't take it - though it looked like God Himself had given Saul into his hand.

SCRIPTURE READING: 1 Peter 3:8-12, Romans 2:1-3

PERSONAL APPLICATION: Pray for the Lord to give you His eyes today. Allow Him to change your perspective. We need to start seeing people the way that God sees people, and sow seeds of forgiveness, patience and humility.

MOVING MOUNTAINS

"And when you stand praying, if you hold anything against anyone, forgive them, so that your Father in heaven may forgive you your sins."
Mark 11:25 NIV

Our study today is based on Mark 11:22-26. Our hearts need to be influenced by the love of God as we forgive everyone who has hurt us. The offence-free heart is more productive than an unforgiving heart. Unforgiveness in the heart will not produce God's Word, rather, it will release whatever was in it in abundance i.e. offences! So the believing with the heart and saying with the mouth should include checking that the heart is free of unforgiveness. Faith works by love. The scriptures say we can speak to mountains of problems or difficulties and they will obey us. In order to appropriate, for example, the provision of divine protection in our lives, we need to engage our words. "I dwell in the secret place of the Most High, I abide under the shadow of the Almighty, I will say of the Lord, He is my refuge and my fortress, my God, in Him will I trust" (Psalm 91:1-2). This must be said, regularly, believing this to be true from the heart of the one who says it. Psalm 91 in its entirety can be personalised when confessing it. This is easier with the *New King James Version*. We start by saying, "I dwell in the secret place of the most High". Then, "He shall deliver me from the snare of the fowler". Then, "He will set me on high, because I have known His name... He will deliver me because I have set my love on Him". The entire Psalm can be so personalised as we speak it over our lives regularly.

SCRIPTURE READING: Matthew 18:21-35
PERSONAL APPLICATION: We must learn to forgive others and to constantly check our hearts for unforgiveness. There is no sin or offence big enough to justify unforgiveness. Receive from God the grace you need to let go of any offence you hold against anyone, and watch your faith grow.

USE IT OR LOSE IT

"Do you see a man who excels in his work? He will stand before kings; He will not stand before unknown men."
Proverbs 22:29

What you can do and what you actually do are two different things; and it isn't what you can do that blesses people, but what you actually do. Every good thing we all enjoy today is available because somebody paid the price. To release your potential, you must be ready for hard work - intelligently directed; nothing good comes cheap or easy. "The hardworking farmer must be first to partake of the crops" (2 Timothy 2:6). You can't avoid hard work, if you will amount to anything in life. Be ready to go the extra mile, be ready to 'burn the midnight oil'; it won't be business as usual - you will be stretched. "Enlarge the place of your tent, And let them stretch out the curtains of your dwellings; Do not spare; Lengthen your cords, And strengthen your stakes. For you shall expand to the right and to the left, And your descendants will inherit the nations, And make the desolate cities inhabited. Do not fear, for you will not be ashamed; Neither be disgraced, for you will not be put to shame" (Isaiah 54:2-4). Success opportunities come in the form of hard work; so when you turn down hard work, you might be turning down success - think about it!

SCRIPTURE READING: Mark 4:26-29
PERSONAL APPLICATION: In the parable of the talents, the master gave his servants talents and told them to do business with them. The two servants doubled the talents they received, but the third servant buried his own. The man called him, lazy; laziness will stop you from releasing your potential. Your potential needs to be discovered and developed before it can be deployed; and that takes hard work.

THE WORD OF GOD AND FAITH

"So then faith comes by hearing, and hearing by the word of God."
Romans 10:17

It is important to know that our needs are not the generator of our faith; the Word of God is the generator for faith. It can produce because it is the Word of God. If you have a need, it will be wrong of you to go from the point of need to prayer. You must go from need to faith, then from faith to prayer. It is not how much you sweat when you pray or how loud you pray that guarantees that your need will be met. But if you know what the Word says concerning your need and allow the reality of that Word to build faith in you, you can from that point of faith go to prayer and get answers to your prayer. Faith does not come by wishing, it comes by hearing the Word of God. The only guarantee you have of having your prayers answered is that it is written in the Word, anything outside that is imaginary.
The Bible tells us in John 1:1-3 *KJV*, "In the beginning was the Word, and the Word was with God and the Word was God. The same was in the beginning with God. All things were made by Him, and without Him was not anything made that was made." The Bible also says that with God all things are possible. If the Word is God, it also means with the Word, all things are possible. The only way to make this Word work for you is through faith, which comes by hearing the Word. It is important for you to build your faith up by the Word because you can only have your life as a believer sustained by faith through the Word of God.

SCRIPTURE READING: Isaiah 55:8-11
PERSONAL APPLICATION: Build up your faith by hearing the Word of God; release your faith by speaking the Word over your life and situation and watch that Word produce for you.

GO FOR EXCELLENCE

"You are the light of the world—like a city on a hilltop that cannot be hidden."
Matthew 5:14 NLT

Always improve on what you have. Be hungry for more - there is more from where that came! You can do better; don't settle for average, go for excellence. Don't be satisfied with the status quo. Don't just settle for what is within your reach, go beyond your immediate environment. Abraham warned his servant not to take a wife for Isaac from among the women around. You must see beyond where you are. Jesus told Peter, speaking, "Launch out into the deep and let down your nets for a catch." And when Peter did that, he caught a great number of fish; from having caught nothing initially! (Luke 5:4-7). Don't settle for less than what God has for you. Don't settle for alternatives. Hannah had no child and her husband, Elkannah would give a double portion of offering to her because he loved her. He said to her, "Hannah, why do you weep? Why do you not eat? And why is your heart grieved? Am I not better to you than ten sons?" (1 Samuel 1:8). But Hannah persevered in prayer, she asked the LORD for a son and she got one - Samuel, and five more! Sometimes, to release your potential, you will have to press in. You must learn to ask; don't always wait to be asked. Be ready to 'sell' your skills; let people know what you can do! Be ready to negotiate; sometimes being good on your job might not be enough. "Life doesn't give you what you deserve, but what you negotiate!" Don't be too dignified to ask. Jesus said if you went to a friend at midnight to ask for bread, though he won't do it for friendship's sake; if you keep knocking long enough, he will get up and give you whatever you need because of your shameless persistence (read Luke 11:9-10).

SCRIPTURE READING: Matthew 5:14-16
PERSONAL APPLICATION: Be bold and stretch out your limits and ask the Holy Spirit to be your Coach today. God has given you an immense capacity for courageousness inside of you. Tap into the LORD's source today and engage everything around you as God is backing you up.

HUMILITY

"I have strength for all things in Christ Who empowers me [I am ready for anything and equal to anything through Him Who infuses inner strength into me; I am self-sufficient in Christ's sufficiency]."
Philippians 4:13 AMPC

Humility, contrary to popular belief, is not about saying, "I am nothing", whilst inside you are bursting to reveal who you truly are. We have very wrong notions about this subject. Humility like meekness is strength under control. It is in knowing who you are and not allowing whatever you think you are affect the correct responses you should give to life's challenges, whether it is in obeying God or dealing with issues or people. David's response to Goliath's challenge was a mark of humility as it demonstrated his dependence on God. When you put yourself under the Lordship of Jesus Christ and humble yourself, you will be teachable and accountable to those who God has put in your life for that purpose. You will not be full of yourself or take pride or significance in your achievements or abilities. You will demonstrate a dependence on God and a subjection to His will for your life.

SCRIPTURE READING: Philippians 2:3-16
PERSONAL APPLICATION: Today, wherever you physically are, find opportunities to do exactly what God says. Speak the words Jesus would speak, do exactly what God says you can do, and expect awesome results today as you demonstrate full dependence on God.

UNDER AUTHORITY

"...I do nothing of Myself; but as My Father taught me, I speak these things." John 8:28

The centurion said to Jesus, "For I also am a man under authority, having soldiers under me. And I say to this one, 'Go,' and he goes; and to another, 'Come,' and he comes; and to my servant, 'Do this,' and he does it" (Matthew 8:9). It looks like we can't exercise more authority in our lives, than we ourselves are under. Jesus Himself was under the authority of God. If you are not a good student, you won't be a good teacher; and if you are not a good servant yourself, you won't be a good leader. Samuel served God under Eli. Who do you serve under? Who do you study after? Who is your teacher or mentor? Who speaks into your life? Who do you check things up with? However, as we move on in life, we don't have the same or just one teacher, and we don't necessarily keep the same associations; life is in phases and seasons. We don't have to stay in bondage to any relationship; in life - we meet to part, and we part to meet. Abraham and Lot parted, to avoid strife; but met again, when Abraham went to rescue Lot. The yardstick for measuring who to follow, is Christ - how much of Christ is reflected in their life? "Be ye followers of me, even as I also am of Christ" (1 Corinthians 11:1 *KJV*).

SCRIPTURE READING: Matthew 8:5-13
PERSONAL APPLICATION: Ask yourself the questions shared in today's reading. Ask God to connect you to the right person of authority and rely on the Holy Spirit to help you make the most of that relationship in the season you are currently in.

FELLOWSHIP WITH THE HOLY SPIRIT

"But the Helper, the Holy Spirit, whom the Father will send in My name, He will teach you all things, and bring to your remembrance all things that I said to you."
John 14:26

We need to listen to the Holy Spirit of God who has been sent to help us in every possible way to experience all that God the Father has provided for us to be and to have. As we get more and more acquainted with God through His Word, we can understand the operations of the Holy Spirit as He wants to help us, guide us and lead us into all God has for us. He is our strengthener, stand by help, teacher and guide in this life. This starts by us recognising the inner witness at the new birth. Then through fellowship, we recognise His voice as He speaks the things that are in harmony with God's Word. He is interested in every subject in our lives; not just our religious life. He wants to teach us about how to succeed in marriage, in parenting, in making correct choices and lead us into every provision of God including divine protection. If we cultivate the habit of listening to Him, we shall enjoy the fullness of the provisions we have in Christ. There have been stories of people who were impressed by the Holy Spirit to move out of a place just before calamity struck in the place. Others have heard instructions inside them that helped them avoid being destroyed by things that have happened. Many others too who did not listen or ignored what they heard have faced calamities that were avoidable.

SCRIPTURE READING: John 16:13-15
PERSONAL APPLICATION: You should pay attention to the Holy Spirit, allow Him to lead you into all truth. It is vital to cultivate intimacy with God by His Spirit to the point of understanding how to respond to His prompting.

LITTLE SIN OR BIG SIN

"For whosoever shall keep the whole law, and yet offend in one point, he is guilty of all."
James 2:10 KJV

In our minds we classify sin and we somehow think our own sins are so small that they don't really matter. Religious devils have so infiltrated the church to such an extent that some people are comfortable with some sins because they are considered not as serious as fornication or adultery. People no longer confess sins of lie telling, exaggeration, pride, anger, etc. When you hear the phrase 'fall into sin' more often than not, it refers to the 'big' sin fornication or adultery. That is deception; sin is sin! Lucifer was kicked out of heaven because of pride. He sought worship. How many of us seek what belongs to God today? For instance many testimonies given in churches today are tailored to give the credit to one person or the other. There is nothing like big sin or small sin (though some sins are more obvious, or more devastating on us, than others). The Bible says, "For whosoever shall keep the whole law, and yet offend in one point, he is guilty of all. For he that said, Do not commit adultery, said also, Do not kill. Now if thou commit no adultery, yet if thou kill, thou art become a transgressor of the law" (James 2:10-11 *KJV*). In context, James was discussing the sin of partiality or favouritism in the church. People were favouring the rich above the poor. We all know we have a lot of that going on in the church today and nobody is sensitive enough to the Spirit to stop it. We all condone it and call it something else. I have even heard well meaning preachers excuse favouritism by saying that Apostle Paul visited rich men in their houses; but the whole truth is that he visited the poor too.

SCRIPTURE READING: John 8:1-11

PERSONAL APPLICATION: Jesus clearly shows us that sin is sin. If there were different categories he would have said something like, "He who hasn't committed adultery cast the first stone". When we judge ourselves according to our standards we are likely to justify any sin - it's our nature. It isn't until we ask God to show us our sin from His point of view and His standard that we really appreciate the magnitude of our actions, and godly sorrow can then work its wonderful course in our lives.

FOSTERING GROWTH

"There is no one greater in this house than I, nor has he kept back anything from me but you, because you are his wife. How then can I do this great wickedness, and sin against God?"
Genesis 39:9

Everything that is legitimate has boundaries. Beyond its boundaries everything becomes erroneous! Joseph shows his understanding of godly boundaries to bring legitimacy to what he was doing. He talked about his master giving him authority over everything except his master's wife. The wife of Potiphar offering herself was a temptation to step beyond his boundaries and come under the disfavour of God. God's Word clearly defines boundaries even in the way things are meant to function here on earth. In the exercise of authority, Apostle Paul said the Corinthian church was within the measure God had given him. He knew the boundaries of his apostolic ministry. Our revelation of what godly boundaries exist around us will greatly help to reduce casualties amongst believers who are on the path of warfare. Remember that revelation is progressive and if we stay within the boundaries of what has been revealed we shall be safe. God is not trying to limit or contain you; rather He wants you to enlarge. All healthy growth is done within certain boundaries. Abnormality exists when growth has no pattern or boundaries. The purpose and focus of growth in anything is to bring about healthy increase, sustain established purpose and cause God's will to be done in the earth. When purpose, focus and motive of any growth is out of order with God's ways and patterns, we have an unhealthy growth that will eventually terminate the life of the thing that is growing.

SCRIPTURE READING: 2 Samuel 6:1-7

PERSONAL APPLICATION: In a world where godly boundaries are being eroded it is more important than ever to recognise worldly influences and resist them. It's not that God wants to stop our fun, He sees the other side of the boundary and the consequences of crossing them - you can't step from underneath an umbrella and complain you're getting wet - it was your choice. God clearly shows us boundaries but He also gives us the free will to choose whether we stay in them.

AVOIDING COMPARISON

"Who then is Paul, and who is Apollos, but ministers through whom you believed, as the Lord gave to each one? I planted, Apollos watered, but God gave the increase."
1 Corinthians 3:5-6

Most of the problems in relationships are caused by unspoken or unrealistic expectations. Know people for who they are for themselves, and treat them as individuals - not collectively. People differ from one another; 'one man's meat is another man's poison' and 'one man's trash is another man's treasure'. Don't impose on people your likes and dislikes, or the likes and dislikes of others. Treat them like they want to be treated. Let them be - they don't have to conform to your image. Don't say or have a disposition that says, "I won't love you, if you are not like me or someone else". Everybody has their place in God's overall scheme; don't force-fit people. Remember there are different categories of relationships. Among those who followed Jesus, were the multitudes and His disciples. Among the disciples were the seventy two, then the twelve; and yet among the twelve were the three - Peter, John and James, who Jesus took with Him to the garden of Gethsemane. Accept people for who they are and respect their individuality if you are going to get the best out of them. For instance, some people thrive under pressure, whereas some might not be able to cope. Some individuals might be able to handle public rebuke, whereas some people's esteem might be damaged by it. You don't treat a horse and a zebra alike! It isn't partiality or favouritism to treat people individually; it's common sense and wisdom!

SCRIPTURE READING: 2 Corinthians 10:12
PERSONAL APPLICATION: Our human nature has a built-in tendency to compare and judge people. Ask the Holy Spirit to help you to treat people and relationships with wisdom and sensitivity.

DIMENSIONS OF GRACE

"For the grace of God has appeared that offers salvation to all people."
Titus 2:11 NIV

To come into a clearer understanding of grace, we need to understand it in more than one dimension. In Titus 2 from verse 11, we see that the grace that brought salvation has appeared to all men, teaching us to say no to all ungodliness. We see four dimensions of grace here.

The first dimension is that it brings Salvation to us all. We are saved by grace through faith; it is the gift of God. As we believe in Jesus as our Lord and Saviour we get saved. We experience the first phase of salvation.

The second dimension of grace is that it teaches us how to deny ungodliness and worldly lusts and live soberly in this present age. The process of this grace teaching can be likened unto knowing Jesus as the Truth.

The third dimension is when we allow Christ to be formed in us and we yield completely to His life. Christ in us is the hope of glory. So now He can do in and through us what He did when He was on earth. We become Sons in the likeness of His person. The Word becomes flesh in us as it was in Him. He is the pattern Son and at the 3rd dimension we become just like He is.

The fourth dimension of grace is when I become a carrier of the grace myself and give myself completely to others for their own good. When I position myself to be a vessel for the Lord, more grace is activated in me. The gifts of the Spirit are called Charismatic because "*Charis*" means grace in the Greek language. The energy of God called grace is at work in all believers and as we cultivate the lifestyle of giving, according to the will of God, more grace will work in our lives. We need to constantly desire to see others healed and getting on well in life. This stance activates God's grace in us and His supernatural energy flows through us to meet the needs of others around us.

SCRIPTURE READING: Ephesians 2:8

PERSONAL APPLICATION: To be a disciple of Christ will cost us something, but we can depend on the grace of God to help us in those times of need. The Bible says God gives grace to the humble, so the key to more grace is the humility or acknowledgment that we need it in the first place.

UNDERSTANDING THE SEED PRINCIPLE

"While the earth remains,
Seedtime and harvest, Cold and heat,
Winter and summer, and day and night
Shall not cease."
Genesis 8:22

Seedtime always precedes harvest, so no matter how bad things are, don't stop sowing or else there will be no harvest. Isaac sowed in the time of famine and he reaped a hundredfold - what if he didn't sow? "He who observes the wind will not sow, and he who regards the clouds will not reap" (Ecclesiastes 11:4). "In the morning sow your seed and in the evening do not withhold your hand" (Ecclesiastes 11:6). God gives seed to the sower, and He multiplies the seed sown. God ordained the seed principle, so He will always put seed into your hand to sow. Decide and position yourself to be a sower - not an eater or a taker. Also, don't eat your seed, sow it; because it is the seed sown that will be multiplied, not the one eaten! Sow the seed of the Word into your heart concerning finances, through study and meditation. Sow the seed of the Word into your situation by speaking the Word of God over your finances, and water the seed by praying, especially in the spirit, over your finances. Sow the seed of finances (or your material stuff) - no matter how little, start from where you are. If you want finances or material things, then sow material things; the Bible says, "whatever a man sows, that he will also reap" (Galatians 6:7). Sow yourself as a seed - by serving the purpose of God; e.g. in soul winning, intercession, holy living, kingdom services, etc. Be consistent with your sowing and don't stop sowing, "and let us not grow weary while doing good, for in due season we shall reap if we do not lose heart" (Galatians 6:9). "If the clouds are full of rain, They empty themselves upon the earth" (Ecclesiastes 11:3).

SCRIPTURE READING: Ecclesiastes 11:1-6, Psalm 112, Psalm 126:5-6
PERSONAL APPLICATION: We all have been given something to bless others with—be it of our time, our talent or our treasure. What can you sow into someone's life today?

THE POWER OF COMMITMENT

"Commit your works to the Lord and your thoughts will be established."
Proverbs 16:3

For God's purpose to be fulfilled in our lives, amongst other things that should be established in our thoughts, the subject of commitment stands out. Somehow commitment is one word that makes a world of difference between success and failure. The point is that it is not usually obvious. Our greatest days are the days when our commitment is at its highest. A great commitment to the great commission produces a great church. When Daniel's friends were confronted with the option to bow or not, to the image of gold, their commitment to God was the key. Their correct concept of God also played a vital role. They had a two-fold concept of God. He is able and no matter the consequences, He expects us to do what is right anyway. When we have the correct concept of God our commitment will be stronger too. Remember, our commitment will always be tried and our God will be glorified. We must forget the things behind; embrace the new things of God with a new level of commitment. Whenever we are at a crossroad of commitment in our lives, these points will help: A personal decision must be made. Only you will live with the commitment you make for your own decision. The decision will cost you something. You can count on that. Others will be influenced by it. Every major commitment will affect others. It is the place God reveals Himself. Commitment starts with little things in our lives. For example, you can commit to winning your next-door neighbour rather than winning the whole world. Let us demonstrate a new commitment to the great commission so that God can be glorified.

SCRIPTURE READING: Genesis 29:15-30, Proverbs 29:18
PERSONAL APPLICATION: When we find our commitment to God wavering, could it be traced back to our concept of God? We have read today that commitment will be tested. How can we strengthen our commitment so that when the tests come we will not waver?

THE BETTER WAY

"A man's heart plans his way,
But the Lord directs his steps."
Proverbs 16:9

Not one of us is just passing through the earth, we each have a destiny in God and there is something about our lives that God wants to use to help humanity. This should create a picture of a future for you. God has invested Jesus Christ in you to activate you to disciplined action. Make up your mind to fulfill your destiny. Many live and die without ever getting near the fulfilment of their destiny. The fact is many don't even know that they have a destiny in God. Discover your destiny in God through prayer and the study of the Word. Ask God in prayer for His plans for your existence and He will answer you.

God may even put a desire in your heart that you don't know how to fulfil, but it's in following Him that you will come to the fulfillment of your dreams. If you try to fulfill it in the strength of your flesh and in your own way, you'll get frustrated because things won't work out the way you want. If you follow Him, you can't miss it. He may lead you in directions opposite to your own plans, just follow Him. He has His own way of fulfilling the dreams He gives. If He gives you a dream, He'll fulfill it, you don't have to try to figure it out yourself. Simply do your best and trust Him to do the rest. Always remember that a man's heart plans his way, but the Lord directs his steps (Proverbs 16:9).

SCRIPTURE READING: Isaiah 55:6, 8

PERSONAL APPLICATION: From today, surrender your own plans to Him and follow what His Spirit is showing you instead. Ask God in prayer to reveal His plans for your existence.

RECEIVING THE WORD OF GOD

"He who receives a prophet in the name of a prophet shall receive a prophet's reward. And he who receives a righteous man in the name of a righteous man shall receive a righteous man's reward."
Matthew 10:41

God's Word will always impose a responsibility on us. Many times, God will use a man or woman to bring His Word to us. Our first responsibility is to receive the Word as His Word and not the Word of a mere human being. It is only when we receive the Word as the Word of God and not of man that we will be in a position to respond to that Word. In 1 Thessalonians 2:13, Paul writes that the Thessalonians received the Word that he spoke as the Word of God not man. This is why the Word was effectual in its working in them. Often, we consider messages or books to be the authors' own ideas or good reasoning. I do not believe it should be so. The Word must be received and believed as the Word of God for it to work effectively in us. Receiving the Word as God's Word immediately unlocks the potential in the Word that only God can release. Our faith must be in the power of God, not in the wisdom of men (see 1 Corinthians 2:5).

After receiving God's Word, it is important that we spend time meditating on what we have believed and received. It is the process of prayerful meditation that causes God's Word to take its root deep into the soil of our hearts. Persecution will come for the Word's sake. Going through persecution at such times is part of the process God expects us to submit to. Unless we realise this, we will easily be offended when such persecution comes (see Mark 4:17).

SCRIPTURE READING: Jeremiah 1:1-19, Psalm 119:105

PERSONAL APPLICATION: The Bible says that the entrance of God's Word brings light and illumination; that means it helps us see ahead. When we can see the goal it will give us the determination to persevere and the humility to ask for the grace to overcome obstacles in the way. Ask God to help you receive the Word with meekness, and for that Word to transform you from the inside out.

TRUST IN THE LORD

"You will keep him in perfect peace, whose mind is stayed on You, because he trusts in You."
Isaiah 26:3

When we choose to trust in God, He keeps us in perfect peace- that is how it works. Trusting that God will take care of me and all that concerns me, is the key to peace. When we are troubled about things going wrong or not working out well, that brings fear, worry and anxiety; but when we choose to entrust those things into God's hands, we will experience His peace. Trust has to do with believing; so trusting God is believing God. Jesus would ask people who needed healing from Him, "Do you believe I am able to do this?". More often than not; it was their faith that healed them! We often go through emotional roller coasters because we are in doubt and unbelief. The Bible says the one who doubts is like a wave of the sea tossed by the wind; he is a double-minded man, unstable in all his ways (James 1:6-8). But if we choose not to be afraid, but to trust in the Lord; our hearts will be established and stable (Psalm 112:7-8). How do you trust God? By not being moved by what you see, hear or feel in the natural or physical. "Trust in the Lord with all your heart, and lean not on your own understanding" (Proverbs 3:5). Trust, like love, is of the heart, and not the head or mind. Your heart can trust God, independent of your mind.

SCRIPTURE READING: Psalm 118:8-9, Proverbs 3:5-6
PERSONAL APPLICATION: Sometimes what your heart is telling you is completely different from what your mind is saying; and you just have to follow your heart as long as it's being led by God. When your head is full of fear, you also can say, "Whenever I am afraid, I will trust in You" (Psalm 56:3). You can also make this a daily exercise to build up your faith. As you confess Psalm 56:3, personalise the verse to include the things you are trusting God for. Faith will rise in your heart as you choose to trust God and His Word through believing, meditating and speaking it.

UNDERSTANDING THE WAYS OF THE SPIRIT OF GOD

"I delight to do Your will, O my God,
And Your law is within my heart."
Psalm 40:8

The many stories in the Bible show the ways of the Spirit of God in operation. The events in the Bible of things that happened to individuals like David, Gideon, and Daniel show the ways of God. The Bible says that Moses knew the ways of God but the children of Israel saw the acts of God. The acts reveal the ways of God. The underlying principles help us to know the ways of God. The greatest desire of our hearts today should be to please God, to be in the centre of His will and fulfil the destiny He has for us. There is no way we can do this without aligning ourselves with His ways. Our ignorance of His ways usually brings about complaining and allowing confusion and bitterness to ruin us. It happened to the men of old as recorded in 1 Corinthians 10:1-13. They missed the purpose of God, failed their tests and perished without getting to the destination God had for them. Our destination in God is called our destiny. It demands our conscious participation, development and willingness to change to fulfil the destiny of God for us. Our participation is our heartfelt obedience, our development is our discovery, development and deployment of our gifts in God, and our willingness to repent, change our minds and do what His Word demands are the keys that will unlock our destinies.

SCRIPTURE READING: 1 Corinthians 10:1-13
PERSONAL APPLICATION: Repent of any sins that come to your mind. Ask the Holy Spirit to show you any un-repented sin. Decide now that you will change and put your belief in God's ability in you to change. Know and say, "I can do all things through Christ who strengthens me. I can turn away from sin (lust of the eyes, lust of the flesh and pride of life) and turn to God in prayer, in thought, in word, in action. I will live for God today, tomorrow and the rest of my life. I will participate with God through the revelation of my destiny in His Word and fulfil the purpose for which He has made me."

GIVE ME THIS MOUNTAIN

"Therefore know that the Lord your God, He is God, the faithful God who keeps covenant and mercy for a thousand generations with those who love Him and keep His commandments..."
Deuteronomy 7:9

"But those who wait upon God get fresh strength. They spread their wings and soar like eagles, They run and don't get tired, they walk and don't lag behind" (Isaiah 40:31 *MSG*). The first level of fellowship, is with God Himself - through the Word, in study and meditation; and His Spirit in prayer and worship. God rubs off on you, and you take on His nature and attributes. "That is why we never give up. Though our bodies are dying, our spirits are being renewed every day" (2 Corinthians 4:16 *NLT*). Forty five years after he was promised the hill country, Caleb, then eighty-five years old, said he was still as strong as he was then; "just as my strength was then, so now is my strength for war, both for going out and for coming in. Now therefore, give me this mountain of which the Lord spoke in that day" (Joshua 14:11-12).
You are not too old to aim higher; "as your days, so shall your strength be" (Deuteronomy 33:25). Abraham was seventy five years old, when he left for Canaan. Remember, age is of the mind - "For as a man thinks in his heart, so is he..." (Proverbs 23:7). You may be old chronologically, but young at heart. It's not too late to start - as long as there is life, there is hope!

SCRIPTURE READING: Hebrews 11:8-12
PERSONAL APPLICATION: Spend time thinking about what Caleb said in Joshua 14:11-12. Remember, he was eighty-five years old when he made that declaration. God's nature had rubbed off on Him and it had affected his expectation and experiences in life. Are there areas in your life where you need to challenge yourself? Areas where you need to aim higher? Spend time fellowshipping with God. Meditate and study on His Word. Spend time in prayer and worship and allow His nature and attributes to rub off on you too.

FELLOWS IN THE SAME SHIP

"As iron sharpens iron, so a friend sharpens a friend." Proverbs 27:17 NLT

The first level of fellowship as we read about yesterday, is with God Himself. The second level of fellowship is with people. You need to hang out with the right people; people who are going in the same direction as you. You need to constantly draw inspiration, counsel, strength, etc. from people to keep aiming higher. "That which we have seen and heard we declare to you, that you also may have fellowship with us; and truly our fellowship is with the Father and with His Son Jesus Christ" (1 John 1:3). When people are in fellowship, they rub minds together, bounce ideas off one another, share dreams and goals together, challenge and encourage one another to go for gold. After Peter and John were released from prison, they went back to their own company and told them all about their experience. Instead of blaming them or asking them to slow down, so as to avoid trouble, they all lifted up their voice in unity praying for boldness to keep on preaching. And when they had finished praying, they were all filled with boldness - what an unusual bunch! You don't fellowship with people who are either going nowhere or going in a different direction - "Can two people walk together without agreeing on the direction?" (Amos 3:3 *NLT*). You can help someone in need without being in fellowship with them. You can be friendly without being a friend. Your friends have the power to influence your thinking, your habits, your vision, your manners and ultimately your life - so choose your friends carefully. "Don't hang out with angry people; don't keep company with hotheads. Bad temper is contagious— don't get infected" (Proverbs 22:24-25 *MSG*). That is why they say, 'show me your friends, and I will show you who you are. "Become wise by walking with the wise; hang out with fools and watch your life fall to pieces" (Proverbs 13:20 *MSG*).

SCRIPTURE READING: Daniel 2:14-23, 46-49

PERSONAL APPLICATION: Having the right company of friends literally saved Daniel and his companions' lives. Daniel went to his company of like-minded believers to pray for the answer to the situation that faced them (the interpretation of the king's dream). God gave Daniel the interpretation because of their prayer together and as a result Daniel was promoted by the King. At Daniel's request, the king also promoted his friends. Make sure to have friends you can pray with, who are like-minded and full of faith. Remember them when you get answers to your prayers and share the reward like Daniel did.

HAVING YOUR LIFE SUSTAINED BY FAITH

"Behold the proud,
His soul is not upright in him;
But the just shall live by his faith."
Habakkuk 2:4

Faith is supposed to be a lifestyle for every believer and not something you try to switch on when there is a need or problem. The believer cannot survive without faith. The Bible says in Hebrews 11:6, "But without faith it is impossible to please Him, for he that cometh to God must believe that He is, and that He is a rewarder of them that diligently seek him." In order to please God, you must relate with Him on the basis of faith, and this can only be possible if you are living your life by faith. How? How do I get this faith?, I hear you ask. "So then faith cometh by hearing, and hearing by the Word of God". (Romans 10:17). You must cultivate a deep walk with God based on His Word and you must be totally dependent on Him. You must fellowship constantly with His Word to build faith in your heart. When you do this, you replace the limitation in your mind with the Word of God. This enables you to see God in the light of His Word and not in the limitation of your mind. You have to make up your mind to leave the realm of the senses because the senses are limiting. Faith on the other hand has no limits; faith is limited only by God. Remember that God is limitless, dynamic in His working and with Him all things are possible.

SCRIPTURE READING: Hebrews 11:1-40
PERSONAL APPLICATION: Ask the Holy Spirit to show you some scriptures to commit to heart today to build up your faith. Ask the Holy Spirit to show you how to act it out in your life. Faith manifests in actions of obedience to God's Word, driven by a loving desire to please our Heavenly Father.

SHOWING APPRECIATION

"In everything give thanks: for this is the will of God in Christ Jesus concerning you."
1 Thessalonians 5:18 KJV

You lose what you don't appreciate, and what you appreciate will increase in value. A lot of times, people don't appreciate what they have, until they lose it. Learn to appreciate people and what they do. Don't wait for them to do something big before you appreciate them - remember that what you appreciate increases. Express your appreciation. Don't wait till you lose a relationship before you tell them how much they mean to you - it might be too late. Let people know what about them you appreciate; be specific. Appreciate their punctuality, appreciate their commitment and loyalty, appreciate their generosity, etc. It can go a very long way in the relationship. Appreciation brings the best out of people, because they know they are valued; it boosts their self-esteem and morale. Be very generous with appreciation, and more economical with criticism and corrections. We live in a very negative world, and every little appreciation helps. In showing we appreciate people, we also give. You must learn to put your time, talent and treasure where your mouth is. You can give without loving, but cannot love without giving!

SCRIPTURE READING: Luke 17:11-19
PERSONAL APPLICATION: Today commit to appreciating all the people God has put in your life by letting them know what you appreciate about them; and thank God right now for all He has given you. Know that what you appreciate (recognise the value of) will appreciate (by rising in value).

A NEW KIND OF PERSON

"Ask and keep on asking and it will be given to you; seek and keep on seeking and you will find; knock and keep on knocking and the door will be opened to you."
Matthew 7:7 AMP

These end-times demand a new kind of person, one who will be willing to pay the price so that God's will can come to pass on the earth. Daniel was God's man for his time. He positioned himself to be one of God's representatives in Babylon. A vital key in Daniel's life was undoubtedly his prayer life. Satan tried to weaken Daniel by keeping him from praying, but satan did not succeed. Prayer is the powerhouse for God's people on earth. It is often said that a prayer-less Christian is a powerless one. We need to build a life of intimacy with God through our prayer life and our study life in Christ. The problem is not a lack of power from God but a lack of character developed in believers. Developing this character will enable us to receive the power that God is willing to release. Accurate praying can enhance character formation. Often, failure in a Christian's life can be traced to a lack of prayer. What we need to see in these days are not those who know how to argue, but those who know how to seek God; not just title lovers, but those who love to travail. We don't need glory seekers, but those who know how to groan. When the Daniels arise, they will travail and groan, seek the face of God and see His will done on earth. They will be obedient like Jesus was to Father God, and they will give their all to see Him glorified. May you be like Daniel in these days!

SCRIPTURE READING: Luke 14:28-33, 2 Timothy 2:4
PERSONAL APPLICATION: There is a divine provision that accompanies divine obedience, but few are willing to truly take that step of faith. As a soldier's needs are taken care of by the army so that he can concentrate on fighting the battle, so our needs are met when we are enlisted as a soldier in God's army in the mission to advance the Kingdom. Ask God to increase your faith in this area.

EMBRACE A FARMER'S ATTITUDE

"The hardworking farmer should be the first to receive a share of the crops."
2 Timothy 2:6

As a Christian, the Word of God is the seed you are to sow, and your heart is the soil, as illustrated in the parable of the sower in Mark 4:3-20. Using the farmer's principles of sowing and reaping, your thoughts are the seeds for the words you speak; the words you speak are the seeds for your actions, and your actions are the seeds for your destiny. Put another way: sow a thought, reap an act; sow an act, reap a habit; sow a habit, reap a character; sow a character, reap a destiny.

Ultimately, your seed-thoughts determine when, where, how and if you will fulfill your God-given destiny. The scriptures warn us to, "take no thought saying..." (Matthew 6:31). That means, do not entertain any ungodly or unscriptural thought even for a moment in your mind otherwise you will eventually say it. And because words have creative power, you must be watchful and careful what you say. "...for the Lord is a God of knowledge, and by Him actions are weighed" (1 Samuel 2:3). Your actions are the seeds for your destiny, so you must really watch the seeds you sow so that you can reach the destiny God has prepared for you. A person who cleans chairs with a bad attitude will most probably remain a cleaner all their life. Their attitude indicates that they will not make progress. But if you see a person who has joy in their heart, who knows they are serving the living God and who does what they do with joy, be sure that God will elevate them and give them more responsibilities.

SCRIPTURE READING: Colossians 3:22-24, 1 Peter 5:5-7

PERSONAL APPLICATION: When we have a revelation that God is our ultimate boss, leader and person of authority and we are ultimately working and serving to please Him, it helps to keep our heart right under unjust leaders or when we feel we aren't getting the recognition we think we deserve. Stay humble and trust that God sees exactly where you are.

BREAKING THROUGH BARRIERS

"For by You I can run against a troop,
By my God I can leap over a wall."
Psalm 18:29

Show me anyone who succeeded in life and I will show you one who had to break through different barriers - of race, class, culture, age, gender, religious traditions and beliefs, etc., to win in life! The Bible is also full of people who were able to break through such barriers, to accomplish what they did. The people around Blind Bartimaeus warned him to be quiet; but he cried out all the more to get Jesus' attention. And when Jesus called him, the same people who told him to be quiet told him to be of good cheer. If you won't allow the opinion and criticisms of others to stop you, they will be the same ones to cheer you on as you break through in life! People are fickle-minded; they change their minds so easily; their opinion should therefore not be strong enough to stop you from going forward! Joseph, a foreigner, a slave and a prisoner, became the prime minister of Egypt! Esther, a Jewish orphan, became a queen of the vast kingdom of king Ahasuerus. Rahab, a foreigner and also a harlot made it into the lineage of Christ! They all faced barriers, but none of them allowed the barriers to stop them, but did what it took to break through. Someone said, you can't stop a man from rising, who has in him enough yeast to rise! The greatest barrier is the one inside you because that is the one that has the power to stop you. It isn't what is outside you that defeats you, but what is inside you - your fears and insecurities, your beliefs, your mindsets, your habits and everything you have accepted to be the reason or reasons for failure or lack of progress. If you could just hang in there and not quit, you will not only learn many ways not to do things but will also succeed eventually! 'Tough times never last, but tough people do!'

SCRIPTURE READING: Mark 10:46-52
PERSONAL APPLICATION: Do you have any barriers stopping you from doing what you know you can or should be doing? Remember, you have it in you to overcome the circumstances and things barring you from making progress in your life.

THE CHURCH

"But you are a chosen generation, a royal priesthood, a holy nation, His own special people, that you may proclaim the praises of Him who called you out of darkness into His marvellous light"
1 Peter 2:9

Anyhow we look at the church, this supernatural organism or corporate entity has tremendous purpose and power at her disposal. In the book of Ephesians the church is described as His body, the new man, the household of God, the dwelling place of God, amongst other things. As His body we are the fullness of Him that fills all in all. Ephesians 1:22 and 4:13 say we have to come to the measure of the stature of the fullness of Christ. When we digest all of the riches of Christ into our being and these riches become part of us, we become the fullness of Christ. The church is the body of Christ, the fullness of a universally great person who fills all in all. We are members of this body. 1 Corinthians 12:12-27 is a great discussion on the unity and diversity of the body. As His body, we require His life to keep the body functioning. The world does not recognize Him partly because His body is not truly expressing Him to them. The church is also the new man in Ephesians 2:15. This is a corporate new man having both the life and the person of Christ. The Jews and the Gentiles are created into one new man, Christ. The church is also the Kingdom of God. This talks about our rights as citizens of the Kingdom. We have rights and responsibilities as citizens. We are also the household of God. Here we enjoy the life of the Father as His household. We are His family as well as Kingdom citizens. We are also His dwelling place. He dwells in our spirits, as well as in a corporate sense; His Church is His dwelling place in the Spirit. We have been called out to be these things and more. This demands local as well as global expressions. We need to agree with God, the builder of His church, as to who we are, who we are meant to serve and what we are called to do. We have a new identity, carry a new authority and should serve the purpose of God on the earth. We should operate with a new mentality so we position ourselves for the release of His ability in and through us. We are to walk in perfect harmony with Him who is the Head of the body. His Name is Jesus Christ.

SCRIPTURE READING: 1 Corinthians 12:12-27
PERSONAL APPLICATION: Ask God to show you the part He wants you to play in building His church. The goal is to grow into the measure of the stature of the fullness of Christ so that we can be carriers of His glory.

MORE THAN A CONTRACT

"For this reason a man shall leave his father and mother and be joined to his wife, and the two shall become one flesh."
Ephesians 5:31

Marriage is a covenant relationship between a man and a woman, with God at the centre of it! The Bible says The LORD is a witness between a man and his wife, "Yet she is your companion and your wife by covenant" (Malachi 2:14); and He hates divorce! It's high time people began to see marriage differently. God has an interest in the marriage of His people. Whatever we do in our marriage is therefore not only our business, but God's! The way we treat each other, our attitude to the marriage, and so forth, really matter to God. Apostle Peter warned the men to treat their wives right so that their prayers would not be hindered (1 Peter 3:7)! Also in Malachi 2:13-14, "So He does not regard the offering anymore, Nor receive it with goodwill from your hands. Yet you say, 'For what reason?' Because the Lord has been witness between you and the wife of your youth, with whom you have dealt treacherously." Covenant is the opposite of convenience. Covenant is more than a contract. It is not subject to the other party's weaknesses or inability to perform. The marriage covenant is not only between the man and his wife, God is included in that covenant. "And a threefold cord is not quickly broken" (Ecclesiastes 4:12). Marriage is like a triangle; with God at the top of it and the two parties at the end of the two base points. The closer each one gets to God, the closer they both get to each other. Marriage is about each person giving their all and not saying, "What about him or her?" It is about each party doing what God commanded them to do, regardless of what the other does - that is why each one must stay connected to God. Marriage is based on the love of God, not on human love! Human love is conditional, very limited and selfish; whereas, the love of God is unconditional, unlimited and very selfless!

SCRIPTURE READING: Ephesians 5:22-31
PERSONAL APPLICATION: What do you feel God is saying to you about your view of marriage? If you are single, ask God for a spouse that also sees marriage the way God ordained for it to be. If you are married, you and your spouse can renew your commitment to one another and decide that you will have a marriage based on the love of God.

POSSIBILITIES THROUGH FAITH

"Ah, Lord God! Behold, You have made the heavens and the earth by Your great power and outstretched arm. There is nothing too hard for You."
Jeremiah 32:17

To be able to experience all that God has and is, you must believe Him and believe in Him. There must always be a great expectation in your heart that He is able to do what He has said in His Word. Faith does not respond until there is an expectation. When your expectation is low, nothing happens for you. The Bible says in Matthew 19:26 (*KJV*), "But Jesus beheld them and said unto them with men this is impossible, but with God all things are possible". It is natural for a preacher to think that God will meet his needs through offerings given to him. A worker expects that God will meet his needs through his salary; in the same way, a child expects his needs to be met though his parents. These natural expectations create limitations in our minds. We limit our expectations to what our minds have conceived. But God is not limited. Remember, with God all things are possible!

You must understand that men have their limitations. For instance, a doctor may diagnose a medical condition and say there is no cure to that particular disease. For man, it is impossible for that situation to change for the better, but not with God—with God all things are possible including healing an incurable disease. You have to stop looking unto men and circumstances. Why? Because things that are seen are temporary, but unseen things are eternal (2 Corinthians 4:18). Men are not God. Situations are in the natural realm and they can change. Move on beyond the natural—move on to God and see possibilities through the eyes of faith.

SCRIPTURE READING: John 16:23-24

PERSONAL APPLICATION: What areas of your life have you looked to the natural? Ask God to help you see things through the eyes of faith.

GOD HAS NOT CHANGED

"I the LORD do not change; Therefore you are not consumed, O sons of Jacob."
Malachi 3:6 NIV

Because Satan through the media and other means has made sin commonplace, we church folks no longer see sin for what it really is. Somehow we get the impression that God no longer hates sin and He now condones sin. The Bible says Jesus loves righteousness and hates sin. Jesus is not indifferent to sin, he hates sin with perfect hatred. God says, "For I am the LORD, I change not" (Malachi 3:6a *KJV*). Satan was hurled or kicked out of Heaven when he rebelled against God. Satan was not advised or counselled or even prayed out of Heaven, he was cast out. Grace does not condone sin, rather it teaches us to live above sin (Titus 2:11-12). God is too Holy to behold sin. Even on the cross, when the sin of the whole world was laid on Jesus (2 Corinthians 5:21) He cried out, "My God, my God, why hast Thou forsaken me?" (Matthew 27:46 *KJV*). Beloved, God has not changed. He loves the sinner, but He still hates sin. Jesus was crushed and bruised for our sin. He had to pay the wages of sin by such a cruel and shameful death on the cross. Salvation is free because somebody has paid the price. Read Isaiah 53 closely and see how much God hates sin.

SCRIPTURE READING: Isaiah 53:1-12
PERSONAL APPLICATION: Are there any areas in your life where you have condoned sin? It could be something you have done knowingly or inadvertently. Ask the Holy Spirit to shine His light and show you. Spend some time thinking about these two questions: What does Isaiah 53 say Christ has done for us? What should our response be?

NOT BOWING TO SIN

"Then Jesus said to him, "Away with you, Satan! For it is written, 'You shall worship the Lord your God, and Him only you shall serve.' "
Matthew 4:10

What do you think people are bowing to today? Money, power or fame? It is all out there, making demands on everyone, asking humanity to bow. Jesus faced the same temptation: Satan offered Him wealth, power and all the kingdoms of the world. In exchange, Satan asked for only one thing, "Bow to me" (see Matthew 4:8-9). The same offer is being made to so many Christians today.

But we need to remember that the three Hebrew children were asked to bow to an image. It is always an image. Satan perverts what God gives; he generates an image of the real thing but with a perverted purpose. He deceives people into thinking the image is the real thing. When they do bow, they realise they do not have what they thought bowing would give them. I have always said that whatever you compromise to get, you are bound to lose.

A consecrated Christian will never compromise his principles or his relationship with God for what the world has to offer. This was the mindset that the apostles had. This is why they gladly gave up their earthly goods and even their lives. They suffered beatings, persecution and shame. They realized that everything they could see was temporal. The real substance is in God. Consecration is a lifestyle that is committed to God.

SCRIPTURE READING: Daniel 3:1-18, Matthew 4:8-10

PERSONAL APPLICATION: Are there any gods you feel pressured to bow to? How can you ensure that you put God above all else?

UNLIMITED POTENTIAL

"So God created man in His own image; in the image of God He created him; male and female He created them."
Genesis 1:27

Don't underestimate yourself. You are capable of greater and better things. You don't know yourself yet, and nobody knows you yet, because you are still evolving. Christ is the express image of God, and you were made in the same image. When He is revealed within you, you will become like Him - because you shall see Him as He is, then you can truly be in this world, just as He is (1 John 3:1-2). Don't limit yourself. You can do all things; "I have strength for all things in Christ Who empowers me [I am ready for anything and equal to anything through Him Who infuses inner strength into me; I am self-sufficient in Christ's sufficiency]" (Philippians 4:13 *AMPC*). You are multi-talented, and you can multi-task. The presence of the Holy Spirit in our lives is the guarantee for huge potential; Jesus said, "And I will ask the Father, and He will give you another Comforter (Counsellor, Helper, Intercessor, Advocate, Strengthener, and Standby), that He may remain with you forever" (John 14:16 *AMPC*). He came into us with all the resources of God; He is the Spirit of wisdom and understanding, of counsel and might, of knowledge and of the fear of The Lord (Isaiah 11:2). "But there is a Spirit within people, the breath of the Almighty within them, that makes them intelligent" (Job 32:8 *NLT*). Everything God has placed within us has unlimited potential - our faith, for instance; "If you can believe, all things are possible to him who believes" (Mark 9:23). And "If ye have faith as a grain of mustard seed, ye shall say unto this mountain, Remove hence to yonder place; and it shall remove; and nothing shall be impossible unto you" (Matthew 17:20 *KJV*).

SCRIPTURE READING: Matthew 17:14-20
PERSONAL APPLICATION: Are there things you face that seem impossible for you? How can today's devotional help you to pray or think differently about your 'mountains'? Just remember, you are equal to anything through Him who infuses inner strength into you! (Philippians 4:13 *AMPC*).

VICTORY IN CHRIST

"Now thanks be to God who always leads us in triumph in Christ, and through us diffuses the fragrance of His knowledge in every place."
2 Corinthians 2:14

There was a story of a man who had been fasting and doing everything he knew to do for his deliverance from tobacco and nicotine. One day after he had fasted a 14 day stretch, he cried out to God and said, "God, I've fasted, I've done everything to be delivered", and the Lord spoke to his heart and said, "That is the problem. You are trying to do it in your own strength". A lot of times, we are trying to get in our own strength what God has already gotten for us. We are supposed to stand on the platform of what He has done for us. The platform of victory is faith. Faith is the victory. Any time the enemy is able to drag you into that battle with himself, he is going to whip you. A lot of the time, he is trying his best to drag you into that place of the flesh, where you want to do it in your own strength; and a lot of times, you are not even aware you are doing it! The Bible says, "this is the victory that has already overcome the world, even our faith" (1 John 5:4 *NIV*). Always stand on the platform of what God has already done for us—that is the victory in Christ.

SCRIPTURE READING: Colossians 2:14-15
PERSONAL APPLICATION: The charges that were against you, your past and your sins have been dropped. If any man be in Christ he is a new creation. Your past is gone and a new beginning has begun. Your beginning is Calvary. Spend some time meditating on Colossians 2:14-15.

FIXING YOUR MIND ON GOD'S WORD

"You will keep him in perfect peace,
Whose mind is stayed on You,
Because he trusts in You."
Isaiah 26:3

What you fix your mind on or think about will determine if you will experience God's peace or not. It's easier to focus on our problems and pains than to focus on God and His Word. What we fix our minds on will determine if we will be in peace or in anxiety; and if we would be in hope or hopelessness. A lot of people are defeated in life because they focus on the negative. We are told to focus on Jesus, so we can run the race set before us with endurance; lest we should become weary and discouraged. You can't develop a strong faith, while thinking on the physical and natural. Abraham was not weak in faith, because he didn't consider his own body or the deadness of Sarah's womb; but was strengthened in faith because he focused on God's promises (Romans 4:19-20). We are told to let the peace of God rule in our hearts, by God's Word dwelling in us richly (Colossians 3:15-16). What is in you in abundance will determine your response when you face a challenge. Jesus said, the mouth speaks out of the abundance of the heart. Jesus said to His disciples, "I have told you these things, so that in Me you may have [perfect] peace and confidence..." (John 16:33 *AMPC*). God wants us to have inexplicable joy, that's full of glory, in spite of the troubles in the world; He said, "These things I have spoken to you, that My joy may remain in you, and that your joy may be full" (John 15:11). Our peace and joy must not be dependent or determined by the world or external circumstances, but on God's Word.

SCRIPTURE READING: Lamentations 3:21-26, Hebrews 12:1-3
PERSONAL APPLICATION: Sometimes we don't even know what is causing us anxiety as we're too busy to sit down and ask the Hoy Spirit to search our hearts and show us. If you are feeling worried or anxious, spend some time with your Creator and meditate on the word He gives you and you will soon be in perfect peace again.

ROAD MAP TO SPIRITUAL MATURITY

*"And Jesus increased in wisdom and stature,
and in favour with God and men."
Luke 2:52*

In developing character as Christians, it is very important that we know what our end product is meant to be. This is necessary so we do not wander off into religious confusion about where we are going and what we are becoming as we mature. Christ-likeness is our goal in character and lifestyle and doing the will of God with the power of God goes along with being Christ-like. The spiritual side of our development should be all encompassing. Any lack of development in any part of our lives will inevitably affect our spiritual development. An emotionally under developed person will be hindered in the expression of spiritual maturity in one-way or the other. If we see spiritual maturity as being conformed to the image of Christ, then all areas are important. Jesus our Lord grew in stature (physical), in wisdom (mental), and in favour with God (spiritual) and with man (social). In the study of human development, one of the marks of a matured person is an ability to love even when the love is not returned. It takes selflessness to love and to keep loving when the love is not reciprocated. This involves a test of motive and an adjustment of the focus of our love. A matured person loves to see others helped and takes it as part of the challenges to love when there is no obvious or immediate return of the love. Our maturity should affect every part of our lives: emotional, mental, social, physical and spiritual. We should mature in all areas. Maturity is not a function of time but of choices, decisions and applications of oneself to principles.

SCRIPTURE READING: 1 John 4:7-11
PERSONAL APPLICATION: If you are having trouble loving someone, ask God to fill you with His agape love (the unconditional love that surpasses human love). When we ask God to fill us with His love and grace, we can truly bless others with the river of life flowing out of us, bringing life to dead places, and we can achieve this even when they don't appreciate it or reciprocate it.

WHAT DO YOU SEE?

"For we walk by faith, not by sight."
2 Corinthians 5:7

Jesus saw a man who was blind from birth and His disciples asked Him if the man was born blind because of his sins or his parents' sins. They had a negative mindset that was more interested in fault-finding, than in finding the solution. They believed the man's problem was because somebody must have sinned. That kind of mindset has the power to lock people in the problem, and block them from seeing the solution. Jesus told them it wasn't because of his sin or his parents' sin, but so that the power of God could be seen in him! And Jesus went on to heal the man. Change the way you see your problems. Do you see a stumbling block or a stepping stone? What you see determines what you get. Jesus said, "whatever things you ask when you pray, believe that you receive them, and you will have them" (Mark 11:24). And it isn't just about what you can see with your physical eyes, but what you can see with your eyes of faith - "For we walk by faith, not by sight" (2 Corinthians 5:7). Believing is seeing! Jesus told Martha, "If you would believe, you would see the glory of God" (John 11:14). What you believe determines what you experience.

SCRIPTURE READING: 2 Kings 4:42-44
PERSONAL APPLICATION: When you feel overwhelmed and all you can see around you are problems and stumbling blocks, its time to look up. Allow God to change your perception of things—what looks like a problem today could be your greatest opportunity for breakthrough and promotion.

FOCUS ON THE PLAN

"Let your eyes look straight ahead,
And your eyelids look right before you."
Proverbs 4:25

Focus produces strength, sharpness, skill, increase, speed, good quality, etc. To focus means to concentrate or to direct at something. You must concentrate on God's plan for your life and direct your energy and resources at it. You cannot afford to deviate or be distracted from God's plans for your life. Don't envy others or try to copy what they are doing, you should rejoice with them and be inspired by them, but please be secure in what God has said to you. Others may seem bigger, wealthier, more popular, etc. but they are not necessarily better. Jesus said to Peter, "If I want him to remain alive until I return, what is that to you? You must follow me" (John 21:22).

You must also be secure in who you are. Don't be intimidated or discouraged because of your race, age, gender, status or your disabilities. You didn't call yourself, God called you and He knew about everything before He called you. Paul said to Timothy, "Don't let anyone look down on you because you are young..." (1 Timothy 4:12). Change what you can change, improve on what can be improved upon, and accept what cannot be changed.

SCRIPTURE READING: Proverbs 4:10-27

PERSONAL APPLICATION: Next time you feel jealous or envious of someone's walk with God, ask the Lord Himself to show you why you're feeling that way. It is in these times of being real with God He can reveal your greatest truths which ultimately lead to freedom and will put you on the right path of your own destiny.

SEEDS

"Then He said to them, "Take heed what you hear.
With the same measure you use, it will be measured to you;
and to you who hear, more will be given."
Mark 4:24

At every moment of your life, you are sowing seeds in your thoughts, words and actions. What kind of seeds are you sowing? Let the Word of God set your mind free because if you know the truth, it will set you free. Let the Word change any mentality you have that is contrary to God's Word, then your attitude will change. Let your mind be free from the bondages that the experiences of your past have kept you in. Knowledge (of the Word of God) is essential. It is said that what you don't know cannot hurt you. That is one of the most destructive lies on the face of this earth; if you say it or have ever said it, stop! Why? Because God's people are destroyed because of a lack of knowledge. Jim Rohn said, "Ignorance is not bliss. Ignorance is poverty, ignorance is devastation. Ignorance is tragedy and ignorance is illness. It all stems from ignorance." He also said, "What you don't know will hurt you." I quite agree. All thoughts come as a result of what you hear, whether it is from inside (your heart) or from outside (the external, the world, people, etc.). So, here is some good advice: "be careful what and how you hear" (Mark 4:24). "As a man thinks in his heart so is he" (Proverbs 23:7). This means that you are what you think. I might not know what you think, but that does not make you someone else. You will always be what you think. None of us can avoid thinking, we just have to, it happens all the time. Well here is some more advice; "whatever things are true, noble, just, pure, lovely, of good report—meditate [think] on these things" (Philippians 4:8 *AMPC* paraphrased). You can't go wrong there, can you?

SCRIPTURE READING: Romans 12:1-2

PERSONAL APPLICATION: When you are alone how do you talk to yourself? Do you put yourself down and doubt your abilities, are you believing a lie that you'll never make it? Stop listening to this and start reading what God says about you. Get into the Word and change this wrong thinking and be transformed as your mind is re-newed.

A LIFE OF SUBMISSION AND OBEDIENCE

"Most assuredly, I say to you, the Son can do nothing of Himself, but what He sees the Father do; for whatever He does, the Son also does in like manner."
John 5:19

Experiencing peace with God comes as we yield to God in every area of our lives. We must embrace God's Word; "Those who love Your instructions have great peace" (Psalm 119:165 *NLT*). All your children shall be taught by the Lord, and great shall be the peace of your children" (Isaiah 54:13). God's Word contains His wisdom; like Paul said to Timothy, "and that from childhood you have known the Holy Scriptures, which are able to make you wise for salvation through faith which is in Christ Jesus" (2 Timothy 3:15). When we embrace God's Word, we are able to deal wisely and be successful in the affairs of life. We must make God's Word the final authority in our lives. The Bible says, "For as many as are led by the Spirit of God, these are sons of God" (Romans 8:14). Jesus is the good Shepherd, and He said His sheep know His voice. The shepherd leads, guards and feeds his sheep; "The Lord is my shepherd; I shall not want. He makes me to lie down in green pastures; He leads me beside the still waters" (Psalm 23:1-2). There are huge benefits in heeding the Shepherd's voice; "Thus says the Lord, your Redeemer, the Holy One of Israel: I am the Lord your God, Who teaches you to profit, Who leads you in the way that you should go. Oh, that you had hearkened to My commandments! Then your peace and prosperity would have been like a flowing river, and your righteousness [the holiness and purity of the nation] like the [abundant] waves of the sea" (Isaiah 48:17-18 *AMPC*).

SCRIPTURE READING: Esther 4:13-17, Psalm 119:165-168
PERSONAL APPLICATION: When we examine our lives and find areas where we are struggling to obey the Word of God, it is actually highlighting an area where we are not trusting God; because we see here the two are linked. Take tithing for example, when we don't give God what is His, it is because we don't trust He will multiply His seed. Ask God to help your faith as you examine your life.

RENEW YOUR MIND

"For "who has known the mind of the Lord that he may instruct Him?" But we have the mind of Christ."
1 Corinthians 2:16

"For though we walk in the flesh, we do not war after the flesh: for the weapons of our warfare are not carnal, but mighty through God to the pulling down of strongholds: casting down imaginations and every high thing that exalteth itself against the knowledge of God, and bringing into captivity every thought to the obedience of Christ" (2 Corinthians 10:3-5 *KJV*).

Battles start in the mind so we must constantly renew our mind with the Word of God. We must also pull down every stronghold and cast down imaginations and every high thing that exalts itself against the knowledge of God and also bring into captivity every thought to the obedience of Christ. Then and only then can the Word of God have a free course in our lives. The Word of God is the seed as it is seen in the parable of the sower. The sower is the Lord Jesus and He is looking for the good hearts, which will not let the cares of this world choke the Word of God in them. He is going to come for the fruit of His seed and He won't stop until He gets a hundredfold. If your heart has thorns or it is hard, it is not the problem of the sower; you are the one who has to get rid of whatever can stop the Word of God from yielding fruit in your heart.

SCRIPTURE READING: 2 Corinthians 10:3-5

PERSONAL APPLICATION: Have you ever had someone tell you something about someone else but you know it wasn't true because you know the heart of that person? As we renew our minds with the Word of God we are developing the mind of Christ so when the enemy attempts to sow a seed that could develop into an imagination, we can recognise straight away that it is from the pit of hell and cast it down.

GENEROUS WITH PRAISE

"Bless the Lord, O my soul,
And forget not all His benefits"
Psalm 103:2

We must be more generous with praise, compliments, acknowledgements and appreciation than we are with correction and rebukes. When we acknowledge the efforts of people, no matter how tiny they are, they are encouraged to want to do more. For example, children rise up to our expectations of them; if we expect nothing of them, they achieve nothing. We must create the right environment for them to thrive and blossom. A child who grows up in an environment of criticism and negative words won't grow up to be a confident adult, but a very insecure person. Let's create an environment of unconditional love and acceptance for our kids. Children respond better to corrections and healthy criticism in such an environment. We must be our children's greatest admirers and cheerleaders. God rewards those who 'diligently' seek Him. God honours those who honour him. God has a reward system. David asked what shall be done for the man who kills Goliath and takes the reproach from Israel? We should not only correct or discipline our children, we must reward them also! We must reward them for being good children. We must acknowledge and reward their efforts, even if they are not quite there yet. We must reward their obedience. We also could introduce incentives; something to look forward to. Let charity begin at home!

SCRIPTURE READING: Psalm 145:8-9
PERSONAL APPLICATION: Not all faults we see in our kids are rebellion or disobedience, so next time you see your child behaving in a way you don't appreciate, seek the Lord's wisdom about what training is required to correct this behaviour and speak words of encouragement to your kids rather than condemn them.

PRINCIPLES OF GOAL SETTING

"Your word I have hidden in my heart,
That I might not sin against You."
Psalm 119:11

The 'becoming' is one of the greatest benefits of goal setting. We set goals for what they force us to become in order to accomplish the goals. When we set the goal to read the entire Bible throughout the year, what do we become by doing so? We get closer to God, we know more about Him and we become really affected by the Word of God. In the same way, we become more spiritual by setting a devotional goal of reading the Bible daily and completing the entire Bible in one year. We become more like Jesus. To achieve is usually preceded by becoming. Things change for good when we set these kinds of goals. We know more, see more things in the spirit and therefore can be more Christ-like in our character. We also need goals that can stretch us and our faith but not goals that are out of reach or beyond our reality. The size of your goal should reflect the size of your God. Take it in little bits so that you do not get presumptuous but rather stay in faith. Purpose in your heart that you will be an effective steward of your time and talents. Make up your mind that you will take responsibility for what happens in your life and future, as much as it lies with you. Embrace God's picture for your life from His Word. Learn to speak to yourself according to the provisions of Calvary - not the opinions of negative people around you. Begin setting godly goals so that you can grow into the fullness of the stature of Christ. Keep a journal or two for recording goals, answers to prayers and other insights you learn as you grow in the Lord. Set goals for the use of your time and for the future you desire in God. Set goals to study the Bible, to pray, to win souls and to help others become better disciples for Christ. May God reward your life with excellence in all areas of your life. Amen.

SCRIPTURE READING: Philippians 3:1-14
PERSONAL APPLICATION: We need action goals that will lead to the overall results we expect. A goal such as reading the entire Bible in one year will bring us closer to God as we meditate on the scriptures we read and broaden our knowledge of the Word of God.

HOW TO BE HAPPY IN LIFE

"Blessed (happy, fortunate, prosperous, and enviable) is the man who walks and lives not in the counsel of the ungodly [following their advice, their plans and purposes], nor stands [submissive and inactive] in the path where sinners walk, nor sits down [to relax and rest] where the scornful [and the mockers] gather."
Psalm 1:1 AMPC

You can be happy, no matter what your state in life is - married or single; rich or poor; young or old, etc. In order to be happy in life, no matter your circumstances, there are certain things you must understand about happiness: happiness is a choice you make in life! It isn't a decision somebody else makes or can make for you; happiness is not a function of what somebody does or doesn't do for you, it is what you do for yourself. Happiness is determined by your response to what happens to you in life.

You must understand that there is a difference between godly happiness and worldly happiness. In the world, you are happy when everything is going your way; everyone is doing what you want; its about you having all you want, doing all you want, etc. And if you can't have it your way, you are not happy. The theme of worldly happiness is you; the focus is you - the 'world' must revolve around you if you are to be happy. "Practically everything that goes on in the world—wanting your own way, wanting everything for yourself, wanting to appear important—has nothing to do with the Father. It just isolates you from him. The world and all its wanting, wanting, wanting is on the way out—but whoever does what God wants is set for eternity" (1 John 2:16-17 *MSG*). In God's kingdom, it's a different ballgame all together. According to God's Word, another word for being happy is, to be 'blessed'. To be 'blessed' means, to be happy; to be prosperous, etc. Happiness is contentment and satisfaction.

SCRIPTURE READING: Psalm 1 *AMPC*

PERSONAL APPLICATION: The key to happiness and contentment is not living for yourself, but for a higher purpose; it is living for God. Agree with God and submit to His plan and purpose for your life. Be in total surrender to Him and His will.

LEARNING THE WORD

"And they continued steadfastly in the apostles' doctrine and fellowship, in the breaking of bread, and in prayers."
Acts 2:42

The early believers continued in the apostles' doctrine. They had a heart posture that enabled them to receive from the apostles. They demonstrated respect, submitted to their God-given authority and were willing to learn and apply the truth of the Word of God. They were not just hearers of the Word but doers also. The doing of the Word of God helps establish the Word in our lives and hearts. God uses His Word to enlighten us, give us direction in life and strengthen us to do His will. The Word is a light unto our path and a lamp unto our feet. There are some internal attitudes that enhance or inhibit the effect of God's Word in the hearts of people. These believers had a right attitude and were eager to do the instructions derived from God's Word through their leaders, the apostles of Christ. Their consecration was a combination of their love for God, balanced with their reverence for Him.

SCRIPTURE READING: Acts 2:41-47
PERSONAL APPLICATION: Ask the Lord to stir up a hunger and desire in you to know and experience Him the same way the early believers did. May we truly be doers and not just hearers of His Word. Make it a daily habit to spend time in the Word of God and to apply it in your daily living.

AN ARK OF SAFETY

"But I will establish My covenant with you; and you shall go into the ark—you, your sons, your wife, and your sons' wives with you."
Genesis 6:18

Jethro said to Moses, "Stand before God for the people, so that you may bring the difficulties to God" (Exodus 18:19). Pray for your children to be all that God wants them to be. Pray for them to overcome their challenges and all the assaults of the enemy. Pray for them to make the right decisions in life. Pray about their future. Stand before God for them, as parents, you have that God-given authority to do so; like the Syrophoenician woman whose daughter was demon-possessed, the father of the epileptic boy, and so forth. Also, stand against the devil in spiritual warfare over them; don't let him steal your kids. The enemy knows that whatever touches your kids, touches you; so if he can't get to you directly, he gets to you through your kids. Jesus said the thief's purpose is to steal, kill and destroy; but you mustn't let him. God told Noah to build an ark for his family to save them from the deluge that was coming on the earth; you must learn to build an ark of safety and deliverance for your family.

SCRIPTURE READING: Psalm 127:1-5
PERSONAL APPLICATION: Spend time today covering your children in prayer. Build that ark of safety around them! Even if you don't yet have kids, begin to pray and speak words over your future children.

POSITIONING IN THE SPIRIT

"But be doers of the word, and not hearers only, deceiving yourselves."
James 1:22

Your every deed and word determine what position or rank you occupy in the realm of the spirit. If someone hurts you and you forgive them whilst obeying the other precepts in the Word of God, you obviously qualify for a higher position than he who metes out revenge. There is no position for pew warmers or those with observer status. Supervisors don't get rewarded in the Kingdom, doers of the Word do. Suffice to say that, your rank in the spirit reveals the kind of life you live as a Christian. The lower your rank, the less of a threat you are to the devil and his minions. Instant obedience to God and His Word will be rewarded with high positioning in the spirit realm. Paul was telling Timothy to endure hardness as a good soldier of Christ (2 Timothy 2:3). Life is hard, that is true. But then that is life! We all get a blow from life at one time or the other, how we respond to it will determine what we learn from it. My candid advice to you is that you set your heart to obey God, doing what the Kingdom of God demands. Not only will you increase in ranking in the spirit realm but you would also be exercising yourself in doing righteously. The question then is, are you a good soldier of Jesus Christ? Are you able to endure hardness? Enduring and tolerating are two very different things and so is enduring and managing. To 'endure' as mentioned in 2 Timothy 2:3, comes from the Greek word '*kakopatheō*' (pronounced kak-op-ath-eh-o) which means to undergo hardship, be afflicted and suffer trouble. You must be able to stand under suffering and affliction. You cannot afford to be weak and sick. Exercise yourself in godliness to be able to stand and having done all, to stand when the going gets tough.

SCRIPTURE READING: Proverbs 4:13, Proverbs 4:20-26
PERSONAL APPLICATION: Ask God for the grace to stand and for the grace and willingness to endure hardship like a true soldier of Christ. Let us seek to be doers of the Word in everything and in every circumstance we may find ourselves, not just when things are rosy.

LEST I BE DISQUALIFIED

"Therefore, confess your sins to one another and pray for one another, that you may be healed. The prayer of a righteous person has great power as it is working."
James 5:16 ESV

It is a lie to believe that our service or good works can outweigh, excuse or cover the sin in our lives. There is a feeling of self-pity we have when we are being rebuked especially if we have been 'labouring for God'. We begin to feel unappreciated when we are being disciplined either by the Lord or the pastor. We also feel that in the light of all we have done our offence should be overlooked. So much so that all our works could be seen as our own way of bribing God or the pastor. The Bible already says that a bribe blinds the eye of the receiver (Exodus 23:8). God can't be bribed by our service or giving. Eli, the old priest, wouldn't discipline or correct his children but he kept on burning incense and giving burnt offerings. But God said, his sins couldn't be atoned for in that way (1 Samuel 3:12–14). To obey God is always better than sacrifice. The Bible tells us clearly in the book of Ezekiel that if a man stops doing what is good and begins to do evil, his good shall be forgotten, and vice versa. You can't cover up the evil with the good (Ezekiel 33:12–19). Apostle Paul said, "But I discipline my body and bring *it* into subjection, lest, when I have preached to others, I myself should become disqualified" (1 Corinthians 9:27). Disqualified from what Paul? From winning the prize. I have discovered that the more good you are doing for God and in God and the greater your kingdom service and input, the more careful you should be. Satan wants you to grow so big before he floors you with sin because he knows that the bigger you are, the greater the fall and many more people will be affected. We should all be like Paul, we should discipline our bodies and make them our slaves; we should crucify the flesh and keep it on the cross! Please remember, no matter how high you go, you can still come down and no matter how big you grow, you can still shrink.

SCRIPTURE READING: James 5:13-20, 1 Corinthians 9:24-27
PERSONAL APPLICATION: Are there any hidden sins in your life you need to repent of? Don't hide or ignore them, bring them before God. "If we confess our sins, He is faithful and just and will forgive us our sins and purify us from all unrighteousness." 1 John 1:9 *NIV*. If it is something you feel is beyond you, get some people of faith you trust to come around you to provide a support network for you and to cover you in prayer.

WHY JESUS CAME

"And suddenly there was with the angel a multitude of the heavenly host praising God and saying: 'Glory to God in the highest, And on earth peace, goodwill toward men!'"
Luke 2:13-14

Jesus came in obedience to God. He came to fulfil the will of God to save the lost by paying the eternal price for the salvation of humanity. He also came to bring us into the commonwealth of Israel. He wants all to enjoy the riches that are found in Christ. He came to live in us and through us express the will of God for humanity. "My little children, of whom I travail in birth again until Christ be formed in you" (Galatians 4:19 *KJV*). He came so He can be born in you. As we remember His birth, may we also let Him grow inside us as we make room for Him to express the will of the Father God in and through us.

SCRIPTURE READING: Isaiah 9:6-7, Luke 2:8-20
PERSONAL APPLICATION: As you remember Jesus' birth, can you think of who He is to you? We are not only to receive Jesus in our hearts, but to let Him grow inside us. The more we know and experience of our Saviour, the more we can live out why He came, as His ambassadors on earth.

THE SALVATION STORY

"For He made Him who knew no sin to be sin for us, that we might become the righteousness of God in Him."
2 Corinthians 5:21

The birth of Jesus Christ brought goodwill to humanity. The great dividing wall between God and man can at last be bridged. Sin has brought eternal separation between God and man. Man in his own effort to get right with God always meets with failure. Religion is the end result of man's attempts. The good news is that God came in the person of His Son Jesus to reconcile us to Himself and is not imputing our trespasses against us. All we need to do is believe in the Lord Jesus Christ, repent of our sins and get saved. A sinner can be redeemed from sin through faith in the Lord Jesus Christ. A lost man can become a child of God by the miracle of the new birth. My meditation today is why this simple truth no longer seems to produce radical changes in people's lives especially in some parts of the world. In fact the simple story of salvation is simply not believed and where some try to believe they meet such repulsion within themselves. I think we need to throw some light on the story; how the death of the Man Jesus on the cross was what dealt a deathblow on Satan's authority on earth. If however he can penetrate a person, family or area with a blinding influence on their minds to the gospel, they will not believe. In 2 Corinthians 4:4-5, Satan is called the god of this world who blinds peoples' minds who do not believe. Satan comes into lives through sin. He is authorized to enter anywhere sin is found. When he enters, he blocks God's program in the area. He tries to escalate individual sin into a corporate sin and thereby establishing a legal hold on the area. Jesus took the nature of sin on Himself and when He died on the cross, the authority of Satan given by sin was destroyed. This is the fulfilment of what was said in Genesis; the seed of the woman would bruise the head of the enemy (Genesis 3:15). Satan's authority came through sin and as sin died on the cross, his authority was crushed. That was eternally settled and it is up to us to enforce it or deny it to our detriment.

SCRIPTURE READING: 2 Corinthians 5:17-21
PERSONAL APPLICATION: The church is God's agent to enforce the victory of Calvary. Let us arise and shine for our light has come. It is time to celebrate our victory in Christ. Merry Christmas!

EVERY JOINT SUPPLIES

"But now God has set the members, each one of them, in the body just as He pleased."
1 Corinthians 12:18

No one can carry out God's plans alone. God needed Joseph, Mary, as well as Ana the prophetess to carry out His plans concerning the birth of Jesus. John the Baptist needed to be prepared to be born and he also was to prepare the way for the coming of Jesus. Everyone's role is very important in God's programme. Always remember that for every phase of God's programme we all have a part to play and no one's part is less important. Remember the role of the widow of Zarephath in carrying out the supply programme of God for the season. Her role ensured the supply for both herself and the prophet Elijah. As long as you fulfil your part in God's programme for your life, you are fulfilling your destiny. The problem is that many want to be in the centre-stage of God's programme. We need to be content with our lot in God. Whatever our roles, we should love God and trust Him enough to do what He wants us to do and enjoy our contribution with gladness and contentment. Even Jesus let the Father take the centre stage in His ministry. John Maxwell says we will get more results if we don't care who takes the credit.

SCRIPTURE READING: 1 Corinthians 12:12-27
PERSONAL APPLICATION: Don't ever underestimate the importance of the role you are assigned in fulfilling the will of God. The body is strengthened as every joint supplies - you are doing a great work no matter how 'small' or 'insignificant' you think it is. In it lies the key to your own fulfilment and destiny.

LEARNING FROM THE MASTER

"Take my yoke upon you. Let me teach you, because I am humble and gentle at heart, and you will find rest for your souls."
Matthew 11:29 NLT

Jesus lived a stress-free life. Even in the storm, He was so sound asleep that His disciples had to wake Him up! He didn't lose His peace when He was told that Lazarus was terribly sick; neither did He lose it when they ran out of wine at the wedding He attended. What was the secret? Jesus Himself said, "the Son can do nothing of Himself, but what He sees the Father do; for whatever He does, the Son also does in like manner. For the Father loves the Son, and shows Him all things that He Himself does" (John 5:19-20). He said it again, "I do nothing of Myself; but as My Father taught Me, I speak these things" (John 8:28). That was the key to His successful and stress-free Ministry; His fellowship with the Father. It was in that place that He saw what the Father was doing, and was also taught by the Father. And that was why He said we too can do nothing, except we abide in Him and His words abide in us. While Martha was worried and troubled about many things, Mary sat at Jesus' feet, hearing His word (Luke 10:38-42)! That is the best place to be; the Psalmist said, "I'm asking God for one thing, only one thing: To live with Him in His house my whole life long. I'll contemplate His beauty; I'll study at His feet" (Psalm 27:4 *MSG*).

SCRIPTURE READING: Psalm 27:1-14
PERSONAL APPLICATION: Take time today to just wait on the Lord and 'sit at His feet'. You will find peace and rest for your soul.

THE WORD AND PRAYER

"But we will give ourselves continually to prayer and to the Ministry of the word."
Acts 6:4

Prayer and the Word must go together, not one can exist without the other. Any believer who will succeed in the last days must give himself or herself to both continually. The Bible says our adversary, the devil walks around like a roaring lion looking for someone to devour, we should therefore be vigilant and sober (1 Peter 5:8). Jesus said if the owner of the house knew when the thief would come he would have watched and not allowed his house to be broken into (Matthew 24:43). The Bible usually links up watching or watchfulness with prayer. Jesus said 'watch and pray' (Mark 13:33, Luke 21:36, Matthew 26:41). The 'watchtower' in the Old Testament, represents the ministry of prayer and intercession. It also represents the place of sensitivity to the Holy Spirit and watchfulness in the spirit. Habakkuk said, "I will stand upon my watch and set me upon the tower, and will watch to see what he will say to me…" (Habakkuk 2:1). People stood on the watchtower to sight anything coming into the city before it comes in, so that nothing took them unawares. That is how we should live as Christians.

SCRIPTURE READING: Habakkuk 2:1, Proverbs 4:20-27
PERSONAL APPLICATION: If we stay in tune with the Holy Spirit, He will show us all things even things yet to come so we can handle things in the spirit before they manifest on the earth.

GET UP AND PRAY

"But while everyone was sleeping, his enemy came and sowed weeds among the wheat and went away."
Matthew 13:25 NIV

In the garden of Gethsemane, before His arrest, Jesus said to His disciples, "Why do you sleep? Rise and pray, lest you enter into temptation" (Luke 22:46). The disciples were sleeping most likely because they were tired and because it was night and that was the normal or natural thing to do. But sleeping connotes in the spirit realm, carelessness, lack of vigilance and sobriety, prayerlessness and lack of spirituality. In the parable of the wheat and the tares, Jesus said the tares were planted 'while men slept'. We need to understand this dimension of warfare. If you live your life in the natural or conduct a normal lifestyle, you will be meat for the devil, because he will be able to predict you. Those who will win are those who won't 'sleep' when men, (i.e. the generality of people) are sleeping. Satan is the enemy of our souls and he attacks when we are most vulnerable. Falling in the time of vulnerability does not excuse or make less our fall. Jesus said, "Pray so that you will not fall into temptation". That tells us that though prayer might not keep temptation away from us, they keep us from falling into them!

SCRIPTURE READING: Luke 22:39-46
PERSONAL APPLICATION: Don't ever underestimate the importance of prayer and warfare. Receive grace and strength from God to be a person of constant prayer. Don't allow the busyness of life to side track your prayer life. Prayer prepares us for the battles ahead of us and guarantees our victory!

A PLACE OF SURRENDER

"Father, if it is Your will, take this cup away from Me; nevertheless not My will, but Yours, be done."
Luke 22:42

Prayer is a place of surrender and yieldedness to the will of God. The voice of flesh is eventually silenced and the voice of the Spirit is heard loud and clear. In prayer all other things become as shadows in the light of Him because we see Him who is invisible. The more prayerful we are, the more yielded we become to God's will. Jesus prayed a prayer of consecration in Gethsemane. He prayed, "nevertheless not My will, but Yours, be done" (Luke 22:42). That is the greatest level of warfare that anyone could engage in. Our lifestyle is actually what binds or looses the devil. The greatest warfare against Satan is to be fully submitted to God's will and His purpose for our lives. The Bible says, "Submit to God, resist the devil and he will flee from you". It is not the other way round, and besides being dangerous, warfare against Satan won't work if we are not in submission to God. The first thing God wants to conquer is our will, that is what it means to seek first God's Kingdom and righteousness. The message of the Kingdom is directed at our will. Jesus said we should turn the other cheek if we are slapped. He said we should go another mile if we are forced to go one mile. He said we should love our enemies; bless those who curse us; do good to those who hate us, and pray for those who despitefully use us and persecute us (Matthew 5)! If we surrender our will and our desires to the Lord then we will always overcome Satan and sin's deceitfulness.

SCRIPTURE READING: Hebrews 10:5-7, Romans 12:1-2
PERSONAL APPLICATION: With our fallen human nature, the 'I want', 'I know', 'I get', etc. is much easier to choose than 'I surrender'. We need to make a conscious effort to follow the pattern of our Lord Jesus who came only to do the will of the Father. Ask the Holy Spirit to help you make the right choices throughout the day.

THE WORD IN YOU

"Let the word of Christ dwell in you richly in all wisdom, teaching and admonishing one another in psalms and hymns and spiritual songs, singing with grace in your hearts to the Lord."
Colossians 3:16

If you don't meditate in the Word, the spiritual essence of faith will not register in your spirit. You need to stay in the Word and allow God to speak to you so that, when the need arises, you have the substance of faith to meet those needs. You must be convinced beyond any shadow of doubt that the Word of God carries power because it carries God Himself.

"Let the word of Christ dwell in you richly in all wisdom..." (Colossians 3:16). 'Dwell' - Greek '*enoikeō*' pronounced [en-oy-keh-o]. It means to inhabit, position, dwell in. 'Richly' - Greek '*plousiōs*', pronounced [ploo-see-oce]. It means the following: copiously, abundantly, richly. Paraphrasing the above-mentioned verse with these meanings in mind renders it as follows, "Let the Word of Christ inhabit or position itself permanently in you in abundance [overflowing, more than enough], copiously [furnished plentifully, abounding] in all wisdom...".

This is the only way faith can grow. The Word of God taken in piecemeal measures and irregularly cannot build faith in you. The amount of Word you hear determines the extent of your faith and your faith determines what you can get from God.

SCRIPTURE READING: Colossians 1:9-23

PERSONAL APPLICATION: What better time than the present to rededicate yourself back to God. Determine today to build your faith daily through meditation in the Word of God—don't wait for the new year to come, do it now. Pray Colossians 3:16 over yourself.

"May the Word of Christ dwell in you richly in all wisdom in the mighty name of Jesus. May you be filled with the knowledge of His will in all wisdom and spiritual understanding; that you may walk worthy of the Lord, fully pleasing Him, being fruitful in every good work and increasing in the knowledge of God. In Jesus' name, Amen."

TOPICAL INDEX

PROCESS
February 13
March 31
April 30
August 16
September 12

PRODUCTIVITY
May 11
August 13
August 25

PROMOTION
January 2

PROVISON
August 23
November 5

PURITY OF HEART
January 15
January 29
April 11
June 3
September 1
September 30

PURPOSE
January 8
March 1
March 4
March 9
April 17
April 19
May 9
August 6
August 14
October 18
November 22

REPENTANCE
July 5

RIGHTEOUSNESS
January 14
September 25

SALVATION
October 8
December 24
December 25

SEEDS
November 20
December 1
December 14

SEEKING GOD
April 15
May 29
October 1

SENSITIVITY TO GOD / HOLY SPIRIT
February 28
September 20
November 13
November 25

SIN
April 9
May 13
June 25
July 5
August 9
October 15
November 14
December 6
December 23

STEWARDSHIP
August 23

STRONGHOLDS
March 17
September 26

SUBMISSION
April 10
April 18
May 12
June 5
June 19
November 12

THANKFULNESS
February 24
April 2
November 29

THE CROSS
February 9
February 15
March 6

September 7

THE MIND / THOUGHTS

January 21
February 26
June 13
June 15
July 30
August 22
December 16

VALUE

May 20
May 27
June 14
August 21
October 14

VICTORIOUS LIVING / WARFARE

January 4
March 3
March 12
March 22
March 28
April 6
April 12
April 26
May 2
May 14
May 26
May 28
June 9
July 1
July 19
July 25
July 30
August 31
September 18
October 10
October 11
December 2
December 8
December 9

WORSHIP

May 18

365 DAILY BIBLE READING PLAN

JANUARY 1
Genesis 1-3; Matthew 1

JANUARY 2
Genesis 4-5; Matthew 2

JANUARY 3
Genesis 6-7; Matthew 3-4

JANUARY 4
Genesis 8-9; Matthew 5

JANUARY 5
Genesis 10-11; Matthew 6-7

JANUARY 6
Genesis 12-13; Matthew 8-9

JANUARY 7
Genesis 14-15; Matthew 10

JANUARY 8
Genesis 16-17; Matthew 11-12

JANUARY 9
Genesis 18-19; Matthew 13

JANUARY 10
Genesis 20-21; Matthew 14-15

JANUARY 11
Genesis 22-23; Matthew 16-17

JANUARY 12
Genesis 24-25; Matthew 18

JANUARY 13
Genesis 26-27; Matthew 19-20

JANUARY 14
Genesis 28-29; Matthew 21-22

JANUARY 15
Genesis 30-31; Matthew 23-24

JANUARY 16
Genesis 32-33; Matthew 25-26

JANUARY 17
Genesis 34-35; Matthew 27-28

JANUARY 18
Genesis 36-37; Mark 1-2

JANUARY 19
Genesis 38-39; Mark 3-4

JANUARY 20
Genesis 40-41; Mark 5-6

JANUARY 21
Genesis 42-43; Mark 7-8

JANUARY 22
Genesis 44-45; Mark 9-10

JANURAY 23
Genesis 46-47; Mark 11-12

JANUARY 24
Genesis 48-49; Mark 13-14

JANUARY 25
Genesis 50; Exodus 1; Mark 15-16

JANUARY 26
Exodus 2-3; Luke 1

JANUARY 27
Exodus 4-5; Luke 2

JANUARY 28
Exodus 6-7; Luke 3-4

JANUARY 29
Exodus 8-9; Luke 5-6

JANUARY 30
Exodus 10-11; Luke 7-8

JANUARY 31
Exodus 12-13; Luke 9-10

FEBRUARY 1
Exodus 14-15; Luke 11-12

FEBRUARY 2
Exodus 16-17; Luke 13

FEBRUARY 3
Exodus 18-19; Luke 14

FEBRUARY 4
Exodus 20-21; Luke 15-16

FEBRUARY 5
Exodus 22-23; Luke 17-18

FEBRUARY 6
Exodus 24-25; Luke 19-20

FEBRUARY 7
Exodus 26-27; Luke 21-22

FEBRUARY 8
Exodus 28-29; Luke 23-24

FEBRUARY 9
Exodus 30-31; John 1-2

FEBRUARY 10
Exodus 32-33; John 3

FEBRUARY 11
Exodus 34-35; John 4-5

FEBRUARY 12
Exodus 36-37; John 6-7

FEBRUARY 13
Exodus 38-39; John 8-9

FEBRUARY 14
Exodus 40; Leviticus 1; John 10

FEBRUARY 15
Leviticus 2-3; John 11-12

FEBRUARY 16
Leviticus 4-5; John 13

FEBRUARY 17
Leviticus 6-7; John 14-15

FEBRUARY 18
Leviticus 8-9; John 16-17

FEBRUARY 19
Leviticus 10-11; John 18-19

FEBRUARY 20
Leviticus 12-13; John 20-21

FEBRUARY 21
Leviticus 14-15; Acts 1

FEBRUARY 22
Leviticus 16-17; Acts 2

FEBRUARY 23
Leviticus 18-19; Acts 3

FEBRUARY 24
Leviticus 20-21; Acts 4

FEBRUARY 25
Leviticus 22-23; Acts 5

FEBRUARY 26
Leviticus 24-25; Acts 6

FEBRUARY 27
Leviticus 26-27; Acts 7

FEBRUARY 28
Numbers 1-2; Acts 8

MARCH 1
Numbers 3-4; Acts 9

MARCH 2
Numbers 5-6; Acts 10

MARCH 3
Numbers 7-8; Acts 11

MARCH 4
Numbers 9-10; Acts 12

MARCH 5
Numbers 11-12; Acts 13

MARCH 6
Numbers 13-14; Acts 14

MARCH 7
Numbers 15-16; Acts 15

MARCH 8
Numbers 17-18; Acts 16

MARCH 9
Numbers 19-20; Acts 17

MARCH 10
Numbers 21-22; Acts 18

MARCH 11
Numbers 23-24; Acts 19

MARCH 12
Numbers 25-26; Acts 20

MARCH 13
Numbers 27-28; Acts 21

MARCH 14
Numbers 29-30; Acts 22

MARCH 15
Numbers 31-32; Acts 23

MARCH 16
Numbers 33-34; Acts 24

MARCH 17
Numbers 35-36; Acts 25

MARCH 18
Deuteronomy 1-2; Acts 26

MARCH 19
Deuteronomy 3-4; Acts 27

MARCH 20
Deuteronomy 5-6; Acts 28

MARCH 21
Deuteronomy 7-8; Romans 1

MARCH 22
Deuteronomy 9-10; Romans 2

MARCH 23
Deuteronomy 11-12; Romans 3

MARCH 24
Deuteronomy 13-14; Romans 4

MARCH 25
Deuteronomy 15-16; Romans 5

MARCH 26
Deuteronomy 17-18; Romans 6

MARCH 27
Deuteronomy 19-20; Romans 7

MARCH 28
Deuteronomy 21-22; Romans 8

MARCH 29
Deuteronomy 23-24; Romans 9

MARCH 30
Deuteronomy 25-26; Romans 10

MARCH 31
Deuteronomy 27-28; Romans 11

APRIL 1
Deuteronomy 29-30; Romans 12

APRIL 2
Deuteronomy 31-32; Romans 13

APRIL 3
Deuteronomy 33-34; Romans 14

APRIL 4
Joshua 1-2; Romans 15

APRIL 5
Joshua 3-4; Romans 16

APRIL 6
Joshua 5-6; 1 Corinthians 1

APRIL 7
Joshua 7-8; 1 Corinthians 2

APRIL 8
Joshua 9-10; 1 Corinthians 3

APRIL 9
Joshua 11-12; 1 Corinthians 4

APRIL 10
Joshua 13-14; 1 Corinthians 5

APRIL 11
Joshua 15-16; 1 Corinthians 6

APRIL 12
Joshua 17-18; 1 Corinthians 7

APRIL 13
Joshua 19-20; 1 Corinthians 8

APRIL 14
Joshua 21-22; 1 Corinthians 9

APRIL 15
Joshua 23-24; 1 Corinthians 10

APRIL 16
Judges 1-3; 1 Corinthians 11

APRIL 17
Judges 4-5; 1 Corinthians 12

APRIL 18
Judges 6-7; 1 Corinthians 13

APRIL 19
Judges 8-9; 1 Corinthians 14

APRIL 20
Judges 10-11; 1 Corinthians 15

APRIL 21
Judges 12-13; 1 Corinthians 16

APRIL 22
Judges 14-15; 2 Corinthians 1

APRIL 23
Judges 16-17; 2 Corinthians 2

APRIL 24
Judges 18-19; 2 Corinthians 3

APRIL 25
Judges 20-21; 2 Corinthians 4

APRIL 26
Ruth 1-2; 2 Corinthians 5

APRIL 27
Ruth 3-4; 2 Corinthians 6

APRIL 28
1 Samuel 1-2; 2 Corinthians 7

APRIL 29
1 Samuel 3-4; 2 Corinthians 8

APRIL 30
1 Samuel 5-6; 2 Corinthians 9

MAY 1
1 Samuel 7-8; 2 Corinthians 10

MAY 2
1 Samuel 9-10; 2 Corinthians 11

MAY 3
1 Samuel 11-12; 2 Corinthians 12

MAY 4
1 Samuel 13-14; 2 Corinthians 13

MAY 5
1 Samuel 15-16; Galatians 1

MAY 6
1 Samuel 17-18; Galatians 2

MAY 7
1 Samuel 19-20; Galatians 3

MAY 8
1 Samuel 21-22; Galatians 4

MAY 9
1 Samuel 23-24; Galatians 5

MAY 10
1 Samuel 25-26; Galatians 6

MAY 11
1 Samuel 27-28; Ephesians 1

MAY 12
1 Samuel 29-30; Ephesians 2

MAY 13
1 Samuel 31; 2 Samuel 1; Ephesians 3

MAY 14
2 Samuel 2-3; Ephesians 4

MAY 15
2 Samuel 4-5; Ephesians 5

MAY 16
2 Samuel 6-7; Ephesians 6

MAY 17
2 Samuel 8-9; Philippians 1

MAY 18
2 Samuel 10-11; Philippians 2

MAY 19
2 Samuel 12-13; Philippians 3

MAY 20
2 Samuel 14-15; Philippians 4

MAY 21
2 Samuel 16-17; Colossians 1

MAY 22
2 Samuel 18-19; Colossians 2

MAY 23
2 Samuel 20-21; Colossians 3

MAY 24
2 Samuel 22-23; Colossians 4

MAY 25
2 Samuel 24; 1 Kings 1; 1 Thessalonians 1

MAY 26
1 Kings 2-3; 1 Thessalonians 2

MAY 27
1 Kings 4-5; 1 Thessalonians 3

MAY 28
1 Kings 6-7; 1 Thessalonians 4

MAY 29
1 Kings 8-9; 1 Thessalonians 5

MAY 30
1 Kings 10-11; 2 Thessalonians 1

MAY 31
1 Kings 12-13; 2 Thessalonians 2

JUNE 1
1 Kings 14-15; 2 Thessalonians 3

JUNE 2
1 Kings 16-17; 1 Timothy 1

JUNE 3
1 Kings 18-19; 1 Timothy 2

JUNE 4
1 Kings 20-21; 1 Timothy 3

JUNE 5
1 Kings 22; 2 Kings 1; 1 Timothy 4

JUNE 6
2 Kings 2-3; 1 Timothy 5

JUNE 7
2 Kings 4-5; 1 Timothy 6

JUNE 8
2 Kings 6-7; 2 Timothy 1

JUNE 9
2 Kings 8-9; 2 Timothy 2

JUNE 10
2 Kings 10-11; 2 Timothy 3

JUNE 11
2 Kings 12-13; 2 Timothy 4

JUNE 12
2 Kings 14-15; Titus 1

JUNE 13
2 Kings 16-17; Titus 2

JUNE 14
2 Kings 18-19; Titus 3

JUNE 15
2 Kings 20-21; Philemon 1

JUNE 16
2 Kings 22-23; Hebrews 1

JUNE 17
2 Kings 24-25; Hebrews 2

JUNE 18
1 Chronicles 1-2; Hebrews 3

JUNE 19
1 Chronicles 3-4; Hebrews 4

JUNE 20
1 Chronicles 5-6; Hebrews 5

JUNE 21
1 Chronicles 7-8; Hebrews 6

JUNE 22
1 Chronicles 9-10; Hebrews 7

JUNE 23
1 Chronicles 11-12; Hebrews 8

JUNE 24
1 Chronicles 13-14; Hebrews 9

JUNE 25
1 Chronicles 15-16; Hebrews 10

JUNE 26
1 Chronicles 17-18; Hebrews 11

JUNE 27
1 Chronicles 19-20; Hebrews 12

JUNE 28
1 Chronicles 21-22; Hebrews 13

JUNE 29
1 Chronicles 23-24; James 1

JUNE 30
1 Chronicles 25-26; James 2

JULY 1
1 Chronicles 27-28; James 3

JULY 2
1 Chronicles 29 ; 2 Chronicles 1; James 4

JULY 3
2 Chronicles 2-3; James 5

JULY 4
2 Chronicles 4-5; 1 Peter 1

JULY 5
2 Chronicles 6-7; 1 Peter 2

JULY 6
2 Chronicles 8-9; 1 Peter 3

JULY 7
2 Chronicles 10-11; 1 Peter 4

JULY 8
2 Chronicles 12-13; 1 Peter 5

JULY 9
2 Chronicles 14-15; 2 Peter 1

JULY 10
2 Chronicles 16-17; 2 Peter 2

JULY 11
2 Chronicles 18-19; 2 Peter 3

JULY 12
2 Chronicles 20-21; 1 John 1

JULY 13
2 Chronicles 22-23; 1 John 2

JULY 14
2 Chronicles 24-25; 1 John 3

JULY 15
2 Chronicles 26-27; 1 John 4

JULY 16
2 Chronicles 28-29; 1 John 5

JULY 17
2 Chronicles 30-31; 2 John 1

JULY 18
2 Chronicles 32-33; 3 John 1

JULY 19
2 Chronicles 34-35; Jude 1

JULY 20
2 Chronicles 36 ; Ezra 1-2; Revelation 1

JULY 21
Ezra 3-5; Revelation 2

JULY 22
Ezra 6-7; Revelation 3

JULY 23
Ezra 8-10; Revelation 4

JULY 24
Nehemiah 1-3; Revelation 5

JULY 25
Nehemiah 4-5; Revelation 6

JULY 26
Nehemiah 6-8; Revelation 7

JULY 27
Nehemiah 9-10; Revelation 8

JULY 28
Nehemiah 11-13; Revelation 9

JULY 29
Esther 1-3; Revelation 10

JULY 30
Esther 4-5; Revelation 11

JULY 31
Esther 6-7; Revelation 12

AUGUST 1
Esther 8-10; Revelation 13

AUGUST 2
Job 1-2; Revelation 14

AUGUST 3
Job 3-4; Revelation 15

AUGUST 4
Job 5-6; Revelation 16

AUGUST 5
Job 7-8; Revelation 17

AUGUST 6
Job 9-10; Revelation 18

AUGUST 7
Job 11-12; Revelation 19

AUGUST 8
Job 13-14; Revelation 20

AUGUST 9
Job 15-16; Revelation 21

AUGUST 10
Job 17-18; Revelation 22

AUGUST 11
Job 19-20; Psalms 1-2

AUGUST 12
Job 21-22; Psalms 3-4

AUGUST 13
Job 23-24; Psalms 5-7

AUGUST 14
Job 25-26; Psalms 8-9

AUGUST 15
Job 27-28; Psalms 10-11

AUGUST 16
Job 29-30; Psalms 12-13

AUGUST 17
Job 31-32; Psalms 14-15

AUGUST 18
Job 33-34; Psalms 16-17

AUGUST 19
Job 35-36; Psalms 18

AUGUST 20
Job 37-38; Psalms 19-20

AUGUST 21
Job 39-40; Psalms 21

AUGUST 22
Job 41-42; Psalms 22-23

AUGUST 23
Ecclesiastes 1-2; Psalms 24

AUGUST 24
Ecclesiastes 3-4; Psalms 25-26

AUGUST 25
Ecclesiastes 5-6; Psalms 27

AUGUST 26
Ecclesiastes 7-8; Psalms 28-29

AUGUST 27
Ecclesiastes 9-10; Psalms 30-31

AUGUST 28
Ecclesiastes 11-12; Psalms 32

AUGUST 29
Song of Solomon 1-2; Psalms 33-34

AUGUST 30
Song of Solomon 3-4; Psalms 35-36

AUGUST 31
Song of Solomon 5-6; Psalms 37-38

SEPTEMBER 1
Song of Solomon 7-8; Psalms 39

SEPTEMBER 2
Isaiah 1-2; Psalms 40-41

SEPTEMBER 3
Isaiah 3-4; Psalms 42

SEPTEMBER 4
Isaiah 5-6; Psalms 43

SEPTEMBER 5
Isaiah 7-8; Psalms 44

SEPTEMBER 6
Isaiah 9-10; Psalms 45

SEPTEMBER 7
Isaiah 11-12; Psalms 46-47

SEPTEMBER 8
Isaiah 13-14; Psalms 48

SEPTEMBER 9
Isaiah 15-16; Psalms 49-50

SEPTEMBER 10
Isaiah 17-18; Psalms 51

SEPTEMBER 11
Isaiah 19-20; Psalms 52-53

SEPTEMBER 12
Isaiah 21-22; Psalms 54-55

SEPTEMBER 13
Isaiah 23-24; Psalms 56-57

SEPTEMBER 14
Isaiah 25-26; Psalms 58

SEPTEMBER 15
Isaiah 27-28; Psalms 59

SEPTEMBER 16
Isaiah 29-30; Psalms 60-61

SEPTEMBER 17
Isaiah 31-32; Psalms 62-63

SEPTEMBER 18
Isaiah 33-34; Psalms 64-65

SEPTEMBER 19
Isaiah 35-36; Psalms 66-67

SEPTEMBER 20
Isaiah 37-38; Psalms 68-69

SEPTEMBER 21
Isaiah 39-40; Psalms 70

SEPTEMBER 22
Isaiah 41-42; Psalms 71

SEPTEMBER 23
Isaiah 43-44; Psalms 72-73

SEPTEMBER 24
Isaiah 45-46; Psalms 74-75

SEPTEMBER 25
Isaiah 47-48; Psalms 76

SEPTEMBER 26
Isaiah 49-50; Psalms 77

SEPTEMBER 27
Isaiah 51-52; Psalms 78

SEPTEMBER 28
Isaiah 53-54; Psalms 79

SEPTEMBER 29
Isaiah 55-56; Psalms 80

SEPTEMBER 30
Isaiah 57-58; Psalms 81

OCTOBER 1
Isaiah 59-60; Psalms 82

OCTOBER 2
Isaiah 61-62; Psalms 83

OCTOBER 3
Isaiah 63-64; Psalms 84-85

OCTOBER 4
Isaiah 65-66; Psalms 86

OCTOBER 5
Jeremiah 1-2; Psalms 87-89

OCTOBER 6
Jeremiah 3-4; Psalms 90

OCTOBER 7
Jeremiah 5-6; Psalms 91

OCTOBER 8
Jeremiah 7-8; Psalms 92

OCTOBER 9
Jeremiah 9-10; Psalms 93

OCTOBER 10
Jeremiah 11-12; Psalms 94

OCTOBER 11
Jeremiah 13-14; Psalms 95

OCTOBER 12
Jeremiah 15-16; Psalms 96-97

OCTOBER 13
Jeremiah 17-18; Psalms 98

OCTOBER 14
Jeremiah 19-20; Psalms 99

OCTOBER 15
Jeremiah 21-22; Psalms 100-101

OCTOBER 16
Jeremiah 23-24; Psalms 102

OCTOBER 17
Jeremiah 25-26; Psalms 103

OCTOBER 18
Jeremiah 27-28; Psalms 104

OCTOBER 19
Jeremiah 29-30; Psalms 105

OCTOBER 20
Jeremiah 31-32; Psalms 106

OCTOBER 21
Jeremiah 33-34; Psalms 107

OCTOBER 22
Jeremiah 35-36; Psalms 108

OCTOBER 23
Jeremiah 37-38; Psalms 109

OCTOBER 24
Jeremiah 39-40; Psalms 110

OCTOBER 25
Jeremiah 41-42; Psalms 111

OCTOBER 26
Jeremiah 43-44; Psalms 112

OCTOBER 27
Jeremiah 45-46; Psalms 113-114

OCTOBER 28
Jeremiah 47-48; Psalms 115

OCTOBER 29
Jeremiah 49-50; Psalms 116-117

OCTOBER 30
Jeremiah 51-52; Psalms 118

OCTOBER 31
Lamentations 1-3; Psalms 119:1-44

NOVEMBER 1
Lamentations 4-5; Psalms 119:45-88

NOVEMBER 2
Ezekiel 1-2; Psalms 119:89-132

NOVEMBER 3
Ezekiel 3-4; Psalms 119:133-176

NOVEMBER 4
Ezekiel 5-6; Psalms 120-121

NOVEMBER 5
Ezekiel 7-8; Psalms 122-123

NOVEMBER 6
Ezekiel 9-10; Psalms 124-125

NOVEMBER 7
Ezekiel 11-12; Psalms 126-127

NOVEMBER 8
Ezekiel 13-14; Psalms 128

NOVEMBER 9
Ezekiel 15-16; Psalms 129

NOVEMBER 10
Ezekiel 17-18; Psalms 130

NOVEMBER 11
Ezekiel 19-20; Psalms 131

NOVEMBER 12
Ezekiel 21-22; Psalms 132

NOVEMBER 13
Ezekiel 23-24; Psalms 133

NOVEMBER 14
Ezekiel 25-26; Psalms 134

NOVEMBER 15
Ezekiel 27-28; Psalms 135

NOVEMBER 16
Ezekiel 29-30; Psalms 136

NOVEMBER 17
Ezekiel 31-32; Psalms 137

NOVEMBER 18
Ezekiel 33-34; Psalms 138

NOVEMBER 19
Ezekiel 35-36; Psalms 139

NOVEMBER 20
Ezekiel 37-38; Psalms 140

NOVEMBER 21
Ezekiel 39-40; Psalms 141

NOVEMBER 22
Ezekiel 41-42; Psalms 142

NOVEMBER 23
Ezekiel 43-44; Psalms 143

NOVEMBER 24
Ezekiel 45-46; Psalms 144

NOVEMBER 25
Ezekiel 47-48; Psalms 145

NOVEMBER 26
Daniel 1-2; Psalms 146

NOVEMBER 27
Daniel 3-4; Psalms 147

NOVEMBER 28
Daniel 5-6; Psalms 148

NOVEMBER 29
Daniel 7-8; Psalms 149

NOVEMBER 30
Daniel 9-10; Psalms 150

DECEMBER 1
Daniel 11-12; Proverbs 1

DECEMBER 2
Hosea 1-2; Proverbs 2

DECEMBER 3
Hosea 3-4; Proverbs 3

DECEMBER 4
Hosea 5-6; Proverbs 4

DECEMBER 5
Hosea 7-8; Proverbs 5

DECEMBER 6
Hosea 9-10; Proverbs 6

DECEMBER 7
Hosea 11-12; Proverbs 7

DECEMBER 8
Hosea 13-14; Proverbs 8

DECEMBER 9
Joel 1-3; Proverbs 9

DECEMBER 10
Amos 1-3; Proverbs 10

DECEMBER 11
Amos 4-6; Proverbs 11

DECEMBER 12
Amos 7-9; Proverbs 12

DECEMBER 13
Obadiah 1; Proverbs 13

DECEMBER 14
Jonah 1-2; Proverbs 14

DECEMBER 15
Jonah 3-4; Proverbs 15

DECEMBER 16
Micah 1-2; Proverbs 16

DECEMBER 17
Micah 3-4; Proverbs 17

DECEMBER 18
Micah 5-7; Proverbs 18

DECEMBER 19
Nahum 1-3; Proverbs 19

DECEMBER 20
Habakkuk 1-2; Proverbs 20

DECEMBER 21
Habakkuk 3; Zephaniah 1; Proverbs 21

DECEMBER 22
Zephaniah 2-3; Proverbs 22

DECEMBER 23
Haggai 1-2; Proverbs 23

DECEMBER 24
Zechariah 1-3; Proverbs 24

DECEMBER 25
Zechariah 4-5; Proverbs 25

DECEMBER 26
Zechariah 6-8; Proverbs 26

DECEMBER 27
Zechariah 9-10; Proverbs 27

DECEMBER 28
Zechariah 11-12; Proverbs 28

DECEMBER 29
Zechariah 13-14; Proverbs 29

DECEMBER 30
Malachi 1-2; Proverbs 30

DECEMBER 31
Malachi 3-4; Proverbs 31

ABOUT THE AUTHORS

Reverend Kola and Reverend Funke Ewuosho are both ministers of the gospel, founding pastors and authors. Rev. Kola was called by God into fulltime ministry in 1986, following his graduation from university in Nigeria as a mechanical engineer. He then went on to a Bible training school and after graduating from there, Rev. Kola pioneered The Word of Faith Christian Centre Church in Kano, Nigeria. Rev. Kola married his wife Rev. Funke, in 1988 (whom he had met before being called into fulltime ministry). Rev. Funke, who had already ministered as a teacher of the Word at her former church, then joined her husband in Kano soon after they were married. There she continued practising her legal profession for another year before joining her husband in fulltime ministry. Since then, they have laboured side-by-side in the ministry.

Their commitment and love for the Word of God is evident throughout their teachings, and they continue to train and disciple a multitude of believers through their sermons, books and discipleship programmes. Many believers who have been discipled by Revs. Kola and Funke have gone on to become leaders in various churches and Christian ministries around the world.

God has also opened the door to many nations, enabling Revs. Kola and Funke to preach and transmit God's Word to every continent of the world. They have both written many anointed and impactful books, including, 'Behind Enemy Lines' (by Rev. Kola) and '31 Diamond Drops' (By Rev. Funke).

Today, Revs. Kola and Funke are based in the UK, leading Harvestime Church in Virginia Water, whilst also giving Apostolic oversight to all the Fountain of Wisdom Ministries churches around the world.

CONNECT WITH THE AUTHORS:

Rev. Kola Ewuosho -

Facebook: RevKolaEwuosho *Twitter: @kolaewuosho*

Rev. Funke Ewuosho -

Facebook: RevFunkeEwuosho *Twitter: @funke_ewuosho*